Interdisciplinary Applications of Electronic Collaboration Approaches and Technologies

Ned Kock
Texas A&M International University, USA

Information Science
REFERENCE

Managing Director:	Lindsay Johnston
Senior Editorial Director:	Heather A. Probst
Book Production Manager:	Sean Woznicki
Development Manager:	Joel Gamon
Assistant Acquisitions Editor:	Kayla Wolfe
Typesetter:	Nicole Sparano
Cover Design:	Nick Newcomer

Published in the United States of America by
Information Science Reference (an imprint of IGI Global)
701 E. Chocolate Avenue
Hershey PA 17033
Tel: 717-533-8845
Fax: 717-533-8661
E-mail: cust@igi-global.com
Web site: http://www.igi-global.com

Library of Congress Cataloging-in-Publication Data

Interdisciplinary applications of electronic collaboration approaches and technologies / Ned Kock, editor.
    p. cm.
  Includes bibliographical references and index.
  Summary: "This book addresses the design and implementation of e-collaboration technologies, assesses their behavioral impact on individuals and groups, and presents theoretical considerations on links between the use of e-collaboration technologies and behavioral patterns"--Provided by publisher.
  ISBN 978-1-4666-2020-9 (hbk.) -- ISBN 978-1-4666-2021-6 (ebook) -- ISBN 978-1-4666-2022-3 (print & perpetual access) 1. Information technology--Management. 2. Computer networks. 3. Information networks. 4. Telematics. I. Kock, Ned F., 1964-
  HD30.2.I5559 2013
  658.4'038--dc23
                                2012009918

British Cataloguing in Publication Data
A Cataloguing in Publication record for this book is available from the British Library.

The views expressed in this book are those of the authors, but not necessarily of the publisher.

Editorial Advisory Board

Table of Contents

Preface..xiv

Acknowledgment..xxvi

Chapter 1
A Semantic E-Collaboration Approach to Enable Awareness in Globally
Distributed Organizations 1
    Eldar Sultanow, University of Potsdam, Germany
    Edzard Weber, University of Potsdam, Germany
    Sean Cox, Mathematicians Anonymous, USA

Chapter 2
An Exploratory Study of How Technology Supports Communication in Multilingual Groups 17
    Milam Aiken, University of Mississippi, USA
    Jianfeng Wang, Indiana University of Pennsylvania, USA
    Linwu Gu, Indiana University of Pennsylvania, USA
    Joseph Paolillo, University of Mississippi, USA

Chapter 3
The Virtual Individual Education Plan (IEP) Team: Using Online Collaboration to Develop a
Behavior Intervention Plan 30
    Robyn M. Catagnus, Arcadia University, USA
    Donald A. Hantula, Temple University, USA

Chapter 4
Measuring Collective Cognition in Online Collaboration Venues..46
    Paul Dwyer, Willamette University, USA

Chapter 5
Using WarpPLS in E-Collaboration Studies: Descriptive Statistics, Settings, and
Key Analysis Results 62
    Ned Kock, Texas A&M International University, USA

Chapter 6
The Influence of Information Technology on Organizational Behavior: Study of Identity
Challenges in Virtual Teams 79
Babak Sohrabi, University of Tehran, Iran
Aryan Gholipour, University of Tehran, Iran
Behnam Amiri, University of Tehran, Iran

Chapter 7
Web Enabled Design Collaboration in India 96
Shaheli Guha, BigMachines Inc., USA
Biswajit Thakur, Meghnad Saha Institute of Technology, India
Tuhin Subhra Konar, Jadavpur University, India
Shibnath Chakrabarty, Jadavpur University, India

Chapter 8
Using WarpPLS in E-Collaboration Studies: Mediating Effects, Control and Second Order
Variables, and Algorithm Choices 112
Ned Kock, Texas A&M International University, USA

Chapter 9
Shared Mental Model Development During Technology-Mediated Collaboration 125
Hayward P. Andres, North Carolina A&T State University, USA

Chapter 10
WikiDesign: A Semantic Wiki to Evaluate Collaborative Knowledge 143
Davy Monticolo, National Polytechnic Institute of Lorraine, France
Samuel Gomes, University of Technology of Belfort-Montbéliard, France

Chapter 11
Industry Perspective-Collaborating from a Distance: Success Factors of Top-Performing
Virtual Teams 155
Darleen DeRosa, OnPoint Consulting, USA

Chapter 12
The Level Paradox of E-Collaboration: Dangers and Solutions 166
Ana Ortiz de Guinea, HEC Montréal, Canada

Chapter 13
E-Collaboration Within, Between, and Without Institutions: Towards Better Functioning of
Online Groups Through Networks 188
Ina Blau, Open University of Israel, Israel

Chapter 14
Towards an Affordance-Based Theory of Collaborative Action (CoAct)..204
  John Teofil Paul Nosek, Temple University, USA

Chapter 15
Working Effectively in a Matrix: Building and Sustaining Cooperation..228
  Jennifer Forgie, OnPoint Consulting, USA

Compilation of References 238

About the Contributors 265

Index...270

Detailed Table of Contents

Preface xiv

Acknowledgment xxvi

Chapter 1

A Semantic E-Collaboration Approach to Enable Awareness in Globally
Distributed Organizations 1

Eldar Sultanow, University of Potsdam, Germany
Edzard Weber, University of Potsdam, Germany
Sean Cox, Mathematicians Anonymous, USA

Collaboration in temporal and spatially distributed environments has consistently faced the challenge of intense awareness extensively more than locally concentrated team play. Awareness means being informed, in conjunction with an understanding of activities, states and relationships of each individual within a given group as a whole. In multifarious offices, where social interaction is necessary to share and locate essential information, awareness becomes a concurrent process that amplifies the exigency for easy routes where personnel can navigate and access pertinent information, deferred or decentralized, in a formalized and context-sensitive way. Even as awareness has become a more pressing topic, extensive disagreement still remains concerning how any type of transparency can be conceptually and technically implemented. This paper introduces an awareness model to visualize and navigate such information in multi-tiers using semantic networks, GIS (Geographic Information Systems) and Web3D. Ultimately, the model presented is used for an evaluation from a business organization's perspective.

Chapter 2

An Exploratory Study of How Technology Supports Communication in Multilingual Groups 17

Milam Aiken, University of Mississippi, USA
Jianfeng Wang, Indiana University of Pennsylvania, USA
Linwu Gu, Indiana University of Pennsylvania, USA
Joseph Paolillo, University of Mississippi, USA

In this paper, the authors study how new technology can support multilingual groups. Their results show that no significant difference was found between group members' comprehension of contributed comments and their stated minimum acceptable understanding. However, comprehension of relevant comments was higher than that for off-topic text, indicating that the sharing of important information was achieved. Further, reading comprehension tests of translations from Chinese, German, Hindi, Korean, Malay, and Spanish to English show that, except for Hindi, the automatic translations achieve accuracies that are acceptable for graduate studies at a university in the United States.

Chapter 3

The Virtual Individual Education Plan (IEP) Team: Using Online Collaboration to Develop a
Behavior Intervention Plan 30

Robyn M. Catagnus, Arcadia University, USA
Donald A. Hantula, Temple University, USA

A team of professional educators in a private school for children with disabilities (a Virtual IEP Team)
used an online platform to collaborate and produce a behavior intervention plan for a student. The collaboration was effective and efficient; the plan was produced in 9 days, rather than the customary 3-6
weeks. Qualitative data yielded four major themes: beneficial augmentation, reflective practice, barriers
to change, and improved interactions. Quantitative results showed that although end user satisfaction
was moderate, educators produced a successful behavior intervention plan that showed positive changes
in both the teacher and student behavior. An increase of in-person staff discussion as a result of online
dialogue was a unique finding in this study warranting further investigation. Now that federal (U.S.)
education law has changed to allow technologically mediated IEP meetings, the Virtual IEP Team may
serve as a model for more efficient use of education professionals' time.

Chapter 4

Measuring Collective Cognition in Online Collaboration Venues... 46

Paul Dwyer, Willamette University, USA

By monitoring online conversations, organizations can receive value from the intellectual activity of their
most interested constituents as they engage in problem solving and ideation. However, since intergroup
dynamics often hinders people from optimizing collaboration, it should be measured and monitored for
quality. Current metrics assess collaborative value solely from the number of collaborators, assuming
that differences between individuals can be ignored. This study found that assumption to be wrong by
identifying three distinct collaborator segments that strongly differ in the timing of their participation
and in the variety of ideas they introduce. Therefore, a new metric is proposed that takes into account
the diverse value individuals add. This new measure is correlated with existing measures only in those
infrequent situations when collaboration productivity is maximized.

Chapter 5

Using WarpPLS in E-Collaboration Studies: Descriptive Statistics, Settings, and
Key Analysis Results 62

Ned Kock, Texas A&M International University, USA

This is a follow-up on a previous article (Kock, 2010b) discussing the five main steps through which a
nonlinear structural equation modeling analysis could be conducted with the software WarpPLS (warp-
pls.com). Both this and the previous article use data from the same E-collaboration study as a basis for
the discussion of important WarpPLS features. The focus of this article is on specific features related
to saving and analyzing grouped descriptive statistics, viewing and changing analysis algorithm and
resampling settings, and viewing and saving the various minor and major results of the analysis. Even
though its focus is on an E-collaboration study, this article contributes to the broad literature on multivariate analysis methods, in addition to the more specific research literature on E-collaboration. The vast
majority of relationships between variables, in investigations of both natural and behavioral phenomena,
are nonlinear; usually taking the form of U and S curves. Structural equation modeling software tools,
whether variancE- or covariancE-based, typically do not estimate coefficients of association based on
nonlinear analysis algorithms. WarpPLS is an exception in this respect. Without taking nonlinearity into
consideration, the results can be misleading; especially in complex and multi-factorial situations such
as those stemming from E-collaboration in virtual teams.

Chapter 6

The Influence of Information Technology on Organizational Behavior: Study of Identity Challenges in Virtual Teams 79

Babak Sohrabi, University of Tehran, Iran
Aryan Gholipour, University of Tehran, Iran
Behnam Amiri, University of Tehran, Iran

This paper attempts to examine the effects of virtual team dimensions on social identities of its members. A review of the literature shows that the geographically dispersed, culturally diverse as well as temporary dimensions of virtual teams do not match with their stability as members have different ethnic, social, or cultural backgrounds. Sources like culture, place, and time seem to continuously acquire social identities. Due to the importance of social identity, an attempt has been made to examine its influence on organizational variables (i.e. job satisfaction, job involvement, job commitment, and organizational citizenship behavior). Questionnaire-based data have been accomplished from 149 members of 44 teams. The hypothesized relationships among the proposed variables are tested via a structural equation model (SEM). Results show that the geographically disperse and culturally diverse variables are negatively related to the social identity as against those of temporary and organizational variables which are related positively.

Chapter 7

Web Enabled Design Collaboration in India 96

Shaheli Guha, BigMachines Inc., USA
Biswajit Thakur, Meghnad Saha Institute of Technology, India
Tuhin Subhra Konar, Jadavpur University, India
Shibnath Chakrabarty, Jadavpur University, India

Designing large scale real estate projects often requires collaboration between consultants and agencies that are located in different geographical areas. The added constraint of geographical distance to a design approach that already involves multiple participants makes design collaboration a particularly challenging task. This study hypothesizes that design collaboration could benefit from harnessing web technologies. Organizational Risk Analyzer (ORA) software was used to identify the key factors of a collaboration network in a design project located in Kolkata, India. The web enabled internet forum system used was compared with the more traditional system of collaboration using mail. The collaborative network factors like connectedness, density, diffusion, centralization degree, and the node level factors like closeness centrality, eigenvector, betweenness and Burt constraint indicate that internet forums provide a more efficient tool of collaboration than traditional mail network systems. A simulation shows that the forum network operated even in an adverse condition, for example, when the project manager, a key member of the collaboration team, was unavailable.

Chapter 8

Using WarpPLS in E-Collaboration Studies: Mediating Effects, Control and Second Order Variables, and Algorithm Choices 112

Ned Kock, Texas A&M International University, USA

This is a follow-up on two previous articles on WarpPLS and E-collaboration. The first discussed the five main steps through which a variancE-based nonlinear structural equation modeling analysis could be conducted with the software WarpPLS (Kock, 2010b). The second covered specific features related to grouped descriptive statistics, viewing and changing analysis algorithm and resampling settings, and viewing and saving various results (Kock, 2011). This and the previous articles use data from the same

E-collaboration study as a basis for the discussion of important WarpPLS features. Unlike the previous articles, the focus here is on a brief discussion of more advanced issues, such as: testing the significance of mediating effects, including control variables in an analysis, using second order latent variables, choosing the right warping algorithm, and using bootstrapping and jackknifing in combination.

Chapter 9
Shared Mental Model Development During Technology-Mediated Collaboration 125
Hayward P. Andres, North Carolina A&T State University, USA

This study examines how collaboration mode – face-to-face and videoconferencing technology-mediated virtual teams - shapes negotiated shared interpretation of ideas needed for shared mental model construction. Social impact theory and group action theory provide a framework for explaining how technology-mediated collaboration constrains or enhances team shared mental model development. Social impact theory suggests that team member behavior is affected by 1) influential members, 2) number of members, and 3) proximity. Group action theory proposes that team member behavior is guided by 1) assessment of task requirements, 2) adopted task strategy, and 3) evaluation of task solution. This study argues that technology-mediated collaboration will exhibit lower participation rates and intra-team communication deficiencies while developing a shared mental model of task requirements, strategy and status. Partial least squares analysis revealed that technology-mediated collaboration does impact shared mental model development. Observers noted that decision making effectiveness and timeliness regarding task execution strategy and solution content was facilitated by a shared understanding of the task context. The study also confirmed the utility of direct observation for studying communication behaviors and social interaction in the development of shared mental model and teamwork.

Chapter 10
WikiDesign: A Semantic Wiki to Evaluate Collaborative Knowledge 143
Davy Monticolo, National Polytechnic Institute of Lorraine, France
Samuel Gomes, University of Technology of Belfort-Montbéliard, France

This paper presents a knowledge evaluation and evolution in a knowledge management system by using a Semantic Wiki approach. The authors describe a Semantic Wiki called WikiDesign which is a component of a Knowledge Management system. Currently WikiDesign is used in engineering departments of companies to emphasize technical knowledge. This study explains how WikiDesign ensures the reliability of the knowledge base thanks to a knowledge evaluation process. After explaining the interest of the use of semantic wikis in knowledge management approach, the architecture of WikiDesign with its semantic functionalities is described. The effectiveness of WikiDesign is proved with a knowledge evaluation example for an industrial project.

Chapter 11
Industry Perspective-Collaborating from a Distance: Success Factors of Top-Performing
Virtual Teams 155
Darleen DeRosa, OnPoint Consulting, USA

Rising travel costs, coupled with the global dispersion of talent, are two of the reasons that organizations have migrated toward virtual teamwork. While numerous organizations have made significant investments in virtual teams and the technology to support them, a surprising number of virtual teams are not reaching their full potential. A new study conducted by OnPoint surveyed 48 virtual teams across industries and found that there are specific practices that are the key ingredients for optimal virtual team performance. If organizations want to maximize their return on investment, they should ensure that these core practices are in place and continually assess the performance of their virtual teams against these factors over time.

Chapter 12
The Level Paradox of E-Collaboration: Dangers and Solutions.. 166
  Ana Ortiz de Guinea, HEC Montréal, Canada

Although e-collaboration phenomena are multilevel in nature, research to date has been conducted from an exclusively single-level focus. This has lead to the level paradox. The dangers of the level paradox are discussed, including the potential that apparent cumulative knowledge may actually be spurious. Solutions to the level paradox are proposed in the form of future opportunities of research from several mixed-level approaches, and the benefits and barriers to mixed-level research are discussed. The article ends with a discussion on the necessity of finding a balance between single-level and mixed-level research, as well as on the necessity of single-level studies explicitly specifying the levels of theory, measurement, and data in their research.

Chapter 13
E-Collaboration Within, Between, and Without Institutions: Towards Better Functioning of
Online Groups Through Networks.. 188
  Ina Blau, Open University of Israel, Israel

This paper discusses different ways for the exchange of knowledge in networks - within, between, and without institutions, as well as their implication on networks in economy and society. Network systems based on technologies and architectures of participation offer a new model of online knowledge sharing, cooperation, and collaboration, that are different from the traditional institutional framework. This paper suggests that this model opens new horizons for both companies and non-profit organizations. By developing an e-networked business model, companies can make as much or even more money in the long tail of power low distribution than they were making at the head of the curve in the traditional business model. This opens to everyone the possibility of participating and contributing content, non-profit organization and online communities, including Communities of Practice and online learning communities, which can ensure reaching the "critical mass" of contributors and involvement level that will keep these communities active. This paper concludes with an example illustrating how the ideas discussed could facilitate knowledge exchange in companies, organizations or educational institutions.

Chapter 14
Towards an Affordance-Based Theory of Collaborative Action (CoAct)... 204
  John Teofil Paul Nosek, Temple University, USA

Collaborative Action provides a novel approach to modeling interaction among users and machines and IT-mediated collaboration among people to solve problems. CoAct extends the notions of affordance and moves away from idiosyncratic, subjective mental models of the world to the notion that actors with similar capacities to act can potentially discern similar action possibilities in the world. It changes the direction from discovery and alignment of internal representations to mutual attunement of collaborators to build sufficient capabilities, share informational structures, and calibrate selectivity to achieve shared affordances. CoAct has the potential to influence such diverse areas as usability engineering, information overload, and group decision making. CoAct can be used at multiple levels of granularity, from fine granularity of a single interaction to tracking intermediate progress and results of a set of interactions. Propositions based on CoAct are presented. An initial experiment provides some support for an affordance-based approach to information sharing/design.

Chapter 15

Working Effectively in a Matrix: Building and Sustaining Cooperation..228
Jennifer Forgie, OnPoint Consulting, USA

The complexities of today's organizations have made it increasingly challenging for leaders to encourage and sustain a culture of cooperation. As organizations become flatter and leaner and people are required to do "more with less," the key to success is the ability to coordinate decisions and actions across organizational boundaries and gain the support of people who often have competing priorities or conflicting goals. Further, the increasing prevalence of virtual teamwork and widespread use of e-collaboration tools have additional implications for how leaders encourage cooperation and coordinate work. This article explores the critical organizational factors and leadership skills that are required to build a culture of cooperation in today's highly matrix, and often virtual, organizations.

Compilation of References 238

About the Contributors 265

Index..270

Preface

One of the most widely cited theories of communication in professional and education contexts is media richness theory (Daft & Lengel, 1986; Daft et al., 1987). Even though the theory was developed well before the emergence of online learning in university contexts, its key propositions can be used to predict the performance of students in those contexts. Among other predictions, media richness theory argues that if equivocal, or knowledge-intensive tasks are accomplished through media of low richness, task outcomes will be negatively affected (Daft & Lengel, 1986). Electronic media in general are considered less rich than face-to-face media. It is reasonable to assume that the task of learning university subjects is equivocal. Therefore one can conclude based on media richness theory that students learning about university topics online will perform more poorly in tests covering those topics than students learning about the same topics face-to-face.

This type of deterministic prediction usually follows logically from media richness theory, even though Daft & Lengel (1986) might not have intended this. Many studies in the past departed from this type of prediction, and reached conclusions that suggest little or no support for media richness theory (Bélanger & Watson-Manheim, 2006; Burke & Aytes, 2001; Crowston et al., 2007; Dennis & Kinney, 1998; El-Shinnawy & Markus, 1998; Hasty et al., 2006; Kock et al., 2006; Markus, 1994). Moreover, the widespread use of online learning in universities (Newlin et al., 2005; Summers et al., 2005) is an indication that this type of deterministic prediction cannot be correct. It would be unlikely that online learning would be widespread in universities if student learning outcomes were being negatively affected in a material way.

Media naturalness theory (Kock, 2004; 2005) is an attempt to move away from the deterministic predictions of media richness theory. The theory explains an intuitive finding; most people have the perception that media that suppress face-to-face communication elements (e.g., the ability to use tone of voice) pose obstacles for the effective communication of knowledge (Daft et al., 1987; Kock & DeLuca, 2007; Kock et al., 2006). It does so by arguing that the biological communication apparatus of modern humans, which includes various brain modules, is largely "designed" for face-to-face communication (Kock, 2004). It follows from this argument that the removal of face-to-face communication elements from a medium will lead to increased communication ambiguity, increased cognitive effort, and reduced excitement associated with knowledge communication interactions (Kock, 2005).

Can one argue based on media naturalness theory that students learning about university subjects online will perform more poorly in tests covering those subjects than students learning about the same subjects face-to-face? The answer is no, for at least two reasons. The first is that media naturalness theory does not make predictions about task outcomes. The second is that media naturalness theory itself argues that low media naturalness effects (e.g., increased cognitive effort) can lead users of unnatural media to develop mental schemas that will make them better users of those unnatural media. That is, users of unnatural media will adapt to those media in a compensatory way. This adaptation is predicted by Carlson & Zmud's (1999) channel expansion theory, and is thus called here compensatory channel expansion.

This preface discusses a study that tests the predictions of the media naturalness and channel expansion theories, and finds general support for them. Data was collected from undergraduate students at the middle and end of a long semester. The students took an introductory course in management information systems; approximately half of the students took the course face-to-face, and the other half took the course online. As predicted based on media naturalness theory, perceived communication ambiguity and cognitive effort were higher in the online than in the face-to-face communication medium condition. As predicted based on channel expansion theory, the difference between mean grades obtained at the middle of the semester, which was significant, subsided at the end of the semester.

The design of this study is similar to that employed by Kock et al. (2007), in that both are longitudinal studies that analyze data at different points of a long semester. However, the data set for this study is both different and much larger, providing a significantly more elaborate test of the underlying theories and related hypotheses. Moreover, the data analysis methods used in this study are considerably more sophisticated than those employed by Kock et al. (2007). The latter study used primarily nonparametric comparison of means tests, whereas this study employs general linear modeling and partial least squares analyses. Nevertheless, in spite of these differences, the results of this study and Kock et al.'s (2007) study reinforce each other, and provide a solid empirical basis on which the basic tenets of the media naturalness and channel expansion theories are supported.

RESEARCH BACKGROUND AND HYPOTHESES

The focus of this study is on hypothesized relationships between communication media used for instruction in an introductory undergraduate university course in management information systems, as well as perceptions and outcomes related to the task of taking the course. The hypotheses of the study are described in this section. A more detailed discussion of the methods employed and of the results is provided in the next section.

The study was aimed at testing four key hypotheses. Three of the hypotheses guiding the study followed directly from media naturalness theory (Kock, 2004; 2005), and one from channel expansion theory (Carlson, 1995; Carlson & Zmud, 1999). Media naturalness' predictions regarding the impact of a medium's degree of naturalness on communication ambiguity, cognitive effort, and physiological arousal led to hypotheses H1, H2 and H3, listed below.

H1: Students in the online course delivery medium will experience higher levels of perceived communication ambiguity than students in the face-to-face medium.

H2: Students in the online course delivery medium will experience higher levels of perceived cognitive effort than students in the face-to-face medium.

H3: Students in the online course delivery medium will experience lower levels of perceived excitement than students in the face-to-face medium.

As it can be seen from hypothesis H3, perceived excitement was used as a proxy for physiological arousal, since it seemed to be a good choice as the basis of a perceptual measurement of physiological arousal. That is, it was assumed that a medium's effect on physiological arousal would manifest itself through an effect on perceived excitement. (This might have been a bad choice, as it will be explained later.)

Channel expansion theory's prediction that over time users of a particular medium will essentially become more adept at using the medium for a particular task, even if the medium poses obstacles for communication (Carlson, 1995; Carlson & Zmud, 1999), opens the door for the prediction that task outcome quality will be moderated by this longitudinal channel expansion effect. This longitudinal prediction is reflected in hypothesis H4, which is stated below.

H4: Students in the online course delivery medium will have lower grades than students in the face-to-face delivery medium in the middle of the semester, but not at the end of the semester.

Hypothesis H4 is not only important because it illustrates the combination of an evolutionary theory with a non-evolutionary one. Its importance also comes from the fact that empirical support for it is in direct contradiction with one of media richness theory's key predictions (Daft & Lengel, 1986; Daft et al. 1987). The prediction in question is that task outcome quality will suffer if the choice of medium is constrained and the medium used is lean, which was the case in this study from the moment students had to choose either the online or the face-to-face course delivery medium. That is, eventual support for H4 illustrates the need for media naturalness theory in combination with channel expansion theory, because the hypothesis addresses one of the chief differences between the media naturalness and richness theories.

As it will be seen in the next section, the results of the study generally supported the combined theoretical model. The only exception was hypothesis H3, which was not supported by the results. The study is one of the first to test media naturalness theory, and also one of the first to test channel expansion theory. Its results are consistent with other studies that tested the theories either fully or partially; see Simon (2006) for a previous test of media naturalness theory, and Hasty et al. (2006) for a previous test of channel expansion theory.

RESEARCH METHODS

A total of 155 undergraduate students participated in the study. Approval was obtained from the IRB at our institution and participants provided written informed consent when participating in this study. Data was collected at the middle and end of a long semester in which the students took an introductory course in management information systems, thus yielding 310 repeated-measure data points. Approximately half of the students took the course face-to-face. The other half took the course entirely online, with no face-to-face meetings. Both media conditions employed the same course materials and covered the same course content. That is, the main difference between media conditions was in the communication medium employed for course delivery.

The online courseware suite used was WebCT. The course materials used in both sections were essentially PowerPoint slides and online papers. No textbook was used in the course; the students were required to review all the course materials provided and discuss them with each other and the instructor (as opposed to read a textbook) to do well in the course. In the online section, audio clips for each of the slides were made available to the students as generic RealMedia files, and discussions on papers were conducted through an online discussion board available in WebCT. No student reported problems playing the audio clips, using WebCT, or accessing any of the course materials.

Forty-six percent of the students were males. The students' ages ranged from 18 to 48, with a mean age of 24. The students' grade point averages (GPAs) ranged from 1.8 to 3.9 (out of 4), with a mean GPA of 2.9. In terms of years of work experience, students ranged from 0 (zero, or no work experience) to 40 years, with a mean of 6 years. Since students self-selected their media conditions, there were small variations in these variables (i.e., gender, age, GPA, and work experience) across media conditions. Given that these variations could have affected grades in the middle and end of the semester, these variables were included as control variables and/or covariates in the analyses.

Communication ambiguity, cognitive effort, and excitement were defined as latent variables and measured through multiple indicators (Hair et al., 1987; Kline, 1998). The media effects on these latent variables (hypothesized through H1, H2, and H3) were tested through quantitative analyses employing the partial least squares technique (Chin, 1998; Chin et al., 2003), a structural equation modeling technique (Kline, 1998) designed to test effects in connection with latent variables.

The media effects on grades (hypothesized through H4) were tested employing the general linear modeling and partial least squares techniques. Midterm and final exam grades were used, and those grades were independent from each other. That is, midterm and final grades were obtained based on exams on topics covered in the first half of the course (midterm), and in the second half of the course (final).

The general linear modeling technique is traditionally used in comparisons of means analyses with no latent variables (Hair et al., 1987; Rencher, 1998), and grades were not measured as latent variables. Nevertheless, the partial least squares technique was also used in the test of media effects on grades for two reasons. The first is completeness, since it was also used in the test of hypotheses H1, H2, and H3. The second and most important is the quasi-experimental design used in this study, which calls for the use of nonparametric methods. The estimation of chance probabilities in the partial least squares technique is done through a nonparametric algorithm, usually bootstrapping or jackknifing (Chin, 1998; Gefen et al., 2000). In this study, the algorithm employed was bootstrapping (Diaconis & Efron, 1983; Nevitt & Hancock, 2001). Nonparametric estimation of chance probabilities is generally considered more appropriate when the study employs a quasi-experimental design (Siegel & Castellan, 1998). This is the case in this study since the student participants were not randomly assigned to each media condition.

Given that media naturalness theory does not make any predictions regarding longitudinal effects, the tests in connection with communication ambiguity, cognitive effort and excitement relied on analyses of the whole dataset. That is, those analyses were run on data at the middle and end of the semester, with a corresponding sample size of 310. Conversely, since channel expansion theory makes predictions regarding longitudinal effects, separate analyses of media effects on grades were conducted in the middle and end of the semester, each with a corresponding sample size of 155.

VALIDATION OF THE MEASUREMENT MODEL

Whenever latent variables are used in data analyses some tests must be conducted in order to assess the validity and reliability of the latent variable measurement model (Kline, 1998). Reliability is usually assessed through the calculation of reliability coefficients, such as Cronbach's alpha and the composite reliability coefficient, and the comparison of those coefficients against a threshold, usually .7 (Fornell & Larcker, 1981; Nunnaly, 1978).

As for validity, two types of tests are normally employed in latent variable measurement model assessment, namely convergent and discriminant validity tests. Convergent validity is normally assessed through the comparison of factor loadings calculated for each latent variable indicator with a threshold value, which is usually .5 (Hair et al., 1987). Discriminant validity usually relies on the calculation and comparison of correlations between each pair of latent variables and square roots of the average variances extracted for each latent variable (Fornell & Larcker, 1981).

Table 1 shows factor loadings associated with each latent variable. The loadings were calculated through a factor analysis employing principal components as its extraction method, and varimax as its rotation method (Ehremberg & Goodhart, 1976; Thompson, 2004). Also shown in the last two columns on the right are reliability coefficients. All factor loadings associated with their respective latent variables are higher than .5, suggesting that the measurement model presents acceptable convergent validity. All reliability coefficients are higher than .7, suggesting that the model also has acceptable reliability.

Table 2 shows correlations between each pair of latent variables and square roots of the average variances extracted for each latent variable. For each latent variable, the square root of the variable's average variance extracted is higher than any of the correlations involving the variable. Therefore it can be concluded that the latent variable measurement model has acceptable discriminant validity (Fornell & Larcker, 1981).

The latent variable measurement model tests above allow for the conclusion that the results of latent variable analysis techniques, such as the partial least squares technique (Chin, 1998; Chin et al., 2003), can be trusted. If our study did not employ latent variables, for example, by focusing only on the media impact on grades, the above measurement model tests would not be necessary (or possible). However, such a study would only address the channel expansion effect (on grades) and no media naturalness effects.

Table 1. Latent variable loadings and reliability coefficients

	Communication ambiguity	Cognitive effort	Excitement	Alpha	CR
Ambig1	.747	.286	.114	.901	.930
Ambig2	.857	.221	.080		
Ambig3	.908	.157	.087		
Ambig4	.886	.085	.077		
Cogeff1	.054	.720	.337	.830	.886
Cogeff2	.145	.829	.185		
Cogeff3	.232	.833	.078		
Cogeff4	.385	.705	.059		
Excite1	.155	.125	.834	.825	.869
Excite2	.038	.111	.827		
Excite3	.088	.246	.862		

Notes:

Alpha = Cronbach's alpha reliability coefficient

CR = composite reliability coefficient

Table 2. Latent variable correlations and square roots of AVEs

	Communication ambiguity	Cognitive effort	Excitement
Communication ambiguity	(.877)		
Cognitive effort	.432	(.813)	
Excitement	.194	.365	(.832)

Notes:

All correlations are significant at the .01 level

Square roots of average variances extracted (AVEs) are shown on diagonal

RESULTS OF THE STATISTICAL ANALYSES

Table 3 summarizes the results of partial least squares analyses of media effects on communication ambiguity (hypothesis H1), cognitive effort (H2), and excitement (H3). The columns labeled "Online" and "Face-to-face" show the means for each latent variable in the online and face-to-face media conditions, respectively. The column labeled "t" shows the t statistics associated with the path coefficients (from the partial least squares technique) between the medium condition (i.e., the independent variable) and the latent variables communication ambiguity, cognitive effort, and excitement (i.e., the dependent variables). These t statistics are equivalent to, but not the same as, the statistics that would be calculated through an independent samples comparison of means t test (Rosenthal & Rosnow, 1991).

As predicted based on media naturalness theory, perceived communication ambiguity and cognitive effort were higher in the online than in the face-to-face communication medium condition. These results provide support for hypotheses H1 and H2. However, no significant difference was found in perceived excitement between media conditions. This latter result is not consistent with hypothesis H3.

Table 4 summarizes the results of general linear modeling and partial least squares analyses of media effects on grades at the middle and end of the semester (hypothesis H4). The columns labeled "Online" and "Face-to-face" show the mean grades at the middle and end of the semester in the online and face-to-face media conditions, respectively.

As predicted based on channel expansion theory, the difference between mean grades obtained at the middle of the semester subsided at the end of the semester. This provides support for hypothesis H4 and the related notion that there was a channel expansion effect. That effect arguably led to no differences in performance observed across media conditions at the end of the semester, when the students in the online condition were more familiar with the use of the online medium for the learning task.

DISCUSSION

The results discussed in the previous section generally support the combined theoretical model on which the hypotheses were developed (see Table 5). Only one out of four hypotheses was not supported by the data, namely hypothesis H3. The lack of support for hypothesis H3 suggests two paths of action. One of them is the refinement of media naturalness theory, perhaps through the removal of the physiological arousal prediction in connection with the theory. The other path of action is to change the measurement model used and conduct future empirical tests using the modified measurement model.

Table 3. Mean online and face-to-face scores for perceptual variables

	Online	Face-to-face	T	P(t)
Communication ambiguity	3.666	3.423	1.630	< .05
Cognitive effort	5.299	5.037	1.587	< .05
Excitement	5.612	5.503	1.041	.149

Notes:

Measurement scale range = 1 to 7

t = t statistic associated with path coefficient (PLS analysis)

P = chance probability associated with t statistic

Table 4. Mean grades obtained online and face-to-face at the middle and end of the semester

	Online	Face-to-face	F	P(F)	t	P(t)
Grade middle	74.23	83.07	11.350	< .001	3.225	< .001
Grade end	76.19	77.60	.336	.563	.590	.278

Notes:

Grade middle = mean grade at the middle of the semester

Grade end = mean grade at the end of the semester

F = F statistic associated with difference between media means (GLM analysis)

t = t statistic associated with path between medium and grade (PLS analysis)

P = chance probability associated with statistic

Table 5. Summary of the results vis-à-vis the hypotheses

Theory	Hypothesis	Supported?
Media naturalness	H1: Students in the online course delivery medium will experience higher levels of perceived communication ambiguity than students in the face-to-face medium.	Yes
Media naturalness	H2: Students in the online course delivery medium will experience higher levels of perceived cognitive effort than students in the face-to-face medium.	Yes
Media naturalness	H3: Students in the online course delivery medium will experience lower levels of perceived excitement than students in the face-to-face medium.	No
Channel expansion	H4: Students in the online course delivery medium will have lower grades than students in the face-to-face delivery medium in the middle of the semester, but not at the end of the semester.	Yes

The combined theoretical model was generally but not fully supported, as indicated by the lack of support for hypothesis H3, and further testing may require a change in the measurement of the construct associated with H3. The key reason for this is the original formulation of the prediction by media naturalness theory that led to hypothesis H3. That original formulation built on the notion of physiological arousal (Kock, 2005), which was measured through a latent variable whose indicators (Hair et al., 1987; Kline, 1998) reflect perceived excitement. For example, one of the question-statements used was: "Taking this course has been very exciting".

The prediction that a medium's naturalness has a positive effect on physiological arousal comes from a key argument made by media naturalness theory. The argument has three main parts. The first part, already discussed earlier, is that we have evolved a biological communication apparatus designed to excel in face-to-face communication, and that apparatus includes a customized vocal tract, brain modules and other elements. The second part of the argument is that evolution is an economical agent that rarely endows an organism right at the moment of birth with all that is needed for the organism to successfully spread genes associated with certain traits (Kock, 2004; 2005). Instead, evolution relies on an organism's interaction with the environment to shape its traits, often creating mechanisms to compel it to engage in practices that will form a biological apparatus, which will contribute to the organism's reproductive success (see also, Wilson, 2000). One such practice in the human species is, arguably, a great deal of face-to-face communication.

The above line of reasoning leads to the third part of the argument in the context of media naturalness theory that: "…evolution must have developed mechanisms to compel human beings to practice the use of their biological communication apparatus, mechanisms that are similar to those compelling animals to practice those skills that play a key role in connection with survival and mating. Among these mechanisms, one of the most important is that of physiological arousal, which is often associated with excitement and pleasure" (Kock, 2005, p. 123). As a corollary, media naturalness theory predicts that the use of media that are unnatural will prevent physiological arousal from being fully experienced, which is expected to lead to a sense of dullness in connection with the task for which the media are used. This is expected to be particularly true in tasks involving a great deal of communication through the media in question.

A substantial amount of evidence exists that is consistent with the above prediction. This evidence suggests that electronic communication media with low degrees of naturalness are generally perceived as less exciting, duller, or less emotionally fulfilling than face-to-face communication (Ellis et al., 1991; Kiesler et al., 1988; Reinig et al., 1995; Sproull and Kiesler, 1986; Walther, 1996). However, most of this evidence associates low naturalness with negative perceptions (e.g., less exciting). This would suggest that a more appropriate proxy latent variable for the study reported here would have been one reflecting perceived *lack* of excitement, or dullness, instead of excitement. This could be incorporated into additional tests of the combined model through a revision of the indicators and related question-statements used to measure physiological arousal.

CONCLUSION

While a number of studies have looked at various aspects of the effects of face-to-face and online learning (Coppola et al, 2004; Day et al, 2004; Mehlenbacher et al, 2000; Shen et al, 2008; Uden, 2003), this study provides a more nuanced understanding of the effects of online learning at the university level;

effects that are often misinterpreted when taken out of context. Critics of the use of online learning in universities frequently point at effects that are analogous to the ones observed in this study at the middle of the semester, in order to justify their opposition to this mode of delivery. Supporters of the use of online learning in universities, on the other hand, usually point at results that are analogous to those observed in this study at the end of the semester, to argue that online learning offers advantages (e.g., time flexibility, access to education in remote areas) without any significant negative effects (as measured by grades). This study shows that both negative and positive effects may occur in the same semester, leading to a final outcome that is generally positive. It is the interplay of positive and negative effects that is clarified by this study and explained by the underlying theoretical framework.

From an organizational perspective, this study is of interest to organizations utilizing tools such as virtual groups and online training for organizational knowledge communication, itself an important goal of effective professional communication. Because online training in organizations is often perceived as being cost effective and efficient as well as readily available to employees and easily replicable, a growing number of businesses currently use this delivery method to impart organizational knowledge (DeRouin et al, 2005; Roberts et al, 2006). Studies such as this can be applied to organizational environments and provide a better understanding of the effects of online training for employees. Based on this study, one would expect perceptions of increased communication ambiguity and cognitive effort to be associated with online training media, at least initially. The final organizational knowledge communication outcomes, however, are likely to be of the same quality as those achieved through traditional face-to-face media. Similarly, virtual groups lasting more than a few days and interacting primarily online are likely to experience increased communication ambiguity and cognitive effort, until channel expansion allows those groups to compensate for the obstacles posed by the online medium, and achieve outcomes of similar quality to traditional face-to-face groups.

Ned Kock
Texas A&M International University, USA

REFERENCES

Bélanger, F., & Watson-Manheim, M. B. (2006). Virtual teams and multiple media: Structuring media use to attain strategic goals. *Group Decision and Negotiation*, *15*(4), 299–321. doi:10.1007/s10726-006-9044-8

Burke, K., & Aytes, K. (2001). Do media really affect perceptions and procedural structuring among partially-distributed groups? *Journal on Systems and Information Technology*, *5*(1), 10–23.

Carlson, J. R. (1995). *Channel expansion theory: A dynamic view of media and information richness perception*. Doctoral Dissertation. Tallahassee, FL: Florida State University.

Carlson, J. R., & Zmud, R. W. (1999). Channel expansion theory and the experiential nature of media richness perceptions. *Academy of Management Journal*, *42*(2), 153–170. doi:10.2307/257090

Chin, W. W. (1998). Issues and opinion on structural equation modeling. *Management Information Systems Quarterly*, *22*(1), vii–xvi.

Chin, W. W., Marcolin, B. L., & Newsted, P. R. (2003). A partial least squares latent variable modeling approach for measuring interaction effects: Results from a Monte Carlo simulation study and an electronic-mail emotion/adoption study. *Information Systems Research, 14*(2), 189–217. doi:10.1287/isre.14.2.189.16018

Coppola, N. W., Hiltz, S. R., & Rotter, N. G. (2004). Building trust in virtual teams. *IEEE Transactions on Professional Communication, 47*(2), 95–104. doi:10.1109/TPC.2004.828203

Crowston, K., Howison, J., Masango, C., & Eseryel, U. Y. (2007). The role of face-to-face meetings in technology-supported self-organizing distributed teams. *IEEE Transactions on Professional Communication, 50*(3), 185–203. doi:10.1109/TPC.2007.902654

Daft, R. L., & Lengel, R. H. (1986). Organizational information requirements, media richness and structural design. *Management Science, 32*(5), 554–571. doi:10.1287/mnsc.32.5.554

Daft, R. L., Lengel, R. H., & Trevino, L. K. (1987). Message equivocality, media selection, and manager performance: Implications for information systems. *Management Information Systems Quarterly, 11*(3), 355–366. doi:10.2307/248682

Day, J., Lou, H., & Van Slyke, C. (2004). Instructors' experiences with using groupware to support collaborative project-based learning. *International Journal of Distance Education Technologies, 2*(3), 11–25. doi:10.4018/jdet.2004070102

Dennis, A. R., & Kinney, S. T. (1998). Testing media richness theory in the new media: The effects of cues, feedback, and task equivocality. *Information Systems Research, 9*(3), 256–274. doi:10.1287/isre.9.3.256

DeRouin, R. E., Fritzsche, B. A., & Salas, E. (2005). E-learning in organizations. *Journal of Management, 31*(6), 920–940. doi:10.1177/0149206305279815

Diaconis, P., & Efron, B. (1983). Computer-intensive methods in statistics. *Scientific American, 249*(1), 116–130. doi:10.1038/scientificamerican0583-116

Ehremberg, A. S. C., & Goodhart, G. J. (1976). *Factor analysis: Limitations and alternatives.* Cambridge, MA: Marketing Science Institute.

El-Shinnawy, M., & Markus, L. (1998). Acceptance of communication media in organizations: Richness or features? *IEEE Transactions on Professional Communication, 41*(4), 242–253. doi:10.1109/47.735366

Ellis, C. A., Gibbs, S. J., & Rein, G. L. (1991). Groupware: Some issues and experiences. *Communications of the ACM, 34*(1), 39–58. doi:10.1145/99977.99987

Fornell, C., & Larcker, D. F. (1981). Evaluating structural equation models with unobservable variables and measurement error. *JMR, Journal of Marketing Research, 18*(1), 39–50. doi:10.2307/3151312

Gefen, D., Straub, D. W., & Boudreau, M.-C. (2000). Structural equation modeling and regression: Guidelines for research practice. *Communications of the AIS, 4*(7), 1–76.

Hair, J. F., Anderson, R. E., & Tatham, R. L. (1987). *Multivariate data analysis* (2nd ed.). New York, NY: Macmillan.

Hasty, B. K., Massey, A. P., & Brown, S. A. (2006). Role-based experiences, media perceptions, and knowledge transfer in virtual dyads. *Group Decision and Negotiation, 15*(4), 367–387. doi:10.1007/s10726-006-9047-5

Kiesler, S., Siegel, J., & McGuire, T. W. (1988). Social psychological aspects of computer-mediated communication . In Greif, I. (Ed.), *Computer-supported cooperative work: A book of readings* (pp. 657–682). San Mateo, CA: Morgan Kaufmann.

Kline, R. B. (1998). *Principles and practice of structural equation modeling.* New York, NY: The Guilford Press.

Kock, N. (2004). The psychobiological model: Towards a new theory of computer-mediated communication based on Darwinian evolution. *Organization Science, 15*(3), 327–348. doi:10.1287/orsc.1040.0071

Kock, N. (2005). Media richness or media naturalness? The evolution of our biological communication apparatus and its influence on our behavior toward e-communication tools. *IEEE Transactions on Professional Communication, 48*(2), 117–130. doi:10.1109/TPC.2005.849649

Kock, N., & DeLuca, D. (2007). Improving business processes electronically: An action research study in New Zealand and the U.S. *Journal of Global Information Technology Management, 10*(3), 6–27.

Kock, N., Lynn, G. S., Dow, K. E., & Akgün, A. E. (2006). Team adaptation to electronic communication media: Evidence of compensatory adaptation in new product development teams. *European Journal of Information Systems, 15*(3), 331–341. doi:10.1057/palgrave.ejis.3000612

Kock, N., Verville, J., & Garza, V. (2007). Media naturalness and online learning: Findings supporting both the significant- and no-significant-difference perspectives. *Decision Sciences Journal of Innovative Education, 5*(2), 333–356. doi:10.1111/j.1540-4609.2007.00144.x

Markus, M. L. (1994). Finding a happy medium: Explaining the negative effects of electronic communication on social life at work. *ACM Transactions on Information Systems, 12*(2), 119–149. doi:10.1145/196734.196738

Mehlenbacher, B., Miller, C. R., Covington, D., & Larsen, J. S. (2000). Active and interactive learning online: A comparison of web-based and conventional writing classes. *IEEE Transactions on Professional Communication, 43*(2), 166–184. doi:10.1109/47.843644

Nevitt, J., & Hancock, G. R. (2001). Performance of bootstrapping approaches to model test statistics and parameter standard error estimation in structural equation modeling. *Structural Equation Modeling, 8*(3), 353–377. doi:10.1207/S15328007SEM0803_2

Newlin, M. H., Lavooy, M. J., & Wang, A. Y. (2005). An experimental comparison of conventional and web-based instructional formats. *North American Journal of Psychology, 7*(2), 327–335.

Nunnaly, J. (1978). *Psychometric theory.* New York, NY: McGraw Hill.

Reinig, B. A., Briggs, R. O., Shepherd, M. M., Yen, J., & Nunamaker, J. F. Jr. (1995). Affective reward and the adoption of group support systems: Productivity is not always enough. *Journal of Management Information Systems, 12*(3), 171–185.

Rencher, A. C. (1998). *Multivariate statistical inference and applications*. New York, NY: John Wiley & Sons.

Roberts, T. L., Lowry, B. E., & Sweeney, P. D. (2006). An evaluation of the impact of social presence through group size and the use of collaborative software on group member "voice" in face-to-face and computer-mediated task groups. *IEEE Transactions on Professional Communication, 49*(1), 28–43. doi:10.1109/TPC.2006.870460

Rosenthal, R., & Rosnow, R. L. (1991). *Essentials of behavioral research: Methods and data analysis*. Boston, MA: McGraw Hill.

Shen, J., Hiltz, S. R., & Bieber, M. (2008). Learning strategies in online collaborative examinations. *IEEE Transactions on Professional Communication, 51*(1), 63–78. doi:10.1109/TPC.2007.2000053

Siegel, S., & Castellan, N. J. (1998). *Nonparametric statistics for the behavioral sciences*. Boston, MA: McGraw-Hill.

Simon, A. F. (2006). Computer-mediated communication: Task performance and satisfaction. *The Journal of Social Psychology, 146*(3), 349–379. doi:10.3200/SOCP.146.3.349-379

Sproull, L., & Kiesler, S. (1986). Reducing social context cues: Electronic mail in organizational communication. *Management Science, 32*(11), 1492–1512. doi:10.1287/mnsc.32.11.1492

Summers, J., Waigandt, A., & Whittaker, T. (2005). A comparison of student achievement and satisfaction in an online versus a traditional face-to-face statistics class. *Innovative Higher Education, 29*(3), 233–250. doi:10.1007/s10755-005-1938-x

Thompson, B. (2004). *Exploratory and confirmatory factor analysis: Understanding concepts and applications*. Washington, DC: American Psychological Association. doi:10.1037/10694-000

Uden, L. (2003). An engineering approach for online learning. *International Journal of Distance Education Technologies, 1*(1), 63–77.

Walther, J. B. (1996). Computer-mediated communication: Impersonal, interpersonal, and hyperpersonal interaction. *Communication Research, 23*(1), 3–43. doi:10.1177/009365096023001001

Wilson, E. O. (2000). *Sociobiology: The new synthesis*. Cambridge, MA: Harvard University Press.

Acknowledgment

Revised text from articles published by the author in the *International Journal of e-Collaboration* and the *International Journal of Distance Education Technologies* has been used in the preparation of this preface. The editor thanks Vanessa Garza, Murad Moqbel, and Miguel Rangel for their valuable help in the data collection for the respective studies and overall development of those articles.

Ned Kock
Texas A&M International University, USA

Chapter 1
A Semantic E-Collaboration Approach to Enable Awareness in Globally Distributed Organizations

Eldar Sultanow
University of Potsdam, Germany

Edzard Weber
University of Potsdam, Germany

Sean Cox
Mathematicians Anonymous, USA

ABSTRACT

Collaboration in temporal and spatially distributed environments has consistently faced the challenge of intense awareness extensively more than locally concentrated team play. Awareness means being informed, in conjunction with an understanding of activities, states and relationships of each individual within a given group as a whole. In multifarious offices, where social interaction is necessary to share and locate essential information, awareness becomes a concurrent process that amplifies the exigency for easy routes where personnel can navigate and access pertinent information, deferred or decentralized, in a formalized and context-sensitive way. Even as awareness has become a more pressing topic, extensive disagreement still remains concerning how any type of transparency can be conceptually and technically implemented. This paper introduces an awareness model to visualize and navigate such information in multi-tiers using semantic networks, GIS (Geographic Information Systems) and Web3D. Ultimately, the model presented is used for an evaluation from a business organization's perspective.

DOI: 10.4018/978-1-4666-2020-9.ch001

INTRODUCTION

The term E-Collaboration was originally introduced by Kock (2005) along with the following six key conceptual elements: the collaborative task, E-collaboration technology, individuals involved in the collaborative task, mental schema possessed by the individuals, the physical environment surrounding the individuals and the social environment surrounding the individuals. The present investigation will focus primarily in the domain of the second and third key elements; namely, E-collaboration technology (especially semantic web, GIS and Web3D) and individuals involved in the collaborative task (roles and responsibilities of personnel of the distributed organization).

An identification of classes for E-Collaboration Systems is given by Riemer (2009). He builds a catalog of classification criteria which he uses to generate a classification scheme using cluster analysis. Based on the cluster results, four main system classes emerged that characterize E-Collaboration systems. The conceptualized system outlined here can be well classified into the class of integrated systems of his developed scheme, especially into a subclass called Real-time collaboration (RTC) systems. RTC systems are mainly used for real-time coordination purposes and for the creation of awareness in the context of distributed work scenarios. These systems purport to present an answer to challenges such as a lack of awareness between co-workers' activities and their respective locations. However, a problem ensues as the communicative complexity increases proportionately to the number of available communication channels and devices introduced, and personnel are thus faced with an increase in communication volume, and work interruptions, which is accompanied by a poor system for identifying the availability of their co-workers. The latter typically impedes information access and the free flow of knowledge. This challenge is ad-

dressed by the awareness model described below. The principle motivation for this article lies in resolving the problem of the major disagreement on how to implement awareness in order to solve many of these problems. Awareness is an integral CSCW (computer Supported Cooperative Work) research component, which Dourish and Bellotti (1992, p. 107) define as follows:

...awareness is an understanding of the activities of others, which provides a con- text for your own activity.

With growth in the area of sensor technology and RFID (Radio Frequency Identification), a new version of the expression awareness has been established dubbed "Real World Awareness" (RWA), a rendition expanded around the ability to perceive information of persons as well as of systems in real time, and to instantaneously react to that information competently (Heinrich, 2005, p. 24):

Real World Awareness is the ability to sense information in real-time from people, IT sources, and physical objects – by using technologies like RFID and sensors – and then to respond quickly and effectively.

RWA is intended to reduce or dissolve media disruptions, and thus minimize, or even close, the gap between natural and virtual worlds. The natural world exists in the physical and operational reality such as persons, products and resources whereas the virtual world exists in information technology such as ERP (Enterprise Resource Planning) and SCM (Supply Chain Management) systems as well as local, regional and global information networks.

The literature (see Heinrich, 2005), reflected the basic idea behind Real World Awareness and can be summarized by following three essential points:

- The natural world is portrayed in current and accurate detail in an IT system.
- The transparency in corporate supply networks or in the entire value chain increases.
- Exceptions occur on both short-termed and constantly-changing business environmental conditions, which can be reacted to accordingly.

The integration of semantic web, and GIS and Web3D technologies against the backdrop of awareness are all characteristics that ultimately outline the model detailed here.

There is a majority consensus on the use of semantic networks in order to portray objects including their relations to each other; see the Aether model (Sandor, Bogdan, & Bowers, 1997), the event oriented model (Fuchs, PankokE-Babatz, & Prinz, 1995) and the Model of Modulated Awareness, abbreviated MoMA (Simone & Bandini, 2002). Semantic networks are well-structured, flexible and intuitive; and as such, are increasingly being used for the development of software products. For instance, Fuchs-Kittowski and Faust (2009) develop a semantic web 2.0-like collaboration tool in order to support the collaboration of all individuals involved in the process of designing an enterprise architecture.

Semantic networks effect transparency in relationships and enhance navigation through concept chains. A concrete implementation of semantic networks is Topic Maps (TM); whose conceptual and technical aspects are held by the Topic Maps standard family. Topic Maps are used to represent dynamically changing engineering contexts and to query by TMQL (Topic Map Query Language). A context-aware computing framework for collaborative virtual engineering services by adopting semantic web-based context-awareness was introduced by Lee, Seo, Kim, and Kim (2005).

A Topic Map consists of Topics, Associations and Occurrences (the so-called TAO principle). Topics illustrate things that exist in reality, which are connected to each other through Associations by their relationships. Occurrences are references to further information on Topics in external documents. The informational content is not included in the Topic Map itself.

The model proposed in this examination brings Web3D into effect with a view to illustrate real-world relationships on a shared virtual globe. Web3D is a generic term for all techniques which identify the threE-dimensional content visualization on the Internet. These techniques involve the use of threE-dimensional computer graphics in web applications. With consideration given to their integration using the model, two aspects of this technique that will be introduced in this paper are:

- The intuitive navigation and visualization of large quantities of information with the help of semantic networks, and;
- The interaction of project members in different location or times, related to reality by means of cartographic geo-visualization.

Applications which come under the heading of GIS are gaining increasingly more inertia. A Geographic Perspectives on E-Collaboration Research has been given by Gilbert and Masucci (2006). Such applications and models have already been implemented. For instance MacEachren (2001) provides an essay on how to extend collaborative tools by means of GIS and cartography to support virtual teams. Diosteanu and Cotfas (2009) created a framework for developing businesses and GIS applications, with their main goal being the assurance of efficient knowledge management by facilitating organization interoperability. They also present an application for supply chain management which was developed using the same framework.

In Bishr (1998), with respect to the worldwide awareness, the aspect "interoperability" is underlined and discussed in the context of GIS. Meanwhile Bishr (1998) introduces layers of interoperability beginning from application semantics over databases down to the lowest level such as hardware and OS and network protocols. In our approach, interoperability is examined on the semantic web layer by inputting and linking all data from different sources into a topic map.

In the course of this contribution the model will be initially defined with regard to its tiers and the elements of its semantic reference system. To this end, collaboration scenarios will be given. The next step entails the technical realization of the model, which will be evaluated during the final phase. The evaluation itself is performed by the implementation of a prototype and subsequently conducting expert interviews in business organizations to gauge competency. Figure 1 shows the organization of this article.

Three Tiers of Awareness

The core requirement of a model for the visualization of collaboration lies in its illustrative aptitude for depicting the essential characteristics of a coalition; including the amount of people involved, activities they do and the objects they use, as well as their relationships to each other.

The model presented here distinguishes three levels of representation, which all serve as a type of detail:

- World view (macro view): Core members of the global network and channels between them;
- Location of view (meso view): Local offices, located partners and relevant sitE-related infrastructure;
- View of an organization unit (micro view): workplace, roles, responsibilities and artifacts.

Personnel and activities are specifically presented to particular cases at each corresponding level. The above threefold division is pragmatic – in very large organizations even intermediate stages could be conceived. Entities in the micro view (roles) are atomic. The elements of a level are wired in a semantic network. An element may, in turn, be described again by elements of a semantic network in a subordinate detail.

The user can filter out information by applying a filter at each level. Relevant filter criteria include projects and their components, departments, skills, industries and artifacts. The filtration itself is based on a search using semantic query languages for Topic Maps, for a more technical description on query language for Topic Maps "TMQL" (Barta, 2007), see "Toma" (Pinchuk et al., 2007), and "Tolog" (Garshol, 2006).

Macro View

The macro view displays the locations of the core members, including their connections and available channels between these locations. Connection types can differ from lines of communication in comparison to those used for people, data or material handling. Figure 2 gives a macro view of an exemplary collaboration scenario that may arise in a state of emergency. In this case topics of the semantic web include offices, hospitals, rescue teams, vehicles and people playing key roles that are all interconnected. An established connection between two entities is a channel in accordance with this model. Data pathways, travel routes consisting of a connecting boat service, a flight connection and intersections (e.g., an international airport) are each represented as a channel.

Figure 1. Procedure for implementing global awareness

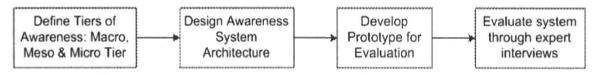

Figure 2. The world-view of global collaboration

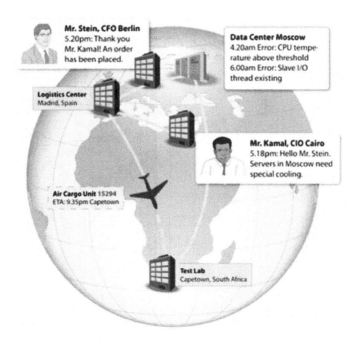

The macro view on a collaboration scenario of business organizations shows topics such as engineering offices and testing divisions overseas with a (possibly automated) transfer of test artifacts and result protocols.

Meso View

The second layer presented provides a detailed view of individual sites. It lists those sites and channels that are only noteworthy for establishments of network development at any one particular regional site. These include agencies, suppliers and depots, which are only interested in this particular regional site to implement and maintain its work. Their existence is not of any interest for network members in other locations as there would already be one's own regional supply network at the other locations.

Similar to the macro view, this view also shows the established link between regional locations. The focus on visualization is once more primarily on the mere existence of these connections rather than their actual design. On the other hand, there are institutions that act as an interface in order to facilitate connecting with other sites and to function as regionally significant sites. Thus, an airport is not part of a regional connection but is an end junction of a separate component of regional infrastructure.

The exemplary scenario displayed in Figure 3 shows an urban area, in the business' warehouse, web design and marketing operation. This is displayed together with flight, bus and taxi connections. Individual documents, such as project reports, flight schedules or delivery confirmations are linked together and are formed in the Topic Map. Other visualized elements, in the second representational level, are links to courier services and telephone accessibility.

Micro View

The third and lowest level is semantically linked to the places of employment, positions, roles and artifacts. This level details the view of in-

Figure 3. Location of view with departments and local infrastructure (rendered with LandXplorer CityGML Viewer)

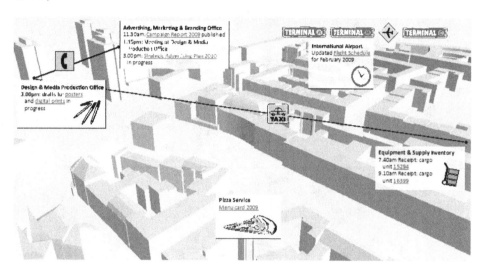

dividual organizational units. It also displays available channels of work flow, prioritized from the principle to the least used pathway. Jobs are associated with artifacts (documents), whereby job descriptions or access rights act as additional information, which can be complemented in the form of occurrences.

As a topic, people are assigned appropriately with accordance to their jobs, positions and roles. Additional links may be added between jobs, positions, given roles and separate actors. Actors have the ability to use the channels that are visually available in the macro, meso and micro views. When they are in the relevant period of use in any one given channel, then they will be visualized. Additional information about the current activity will then be treated as an occurrence, and suitably displayed.

Activities are always addressed by at least one actor and are treated as Topics. The visualization not only shows directly neighboring objects of the involved actors, but also depicts the connection lines that offer the channel for this activity. Topics, and in particular, activities, may vary according to their temporal occurrence and can be faded in and out. This provides an opportunity to visualize temporal relationships.

Figure 4 shows the structure of a business unit in a static and dynamic view. The static view illustrates employees, roles and artifacts. The dynamic view serves to show how actors interact with each other. This could be, for example, a phone call or a sent fax.

Various activities of actors have already been featured in Figure 2. The communication aspect was related to the first level (macro view) of project members blended in at globally distributed sites to synchronously communicate with each other using devices such as instant messaging or VoIP (Voice over IP)-conferences.

Awareness About Informal Activities

In order to record and describe information about informal and knowledgE-intensive activities, a method has been developed (Gronau, Müller, & Korf, 2005), which is called Knowledge Modeling and Description Language (KMDL). This language describes knowledge and information processes found in reality. Special attention is paid to those processes which are not described by information systems. These processes are principally unconscious and become only transparent due to modeling. Thus, transparency is one of the zenith

Figure 4. Employees, artifacts within an institution (Static View on the left) and employees, artifacts and activities (Dynamic View on the right)

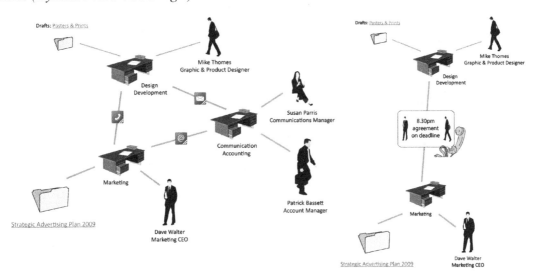

reasons for choosing the KMDL-method. Human activity and output, along with skills brought in and subsequent knowledge applied, are the essential building blocks of these processes. Figure 5 shows a process model for the requirement specification noted in KMDL. The actors in this example range from customers, innovation research managers and project managers. Information and explicit knowledge are modeled as information-objects in KMDL. In this case, the requirement specification is an information-object. The knowledge implemented, which is tacit, is represented as a knowledgE-object in KMDL method. This encompasses customer needs, product ideas and product knowledge. According to Leidner, Alavi, and Kayworth (2006) the practical approach to knowledge management assumes that a great deal of organizational knowledge is tacit.

Although an automated acquisition and linkage of informal activities (e.g. informal floor talks, instant messages) and hence an automated extraction of tacit knowledge into a semantic web seems to be among the most difficult problems facing awareness, there are a number of approaches for solving this. For instance Böhm and Maichner (2006) introduce a system called SemanticTalk

for Real-time Generation of Topic Maps from Speech Streams. Similarly, there are approaches for content monitoring and qualitative analysis of instant messaging (see Kucukyilmaz, Cambazoglu, Aykanat, & Can, 2008). An approach going beyond linguistic analyses of computer-mediated communications is given by Marcoccia, Atifi, and Gaducheau (2008), which takes the kinesic behaviors of participants into account.

The Topic Map stores information about relations between persons, actors, objects or artifacts. KMDL covers a specific conjunction which concretely describes the relations in knowledgE-intensive processes and subsequently captures informal interactions.

The KMDL-objects, (i.e. actors, activities, information-objects and knowledgE-objects) were enhanced with geo-attributes (positions and directions) in order to use them for awareness functions. As demonstrated by the example in Figure 6, these objects are placed accordingly based upon their actual threE-dimensional position. If temporal information is available then model elements can incrementally fade in or fade out to mimic real-time relationships.

Figure 5. KMDL Process model for requirement specification

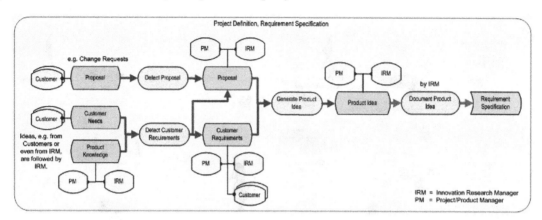

Architecture

As shown in Figure 7, the system architecture is layered: External applications generate collaboration data due to organizational processes. Interaction in collaboration processes can be distinguished in formal and informal interaction. The first case means the exchange of emails and documents, which can be automatically analyzed and from which metadata can be extracted. The second case, informal interactions include face to face discussions and chats. Informal interactions can to a specific extend be captured automatically, by analyzing SkypE-logs or the conversation-history of other chat systems for example. Manual capture of relations in informal processes can be achieved by using K-Modeler, a KMDL-modeling platform designed for this purpose. This data flows together in a KMDL-repository as shown in Figure 7.

Third party services and mobile devices generate data such as the updating of environmental/weather conditions, vehicle/vessel/aircraft positions, etc. Collaboration data extracted from different sources meet together in a common pool, which is located in the data tier. This pool includes the KMDL-repository, a skill database, customer data from CRM, metadata of and references to documents from a DMS (Figure 7). To ensure that all of this information is linked in a semantic network and can be visualized, they are intertwined within the topic map layer. The linking is actualized, for example, if an employee links reports or evaluation documents through web-uploads in a DMS. Finally, the graph representation of the information or the web-based search is carried out in the visualization tier, filtering and accessing information and the relevant documents. The technical basis on which each of the three representation views are built upon is:

- A web-enabled visualization system – a Java Applet or Webstart application; and
- A TM-Framework – an ISO-13250 implementation, which allows creation, editing and processing of Topic Maps.

All delivered content is requested and displayed over filters and are managed in different systems and formats. Geographical information is displayed as spatial data, which can be obtained on the World Wide Web – and in many cases free of charge (Amirian & Alesheikh, 2008). Event messages are delivered by monitoring and warning systems, similar to those exposed by the Nagios software in the technical administration environment.

The Topic Map also contains all staff contact information, instant messaging profiles (Skype or ICQ usernames) and data pertinent to their skills.

Figure 6. Meso View on the process of requirement specification

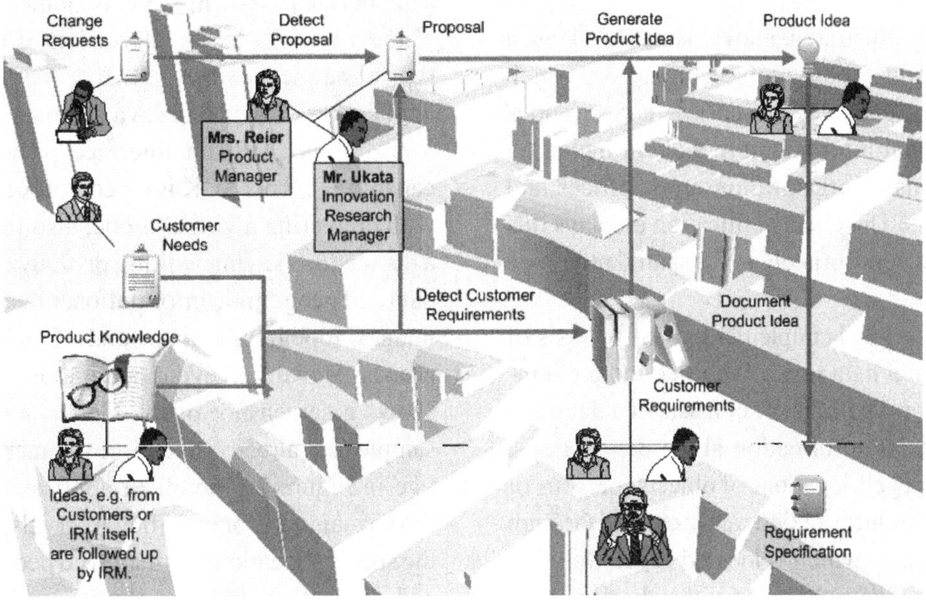

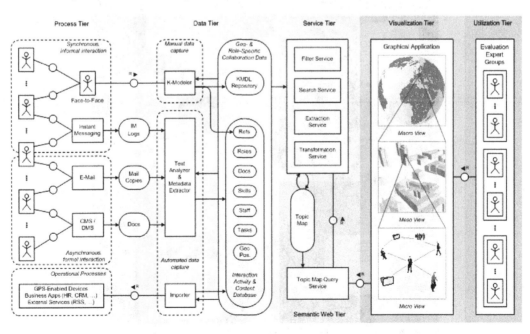

Figure 7. Multi layered architecture of the collaborative web system

Realizing a Prototype for Evaluation

The model illustrated above is realized as a demonstration prototype (see Figure 8), which introduces separate Web Services and provides specific visual information to a client including geo positions of organization units, offices and notifications. The client application displays this information appropriately in the spatial reference system.

The prototype is implemented on the basis of three layers: a data tier, a Web tier and a client-side GUI tier. The first tier consists of a database which contains information about descriptions, relations and geo-locations of objects (persons or artifacts). This information can be entered through a web interface, which is located in the web tier. There is an additional service within the tier which delivers the information from the database under a predefined URL in CSV (Comma Separated Values) format. The final version of this prototypical service will use XML. The GUI client application is written in Java and uses the NASA World Wind API, an interface providing GIS capabilities. This SDK is Open Source and along with delivering a virtual globe, also functions as a device for viewing, editing or analyzing spatial data and geographic information, meteorological images, topographic maps and 3D scientifically processed natural event animations. Figure 8 shows a screenshot of the GUI client with the sample data already given from a macro perspective in Figure 2. The client application updates the virtual world at specified intervals, including the specific locations of displayed people, offices and connections between them.

Figure 8. Screenshot of implemented prototype

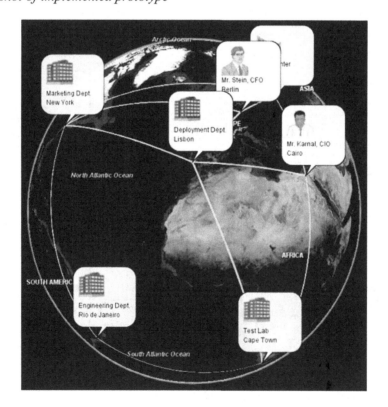

Evaluation in Business Organizations

Within scientific literature, different sources are often cited regarding models with respect to the identification and classification of their benefits to business software. Some such benefit models were developed by Shang and Seddon (2002), Gable, Sedera, and Chan (2008) as well as Williams and Schubert (2010). The Williams and Schubert model subdivides the benefit into levels similar to that of Shang and Seddon. As a result, five levels are distinguished (Table 1) in which tangible benefits can be clearly obtained through the use of the business software. Measurable criteria can be determined for every beneficial element, such as the availability of information on the level of management. In this manner different benefit-describing triplets (level, element, criterion) can be formed. The specification capacity and intuitive structure of the model led to the decision to use it as a basis for the evaluation displayed

For the evaluation, staff in eight small to medium sized businesses in the areas of development, leadership and organization were introduced to a prototype and interviewed. Subsequently, a discussion took place regarding the benefits to the specific business needs. To this extent, the general reaction of the participants was positive in the way that they took on the 3D-Visualisation and GUI, acknowledging it and using it intuitively. There were at least two occurrences where participants raised concerns about data protection.

Knowledge related to the current location of persons, documents and products was perceived as especially useful because, hypothetically, one could be directly led to immediate or presumed accessibility.

On the management level of the model of Williams and Schubert, benefits were identified in all of the companies assessed. Companies noted an increase of the volume, availability and depth-of-detail of information which generated an

Table 1. Levels of benefit from using business software (Williams & Schubert, 2010)

Level	Beneficial-elements
Business Design	Structure and Processes: Control structures, Business Processes and Workflow
Management	Resources: Finance, Staff, Information, Products and Strategy
Department	Functions: PR/Marketing, procurement, Production and Sale
Supply Chain	Participants: Suppliers, Partners und Customers
Information Technology	Technological elements: Applications, Databases and Operating Systems

increased awareness for information that is likely to be sought out. In addition, three companies identified a financial benefit on the same level, namely the cost-cutting through dissolution of media gaps.

A pharmaceutical distributor identified the quality-security and forgery-security of their products as an enhanced benefit. By invoking the visualization, medicine flow irregularities could be detected, such as the purchase of large quantities that do not rE-appear on the market. Such "black holes" within this industry can lead to illegal export, forgery and manipulation of the products. By implementing the threE-dimensional real time presentation, staff stated that they could quickly grasp visual information and would prefer this to previous information representation methods on the basis of number tables. Four Companies identified a benefit on the level of the information technologies that exists within the model, stating that the meaningfulness of stored data (in databases) would increase through semantic networking. Furthermore, the model made existing data more meaningful in existing business applications. A company in the E-commercE-area named the use of the real-time delivery data for SCM and CRM applications as an example where a benefit arose at the department level due to increased awareness for procurement and sale.

Another example presents a company operating in the worldwide import/export of construction material. This company expressed a desire to visualize cargo at specific locations, storage depots and routes for supply transportation on an interactive globe. Furthermore, they needed an accurate real-time visualization of weather and traffic conditions on their major routes, all of which can be retrieved by several external services through third party sources (Table 2).

Outlook

On one hand, this evaluation has demonstrated specific needs for a collaborative system similar to the one presented here which builds upon RWA concepts. On the other hand, it also presents skepticism, with respect to privacy rights and data protection, as to how such a system could be implemented. One major problem is how to coordinate the paradigmatic necessity of transparency in order to support work coordination, juxtaposed against observing the privacy rights of the personnel involved (Dourish & Bellotti, 1992). When personal data is at hand, data protection rules must sufficiently be taken into account. Steps to provide privacy for members, as well as their locations, include a security component based on policies for users and roles that may access appropriate information. Not unlike the settings of a social networking site, a user assigns others the right of accessing private information to a certain required extent.

Awareness and transparency support need not be limited to the constraints of business organizations. An evaluation from a scientific perspective (e.g. on disaster recovery) is also relevant due to the extensive global collaboration within scientific organizations.

An evaluation of this model in relation to different situations is currently being discussed from a scientific vantage point. In this case, the model is being used to evaluate disaster response scenarios. The purpose, benefit and possible implementation potential are ascertained by means of expert interviews, using the aforementioned procedures carried out in business organizations. Preliminary results are taken from interviews conducted with the administration of the Astronomical Center in Potsdam as well as with researchers from the Potsdam Geographic Research Institute. Despite thorough monitoring and calculations, last year a meteorite chaotically plunged into the Baltic Sea. A similar situation occurred two years ago

Table 2. Business profiles of interviewed companies

Area of operation	Activities
E-Commerce	Portal development: Provision of product, offer and consumer information
Search Engine Optimization (SEO)	Online Marketing, competition analysis, structural optimization of web pages for search engines
Pharmaceutical distribution	Forgery security, web-based real time QS, Track-&-Trace and condition control of medicine
Online Community	Portal for organizing and administrating interests-group-specific events
Design Led Innovation (DLI)	Elevation of market and user demands, solution conception, user feedback driven software development
Intercultural exchange	Assisting international communication, construction of culture spreading cooperations, organizing culture events
Global import/export of construction material	Storage, international sales, marketing and import/export of construction materials
Customer Acquisition in WWW	Online marketing of security technologies and systems for renewable energies

when another meteorite unexpectedly struck land in Sudan. The model could be integrated with a stochastic system which would allow a visualization of a meteorite's calculated trajectory; thus aiding in protecting settled areas from possible collisions. Debris such as astro-garbage (for example spent-propulsion-stage rockets and broken satellite components) regularly falls down to earth as a consequence of the effects of solar winds. Planning and coordinating launch routes and orbit paths of satellites is becoming increasingly difficult as a result of the vast increase in volume of objects entering and leaving space. Using the awareness model would greatly aid visualization of their launches as well as orbit paths, thus ensuring safer and more efficient cycles. Greater coordination of space programs could also become possible through implementation of the model, which would facilitate sharing of project-related artifacts and discoveries (such as spectral analyses) between diverse institutions.

During an interview at the Geo Institute, experts for Tsunami Research proposed the integration of the model with a Tsunami early-warning system called GITEWS, which collects data from diverse Sensor Systems such as earthquake detectors, GPS and water-level meters, and transfers them via satellite in order to forecast their severity. The model allows visualization of endangered regions and unaffected areas. A benefit of implementation would be the ability to deliver this information to the relevant agencies, administrative bodies and ultimately, to business organizations and citizens. Moreover, coordination of resources for rescue teams, temporary accommodation services, medical aid providers and technical emergency services would be possible, as shown in Figure 9.

Search engines are used to quickly locate required objects and always exist in data from a collected part and from a query part. The method introduced for the visualization of collaborative networks as well as the navigation through the functions of these networks is covered by a search engine. However, it is a semantic search, which provides users a unique entry point into the Topic Map from which they may navigate through

Figure 9. In an emergency case multinational organizations collaborate on disaster recovery (macro view)

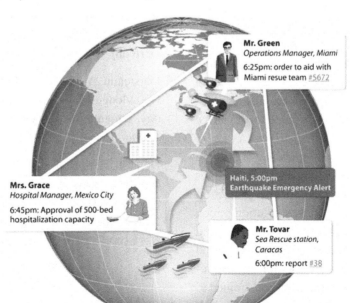

relevant neighboring objects. The visual background of using Web3D technologies provides an extensive GUI for semantic search which further prepares the search results without omitting the visual context.

An implementation of the approach presented in this work is currently being carried out at the University of Potsdam, which addresses various sub-disciplines of applied and practical computer sciences, such as semantic technologies, process management, geographic information systems, and experience in the software engineering, knowledge management and web technologies.

CONCLUSION

Awareness in collaborations of globally distributed organizations has always been a challenge and hitherto the research centered around CSCW has yet to provide any concrete reform for the original problem. There is, however, a consensus that using semantic networks will facilitate awareness in complex relations. Nevertheless, the technical implementation of such a system has until now yet to be agreed upon.

The conception in this study establishes a proven way to implement higher levels of awareness. The evaluation of a prototype in various business organizations, which operate globally, clearly demonstrates that the introduced model is applicable for specific business needs, notably in the field of quality assurance for sensitive products, such as medicine distribution, where real world awareness techniques like RFID are involved. Although effective, these techniques expose difficulties that concern the protection of personal privacy. A proposed solution which involves implementing a rolE-based identity and access management system has been suggested in order to secure privacy rights for all personnel. The model's application is not constrained to businesses organizations but also, as demonstrated,

may be implemented for a multitude of diverse research and scientific purposes.

REFERENCES

Amirian, P., & Alesheikh, A. A. (2008). Publishing Geospatial Data through Geospatial Web Service and XML Database System. *American Journal of Applied Sciences, 5*(10), 1358–1368. doi:10.3844/ajassp.2008.1358.1368

Barta, R. (2007, October 11-12). Towards a Formal TMQL Semantics. In L. Maicher, A. Sigel, & L. M. Garshol (Eds.), *Leveraging the Semantics of Topic Maps: Second International Conference on Topic Maps Research and Applications, TMRA 2006,* Leipzig, Germany (pp. 90-106). Berlin: Springer.

Bishr, Y. (1998). Overcoming the semantic and other barriers to GIS interoperability. *International Journal of Geographical Information Science, 12*(4), 299–314. doi:10.1080/136588198241806

Böhm, K., & Maicher, L. (2006, October 6-7). Real-Time Generation of Topic Maps from Speech Streams. In L. Maicher & J. Park (Eds.), *Charting the Topic Maps Research and Applications Landscape: First International Workshop on Topic Map Research and Applications, TMRA 2005,* Leipzig, Germany (pp. 112-124). Berlin: Springer.

Diosteanu, A., & Cotfas, L. (2009). Agent Based Knowledge Management Solution using Ontology, Semantic Web Services and GIS. *Informatica Economica, 13*(4), 90–98.

Dourish, P., & Bellotti, V. (1992). Awareness and coordination in shared workspaces. In M. Mantel & R. Baecker (Eds.), *Proceedings of the 1992 ACM Conference on Computer-supported Cooperative Work* (pp. 107-114). New York: ACM Press.

Fuchs, L., PankokE-Babatz, U., & Prinz, W. (1995). Supporting Cooperative Awareness with Local Event Mechanisms: The GroupDesk System. In H. Marmolin, Y. Sundblad, & K. Schmidt (Eds.), *Proceedings of the Fourth European Conference on Computer-Supported Cooperative Work* (pp. 247-262). Norwell, MA: Kluwer Academic Publishers.

Fuchs-Kittowski, F., & Faust, D. (2009). Collaborative Enterprise Architecture Design and Development with a Semantic Collaboration Tool. *International Journal of E-Collaboration, 5*(4), 53–66.

Gable, G. G., Sedera, D., & Chan, T. (2008). RE-conceptualizing Information System Success: The IS-Impact Measurement Model. *Journal of the Association for Information Systems, 9*(7), 377–408.

Garshol, L. M. (2006, October 6-7). tolog – A Topic Maps Query Language. In L. Maicher & J. Park (Eds.), *Charting the Topic Maps Research and Applications Landscape: First International Workshop on Topic Map Research and Applications, TMRA 2005,* Leipzig, Germany (pp. 183-196). Berlin: Springer.

Gilbert, M., & Masucci, M. (2006). Geographic Perspectives on E-collaboration Research. *International Journal of E-Collaboration, 2*(1), i–v.

Gronau, N., Müller, C., & Korf, R. (2005). KMDL – Capturing, Analysing and Improving KnowledgE-Intensive Business Processes. *Journal of Universal Computer Science, 11*(4), 452–472.

Heinrich, C. E. (2005). *RFID and Beyond: Growing Your Business Through Real World Awareness*. Indianapolis, IN: Wiley Publishing.

Kock, N. (2005). What is E-collaboration? *International Journal of E-Collaboration, 1*(1), i–vii.

Kucukyilmaz, T., Cambazoglu, B. B., Aykanat, C., & Can, F. (2008). Chat Mining: Predicting User and Message Attributes in Computer-Mediated Communication. *Information Processing and Management: an International Journal, 44*(4), 1448–1466. doi:10.1016/j.ipm.2007.12.009

Lee, J. Y., Seo, D. W., Kim, K., & Kim, H. (2005). A Ubiquitous and Context-Aware Framework for Supporting Virtual Engineering Services. *Computer-Aided Design & Applications, 2*(6), 769–776.

Leidner, D., Alavi, M., & Kayworth, T. (2006). The Role of Culture in Knowledge Management: A Case Study of Two Global Firms. *International Journal of E-Collaboration, 2*(1), 17–40.

MacEachren, A. M. (2001). Cartography and GIS: extending collaborative tools to support virtual teams. *Progress in Human Geography, 25*(3), 431–444. doi:10.1191/030913201680191763

Marcoccia, M., Atifi, H., & Gaducheau, N. (2008). Text-Centered versus Multimodal Analysis of Instant Messaging Conversation. *Language@Internet, 5,* article 7. Retrieved from http://www.languageatinternet.de/articles/2008/1621/marcoccia.pdf

Pinchuk, R., Aked, R., de Orus, J.-J., Dessin, E., de Weerdt, D., Focant, G., et al. (2007, October 11-12). Toma – TMQL, TMCL, TMML. In L. Maicher, A. Sigel, & L. M. Garshol (Eds.), *Leveraging the Semantics of Topic Maps: Second International Conference on Topic Maps Research and Applications, TMRA 2006,* Leipzig, Germany (pp. 107-129). Berlin: Springer.

Riemer, K. (2009). E-Collaboration Systems: Identification of System Classes using Cluster Analysis. *International Journal of E-Collaboration, 5*(3), 1–24.

Sandor, O., Bogdan, C., & Bowers, J. (1997). Aether: An Awareness Engine for CSCW. In J. A. Hughes, W. Prinz, T. Rodden, & K. Schmidt (Eds.), *Proceedings of the fifth European Conference on Computer-Supported Cooperative Work* (pp. 221-236). Norwell, MA: Kluwer Academic Publishers.

Shang, S., & Seddon, P. B. (2002). Assessing and managing the benefits of enterprise systems: the business manager's perspective. *Information Systems Journal*, *12*(4), 271–299. doi:10.1046/j.1365-2575.2002.00132.x

Simone, C., & Bandini, S. (2002). Integrating awareness in cooperative applications through the reaction-diffusion metaphor. *Computer Supported Cooperative Work*, *11*(3), 495–530. doi:10.1023/A:1021213119071

Williams, S. P., & Schubert, P. (2010). Benefits of Enterprise Systems Use. In R. H. Sprague (Ed.), *Proceedings of the 43rd Hawaii International Conference on System Sciences* (pp. 1-9). Los Alamitos, CA: IEEE Computer Society Press.

This work was previously published in the International Journal of e-Collaboration, Volume 7, Issue 1, edited by Ned Kock, pp. 1-16, copyright 2011 by IGI Publishing (an imprint of IGI Global).

Chapter 2

An Exploratory Study of How Technology Supports Communication in Multilingual Groups

Milam Aiken
University of Mississippi, USA

Jianfeng Wang
Indiana University of Pennsylvania, USA

Linwu Gu
Indiana University of Pennsylvania, USA

Joseph Paolillo
University of Mississippi, USA

ABSTRACT

In this paper, the authors study how new technology can support multilingual groups. Their results show that no significant difference was found between group members' comprehension of contributed comments and their stated minimum acceptable understanding. However, comprehension of relevant comments was higher than that for off-topic text, indicating that the sharing of important information was achieved. Further, reading comprehension tests of translations from Chinese, German, Hindi, Korean, Malay, and Spanish to English show that, except for Hindi, the automatic translations achieve accuracies that are acceptable for graduate studies at a university in the United States.

DOI: 10.4018/978-1-4666-2020-9.ch002

INTRODUCTION

Businesses in today's global economy must take into consideration differences in time zones, languages, and cultures. For example, 75% of multinational companies managed networks of 20 or more overseas operations over ten years ago (John et al., 1997), and Microsoft conducts business in about 80 different languages (Feely & Harzing, 2003). Other organizations must communicate over large distances with different cultures, as well. The United Nations used a distributed, electronic meeting in January 1998 to link 10 Pacific island countries, and officials saved time and over US $25,000 in travel costs (Wescott, 2001). Development Decision Centers (DDC) equipped with electronic meeting technology help to improve communication, increase effectiveness and efficiency of public and private administration, and support democratization and political stability in Africa (de Vreede et al., 2003; Splettstoesser, 1998), and electronic meeting systems have been used throughout the world (Nunamaker et al., 1996).

Meetings with cultural diversity have a positive influence on decision-making as these groups generate more ideas in electronic discussions than do homogenous groups (Daily & Steiner, 1998). However, this diversity can also have a negative influence on communication, often due to differences in the members' native languages (Shachaf, 2008; Shigenobu et al., 2007). Further, there is an emerging shortage of human translators (Levin, 2009), resulting in fewer interpreted encounters (Fügen et al., 2007).

Incorporating automatic translation into electronic meetings can reduce this negative influence on intercultural communication (Morikawa et al., 2008). For example, Pangaea, a non-profit organization that enables children around the world to communicate across language boundaries, has been using a machine-translation-embedded chat system called *AnnoChat* for several years (Pangaea, 2009). Language needs are likely to become one of the essential requirements of mature information societies with global communications infrastructures, and access to information in a user's chosen language will become a prerequisite (Tiffin & Terashima, 2001). It is now widely accepted that global communications must be accessible and transferable, in a timely manner, in as many languages as feasible (Sert & Açıkgöz, 2006).

This paper describes how machine translation (MT) can support electronic meetings and introduces a new multilingual system that provides communication in 51 different languages. Such a system could be especially useful in many multinational meetings such as those within the European Union where 23 languages are spoken and the United Nations that has over 350. We also discuss the minimum comprehension necessary for meeting success, and illustrate how the technology can be used in multilingual discussions.

MT COMPREHENSION

One of the first demonstrations of a translation system occurred in January 1954 (Hutchins, 2007), and MT was implemented on personal computers in 1981 and on the Web in 1997 (Yang & Lange, 1998). *Google Translate* (http://translate.google.com/) appeared on the Web a few years later, and accuracy improved considerably when the service began to use statistical machine translation (Lopez, 2008), as tests of 20 MT systems involving translations between English and Chinese or Arabic showed that it was often the most accurate (NIST, 2006). Currently, *Google Translate* supports 51 languages in 2,550 language-pair combinations, but accuracies vary considerably (Aiken et al., 2009).

It is difficult to determine the minimum level of translation accuracy required. Obviously, 100% is sufficient and 0% is not, and the importance of accuracy varies with the topic and task. Medical or legal matters require more attention than do informal, ad hoc communication. In some cases, interpreters might be expected to be 80% accurate in meetings (Fügen et al., 2007), and in other situations, such as intelligence analysis, just 40% accuracy might be enough (Caulfield & Reeder, 2001).

Tests of reading comprehension can provide a direct measure of the usefulness of translations (Somers, 2007). For example, in one test of comprehension (Fügen et al., 2007), questions were answered correctly 74% of the time when a human translated material (presumably with 100% accuracy), but when MT was used, only 58% was comprehended and 52% of the questions were answered correctly.

In order to assess the validity of reading comprehension tests, we chose the Test of English as a Foreign Language (TOEFL) to evaluate the accuracies of translations from Chinese, German, Hindi, Korean, Malay, and Spanish to English. Samples of the reading comprehension portion of the test were obtained online (TOEFL, 2009), and human experts translated the English text to each of the six languages. Then, we translated each back to English with *Google Translate* and asked 75 undergraduate business students whose primary language is English to evaluate the resulting text. Appendix 1 shows a portion of the test translated from German, and Table 1 shows a summary of the evaluations.

As expected, there was a significant positive correlation between the percentage of the text understood and the TOEFL reading comprehension score (R = 0.511, p < .001), and therefore, self-assessed values of understanding are valid measures. Given a subjective value of comprehension, the hypothetical reading score can be determined by (F = 25.5, p < 0.001):

(TEOFL reading score) = 12.9 + 13.9 * (percentage understood)   (1)

All of the mean student TOEFL reading comprehension scores except those for Hindi were

Table 1. Summary of TOEFL reading tests

Test translated from	N	Percentage Understood		TOEFL Reading Score	
		Mean	Std Dev	Mean	Std Dev
English (no translation)	9	97.1%	5.0%	28.90	3.30
Spanish	9	95.0%	8.7%	28.89	3.33
German	11	79.5%	24.5%	23.60	6.70
Chinese	12	57.1%	28.8%	20.80	7.90
Malay	12	54.6%	28.2%	17.50	12.20
Korean	11	28.6%	24.6%	20.90	7.00
Hindi	11	27.6%	26.6%	12.70	10.10
Average	10.7	62.8%	20.9%	21.90	7.22

above the 16 (out of a maximum 30) required by Auburn's MBA program (Auburn University, 2009), but only English, Spanish, and German met UCLA's 21 minimum for their graduate programs (UCLA, 2009). Thus, we believe that the translations from Spanish and German to English might be sufficient for many purposes.

The 75 students in the study got 73% of the reading comprehension questions correct, despite reporting being able to understand only about 63% of the text. The students might have underestimated how much they actually understood, perhaps because emotional reactions to the poor grammar affected their judgments (Pfafflin, 1965). However, it is clear that MT users can often pick up some meaning from a translation, even if the quality is poor (Nomura et al., 2003).

TRANSLATION IN A MULTILINGUAL ELECTRONIC MEETING

Prior Studies

The first electronic meeting to include the automatic translation of comments appeared in 1992 (Aiken et al., 1992), but the system accommodated only Spanish and English. Tests showed that meeting participants were able to comprehend 81% to 100% of the conversations, despite several misspellings in the original comments (Aiken, 2008).

Amikai's *AmiChat* multilingual Internet chat program was developed in the late 1990s (Flournoy & Callison-Burch, 2000), and *TransBBS* (perhaps the first fully automated, Web-based multilingual electronic meeting system) appeared a few years later, allowing group members to exchange comments in Chinese, Korean, English, Japanese, and English. A test of this latter system using a scale of very good, good, not bad, and bad found that translations from Japanese to Chinese, Japanese to Korean, and Korean to Japanese were good, and Chinese to Japanese translations were not bad (Ogura et al., 2004). Presumably, translations in the other language-pair combinations were bad. In another study with eight pairs of participants from China, Korea, and Japan using English as a common language, Japanese to English translations with the system were rated good and Chinese to English translations were not bad (Yamashita & Ishida, 2006).

In a third study (Shigenobu et al., 2007), three pairs of Japanese and Korean speakers, six pairs of Chinese and Japanese speakers, and 10 pairs of Korean and Chinese speakers used *Annochat* to provide automatic translations. Results showed that on a 5-point scale, the Japanese/Korean pairs could communicate best with a score of 4.0, while the Japanese/Chinese and Korean/Chinese pairs had scores of 3.3 and 2.5, respectively. When asked "I could understand my partner's message through translation like my own mother tongue," the Japanese/Korean pairs reported on average a score of 3.8, Japanese/Chinese pairs reported 2.8, and Korean/Chinese pairs reported 2.0.

A fourth study (Yamashita et al., 2009) with *Annochat* found that for 13 Chinese, 13 Korean, and 13 Japanese participants living in Japan, it was virtually impossible to conduct a group meeting when the total number of languages within the group was larger than two.

In a study using a different system with multilingual support (Lim & Yang, 2008), 90 undergraduate students in 45 sessions typed English and Chinese comments in a series of negotiations, and results showed that while the quality of outcomes improved, the time needed was longer. Finally, a study with *TransBBS*, a multilingual bulletin board system incorporating MT, Malay, Korean, Japanese, and Chinese users posted 755 messages in their native languages, but they found the translations were poor (Funakoshi et al., 2009).

Usefulness of MT in Electronic Meetings

We believe that electronic meetings with machine translation become even more useful as the group size and the number of languages increase. Large oral meetings with human interpreters are very slow, but a large multilingual electronic meeting could be a very effective means of communication. In most electronic meetings, the number of comments per person stays roughly the same regardless of group size, while in an oral meeting, comments per person decreases linearly (Aiken & Vanjani, 2002). It is clear that many people typing and reading text at the same time can share much more information than one person speaking at a time. If human interpretation were used in an electronic meeting, a linguist for each language pair and for each participant would be needed. Thus, only machine translation is practical in large meetings with many languages.

Even with less than optimal translation accuracy and with smaller groups, the anonymity provided in an electronic meeting could be important for discussions involving participants from many Asian cultures based upon Confucianism (Watson et al., 1994). For example, comments from women or younger people are given less importance in Confucian societies, but in an electronic meeting, the gender and age of the contributor might not be known. With anonymity, criticism of an idea can be deflected from the originator to the idea itself, preserving the person's "face," and several studies conducted on Chinese, Japanese, Korean, and Malaysian groups using their native languages in electronic meetings showed that participants enjoyed the same benefits of GSS use reported by English-speaking groups (Aiken et al., 1994).

Finally, nothing precludes the use of a traditional, oral meeting with a human interpreter in addition to a multilingual meeting system, as each environment has strengths and weaknesses (Hong, 1999). For example, the technology can be used first to generate as many anonymous, rough ideas as possible toward the solution of a problem. After these suggestions are organized and voted upon, a human-interpreted meeting can be held to hone the most important outcomes into a final group decision, where high accuracy counts most.

A NEW MULTILINGUAL ELECTRONIC MEETING SYSTEM

Description

We have developed a new Web-based electronic meeting system implementing gallery writing (Aiken et al., 1996) that enables users to read and submit comments simultaneously and anony-

mously, wherever in the world the Internet is available. Linked to *Google Translate*, the software automatically provides translations between any two of 51 languages (2,550 language pair combinations) currently implemented on that service.

To use the software, a group member selects a language in the drop down box, types a comment in the text box, and clicks the "Submit Comment" button (see Figure 1). Within about two seconds, the comment has been translated and stored in a file and is immediately available in any other language used by the group. If the participant wishes to read comments, he or she simply clicks the "Read Comments" button, and the comments written by the group appear on a separate Web page in that participant's language (see Figure 2).

Methodological Procedures

We conducted five multilingual meetings with 71 undergraduate business students using the new software at a college in the northeastern United States. Group 1 (consisting of 10 Chinese and 6 English speakers) and Group 2 (2 Chinese and 2 English) were asked to discuss "How can we improve the parking situation on campus?" Group 3 (5 English, 3 Chinese, and 1 Malay) and Group 5 (10 Chinese, 9 Arabic, 3 Indonesian, and

Figure 1. English user's comment entry screen

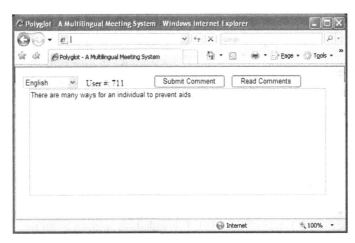

Figure 2. Chinese user's view of meeting comments

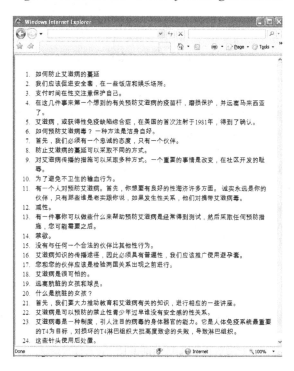

3 English) were asked to discuss "How can we prevent AIDS?" Group 4 (6 Hindi, 3 English, 3 French, 2 Chinese, 1 Spanish, 1 Indonesian, and 1 German) discussed "Should tuition be raised next semester?" We attempted to study a variety of group sizes (4 to 25) focused on different topics with a good balance of languages, subject to the limitations of the number of native speakers available.

After each meeting, the students were asked (in English):

1. How much of the comments did you understand? (0-100%)

2. How much should you be able to understand for a successful meeting? (0-100%)

3. How long (in minutes) do you think a human-interpreted, verbal meeting with this many people and this many languages would take to exchange the equivalent number of comments?

4. How easy was it to use this meeting software? (1 = extremely hard, 4=neutral, 7 = extremely easy)

Results

Table 2 shows a summary of the meetings. Group members thought the system was easy to use, and believed an equivalent oral meeting with a human interpreter would have taken 3.77 times longer than the 17.2 minutes average for an electronic meeting. In addition, the participants' stated comprehension of the meeting transcripts varied by group and by language: Arabic (9 speakers: 78%), Chinese (27: 70%), English (19: 89%), French (3: 95%), German (1: 65%), Hindi (6: 84%), Indonesian (4: 74%), Malay (1: 90%), and Spanish (1: 70%). However, direct comparisons are not possible due to small sample sizes in some cases, as well as differences in the comments' vocabulary and sentence complexity. Further, we cannot determine how many of the comments were translated, as some were written by group members speaking the same language.

Those who understood the comments more tended to think an oral meeting would have been shorter ($R = -0.255$, $p = 0.032$) and tended to think the system was easier to use ($R = 0.422$, $p < 0.001$). Otherwise, there were no significant correlations among the variables of the meetings.

There were no significant differences (at $\alpha = 0.05$) among the groups in terms of comprehension ($F = 2.44$, $p = 0.055$), feelings of how easy the system was to use ($F = 1.88$, $p = 0.124$), or estimates of how long an equivalent oral meeting would have taken ($F = 1.14$, $p = 0.347$), but there was a difference among the groups in terms of how much the students thought they should be able to comprehend ($F = 3.22$, $p = 0.018$). Students' opinions on how much they should understand when they discussed the parking problem was fairly similar (77.5% vs. 79.1%), but the two groups that discussed how to prevent AIDS had widely different opinions (80.0% vs. 94.9%).

Table 2. Summary of electronic meetings

Group	N	Time (mins)	Comprehended		Should Comprehend		Oral Meeting Time (mins)		Ease of Use (1 to 7 scale)	
			Mean	Std. Dev.	Mean	Std. Dev.	Mean	Std. Dev.	Mean	Std. Dev.
1	16	15	77.30%	14.90%	79.10%	9.80%	64.38	34.97	5.00	1.41
2	4	28	90.50%	16.40%	77.50%	21.80%	37.50	9.57	6.75	0.50
3	9	11	86.20%	16.40%	94.90%	7.40%	65.00	41.53	5.33	1.89
4	17	20	83.70%	23.10%	87.00%	12.70%	77.65	41.16	5.24	1.39
5	25	12	71.30%	13.90%	80.00%	14.50%	79.80	49.63	5.80	1.19
Average	14	17.2	81.80%	16.90%	83.70%	13.20%	64.86	35.37	5.62	1.28

Although the comprehension rate overall was lower than the participants' acceptable comprehension rate (81.8% vs. 83.7%), the difference was not significant (T = -1.89, p = 0.063). Also, using Equation (1) above, the equivalent TOEFL reading comprehension score for the meetings was 24.3, well above the 21 minimum for UCLA. Many comments were not relevant to the topics, resulting in lower comprehension overall. For example, the smallest group with four students shared comments that were nearly all on topic and indicated the highest understanding rate. Students who are able to contribute text anonymously in a meeting for the first time have often generated irrelevant comments. For instance, in 14 meetings on a variety of topics with a total of 110 students, 26.1% of the comments on average were extraneous to the discussion, with a minimum of 11% and a maximum of 46% (Gu et al., 2007). In another study (Alonzo & Aiken, 2004), 37% of approximately 780 comments generated by 20 groups of 8 were not relevant.

First-time users often become uninhibited through the use of the anonymity feature in the software and wish to try out the feature to for sensation seeking, relaxation, entertainment, escape, social interaction, companionship, time consumption, or other purposes (Aiken & Waller, 2000). Therefore, they sometimes contribute comments that they would not say when face-to-face (Hiltz et al., 1989). Further, the meeting environment fosters deindividuation as members of the group submit more off-topic comments because they see that others are getting away with it (Postmes & Spears, 1998).

Two objective evaluators reviewed the 387 comments generated in the meetings. When they reviewed the comments in English, they found 30.3% to be not relevant, and only 13.2% of the off-topic text was understood. On the other hand, 82.5% of the relevant comments were understood, giving an overall average of 47.9% understood for all text in English, considerably less than the 89% average understood by the 19 English-speaking participants. Examples of these comments are shown in Table 3. The relevant comments had some relationship to parking, but the non-relevant text included references to a popular television show in the United States called "Gossip Girl" (e.g., "Gossip girl's here~" and "DJ is so handsome!"), a common Chinese desert (e.g., "I also want to eat double-yolk moon cake!"), and other off-topic issues.

The evaluators considered 31.4% of the comments to be irrelevant when they reviewed the text in Chinese, and the slight disparity might be due to differences in translations, variations in opinion over the intervening time, errors, or other reasons. They understood only 2.5% of the irrelevant comments, but could comprehend 80.3% of those that were on the topic, giving an overall average of 41.4% understood for all of

Table 3. Examples of relevant and irrelevant comments. Topic: "How can we improve the parking situation on campus?"

Relevant		Irrelevant	
Under-stood	Misunder-stood	Understood	Misunder-stood
Increase in parking spaces	Multi-stop at school	Gossip girl's here~	Sang, like the Chicago
parking a problem here on the campus	american is a country in a car, or more than a car!!	DJ is so hand-some!	hotpot!!!!
How kind of under-ground parking	Wants to drive to the pay parking fees.	I also want to eat double-yolk moon cake! ! ! !	rinsy like the Big Dip-per!!!
Should we be charged for park-ing?	Parking card to buy it.	Interesting test~	Yunnan Ham can be!

the text, also less than the 70% understood by the 27 Chinese participants.

The 30.85% average of comments found to be irrelevant to the conversations was very close to the 31.55% average of the two studies cited above, and it appears that up to a third of first-time users' anonymous comments in many electronic meetings might be off-topic. These results show that the amount of participants' understanding of the material that matters most is probably much higher than that indicated for the text overall.

During the meetings, some participants wrote positive remarks about the system, e.g.:

- "Yeah!! I like the system so that my baby will not have to learn English in the future!"
- "This system is good, but with it we won't want to study English anymore."
- "This is a fantastic system, to be perfected."

Others wrote negative thoughts, probably because they were dissatisfied with the quality of the translations they viewed:

- "This system is not at easy to use, no trans-lation of the words!"
- "I don't want to speak like this. It's not so convenient as QQ."
- "This translation system rotten."

Although the translations in the meetings were poor in many cases, we believe that comprehension was sufficient for their purposes, especially if the alternative is no translation and participants cannot communicate with all members of their groups. Just as people speak using slang and make grammatical errors while still being understood, MT quality should be assessed in the context of the importance of the conversation. When information is exchanged in a group using e-mail or a chat room, for example, more translation errors can be tolerated (Levin, 2009). Further, if translations are not understood during a meeting, group members can submit a comment asking the unknown author for more explanation.

Translation problems occurred in the meetings due to the inadequacies of *Google Translate* with some language pairs, unknown vocabulary, complex sentences, and source comment errors (misspellings, incorrect grammar, etc.). Many more errors occurred with irrelevant comments as these tended to have more slang, abbreviations, and spelling errors, for example. However, the incidence of irrelevant comments can be reduced significantly when the meeting facilitator admonishes the group to refrain from such non-productive conduct, when smaller groups use the software and there is less deindividuation, and when the novelty of the meeting software begins to wear off (Reinig et al., 1997).

CONCLUSION

Summary

This paper shows how 71 speakers from different countries using their native languages can communicate efficiently and effectively with the use of meeting software integrated with machine translation. Although comprehension varied by meeting and language, overall, the group members were able to understand as much as they thought was necessary, and their reading comprehension of the translated comments was sufficient for many graduate schools in the United States. In addition, the group members were satisfied with the meeting technology, and they thought equivalent oral meetings with human interpreters would have taken 3.77 times longer. Another major finding was that relevant comments were understood better than those deemed irrelevant.

Limitations

Students were used as subjects of convenience, but this is a wide-spread practice in electronic meeting research (Pervan, 1998), and many experimental results have been validated by field studies in real-life organizations (e.g., Grohowski et al., 1990). Also, there is no reason to believe that these meeting participants who focused on problems that concerned them and they knew about behaved any differently than group members might in business meetings.

However, several meeting moderators were not investigated, such as the effect of the topic and the combination of languages in a meeting. Thus, it is not clear which language combinations can be used most effectively in multilingual settings. In addition, the group members evaluated overall comprehension, including original and translated comments. A higher proportion of non-translated comments would probably result in greater understanding.

Future Research

The goal of multilingual electronic meeting research is to allow group members to communicate in any mixture of languages as efficiently and effectively as English-only groups have in the past.

For example, we hope to be able to show how a 10-language or even a 52-language electronic meeting can be more productive and satisfying than an oral meeting with humans providing interpretation. In addition, future research should investigate how the technology can be used in multinational business meetings.

ACKNOWLEDGMENT

The authors would like to thank the reviewers for their valuable suggestions for improvement on a previous version of this article.

REFERENCES

Aiken, M. (2008). Multilingual collaboration in electronic meetings. In Kock, N. (Ed.), *Encyclopedia of E-Collaboration* (pp. 457–462). Hershey, PA: Information Science Publishing.

Aiken, M., Hwang, C., Paolillo, J., & Lu, L. (1994). A group decision support system for the Asian Pacific rim. *Journal of International Information Management, 3*(2), 1–13.

Aiken, M., Martin, J., Reithel, B., Shirani, A., & Singleton, T. (1992, November 22-24). Using a group decision support system for multicultural and multilingual communication. In *Proceedings of the 23rd Annual Meeting of the Decision Sciences Institute,* San Francisco (Vol. 2, pp. 792-794).

Aiken, M., Park, M., Simmons, L., & Lindblom, T. (2009). Automatic translation in multilingual electronic meetings. *Translation Journal, 13*(9).

Aiken, M., & Vanjani, M. (2002). A mathematical foundation for group support system research. *Communications of the International Information Management Association, 2*(1), 73–83.

Aiken, M., Vanjani, M., & Paolillo, J., J. (1996). A comparison of two electronic idea generation techniques. *Information & Management, 30*(2), 91–99. doi:10.1016/0378-7206(95)00048-8

Aiken, M., & Waller, B. (2000). Flaming among first-time group support system users. *Information & Management, 37*(2), 95–100. doi:10.1016/S0378-7206(99)00036-1

Alonzo, M., & Aiken, M. (2004). Flaming in electronic communication. *Decision Support Systems, 36*(3), 205–213. doi:10.1016/S0167-9236(02)00190-2

Auburn University. (2009). *Auburn University MBA program.* Retrieved November 9, 2009, from http://www.mba.business.auburn.edu/FAQ/OnCampus/oncampus.cfm

Caulfield, H., & Reeder, F. (2001). *Evaluation of endogenous systems.* Retrieved November 9, 2009, from http://www.mitre.org/work/tech_papers/tech_papers_01/reeder_evaluation/index.html

Daily, B., & Steiner, R. (1998). The influence of group decision support systems on contribution and commitment levels in multicultural and culturally homogeneous decision-making groups. *Computers in Human Behavior, 14*(1), 147–162. doi:10.1016/S0747-5632(97)00037-X

de Vreede, G., Mgaya, R., & Qureshi, S. (2003). Field experiences with collaboration technology: A comparative study in Tanzania and South Africa. *Information Technology for Development, 10*(3), 201–219. doi:10.1002/itdj.1590100306

Feely, A., & Harzing, A. (2003). Language management in multinational companies. *Cross Cultural Management: An International Journal, 10*(2), 37–52. doi:10.1108/13527600310797586

Flournoy, R., & Callison-Burch, C. (2000, November 16-17). Reconciling user expectations and translation technology to create a useful real-world application. In *Proceedings of the 22nd International Conference on Translating and the Computer*, London.

Fügen, C., Waibel, A., & Kolss, M. (2007). Simultaneous translation of lectures and speeches. *Machine Translation, 21*, 209–252. doi:10.1007/s10590-008-9047-0

Funakoshi, K., Yamamoto, A., Nomura, S., & Ishida, T. (2009). *Lessons learned from multilingual collaboration in global virtual teams.* Retrieved November 9, 2009, from http://www.ai.soc.i.kyoto-u.ac.jp/ice/slides/kfHCII2003.pdf

Grohowski, R., McGoff, C., Vogel, D., Martz, B., & Nunamaker, J. (1990). Implementing electronic meeting systems at IBM: Lessons learned and success factors. *Management Information Systems Quarterly, 14*(4), 369–384. doi:10.2307/249785

Gu, L., Aiken, M., & Wang, J. (2007). Topic effects on process gains and losses in electronic meetings. *Information Resources Management Journal, 20*(4), 1–11.

Hiltz, S., Turoff, M., & Johnson, K. (1989). Experiments in group decision making, 3: Disinhibition, deindividuation, and group process in pen name and real name computer conferences. *Decision Support Systems, 5*, 217–232. doi:10.1016/0167-9236(89)90008-0

Hong, I. (1999). Information technology to support any-time, any-place team meetings in Korean organizations. *Industrial Management & Data Systems, 99*(1), 18–24. doi:10.1108/02635579910247145

Hutchins, J. (2007). Machine translation: A concise history. In Wai, C. (Ed.), *Computer Aided Translation: Theory and Practice*. Hong Kong: Chinese University of Hong Kong.

John, R., Ietto-Gillies, G., Cox, H., & Grimwade, N. (1997). *Global Business Strategy*. London: International Thomson Press.

Levin, R. (2009). Tools for multilingual communication. *Multilingual Magazine, 16*(2). Retrieved November 9, 2009, from https://www.multilingual.com/articleDetail.php?id=715

Lim, J., & Yang, Y. (2008). Exploring computer-based multilingual negotiation support for English-Chinese dyads: Can we negotiate in our native languages? *Behaviour & Information Technology, 27*(2), 139–151. doi:10.1080/01449290601111135

Lopez, A. (2008). Statistical machine translation. *ACM Computing Surveys, 40*(3), 1–49. doi:10.1145/1380584.1380586

Morikawa, H., Suo, Y., Miyata, N., Ishida, T., & Shi, Y. (2008). Supporting remote meeting using multilingual collaboration tool. *Institute of Electronics, Information, and Communication Engineers Technical Report, 107*(428), 19–24.

NIST. (2006). *Machine translation evaluation official results*. Retrieved November 9, 2009 from http://www.itl.nist.gov/iad/mig//tests/mt/2006/doc/mt06eval_official_results.html

Nomura, S., Ishida, T., Yamashita, N., Yasuoka, M., & Funakoshi, K. (2003, June 22-27). Open source software development with your mother language: Intercultural collaboration experiment. In *Proceedings of the International Conference on Human-Computer Interaction (HCI-03)*, Heraklion, Crete, Greece (Vol. 4, pp. 1163-1167).

Nunamaker, J., Briggs, R., Mittleman, D., Vogel, D., & Balthazard, P. (1996). Lessons from a dozen years of group support systems research: A discussion of lab and field findings. *Journal of Management Information Systems, 13*(3), 163–207.

Ogura, K., Hayashi, Y., Nomura, S., & Ishida, I. (2004). User adaptation in MT-mediated communication. In *Proceedings of the First International Joint Conference on Natural Language Processing* (pp. 596-601).

Pangaea. (2009). *NPO Pangaea*. Retrieved November 9, 2009, from http://www.pangaean.org/

Pervan, G. (1998). A review of research in group support systems: Leaders, approaches and directions. *Decision Support Systems, 23*(2), 149–159. doi:10.1016/S0167-9236(98)00041-4

Pfafflin, S. (1965). Evaluation of machine translation by reading comprehension tests and subjective judgments. *Machine Translation, 8*(2), 2–8.

Postmes, T., & Spears, R. (1998). Deindividuation and anti-normative behavior: A meta-analysis. *Psychological Bulletin, 123*, 238–259. doi:10.1037/0033-2909.123.3.238

Reinig, B., Briggs, R., & Nunamaker, J. (1997). Flaming in the electronic classroom. *Journal of Management Information Systems, 14*(3), 45–59.

Sert, O., & Açıkgöz, F. (2006). Interlingual machine translation: Prospects and setbacks. *Translation Journal, 10*(3).

Shachaf, P. (2008). Cultural diversity and information and communication technology impacts on global virtual teams: An exploratory study. *Information & Management, 45*(2), 131–142. doi:10.1016/j.im.2007.12.003

Shigenobu, T., Fujii, K., & Yoshino, T. (2007, July 22-27). The role of annotation in intercultural communication. In N. Aykin (Ed.), *Usability and internationalization: HCI and Culture: Proceedings of the Second International Conference on Usability of Internationalization*, Beijing, China (pp. 186-195). Berlin: Springer.

Somers, H. (2007). The use of machine translation by law librarians—a reply to Yates. *Law Library Journal, 99*, 611–619.

Splettstoesser, D. (1998). Electronic decision-making for developing countries. *Group Decision and Negotiation*, *7*(5), 417–433. doi:10.1023/A:1008699902917

Tiffin, J., & Terashima, N. (2001). *HyperReality: Paradigm for the third millennium*. London: Routledge.

TOEFL. (2009). *TOEFL Test Review*. Retrieved November 9, 2009, from http://www.toeflprepinfo.com/toefl-reading-comprehension1.htm

UCLA. (2009). *UCLA graduate division English requirements*. Retrieved November 9, 2009, from http://www.gdnet.ucla.edu/gasaa/admissions/ENGREQ.HTM

Watson, R., Teck, H., & Raman, K. (1994). Culture: A fourth dimension of group support systems. *Communications of the ACM*, *37*(10), 45–55. doi:10.1145/194313.194320

Wescott, C. (2001). E-Government in the Asia-Pacific region. *Asian Journal of Political Science*, *9*(2), 1–24. doi:10.1080/02185370108434189

Yamashita, N., Inaba, R., Kuzuoka, H., & Ishida, T. (2009, April 4-9). Difficulties in establishing common ground in multiparty groups using machine translation. In *Proceedings of the 27th International Conference on Human factors in Computing Systems,* Boston (pp. 679-688).

Yamashita, N., & Ishida, T. (2006, November 4-8). Effects of machine translation on collaborative work. In *Proceedings of the 2006 20th Anniversary Conference on Computer Supported Cooperative Work*, Banff, Alberta, Canada (pp. 515-524).

Yang, J., & Lange, E. (1998, October 28-31). SYSTRAN on AltaVista: A user study on real-time machine translation on the Internet. In *Proceedings of the 3rd Conference of the Association for Machine Translation in the Americas,* Langhorne, PA (pp. 275-285).

APPENDIX 1

Sample Comprehension Passage – Translated from German

Please read the following passage and answer the questions below:

Have you ever heard of Frank Towers? He is the questionable figure who in the 19th Century supposedly survived three shipping accidents. Some people see him as the happiest man in the world. As a middle-aged man, he was as a stoker in the engine room hired. Some people saw him as a normal, hardworking person. Yet he possessed the ability not to die in some of the most terrible ever documented maritime accidents.

Some said that he was once a crew member on the *Titanic* when the vessel an iceberg rammed. Two years later he worked on the *RMS Empress of Ireland* when that ship with the *Storstad* collided. About one thousand people lost their lives during the disaster. In May 1915 he was employed on the *Lusitania* when she by a German submarine, U-20, was torpedoed. Apparently Frank Towers does not even have a scratch away. When you begin the existence of this man in question, they are tight on the truth of the track. There were no records, a Frank Towers on all three vessels suggest ever found.

The Legend of Frank Towers seems another case of those folk tales to be the desire of humankind to see triumph over a tragic situation. Fact or fiction, Frank Towers is one of those characters who help us understand the history books to be illustrative better.

1. **How much of the text did you understand? (0 – 100%) _____**
2. **Which of the following phrases best captures the intent of the passage?**
   A.   A stitch in time saves nine.
   B.   Don't believe everything you read.
   C.   Seeing is believing.
   D.   There are many layers of an onion.
3. **The article states that urban folk tales are created because**
   A.   They are fun to hear.
   B.   Humanity likes to see someone triumph over tragedy
   C.   They trick people into believing lies.
   D.   People do not remember details clearly.
4. **This passage sheds doubt on**
   A.   The fact that three ships sank.
   B.   The thought that America was at war with other countries.
   C.   Frank Towers causing the ships to sink.
   D.   Urban folk tales are not always based on real people.

This work was previously published in the International Journal of e-Collaboration, Volume 7, Issue 1, edited by Ned Kock, pp. 17-29, copyright 2011 by IGI Publishing (an imprint of IGI Global).

Chapter 3
The Virtual Individual Education Plan (IEP) Team:
Using Online Collaboration to Develop a Behavior Intervention Plan

Robyn M. Catagnus
Arcadia University, USA

Donald A. Hantula
Temple University, USA

ABSTRACT

A team of professional educators in a private school for children with disabilities (a Virtual IEP Team) used an online platform to collaborate and produce a behavior intervention plan for a student. The collaboration was effective and efficient; the plan was produced in 9 days, rather than the customary 3-6 weeks. Qualitative data yielded four major themes: beneficial augmentation, reflective practice, barriers to change, and improved interactions. Quantitative results showed that although end user satisfaction was moderate, educators produced a successful behavior intervention plan that showed positive changes in both the teacher and student behavior. An increase of in-person staff discussion as a result of online dialogue was a unique finding in this study warranting further investigation. Now that federal (U.S.) education law has changed to allow technologically mediated IEP meetings, the Virtual IEP Team may serve as a model for more efficient use of education professionals' time.

INTRODUCTION

Investigations of e-collaboration often use measures of member attitudes or intentions as their dependent variables. However, measures such as perceived ease of use or usage intent are not necessarily synonymous with actual technology usage behavior (Sauter, 2008). As Hantula, Kock, D'Arcy and DeRosa (in press) observe, although attitudinal and process measures may be important in their own right, they should not be explicitly or implicitly equated with actual work products or outcomes of e-collaboration. Indeed, from a

DOI: 10.4018/978-1-4666-2020-9.ch003

media compensation theory perspective, they should be expected to diverge (DeLuca, Gasson, & Kock, 2006). Fortunately, studies employing behavioral usage measures are increasing. The next step in e-collaboration research is incorporating and measuring organizationally important outcomes of e-collaboration. For example, Nikas and Poulymenakou (2008) studied the institutionalization (or lack thereof) of e-collaboration in a construction company and Kock, Verville, Danesh-Pajou, and DeLuca, (2009) studied the effects of e-collaboration on the success of business process redesign. Other organizationally important outcomes of e-collaboration include work/decision quality and time use. These outcomes are especially important in the case of collaborative work that demands a high degree of knowledge and expertise.

The current study is an action research project designed to establish and evaluate an e-collaboration in a special education organization. The study was based on an action research cycle of thoughtfully planned activities to gather, interpret, and explore data about online group collaboration in order to facilitate an innovative solution. As an intensive study of a single e-collaboration (the "virtual IEP team"), it includes measures of attitude, process, usage and outcome. However, the outcome data extend beyond an evaluation of the work product to include measures of changes in teacher behavior and student behavior as a result of the behavior intervention plan developed in the e-collaboration.

The IEP Process

Special education services for more than 6 million students between the ages of 3 and 21 are provided under the Individuals with Disabilities Act of 1997 (IDEA) (US Department of Education, Office of Special Education, 2004). Each student identified as eligible for and receiving special education services is required by federal (USA) law to have an Individualized Education

Plan (IEP). The IEP is a written plan detailing a student's special education goals, current educational performance, methods of assessment, and related services required to individualize instruction. A team of professionals including parents, a regular education teacher, a special education teacher, local education agency specialists (LEA), and related services personnel (speech therapists, psychologists, and occupational therapists) must meet, develop, and plan for the education and any related or necessary services required for the student to benefit from a public school education (Gartin & Murdick, 2005). USA education law mandates interdisciplinary collaboration (U.S. Department of Education, 2004: Pub. L. 108–446, Dec. 3, 2004, 118 Stat. 2662 § 609(b)(4)). Additionally, when there is a behavior problem that affects learning, a functional behavioral assessment and a plan for behavior change (behavior intervention plan) are required products of this collaborative process.

The Virtual IEP Team

Collaboration for interdisciplinary teams in special education is especially challenging due to a historical mandate of face-to-face collaboration, scheduling, and time constraints (Glazer & Hannafin, 2006; Harfitt & Tavares, 2004; Odom & Bailey, 2001; Romiszowski & Mason, 2003; Smith, 1990). Overall, it is difficult to arrange for groups of people to be in the same place at the same time. Typically, collaborative teams have met in person to complete tasks and plan for the education of students with disabilities. Changes in federal rules and regulations now allow utilization of alternatives to meeting in person, such as conferences calls, videoconferences, and online collaboration; until 2005, federal (USA) law prohibited virtual collaboration in this context. Further, changes in educational mores and the increased cultural use of computers have served to increase the perceived value of online collaboration among educators (Haythornthwaite,

2005). These new legal and cultural trends have set the stage for e-collaboration to facilitate IEP collaboration among educators.

In this study, an online platform served as a tool to foster collaborative interactions among professional education staff to overcome the common major obstacles of time and scheduling. While e-collaboration may serve to save resources, and the inconvenience of traditional face-to-face meetings (Campbell & Halbert, 2002; DeWert, Babinski & Jones, 2003; Fjermestad, 2004; Ocker & Yaverbaum, 1999), it also yields other benefits. During behavioral consultation with educators, addition of Internet technology for completing documents and collaborating by email saves time overall and results in improved student outcomes (Meers & Nelson, 1998). Educators also report improved communication, high levels of reflection, knowledge building, and improvement in practice through use of online communication, noting that the format is easy to use and helpful for collaboration (Hawkes & Romiszowski, 2001; Meers & Nelson, 1998; Poling, 2005) and can be preferable to in-person meetings. For some participants of collaborative endeavors, the optimum format for teaming is described as a combination of online and in-person meetings (Pinsonneault & Caya, 2005).

Blanchard (2004) cited benefits of asynchronous discussion as the ease of use and comprehension for first time users and the ability to participate without the simultaneous presence of other members online. Users can choose to post messages or comment in limitless ways, can engage in research, thinking, and reviewing messages prior to sending a post, or can respond immediately. Not only are participants unhindered by time, they are also unhindered by geographic place. Participants in an asynchronous collaboration can be anywhere with Internet access and a computer (Hawkes, 2000). Additionally, the text of the discussion remains online in an archival format for members to review at any time. There is a "group memory" as members can refer to previ-

ous ideas and not miss any pertinent information (Dennis & Valacich, 1993; Stowitscheck & Guest, 2006). The text accumulated online becomes a group archive, facilitating memory and reflection for all and increasing participants' time to process and respond thoughtfully (Ocker & Yaverbaum, 1999; Romiszowski & Mason, 2003; Winter & McGhie-Richmond, 2005; Zhao, Alvarez-Torres, Smith, & Tan, 2004).

The goals of the study were to improve practice and understanding of e-collaboration used for interdisciplinary teaming and problem solving. The ultimate goal was engagement in future action to solve problems of scheduling and time via online discourse. The self-reflection used during this process was also a powerful tool for improvement of practice (Schon, 1983) and a method of action research (Altricher, Posch, & Somekh, 2003; Sagor, 2000). The primary research question was, "How does the addition of online asynchronous discussion affect collaborative behavioral intervention planning by IEP team members in terms of student outcomes and professional learning?" Supporting questions included:

1. How do online asynchronous discussion participants feel about their experience and participation in these discussions?
2. Does the process result in changes in teacher and student behavior in the classroom?
3. What is the content and development of the online discussion?
4. How do characteristics of the online format affect participation in a team's intervention planning?
5. In what ways does the discussion result in professional learning?

METHOD

Participants. A pre-existing interdisciplinary team consisting of a teacher ("Serena," female, early 30s, BA in Psychology; Special Education certification), a speech and language therapist ("Rebecca," female, early 30s, MA in Speech-Language Pathology), and an occupational therapist ("Enid," female, late 20s, BS in Occupational Therapy) working in the same building was chosen. Selection of the participating teacher was based on four criteria: school administration approval, teacher willingness to participate, personal Internet access, and existence of a qualifying student with behavioral concerns in her classroom. Selection of the other team members was based on willingness, Internet access, and existing assignment to the nominated student's IEP team.

Setting. A private, tuition-based non-residential school for students with intellectual disabilities that provides educational and related services to 473 students in grades K through 12. The staff was comprised of professional educators, including 57 certified special education teachers and 44 related service personnel, such as speech and language pathologists, occupational therapists, psychologists, and physical therapists.

The interdisciplinary team focused on developing a behavior intervention plan for a student named "Eddie," a 14-year-old male diagnosed with an intellectual disability and autism who had been a student in the teacher's classroom for four months. He frequently initiated inappropriate and contextually unrelated topics of conversation or responded to others' conversations with off-topic comments. This behavior was a formal IEP goal for the student because it significantly concerned the parent, interfered with learning time, impeded social participation, and disrupted routines. This student was chosen based on three criteria. First, the teacher was unable to solve the student's behavior problem on his or her own or with the informal, typical support of colleagues and senior teachers. Second, school administrators approved the student's potential participation based on their knowledge of the student and family's history and relationship with the school. Finally, the student exhibited problem classroom behaviors of moderate, non-dangerous intensity and moderate to high frequency. The criterion of non-dangerous intensity was established to protect the student and staff in case the use of an online discussion in some way failed to be as effective as a traditional meeting. Eddie's parents were fully informed of the virtual IEP team project, its discussions and resulting behavior plan, and consented to this collaboration.

Collaborative Technology. CryptoHeaven (www.CryptoHeaven.com) hosted the online asynchronous discussion board, email, chatting, messaging, file sharing, and discussion forum options. The site was encrypted, password protected, private, and Health Insurance Portability and Accountability Act (HIPAA) compliant. A shared file was created, named "Behavior Plan Development." Inside the file, specific documents including behavior graphs, narrative data, and a completed behavioral consultation request form were posted.

CryptoHeaven was set up so a daily email notification was sent to individuals when someone posted a group message or sent a private email. The environment had an "Inbox" link similar to other email clients. All messages (group, posted to the folder, or private) were also sent to the email box and participants could respond by opening the email message as well as by clicking a message on the discussion board.

Quantitative Measures

IEP Team Surveys. Pre and post-surveys were collected online at www.SurveyMonkey.com. The pre-survey was designed to collect data on variables potentially related to satisfaction with and use of technology by educators. The post-survey collected information about participants' attitudes and reports of their experience using the discussion forum, including perceptions of value, usefulness, effectiveness of the online teaming process, and Doll and Torkzadeh's (1998) end user satisfaction scale as modified for Internet use by Davis and Hantula (2001). The two survey instruments were piloted with education professionals enrolled in a doctoral program in order to resolve issues such as misleading, unclear, leading, or problematic questions or questions resulting in difficult to analyze data.

IEP Team Time Tracking. Time spent online or meeting in person was recorded for each participant. Participants were asked to record the start and stop time of any face-to-face meeting held to discuss the target student's behavior intervention planning (Meers & Nelson, 1998). Additionally, the discussion board automatically recorded the first date and time participants viewed the questions and the dates and times of all postings to the board. The combination of these data collection methods allowed tracking of discussion board visits, time spent posting, and time spent meeting.

Student and Teacher Behavior Change. Observational data were collected for the teacher's responses to both inappropriate initiation and off-topic responding. Based on recommendations of DeWever, Schellens, Valcke, and Van Keer (2006) inter-observer agreement (IOA) was gathered on the video observational data of teacher and student behavior by second and third observers. They worked with the study author while reviewing the tapes until 90% agreement was obtained on the rate (and duration, if relevant) of identified and defined teacher and student behaviors.

Qualitative Measures

Qualitative data collection techniques included rich descriptive observations, online discussion transcript, a focus group with the interdisciplinary team and surveys that asked participants to relate their experiences. Field notes and observations of activities documented the relationships, processes, and social interactions of participants as they engaged in the activities of the study (Emerson, Fretz, & Shaw, 1995). The investigator's use of a reflective journal was an effective method of exploring research biases, focusing reflections,

and deepening the understanding of role as a researcher (Sagor, 2000).

Focus Group. The group convened for a focus group interview after completing their collaborative activities online and in person. Interviews were audio-taped for transcription and detailed field notes were collected. The text and transcriptions from these interviews were coded and recoded as categories and themes emerged from the data (Hawkes & Romiszowski, 2001).

Online Discussion Board. The online discussion tool was structured on a functional assessment problem-solving model (Sugai & Tindal, 1993) and a model of problem solving synthesized from the literature (Hobbs, Day, & Russo, 2002; Welch, 1998; Veerman & Veldhuis-Diermanse, 2001). By overlaying the functional assessment approach of Sugai and Tindal and the problem-solving approach of Welch onto Hobbs et al.'s recommendations for team analysis prompts, a structure for the study's online problem-solving format was developed. The teacher posted online a structured request for a behavioral consult. Files with graphs of the problem behavior and anecdotal data were posted separately on the board for participant review. Additionally, historical attempts to solve the problem were described on the board. The structured online format included a measurable and objective behavioral definition for the problem behavior, written reports of observations of the behavior, setting events possibly related to the behavior, immediate triggers for the behavior, and common events following the behavior. Guiding questions for the team included prompts to facilitate identification of the problem, generation of potential solutions, and selection and evaluation of a final solution.

Reliability. Online conversations were analyzed by coding of content and identification of common themes (Brownell, Adams, & Sindelar, 2006; Häkkinen, 2003; Meers & Nelson, 1998; Selwyn, 2000). Summaries of the online discussion included the number of messages posted and responses to each thread and threads were analyzed in terms of content, quality, and types of interactions. A coding tool and professional learning rubric were developed (Yang & Liu, 2004). For the interview and focus groups, a grounded theory approach to the analysis of the data was accomplished by reading, rereading, coding, categorizing, and ultimately developing a theory detailing the perceptions of participants (McConnell, 2002).

RESULTS

An evaluation of the IEP team's use of the collaborative technology and their reactions is presented first. Because the goal of this e-collaboration was development of a suitable behavior intervention plan for the student and subsequent successful implementation of that plan by the teacher, data on student and teacher behavior relevant to the IEP are also presented.

IEP Team's Use of e-Collaboration

Emerging Themes

The data from the study were reduced through a process of coding and categorization, eventually yielding four major themes: *beneficial augmentation, reflective practice, barriers to change,* and *improved interactions*. The first theme, beneficial augmentation, addressed how the online forum augmented the participants' traditional face-to-face meetings, but did not replace them. The theme of reflective practices addressed the benefits of the requirement of reading and writing, which increased the depth of reflection and expanded the time available for consideration of the problem. The third theme dealt with barriers to change; use of the discussion board was not easy because Internet access, technical difficulties, participant characteristics, and time impediments were barriers to participation. The fourth theme

was improved interactions between staff and student, in both quality and quantity.

Beneficial Augmentation. The data included under beneficial augmentation allowed for a brief comparison of the perceptions of both the traditional face-to-face and the online consultation processes. Although the group members cited time constraints and technical difficulties as negatives, overall they viewed the online discussion process in a very favorable light, as shown in Table 1.

The group consensus was that the addition of the online discussion shortened the overall span of time required to complete a behavior consultation at the school and could speed up the process. In addition, online discussion was easier to schedule than in-person discussions. Figure 1 indicates time spent and numbers of responses made during online discussion.

The format of the online process focused and cued the group to develop and finalize a plan for the student when their in-person collaboration had not been successful. One particularly beneficial aspect of the online collaboration was the fact that it required commitment by the participants and provided regular reminders of required activities.

Reflective Practice. The second theme identified in the project, reflective practice, was closely related to the nature of online discussions. Participants had to read and write about the behavior problem in order to communicate and collaborate. The visual input and act of writing affected their depth of thinking about the issue. Their use of time was also different for the online discussion. The visual input of the words helped Enid to

Table 1. Representative commentary illustrating beneficial augmentation

> I could read the responses online, without having to physically 'find' my other team members and it was interesting to read things that we didn't necessarily discuss in person, as well as to hear other points of view. Also, this process helped me look at different aspects of the behavior (when, where, who it occurred with and why) that I hadn't already thought about.

Figure 1. Number of visits by each participant to the online forum, total minutes spent online, and number of posts

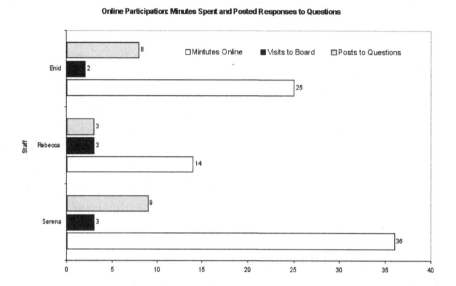

Online Participation: Minutes Spent and Posted Responses to Questions

develop the behavior plan because "by reading each member's answer and actually seeing the information written, I was able to get a good grasp on the analysis and planning of the project." During the focus group, participants agreed the written format was particularly important and the act of writing helped to clarify their thoughts as illustrated in Table 2.

Serena added that the written format allowed them to have a shared storage place, like a shared document. She said it was "like where I keep my behavior data in a section of the classroom or a binder or something." They reported the online aspect was equally important because a written document on the classroom or office wall would not have been as salient to them as the shared discussion board. In addition, the fact that members had several days to think about posted questions gave them plenty of time to ponder the questions in depth. Figure 2 details this time gap between question and response. Finally, the online format prompted the members to think in new ways about behavior and intervention.

Barriers to Change. The third theme, barriers to change, concerned technical aspects of the study. Participants were not particularly adept at computer technology. Setting up and using the discussion board system was easy for some and difficult for others, and technical challenges arose during both its creation and its use. Posting messages was just one area in which participants had difficulty. Several test messages were posted in order to learn the system, but the number of posts was modest as Figure 3 depicts.

The professionals' postings included only three major types: answers to a discussion question, agreement with a peer, and clarification of or addition to a peer's statement as shown in Figure 4.

The group found some characteristics of the discussion software satisfactory and some less satisfactory. Figure 5 shows the mean user satisfaction ratings. It can be seen from Figure 5 that output format and ease of use were the only aspects rated below acceptable.

Improved Interaction. The fourth theme emerging from the study was improved interaction. Lack

Table 2. Representative commentary illustrating reflective practice

> Robyn: So what I got from your answers is that it helped you to be more reflective because it was a structured process. Do you think it made any difference that you were reading the material and seeing it visually rather than talking about it? [Pause of a few seconds]
> Rebecca: I think it helped because some people are visual learners.
> Enid: Yeah.
> Rebecca: I am kind of both, auditory plus visual, but I think it helped a little bit for me personally.
> Enid: I liked being able to think about it on my own….and then reading what everyone else wrote and being like "yeah," that is what I was thinking and "oh," that is interesting, too. So, … I liked that aspect.
> Serena: Where if we were all just talking, we would be shooting things out and you don't think before you… A lot of, I mean especially during our "collab" meeting which is only a half hour, we don't think a lot as we are talking about it but when you are sitting down and you know, ok, I am typing all this out and this is going to be there for people to read and re-read.
> [Several sounds of assent from the other two]
> Serena: Let me make sense of this and put down exactly what I want to say so…
> Robyn: The act of writing also helps you clarify.
> [Group "Mm Hmm"]

of time to participate in discussions as fully as they desired was a problem that worked against interaction for all group members. The addition of online discussion to face-to-face collaboration in the context of this study had positive effects for both participants and the student because of the improved interaction that the combination of methods allowed.

The changes due to participation in the process were not limited to behavioral change in the classroom. Interplay between participant concepts of 'team' and 'self' was apparent online in the discussion. Collegiality and cohesion among the interdisciplinary team members increased, too. The women felt very strongly that they had bonded by participating in the study. The process was further facilitated because the online discussion stimulated increased frequency of face-to-face collaboration about the student's behavior intervention plan.

Figure 2. Number of days for each participant between their first view of the questions, first post, and plan development

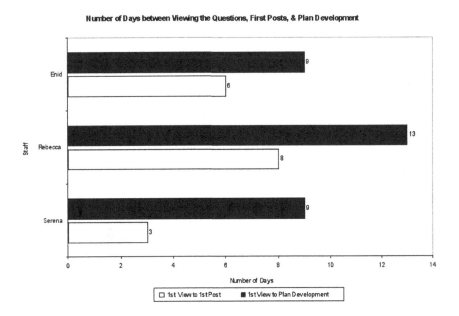

Figure 3. Number of responses to each online question in order of the questions' posting date and physical position on the discussion board

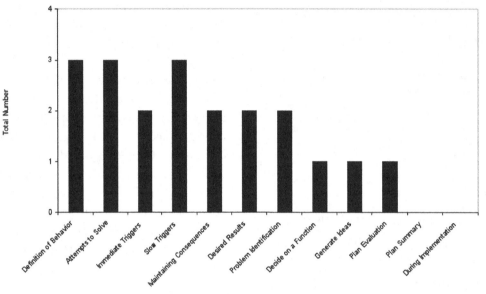

Figure 4. Type and frequency of posts for participants

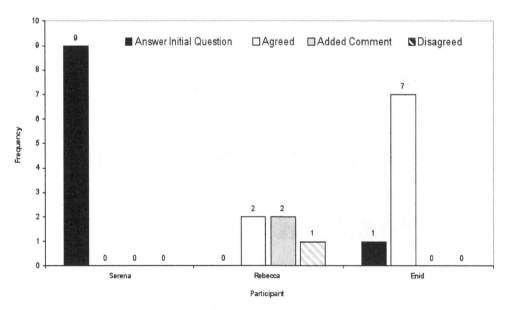

Figure 5. Mean user satisfaction ratings for various aspects of the CryptoHeaven environment

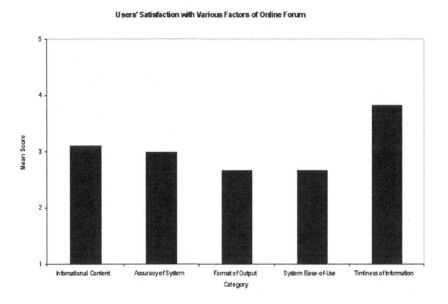

IEP Team Time Tracking

The addition of online discussion resulted in a behavior consultation completed more quickly than the traditional face-to-face format. Each of the participants had experienced the traditional in person, face-to-face behavior consult process at the school, and each reported the process to be effective, but slow to start and slow to finish. As the Director of Training and Supervision of the school explained, the typical consult process could take up to six weeks to complete. Serena reported that the face to face IEP process was slow to complete, taking up to 3 weeks and Rebecca recalled the entire process was effective but slow, usually taking a couple of months to complete. Enid also reported the process to be too slow and viewed time as the most difficult aspect of the collaborative process. In stark contrast, the online behavior planning was completed in nine days from the time the information was posted and all members had joined. As Rebecca remarked, "that was quick" as compared to the traditional consult.

Not only was the process shorter overall while requiring similar effort, it was easier to schedule, as well. Enid particularly enjoyed being able to access the project information at any time of her choice and she did so from home. Serena liked "how we could access the project any time we wanted" and Rebecca liked the process more than the face-to-face consult because:

I could read the responses online, without having to physically 'find' my other team members and it was interesting to read things that we didn't necessarily discuss in person, as well as to hear other points of view. Also, this process helped me look at different aspects of the behavior (when, where, who it occurred with and why) that I hadn't already thought about.

She and Serena both used work time to collaborate online, but Enid chose to do so from home. The group consensus was that the addition of the online discussion shorted the span of time required to complete a behavior consultation at

Table 3. Representative commentary illustrating the e-collaborations effect on time

> Serena: I know for me, I am on both ends. I will complete a behavior consult and I will request a behavior consult. So, as far as maybe requesting a behavior consult, you have to – it could take a few days before the person who receives that consult to notify you. Within that, you have to coordinate a time that is good for them to come observe or a time that you can sit with them and discuss those issues. At that point, the person will come and observe and talk with you and maybe look over data and maybe reschedule another meeting time where you can actually sit down and discuss everything that you've observed and all the data that you've collected. And, then maybe by the third time you can actually sit and write something. You know, you can toss ideas out and about and see how that works. So it might take three meetings? Between two or three meetings which could go, you know, between a few weeks before you actually have a plan developed.
> Robyn: So it stretches out in time and takes, face-to-face, at least an hour to an hour and a half or more.
> Serena and Rebecca: Yeah.
> Serena: Typically you'll schedule like a half hour.
> Rebecca: So, definitely, definitely more.
> Robyn: So this forum, if you could work it out, might be a way to speed that process along for some things?
> Serena: I think not so much time as in minutes, but time as in the span [moves arms and hands apart in a spreading gesture].
> Rebecca: Mm Hmm.

the school and could speed up the process overall, as shown in Table 3.

The time of active participation required was about the same using the online format as it was for the traditional process. Traditionally, two or three meetings of a half hour each accumulated to one or one and a half hours of meeting times stretched across several weeks. By adding the online process, Enid spent 28 minutes during one day to post eight responses. Rebecca posted three times over two days, taking 14 total minutes, and Serena was at the board on two different days for 36 total minutes while answering nine questions.

Overall, participants viewed the online process very positively. They described the team's collaborative process as intuitive, consistent, holistic, concise, effective, helpful, and informative and found that it fostered open-mindedness. Although not in complete agreement about the effectiveness of the online process as a stand-alone system, the participants were happy with their collaborative process and the resultant plan and were excited to

see if their strategies would work and interested in using the online forum again for collaboration.

STUDENT AND TEACHER BEHAVIOR CHANGE

Behavior Intervention Plan. The IEP team collaboration was successful. Using a combination of online and in-person discussions, the members developed a behavior plan to deal with Eddie's inappropriate conversational habits. They decided on use of a visual clue for the student—a happy face and thumbs-up to indicate his behavior was acceptable, and a "No" symbol for unacceptable conversation. They coupled the symbols with appropriate attention or redirection of the conversation. The plan was suitable for inclusion in an IEP document.

Teacher Behavior. In order to assess teacher behavior change outcomes, we examined the teacher's classroom behavior before and after participation in the online discussion. The teacher behaviors in responding to the student's inappropriate conversational habits were coded and scored, with acceptable reliability (interobserver agreement = 91.7%.)

Because there were two target behaviors for the student, baseline data were collected for the teacher's responses to both *inappropriate initiation* and *off-topic responding*. Three post-treatment observations of teacher responses to each of the student's target behaviors were conducted. During 2 days of baseline observation the behaviors occurred at a sufficient rate, and five examples of each were quickly obtained. The teacher responded to *inappropriate initiation* with a related verbal response 80% of the time or a verbal redirection 20% of the time. When *off-topic responding* occurred, the teacher engaged in a verbal redirection 50% of the time or a related verbal response 20% of the time. After the IEP was developed and implemented, verbal redirection and interaction by the teacher ceased for both target behaviors,

Figure 6. Mean rate and standard deviations (SD) of inappropriate initiation and off-topic responses in each treatment condition. Bars represent +/- 1 SD. IT = inappropriate conversation; OT = off-topic conversation.

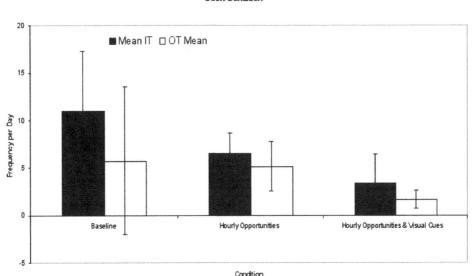

Mean Rate and Standard Deviations of of Inappropriate Initiation and Off Topic Responses in Each Condition

and the use of the visual cue and withholding attention became a consistent approach.

Student Behavior. After developing the plan, the staff implemented it in two phases. For 7 days, they first implemented an hourly opportunity for the student to talk about a preferred topic. The student's rate of *inappropriate initiation* during this condition ranged from 2-8 per day, and *off-topic responding* ranged from 2-10. Next, they implemented additional visual cues, and the range for *inappropriate initiation* was unchanged at 2-9/ day, however *off-topic responding* was reduced to 0-3/day. Although the range of behaviors showed a slow decrease in high values from baseline to intervention phases and a decrease in variability, the average rates in each condition reveal a decrease overall for each condition. Over time, the behavior plan decreased both problem behaviors noticeably in the classroom, in average daily rate of *inappropriate initiation* from 11 to 3.4, and *off-topic responding* from 5.75 to 1.7 as shown in Figure 6.

DISCUSSION

Collaboration between IEP team members was augmented with online asynchronous discussion. Attitudinal, behavioral, learning and work outcomes were assessed. This study found the e-collaboration to be a beneficial and effective addition to collaborating in person, and participation in the online discussion increased reflective practice. The behavior intervention plan developed as a part of this study improved both the teacher's and student's behavior. Barriers to change emerged but there were also improved interactions among the participants of this study. The increase of in-person staff discussion as a result of online dialogue was a unique finding in this study warranting further investigation. Very little research has investigated observable behavioral outcomes for online problem solving in discussion forums or by educators. The findings and implications of the current study contributed to the body of knowledge in the field and may act as a catalyst for a new line of research into multiple levels of outcomes for online collaboration.

Affective/attitudinal response to the e-collaboration was mixed. While the overall reaction to the technology was positive, difficulties with time constraints were noted and end-user satisfaction was fair; neither very positive nor very negative. If the evaluation of this e-collaboration stopped at these data, it could be concluded that the implementation not successful. Usage data showed that the virtual IEP team did not spend much time online nor did they post on the discussion board often. A period of days intervened between posts and answers to questions. At first glance this finding may also appear to show that the e-collaboration was unsuccessful. However, when taken in the context of education professionals collaborating to develop a behavior intervention plan, the lags between posts may be evidence of a constructive outcome: reflective practice. Participants noted that a benefit of e-collaboration was that the asynchronous interaction allowed for consideration of other members' input and time to think. Having the time to reflect on one's own input and that of collaborators offers an additional explanation for why technologically mediated idea generation groups outperform traditional face-to-face groups (DeRosa, Smith & Hantula, 2007).

The e-collaboration was efficient; the behavior intervention plan developed was accomplished in less time than usual. The e-collaboration was also effective; the behavior intervention plan was acceptable to the student and resulted in positive behavior changes for the student and the teacher. The particular behavior chosen by this virtual IEP team was of moderate, non-dangerous intensity for ethical reasons. Education lags industry in adopting technology (Hantula & Pawlowicz, 2004), and since any kind of technologically mediated communication was not permitted in the IEP process until 2005 the possibility that this new technology could compromise the IEP process and potentially harm the student was minimized.

In addition to a successful IEP and behavior intervention plan, other advantages emerged. Glazer and Hannafin (2006) recommend collaboration as a particularly good way to provide ongoing professional development for educators, which was an additional benefit of this e-collaboration. The participants reported improved interaction in their face-to-face communication as a result of participating in the virtual IEP team. However, difficulty with accessing and using technology was also evident. These perhaps more prosaic issues should be given special consideration when working with an organization or profession that is new to e-collaboration.

These results should be viewed in context of the study's limitations. As an action research project combining qualitative and quantitative methodologies, the sample size was necessarily limited, constraining generality. And because this was an action research project, the investigator was not an objective observer, but rather an involved participant in the project. Although the IEP team collaboration process is standard in USA educational settings, as a private institution, this particular school may not be representative of the "typical" special education environment. Study limitations constrain drawing broad conclusions about virtual IEP teams in general; replicating and extending the findings will address these limitations as a body of knowledge is built systematically.

CONCLUSION

Special education teachers and other educational personnel are highly trained professionals whose time is a precious resource. Time spent arranging meetings, travelling to meetings, and sitting in meetings is time taken away from working with students or on behavior plans. This raises an important operational, if not ethical issue: is it appropriate to squander such important professional time and expertise for the sake of face-to-face meetings that can be accomplished more efficiently and effectively via e-collaboration? As the old assumptions of the importance of spatiotemporal contiguity fade and the advantages of technologically mediated communication and collaboration accrue, we should expect to see the special education population served much more effectively.

ACKNOWLEDGMENT

We thank the educators who made this study possible.

REFERENCES

Achenbach, T. M., Altrichter, H., Posch, P., & Bridget, S. (2003). *Teachers investigate their work.* New York: Routledge.

Altrichter, H., Posch, P., & Somekh, B. (1993). *Teachers investigate their work. An introduction to the methods of action research NewYork.* Routledge.

Blanchard, A. (2004). Virtual behavior settings: An application of behavior setting theories to virtual communities. *Journal of Computer-Mediated Communication, 9*(2).

Brownell, M. T., Adams, A., & Sindelar, P. (2006). Learning from collaboration: The role of teacher qualities. *Exceptional Children, 72*(2), 169–185.

Campbell, P. H., & Halbert, J. (2002). Between research and practice: Provider perspectives in early intervention. *Topics in Early Intervention and Childhood Education, 22*(2), 213–220. doi:10.1177/027112140202200403

Davis, E. S., & Hantula, D. A. (2001). The effects of download delay on performance and end-user satisfaction in an Internet tutorial. *Computers in Human Behavior, 17*, 249–268. doi:10.1016/S0747-5632(01)00007-3

DeLuca, D., Gasson, S., & Kock, N. (2006). Adaptations that virtual teams make so that complex tasks can be performed using simple e-collaboration technologies. *International Journal of e-Collaboration, 2*(3), 64–90.

Dennis, A., & Valacich, J. S. (1993). Computer brainstorms: More heads are better than one. *The Journal of Applied Psychology, 78*(4), 531–537. doi:10.1037/0021-9010.78.4.531

DeRosa, D. M., Hantula, D. A., Kock, N., & D'Arcy, J. (2004). Trust and leadership in virtual teamwork: A media naturalness perspective. *Human Resource Management, 43*, 219–232. doi:10.1002/hrm.20016

DeRosa, D. M., Smith, C., & Hantula, D. (2007). The medium matters: Mining the long-promised merit of group interaction in creative idea generation tasks in a meta-analysis of the electronic group brainstorming literature. *Computers in Human Behavior, 23*(3), 1549–1581. doi:10.1016/j.chb.2005.07.003

DeWert, M. H., Babinski, L. M., & Jones, B. D. (2003). Safe passages: Providing online support to beginning teachers. *Journal of Teacher Education, 54*(4), 311–320. doi:10.1177/0022487103255008

DeWever, B., Schellens, T., Valcke, M., & Van Keer, H. (2006). Content analysis schemes to analyze transcripts of online asynchronous discussion groups: A review. *Computers & Education, 46*(1), 6–28. doi:10.1016/j.compedu.2005.04.005

Doll, W. J., & Torkzadeh, G. (1988). The measurement of end-user computing satisfaction. *Management Information Systems Quarterly, 12*(2), 259–274. doi:10.2307/248851

Emerson, R. M., Fretz, R. I., & Shaw, L. L. (1995). *Writing Ethnographic Fieldnotes.* Chicago: University of Chicago Press.

Fjermestad, J. (2004). An analysis of communication mode in group support systems research. *Decision Support Systems, 37*(2), 239–263.

Gartin, B., & Murdick, N. (2005). IDEA 2004: The IEP. *Remedial and Special Education, 26*(6), 327–331. doi:10.1177/07419325050260060301

Glazer, E. M., & Hannafin, M. J. (2006). The collaborative apprenticeship model: Situated professional development within school settings. *Teaching and Teacher Education: An International Journal of Research and Studies, 22*(2), 179–193. doi:10.1016/j.tate.2005.09.004

Häkkinen, P. (2003). Collaborative learning in networked environments: Interaction through shared workspaces and communication tools. *Journal of Education for Teaching, 29*(3), 279–281. doi:10.1080/0260747032000120178

Hantula, D. A., Kock, N. F., D'Arcy, J., & DeRosa, D. M. (in press). Media Compensation Theory: A Darwinian perspective on adaptation to electronic communications and collaboration. In Saad, G. (Ed.), *Darwinian theory in the organizational sciences*. New York: Springer.

Hantula, D. A., & Pawlowicz, D. M. (2004). Education mirrors industry: On the not-so surprising rise of Internet distance education. In Monolescu, D., Schifter, C., & Greenwood, L. (Eds.), *The distance education evolution* (pp. 142–162). Hershey, PA: Information Sciences Publishing.

Harfitt, G. J., & Tavares, N. J. (2004). Obstacles as opportunities in the promotion of teachers' learning. *International Journal of Educational Research, 41*(5), 353–366. doi:10.1016/j.ijer.2005.08.006

Hawkes, M. (2000). Structuring computer-mediated communication for collaborative teacher development. *Journal of Research and Development in Education, 33*(4), 268–277.

Hawkes, M., & Romiszowski, A. (2001). Examining the reflective outcomes of asynchronous computer-mediated communication on inservice teacher development. *Journal of Technology and Teacher Education, 9*(2), 285–308.

Haythornthwaite, C. (2005). Introduction: Computer-mediated collaborative practices. *Journal of Computer-Mediated Communication, 10*(4).

Hobbs, T., Day, S. L., & Russo, A. (2002). The virtual conference room: Online problem solving for first year teachers. *Teacher Education and Special Education, 25*(4), 352–361. doi:10.1177/088840640202500404

Kock, N., Verville, J., Danesh-Pajou, A., & DeLuca, D. (2009). Communication flow orientation in business process modeling and its effect on redesign success: Results from a field study. *Decision Support Systems, 46*(2), 562–575. doi:10.1016/j.dss.2008.10.002

McConnell, D. (2002). Action research and distributed problem-based learning in continuing professional education. *Distance Education, 23*(1), 59–83. doi:10.1080/01587910220123982

Meers, D. T., & Nelson, M. (1998). *Using the Internet as a medium to support teachers in the management of students with challenging behaviors*. Lexington, KY: University of Kentucky. Retrieved May 13, 2006, from http://sweb.uky.edu/~dtmeer0/meers98.html

Nikas, A., & Poulymenakou, A. (2008). Technology adaptation: Capturing the appropriation dynamics of web-based collaboration support in a project team. *International Journal of e-Collaboration, 4*(2), 1–28.

Ocker, R. J., & Yaverbaum, G. J. (1999). Asynchronous computer-mediated communication versus face-to-face collaboration: Results on student learning, quality, and satisfaction. *Group Decision and Negotiation, 8*, 427–440. doi:10.1023/A:1008621827601

Odom, S. L., & Bailey, D. (2001). Inclusive preschool programs: Classroom ecology and child outcomes. In Guralnick, M. J. (Ed.), *Early childhood inclusion: Focus on change* (pp. 253–276). Baltimore, MD: Brookes.

Pinsonneault, A., & Caya, O. (2005). Virtual teams: What we know, what we don't. *International Journal of e-Collaboration, 1*(3), 1–16.

Poling, C. (2005). Blog on: Building communication and collaboration among staff and students. *Learning and Leading with Technology, 32*(6), 12–15.

Romiszowski, A. J., & Mason, R. (2003). Computer-mediated communication. In Jonassen, D. H. (Ed.), *Handbook of research for educational communications and technology: A project of the Association for Educational Communications and Technology* (2nd ed., pp. 397–431). New York: Lawrence Erlbaum Associates.

Sagor, R. (2000). *Action Research.* Alexandria, VA: Association for Supervision and Curriculum Development.

Sauter, V. (2008). Information technology adoption by groups across time. *International Journal of e-Collaboration, 4*(3), 51–76.

Schon, D. A. (1983). *The reflective practitioner: How professionals think in action.* New York: Basic Books.

Selwyn, N. (2000). Creating a 'connected' community? Teachers' use of an electronic discussion group. *Teachers College Record, 102*(4), 750–778. doi:10.1111/0161-4681.00076

Smith, S. (1990). Individualized education programs (IEPs) in special education—from intent to acquiescence. *Exceptional Children, 57*(1), 6–14.

Stowitschek, J. J., & Guest, M. A. (2006). Islands with bridges: Using the web to enhance ongoing problem solving among educators of young children with special needs. *Infants and Young Children, 19*(1), 72–82. doi:10.1097/00001163-200601000-00008

Sugai, G. M., & Tindal, G. A. (1993). *Effective school consultation: An interactive approach.* Belmont, CA: Brooks/Cole.

U.S. Department of Education. (2004). *Individuals with Disabilities Education Improvement Act of 2004.* Retrieved July 1, 2006, from http://frwebgate. access.gpo.gov/cgibin/getdoc.cgi?dbname=108_ cong_public_laws&docid=f:publ446.108

Veerman, A., & Veldhuis-Diermanse, E. (2001). Collaborative learning through computer-mediated communication in academic education. In *Proceedings of Euro CSCL 2001.* Retrieved July 2, 2006, from http://www.ll.unimaas.nl/euro-cscl/ Papers/166.doc

Welch, M. (1998). Collaboration: Staying on the bandwagon. *Journal of Teacher Education, 49*(1), 26–37. doi:10.1177/0022487198049001004

Winter, E. C., & McGhie-Richmond, D. (2005). Using computer conferencing and case studies to enable collaboration between expert and novice teachers. *Journal of Computer Assisted Learning, 21*(2), 118–129. doi:10.1111/j.1365-2729.2005.00119.x

Yang, S. C., & Liu, S. F. (2004). Case study of online workshop for the professional development of teachers. *Computers in Human Behavior, 20*(6), 733–761. doi:10.1016/j.chb.2004.02.005

Zhao, Y., Alvarez-Torres, M. J., Smith, B., & Tan, H. S. (2004). The non-neutrality of technology: A theoretical analysis and empirical study of computer mediated communication technologies. *Journal of Educational Computing Research, 30*(1-2), 23–55. doi:10.2190/5N93-BJQR-3H4Q-7704

This work was previously published in the International Journal of e-Collaboration, Volume 7, Issue 1, edited by Ned Kock, pp. 30-46, copyright 2011 by IGI Publishing (an imprint of IGI Global).

Chapter 4
Measuring Collective Cognition in Online Collaboration Venues

Paul Dwyer
Willamette University, USA

ABSTRACT

By monitoring online conversations, organizations can receive value from the intellectual activity of their most interested constituents as they engage in problem solving and ideation. However, since intergroup dynamics often hinders people from optimizing collaboration, it should be measured and monitored for quality. Current metrics assess collaborative value solely from the number of collaborators, assuming that differences between individuals can be ignored. This study found that assumption to be wrong by identifying three distinct collaborator segments that strongly differ in the timing of their participation and in the variety of ideas they introduce. Therefore, a new metric is proposed that takes into account the diverse value individuals add. This new measure is correlated with existing measures only in those infrequent situations when collaboration productivity is maximized.

INTRODUCTION

Academic research recognized the existence of *collective cognition*, the thinking of a group, before it became a major byproduct of the interpersonal connectivity provided by the Internet. It was observed that people collaborated through word-of-mouth and engaged in sensemaking over whatever new ideas, things and events they encountered. Organizations want to join in these deliberations as a means of gaining feedback and informing constituents more efficiently. However, gaining value from a collaborative venue poses a challenge. Scoble and Israel (2006), the authors of *Naked Conversations*, caution that online communities may only reflect the views of a vocal minority, a phenomenon they call the *echo chamber*. Currently, the only way to detect the presence of this problem is through the time-consuming, skill-demanding and possibly subjective qualitative analysis of content. This

DOI: 10.4018/978-1-4666-2020-9.ch004

article seeks to augment qualitative analysis by proposing a more objective quantitative measure of the collaborative value inside an online venue.

This article is organized as follows. First, literature is reviewed that explains participation in online communities, noting the prevalence of certain oft-discussed constructs in that literature that reveal the presence and influence of collective thinking. Second, this study's primary argument is introduced: extant measures of collaborative value are wrongheaded because they assume that the only relevant correlate of collaborative value is the number of collaborators. Third, this study demonstrates that significant differences exist between collaborators on the basis of the information content and timing of their contributions. Fourth, a new measure of collaborative value based on information content is proposed that is correlated with existing measures only in those infrequent situations when information content is maximized. Finally, the findings and their implications are discussed.

CONCEPTUAL UNDERPINNINGS

This section begins by briefly summarizing what is known about what motivates consumers to engage in online participation. It is argued that giving consumers an opportunity to engage in collective cognition is a powerful attractor. However, lest it be assumed that high quality collaboration always occurs, two examples of natural socio-psychological processes that explain why collaboration is often suboptimal are described. These considerations are the foundation for this study's relevance.

Motives for Virtual Community Participation

Drawing from the realms of economics and sociology, Balasubramanian and Mahajan (2001) explain virtual community participation in terms of individual utility as the sum of three sources of value: (1) focus-related, where the community as a whole benefits from everyone's contribution, (2) consumption, the benefit individuals receive personally, and (3) approval, the satisfaction from seeing others approve of one's contributions.

In explaining the emergence of interactive media, like blogs, Jenkins (2006) builds on Balasubramanian's and Mahajan's (2001) first source of value by focusing on the phenomenon of *fandom*, camaraderie between people with common interests, as the basis for an emerging *participation culture*. This participation culture leverages new technologies that allow "more active modes of spectatorship" (p. 136). Jenkins also builds on Levy's (1997) concept of *collective intelligence*, the capacity of human communities to cooperate intellectually in creation, innovation and invention. This capacity often causes self-organized groups to spontaneously emerge around "common intellectual enterprises and emotional investments. Members may shift from one community to another as their interests and needs change, and they may belong to more than one community at the same time. Yet, they are held together through the mutual production and reciprocal exchange of knowledge" (Jenkins, p. 137). However, as the next section describes, communities may also form around deliberately planted intellectual seeds.

Cognitive Stimulation Inspires Co-Creation and Sensemaking

Need-for-Cognition and Co-Creation. Cacioppo and Petty (1982) note that a goal-directing problem statement will arouse those with a relatively high need-for-cognition, causing them to expend cognitive effort under the pressure of an inner tension to meet the goal. It is to be expected that blog readers, having signaled by their presence some threshold level of personal relevance for the blog's theme, are susceptible to being lured into a need-for-cognition state by a blog author who provides an impetus, often in the form of an invitation to joint problem-solving, which stimulates thought. People with knowledge of the subject matter are then drawn to contribute because it is an opportunity for them to gain recognition for their expertise and provide help (i.e., Balasubramanian's and Mahajan's (2001) third and first sources of value). As more perspectives are voiced, the thoughts of participants are even more stimulated and lively debate may ensue. From a business perspective, Prahalad and Ramaswamy (2004) note that the interaction between consumers and firms is a unique and valuable co-creation experience for the consumer as well as an opportunity for knowledge capture by the firm. Consumers are, however, limited in the time they can spend in the blogosphere. Hence, attracting the attention and interest of consumers in their target markets, and drawing them to interact in the blogosphere is likely to emerge as a new domain of competition between rivals.

Sensemaking. Overt invitation to joint problem solving is not the only inspiration for need-for-cognition. Writing from a business perspective, Rosa, Spanjol and Saxon (1999) observed that continually evolving products and categories often confuse consumers. Producers are uncertain as to whether consumers appreciate the value of new products. It has been observed that many corporate blog authors introduce new products in their entries. This suggests that sensemaking will gravitate toward blogging because it allows producers and consumers to converse more directly, and thus resolve uncertainty with greater efficiency. However, it should be noted that sensemaking does not exclusively occur between producers and consumers. Sensemaking between people is also a common scenario as described by Weick, Sutcliffe and Obstfeld (2005) where, as predominantly a social process, sensemaking involves individuals collaborating to form coherent thought structures about a newly encountered entity or concept because individuals do not always have enough

knowledge to make sense of the new. The forming of a community does not guarantee optimal or even fruitful collaboration. In the next section two examples of natural processes that hinder maximizing collaborative value are described.

Hindrances to Creating Collaborative Value

Cultural Tribalism. Scoble and Israel's (2006) "echo chamber" effect refers to the illusion of vibrant community that frequent communication between a few parties can create:

Blogging can fool you. You may think you are conversing with the world, when it's just a few people talking frequently, back and forth to each other, creating the illusion of amplification. The echo chamber can deceive a business into thinking it is either more widely successful or further off the mark than it is in reality, because a few people are making a lot of noise. (p. 134)

This phenomenon has been addressed in academic research as *cultural tribalism.* Kitchin (1998) described\cultural tribalism in this way:

...communities based upon interests and not localities might well reduce diversity and narrow spheres of influence, as like will only be communicating with like. As such, rather than providing a better alternative to real-world communities cyberspace leads to dysfunctional on-line communities ... (p. 90)

Cultural tribalism is thus portrayed as the ultimate equilibrium condition of all online communities. Since the cost of trial and switching are low, people will sample a large number of online communities and migrate to the ones wherein they feel most at home, those where they hear enough of what they want to hear to feel cognitively at ease. Matz and Wood (2005) supported this view by finding that heterogeneous attitudes create dissonance or tension and discomfort between members of a group. They found that the level of such discomfort was proportional to the numerical minority status of those with atypical views. The discomfort is partly relieved if the minority view-holders felt free to affirm their attitudes without pressure to conform. But, true relief of discomfort was only achieved if the minority could persuade the majority of their error, the majority could present more convincing support for their position, or if the minority could leave and join a more compatible group. The migratory aspect of cultural tribalism, given its ease among internet blogs, seems to be the result of a natural, unavoidable coping mechanism that will cause communities characterized by diverse thought to diminish over time with high cognitive diversity being only temporary.

Flocking Theory. Reynolds (1987) proposed *flocking theory* as a computational model that explains how the coordinated movement of a group can emerge from individuals making decisions based on personal information. He discovered that by using three simple "steering behaviors," coordination would emerge without any explicit management activity: *separation* ("steer to avoid crowding local flockmates"), *alignment* ("steer toward the average heading of local flockmates"), and *cohesion* ("steer toward the average position of local flockmates"). These steering behaviors are really just heuristic components of the more complicated calculation of which direction an individual should move to be in its desired location, relative to the group, one unit of time in the future.

Although flocking theory was developed as a solution to modeling the behavior of flocking birds and animals in computer graphics, it has been extensively investigated in a variety of academic disciplines and mathematically modeled by physicists Toner and Tu (1998). Rosen (2002) proposed that flocking theory was a good explanation for self-organization in human social systems. His proposal was based on the idea that communication

is the mechanism of cohesion in human society where a social network of individuals shares access to a collective body of knowledge that acts as a "roadmap" for coordinated action with little centralized control.

Rosen based his model on multiple literature streams. Simmel and Levine (1972) said that for social relationships to occur "the personalities must not emphasize themselves too individually … with too much abandon and aggressiveness." Eisenberg and Phillips (1990) proposed that community cohesion is always a balance between autonomy and interdependence, corresponding to Reynold's (1987) separation and cohesion steering behaviors. Rosen concludes that to some extent uniformity and common interest is essential to flock maintenance and that individuals must sacrifice some autonomy to keep group acceptance.

In summary, people whose behavior results in cultural tribalism are motivated by a need for cognitive support (i.e., they look for people who will say "You are correct."), while those who engage in flocking are motivated by a need for social belonging (i.e., they moderate self-expression to preserve a relationship). These two processes lead to the expectation that collective cognition has limits and is therefore measurable. In the next section, existing methods of measuring collaborative value are described along with the suspected shortcomings that inspired this study.

Metcalfe's Law

Other attempts have been made to measure the value gained from collaboration. Gilder (1993) introduced the concept of *Metcalfe's Law*: "the systematic value of compatibly communicating devices grows as the square of their number" based on Metcalfe's original statement of this "law," in a slide presentation sometime in the 1980's, referring specifically to communication technology like fax machines (Metcalfe, 1995). Gilder expanded the definition by substituting "users" for "compatibly communicating devices," thus making Metcalfe's Law relevant to the context of social networks and collaboration. Odlyzko and Tilly (2005) argued that Metcalfe's Law overestimated the value of adding connections to a network by observing that the efficiency of communication across network connections is always suboptimal. They suggested the true value (V) is better estimated by using Equation 1, where n_c is the number of collaborators.

$$V = n_c \ln n_c \qquad (1)$$

Metcalfe's Law and its variants estimate collaborative value solely from the number of collaborators, seeming to assume that differences in individuals' contributions can be disregarded. However, flocking theory and inherent variation in the knowledge possessed by individuals leads to the expectation that community participants will differ in the amount of unique collaborative value they add. In the next section, a means of measuring the information content of participant contributions is described. This will allow the speculation that participants substantially differ in their collaborative value to be tested.

Bag-of-Words Modeling and Information Theory

Bag-of-words modeling translates a body of text into a probability distribution by "classifying [its] words into a smaller number of thematic categories [i.e., bags] ... the relative occurrence of the different categories indicates the underlying thematic content" (Genovese, 2002, p. 110). The mapping of words into thematic categories is facilitated by looking them up in a *tag dictionary*, a collection of words that have been previously assigned to one or more thematic categories. This study used the Harvard-Lasswell IV (HL-4) dictionary, which categorizes 11,788 of the most-used words in the English language into 182 psychographic categories.

After the words in a body of text have been grouped into categories, the probability of occurrence of each category can be calculated by dividing the number of words in each category by the total number of words. This set of probabilities forms a probability distribution for a body of text. This probability distribution can be reduced to a single value H(X) denoted *information entropy*, or simply *entropy* (its expected information content), using Equation 2 (Shannon, 1948):

$$H\left(X\right) = -\sum_{i=1}^{n} p\left(x_i\right) \ln(p(x_i)), \qquad (2)$$

where *X* is a body of text with words categorized into *n* themes, and the probable occurrence of any theme *i* is $p(x_i)$. If the words in a body of text belong to one category, entropy is minimized at 0. If the words are uniformly distributed across *n* categories, entropy is maximized at the logarithm of *n*. This model of information content assumes that a body of text with more than one theme (i.e., categories of words) contains more information than text with a single theme.

The difference between the thematic probability distributions of two bodies of text can be measured by their *Kullback-Leibler divergence* (D_{KL}) using Equation 3 (Kullback & Leibler, 1951):

$$D_{KL}(P \,\|\, Q) = \sum_{i=1}^{n} p\left(x_i\right) \ln(p(x_i) / q(x_i)), \qquad (3)$$

where *P* and *Q* are bodies of text with words categorized into the same set of *n* themes, and the probability of occurrence of any theme *i* is $p(x_i)$ and $q(x_i)$ respectively. It should be noted that Kullback-Leibler divergence is a non-symmetric measure, that is $D_{KL}(P\|Q)$ is not equal to $D_{KL}(Q\|P)$. That makes D_{KL} particularly appropriate as a measure of *information gain* between subsequent additions (i.e., comments) to a conversation over time where P is followed by Q.

The next section describes the dataset used and the rationale used to select it.

DATA

A *blog*, a shortened form of *weblog*, is a website where an author displays articles, called *posts* or *entries*. The collection of all blogs is often called the *blogosphere*. Most blogs permit readers to add comments to posts and thereby be a vehicle for *collective cognition*, a process where individual knowledge and thought is augmented by social collaboration. Blogs are therefore used as the source of data to demonstrate the methodology proposed in this study.

Selection of Blogs Used as Data

Kozinets (2002) introduced *netnography* as a methodology where the principles of ethnography, or unobtrusive observation, are applied to study virtual communities. He specified a selection criterion for subject communities that differed from the practice of standard ethnography: select communities that are focused on a research question-relevant topic, receive above average posting traffic, have a large number of contributing members, contain descriptively rich content and enjoy a high level of member-to-member interaction. This criterion was adopted for the selection of the fourteen blogs (see Table 1) used in this study.

The Data Gathering Process

The data was gathered using a custom computer program that retrieved the entire archive of blog web pages as HTML and then parsed the HTML for author and commenter identification, origination dates and intellectual content. This is commonly called *screen scraping*. Most blogs are implemented using a standardized template for information layout, easing the task of HTML parsing. All data was written to a Microsoft SQL Server database as it was gathered. The data gathering phase took approximately three months of continuous computer program operation.

The next section describes the analysis using Shannon's entropy, Kullback-Leibler divergence and bag-of-words modeling on the content of text posted to these blogs. The results are then compared with a simulation of blog activity. Since this study proposes a new means of measuring collective cognition through the collaborative value it creates, the results are also compared with the existing measures of collaborative value already discussed.

ANALYSIS AND DISCUSSION

Collaboration Value Clusters

Since flocking theory and innate knowledge variation prompted the speculation that people would differ in the collaborative value they provided, the analysis began by determining whether natural segments or clusters would be detected among blog collaborators and what differences might exist between them. Three clustering algorithms—McQueen's (1967) *k*-means; Chiu, Fang, Chen, Wang and Jeris' (2001) two-step algorithm; and, Kohonen's (1982) neural network-based algorithm as implemented in IBM SPSS Modeler 14—were run separately on the mean information content across the comments each participant wrote. The results of the three algorithms applied to a 40% testing partition were compared on the basis of *silhouette coefficient* to find the best clustering scheme (Kaufman & Rousseeuw, 1990). Kaufman and Rousseeuw recommended that a silhouette coefficient greater than .5 be considered a strong assertion of cluster validity. It was found that Chiu et al.'s two-step algorithm achieved the best results (silhouette = .653) segmenting participants into three clusters occupying low, medium and high positions along the spectrum of the mean information content contributed by all collaborators.

Table 1. Blogs used and correlates of collective cognition

Name	Description	Final Envelope Area	Total Words	Unique Commenters	Info. Gain & N ln(N)	
					Mean Gain	Max. Gain
AutoBlog	Auto test drives and commentary.	36.5	ns	.057	ns	.304
Blog for America	US Democratic Party blog.	320.8	.247	.343	ns	.494
Blogoscoped	News about Google.	49.5	.045	ns	ns	.673
Consumerist	Consumer advocacy.	54.1	ns	ns	ns	.356
EnGadget	High tech product reviews and news.	100.0	.098	.247	ns	.456
Evangelical Outpost	Politics, religion, society	158.0	.319	ns	-.084*	.390
FastLane	GM Vice Chairman Bob Lutz's blog.	137.3	.515	.630	.123	.492
Freakonomics	Blog for the book.	134.7	.234	.383	.065	.534
Gizmodo	High tech product reviews and news.	50.0	0.039*	.075	ns	.412
Maverick	Entrepreneur Mark Cuban's blog.	82.7	.336	.281	ns	.391
Paul Stamatiou	Product reviews and technical support.	41.8	.066*	.092	ns	.335
Townhall	Politics, religion, society.	71.6	.229	.108	ns	.485
TUAW	Unofficial Apple Weblog	53.0	ns	.134	ns	.557
TV Squad	TV commentary.	111.2	.092	.216	ns	.427

Note. All $p < .01$, except $*p < .1$ and non-significant(ns) $p > .1$. The right-most column shows that only the maximum levels of information gain across all conversations were correlated with Metcalfe's Law. The remaining columns demonstrate how changes in the area of a blog collaboration envelope due to each new blog entry conversation do not redundantly reflect the information conveyed by simpler measures such as the number of collaborators and the number of words associated with the blog entry and its comments.

It has already been noted that this study's use of information entropy ascribes greater information content to a body of text with a variety of themes. When this idea was applied to people whose information contributions placed them at the lower end of the entropy spectrum it was concluded that they tend to focus their contributions on a single theme. That lead to them being denoted *focused* contributors while those at the high end were *broad* contributors, and those in the middle were *balanced* contributors. Figure 1 shows the time line for the three types of participants across all blog conversations. It was no surprise that the populous balanced cluster played an important role. However, the shift in the prominence of broad and focused clusters was interesting. Focused contributors tended to grow more prevalent toward a conversation's later stages, drawing it to a conclusion. Broad contributors were prevalent earlier when expanding the variety of ideas is generally considered to be critical to productive collaboration. Note also how the participation of broad contributors (the middle line in Figure 1B) seemed to follow Rogers' (1962) classic *diffusion curve* where broad commenters gradually increased in number until a peak was reached and their activity declined.

Now that it has been demonstrated that individual differences in collaborative production are worthy of note, the next section discussing the

Figure 1. Contributor cluster participation patterns and histogram. This is the participation time line for the three types of participants across all blog conversations. Focused contributors tend to grow more prevalent toward a conversation's later stages, drawing conversation to a conclusion. Broad contributors are prevalent earlier when expanding the variety of ideas is critical to productive collaboration.

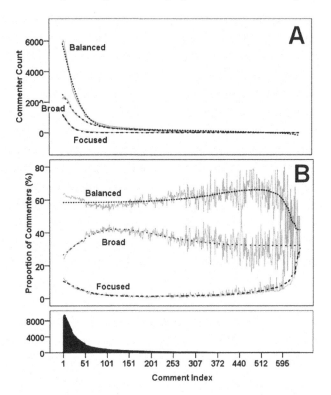

findings that led to introducing a new metric for collaborative value that focuses on the information content of what the collaboration produces rather than the number of collaborators.

The Collaborative Envelope

Figure 2 shows the range of information gain contributed by collaborators in the blog entries and associated comments (i.e., conversations) of The Unofficial Apple Weblog (TUAW, 2A) and the Blog for America (BFA, 2B). The graphs in Figure 2 use information gain as the vertical axis and a timeline relative to the point when each conversation began as the horizontal axis. Below each information gain timeline is a histogram showing the volume of content at each comment

interval. It was observed that the maximum and minimum levels of information gain across all the conversations in a blog form the upper and lower boundaries of a *collaboration envelope*. The upper boundary indicates how broad an array of thematic associations has been connected to a blog's subject. The lower boundary indicates the extent to which conversation has also focused on specific themes. A reference to a specific data point makes this explanation more explicit: TUAW had 45 blog entries that inspired 50 comments or more. In Figure 2A it is shown that the maximum information gain provided by one of the 50th comments was .074 while the minimum was -.364. The positive maximum indicates the greatest extent that a 50th comment expanded the variety of themes introduced to its associated conversation while the negative minimum reflects the extent that a 50th comment focused most narrowly on a specific theme relative to the conversation as a whole.

A measure of the area between the two boundaries was surmised to be an indicator of the extent to which conversants have explored a blog's subject, alternating between adding new themes to keep a discussion alive and deeply delving into specific themes already introduced. Even though each blog in the data set revealed such a collaboration envelope, it was uncertain whether this effect was a general phenomenon and what process could explain its shape. The next section describes how agent-based modeling was used to simulate blog conversations to determine whether similarly shaped collaboration envelopes appeared, thereby defining a process that could explain them.

Explaining the Envelope with Agent-Based Modeling

It was noted that Rosen (2002) proposed that communication was the mechanism of cohesion in human society where a social network of individuals shares access to a collective body of knowledge that acts as a "roadmap" for coordinated action with little centralized control. It was also noted that in the sensemaking process collaborators incrementally create a collective body of knowledge by searching their personal knowledge and uttering relevant cognitive associations. Collaborators thus try to assemble a common understanding that approximates all the knowledge known about a subject. This study used Wilensky's (1999) *Net-Logo* modeling environment (Version 4.1) to create an *agent-based model (ABM)* of a population's

Figure 2. Blog collaboration envelopes and participation histograms. Information gain is the vertical axis and a timeline relative to the point when each conversation began is the horizontal axis. Below each information gain timeline is a histogram showing the volume of content at each comment interval.

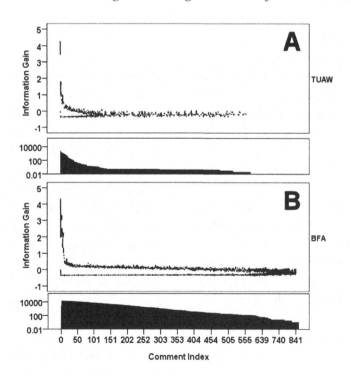

Figure 3. Simulation logic flow

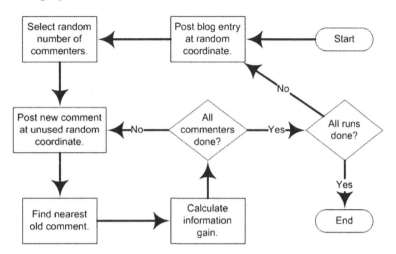

piecemeal construction of a collective body of knowledge. ABM is a simulation technique where system behavior emerges from the interaction of multiple decision-making entities called *agents*, each following a behavioral script with little or no synchronization. ABM is also a way of thinking about modeling: it is a bottom-up methodology that describes a system as the outcome of individuals acting autonomously, rather than the result of system-wide laws that dictate individual behavior from the top down. As a result, it is easy to learn to use ABM because only the behavior of a single agent need be programmed and as many agents as desired can be replicated and set loose within the simulation. Many theorists (e.g., Bonabeau, 2002; Casti, 1997; Epstein & Axtell, 1996) view ABM as providing the most natural way of modeling a system. This study's simulation followed the steps depicted in Figure 3.

The results of an ABM simulation can often be unexpected and counterintuitive. These are attributes of *emergent* behavior, that is, behavior resulting from interactions between unsynchronized autonomous entities. Such interactions are often nonlinear, sensitive to initial conditions and stochastic. This aspect of ABM makes it a powerful utility for testing theoretical models by revealing what Krippendorf (1986) called a *behavior space*:

The collection of behaviors a system can follow, the set of paths a system is capable of taking. A behavior space represents, sometimes graphically, and/or abstractly, and, often within many dimensions, just what a system can do so that what it actually does can be seen as a special case determined by initial conditions (Behavior Space section, para. 1).

If a behavior space is defined as a function of theory-based agent parameters, simulation can determine which parameters most influence the shape of the space. Then an attempt can be made to locate empirical data within the space. If the data does not fit the space, then the model must be modified. This procedure is consistent with Carley's (1996) observation that *validation*, the extent to which a model is true, can have more than one form, depending on the model's intended use. This study focuses on *theoretical validity*, the extent to which a model characterizes the real world and *external validity*, the extent to which simulated data matches real world data. This model's provisions for theoretical validity are discussed in the next paragraph, while its external validity is discussed in the one that follows.

This study's simulation was configured to take place within a 100 by 100 cell toroidal (i.e., doughnut-shaped) information space representing all the knowledge about a subject. Each coordinate within the space mapped a unit of knowledge, the difference in information content between units varied with the Euclidean distance between each unit's coordinates. To be consistent with blogs the space was populated with two classes of agent: many commenters and one author. Collectively, commenters were assumed to add knowledge from the entire knowledge space after an author initiated discussion. Under the assumption that commenter knowledge is randomly triggered as conversation proceeds, the coordinates of each simulated unit of knowledge were selected at random as the simulation ran. The simulation was reset to initial conditions and run 1000 times with commenter populations randomly sampled from a long-tailed distribution with a mean of 50 people. This simulation yielded the collaboration envelope shown in Figure 4A.

When the envelope of Figure 4A was compared with those in Figure 2 it was apparent that while the general shape matched, the lower boundary of the envelope did not dip below zero like those

in Figure 2. As a result, the simulation was modified in the way it calculated the information gained from each comment. Rather than assume that every comment added information gain equal to its distance from the nearest previous comment (its nearest neighbor), gain was calculated after the location of each new comment was found in one of the quadrants depicted in Figure 5, with its nearest neighbor positioned at the origin. Figure 5 assumes that comments only add new information content to the extent they are in front of existing content (i.e., located at coordinates with greater numeric value), while those placed behind explain ideas already expressed. The quadrant labels (i.e., exploration, elaboration and explanation) and their meaning are taken from Bybee's (1997) model of *constructivist learning*, another example of collective cognition.

The modified simulation produced the collaboration envelope in Figure 4B. Note that its lower boundary mimics those of the envelopes of Figure 2. Note also that by recognizing that comments often elaborate on and explain existing

Figure 4. Simulated collaboration envelopes. The original simulation yielded the collaboration envelope shown in 4A. When 4A was compared with Figure 2 it was apparent that while the general shape matched, the lower boundary of the envelope did not dip below zero. As a result, the information gain calculation was modified with results in 4B.

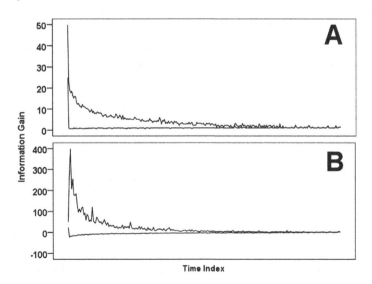

Figure 5. Simulated information gain grid. Rather than assume every comment added information gain equal to its distance from the nearest previous comment, gain was calculated after the location of each new comment was found in one of the four quadrants, with its nearest neighbor positioned at the origin. Comments are assumed to add new information content only to the extent they are in front of existing content, while those placed behind explain ideas already expressed.

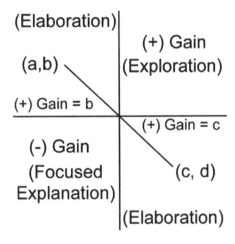

content rather than always adding new information, the area of the collaboration envelope is enlarged. This larger envelope is also more consistent with the empirical data displayed in Figure 2.

As already stated, this study interprets the area of the collaboration envelope to be an overall measure of the collective thinking inspired in a blog. Note that the collaboration envelope in Figure 2B seems larger than that of 2A, leading to the supposition that the BFA participants perceive, and draw from, a much larger thought space than TUAW's and in so doing add more value with their collective cognition. The next section proposes a means of measuring the size of the envelope thereby testing this supposition.

Calculating the Area of the Collaboration Envelope

It is readily apparent from Figure 2 that a collaboration envelope is bounded top and bottom by rough edges that can be approximated by non-linear mathematical models, but never fully described by them. As a result, the use of integral calculus to find the area below each curve is difficult and even if it was achieved, would not yield a general solution applicable to all collaboration envelopes. As a result, this study uses the trapezoidal rule (Hoffman, 2001, p. 291) to approximate the area under each bounding curve and then subtracts the smaller from the larger.

The trapezoidal rule approximates the area under the graph of a function (denoted *f(x)*) by modeling it as a collection of trapezoids, that is, four sided figures with one pair of parallel sides, where the area of each trapezoid is found using Equation 4:

$$\int_a^b f(x)\,dx \approx (b-a)((f(a)+f(b))/2), \qquad (4)$$

where *a* and *b* mark the position of two parallel sides along the x-axis. The results of the calculation are given in Table 1, confirming the speculation that BFA's envelope is larger than TUAW's.

Thus far the proposition that the collaborative envelope measures the collective cognition of a community has been supported by its information theory underpinnings and its qualitative similarity to the results of an agent-based model designed to simulate collaborative thinking. How does the area of the collaborative envelope compare to existing methods of measuring collaborative value? As one dimension of validation, this study calculated the correlation between information gain during blog conversations (i.e., the Kullback-Leibler divergence between comments to a blog entry) and Odlyzko and Tilly's estimate of collaborative value. The results of the calculation are given in Table 1.

It was expected that there would be positive correlation between the information gained during blog conversations and Odlyzko and Tilly's (2005) estimate of collaborative value. However, the right-most column of Table 1 shows that only the maximum levels of information gain across all conversations were reliably and substantially correlated with Odlyzko and Tilly's model. This study cannot support the proposition that Odlyzko and Tilly's model is more realistic than Metcalfe's Law because the correlation between Metcalfe's Law and maximum information gain was observed to generally be similar and often better. However it must be concluded that Metcalfe's Law and its variants only estimate ideal levels of collaborative value not those typically achieved, highlighting the need for a more empirically accurate measure.

The remaining columns of Table 1 demonstrate how changes in the area of a blog collaboration envelope due to each new blog entry conversation do not redundantly reflect the information conveyed by simpler measures such as the number of collaborators (column 5) and the number of words associated with the blog entry and its comments (column 4). The collaboration envelope seems to measure the content written while still being consistent with theoretical expectations that prompted Metcalfe's Law and its variants to estimate collaborative value solely from the number of collaborators.

CONCLUSION

When considering the implications of this study's findings it is important to be mindful that the scope of this investigation is narrow and that conclusions' must not overflow its limited bounds. This study primarily sought to make a methodological contribution to the electronic collaboration literature motivated by a problem: that human

collaboration often has limited value because natural socio-psychological processes cause people to limit the range of ideas they introduce into their deliberations; and, by the observation that existing collaboration value metrics cannot detect this phenomenon because they assume assessing content is unimportant. A new metric, the area of a collaboration envelope, is proposed that address this issue. It is supported by information theory, its qualitative similarity to the results of an agent-based model designed to simulate collaborative thinking, and its correlation with existing metrics, albeit only in those infrequent situations when collaborative production is maximized.

It is an axiom that for something to be managed it must be measured. However, it cannot be assumed that axiom is symmetric: that everything measurable is manageable. It is understandable that this study would be looked to for insight into how collaborative value, now that it can be measured, might be optimized. Attempting to provide such insight would overflow the bounds of this study, however there are clues for the direction of future research that could begin to provide this needed insight. It was noted that the problems that arise in human collaboration are natural phenomena both internal and external to the individuals involved. However, not all natural phenomena seem directed at undermining collaboration. It was noted in the discussion of Figure 1 that broad contributors seem to naturally enter a collaboration early expanding the array of ideas considered, while focused collaborators enter later when the drawing of conclusions seems most needed. The interplay of these collaborator segments seems directed at optimizing collaborative outcomes. Can these seemingly productive influences be magnified while those that seem counterproductive be minimized? Or are all these natural processes, both productive and non, properly balancing a system that the evolution of our social behavior has already optimized? These questions must be answered before the implications of being able to measure collaboration can be fully assessed.

Limitations and Further Opportunities

The blogs in this study's dataset are merely a sample of one type of high volume collaboration venue. There are many other such venues including wikis, forums (threaded discussions where any collaborator can initiate a topic of discussion) and Twitter *retweets* where Twitter messages are forwarded to new recipients sometimes with comments added. In all these contexts it might be asked "Is this discussion a productive collaboration?" It would be interesting to investigate whether different types of collaboration venues exhibit unexpected differences in the pattern of participation and shape of collaboration envelope from those observed here.

The methodology described is intended to be subject-matter agnostic. As a result it cannot qualitatively differentiate (e.g., good or bad) between ideas expressed in online communities, nor predict the commercial value of insights derived from the content of user-generated media. Only human judgment and market testing can address those issues. As noted in the narrative, this methodology is not intended to replace the qualitative analysis of what collaborators write but assist such methods to expand their productive scope to encompass high volume collaboration venues. Another valuable step beyond this study might involve pairing the calculation of collaborative envelope area with a qualitative analysis of content and thereby determine what area magnitudes correspond with poor collaboration outcomes.

REFERENCES

Balasubramanian, S., & Mahajan, V. (2001). The economic leverage of the virtual community. *International Journal of Electronic Commerce, 5*(3), 103–138.

Bonabeau, E. (2002). Agent-based modeling: Methods and techniques for simulating human systems. *Proceedings of the National Academy of Sciences of the United States of America, 99*(3), 7280–7287. doi:10.1073/pnas.082080899

Bybee, R. W. (1997). *Achieving scientific literacy: From purposes to practices*. Portsmouth, NH: Heinemann Educational Books.

Cacioppo, J. T., & Petty, R. E. (1982). The need for cognition. *Journal of Personality and Social Psychology, 42*, 116–131. doi:10.1037/0022-3514.42.1.116

Carley, K. M. (1996). *Validating computational models*. Retrieved July 21, 2010, from http://citeseerx.ist.psu.edu/viewdoc/summary?doi=10.1.1.87.9019

Casti, J. (1997). *Would-be worlds: How simulation is changing the world of science*. New York: Wiley.

Chiu, T., Fang, D. P., Chen, J., Wang, Y., & Jeris, C. (2001). A robust and scalable clustering algorithm for mixed type attributes in large database environments. In *Proceedings of the Seventh ACM SIGKDD International Conference on Knowledge Discovery and Data Mining,* San Francisco (p. 263). New York: ACM Press.

Eisenberg, E. M., & Phillips, S. R. (1990). What is organizational miscommunication? In Wiemann, J., Coupland, N., & Giles, H. (Eds.), *Handbook of miscommunication and problematic talk* (pp. 85–103). Oxford, UK: Multilingual Matters.

Epstein, J. M., & Axtell, R. L. (1996). *Growing artificial societies: Social science from the bottom up*. Cambridge, MA: MIT Press.

Genovese, J. E. (2002). Cognitive skills valued by educators: Historical content analysis of testing in Ohio. *The Journal of Educational Research, 96*(2), 101–115. doi:10.1080/00220670209598797

Gilder, G. (1993, September 3). Metcalfe's law and legacy. *Forbes ASAP*.

Hoffman, J. D. (2001). *Numerical methods for engineers and scientists*. New York: McGraw-Hill.

Jenkins, H. (2006). *Fans, bloggers, and gamers: Exploring participatory culture*. New York: New York University Press.

Kaufman, L., & Rousseeuw, P. (1990). *Finding Groups in Data: An Introduction to Cluster Analysis*. London: John Wiley & Sons.

Kitchin, R. (1998). *Cyberspace the world in the wires*. Chichester, UK: Wiley.

Kohonen, T. (1982). Self-organized formation of topologically correct feature maps. *Biological Cybernetics*, *43*, 59–69. doi:10.1007/BF00337288

Kozinets, R. V. (2002). The field behind the screen: Using netnography for marketing research in online communities. *JMR, Journal of Marketing Research*, *39*, 61–72. doi:10.1509/jmkr.39.1.61.18935

Krippendorf, K. (1986). *A dictionary of cybernetics*. Retrieved February 11, 2010, from http://pespmc1.vub.ac.be/ASC/indexASC.html

Kullback, S., & Leibler, R. A. (1951). On information and sufficiency. *Annals of Mathematical Statistics*, *22*(1), 79–86. doi:10.1214/aoms/1177729694

Levy, P. (1997). *Collective intelligence: Mankind's emerging world in cyberspace*. New York: Plenum Publishing.

Matz, D. C., & Wood, W. (2005). Cognitive dissonance in groups: The consequences of disagreement. *Journal of Personality and Social Psychology*, *88*(1), 22–37. doi:10.1037/0022-3514.88.1.22

McQueen, J. B. (1967). Some methods for classification and analysis of multivariate observations. In *Proceedings of the Fifth Berkeley Symposium on Mathematical Statistics and Probability* (pp. 281-297).

Metcalfe, R. (1995, October 2). Metcalfe's law: A network becomes more valuable as it reaches more users. *Infoworld*.

Odlyzko, A., & Tilly, B. (2005). *A refutation of Metcalfe's law and a better estimate for the value of networks and network interconnections*. Retrieved February 11, 2010, from http://www.dtc.umn.edu/~odlyzko/doc/metcalfe.pdf

Prahalad, C. K., & Ramaswamy, V. (2004). Co-creation experiences: The next practice in value creation. *Journal of Interactive Marketing*, *18*(3), 5–14. doi:10.1002/dir.20015

Reynolds, C. W. (1987). Flocks, herds, and schools: A distributed behavioral model. *SIGGRAPH '87 Conference Proceedings. Computer Graphics*, *21*(4), 25–34. doi:10.1145/37402.37406

Rogers, E. M. (1962). *Diffusion of innovations*. Glencoe, IL: Free Press.

Rosa, J. A., Spanjol, J., & Saxon, M. S. (1999). Sociocognitive Dynamics in a Product Market. *Journal of Marketing*, *63*, 64–77. doi:10.2307/1252102

Rosen, D. (2002). Flock theory: Cooperative evolution and self-organization of social systems. In *Proceedings of the 2002 CASOS (Computational Analysis of Social and Organizational Systems) Conference*. Pittsburgh, PA: Carnegie Mellon University Press.

Scoble, R., & Israel, S. (2006). *Naked conversations*. Hoboken, NJ: John Wiley & Sons.

Shannon, C. E. (1948). A mathematical theory of communication. *Bell System Technical Journal*, *27*, 379-423 & 623-656.

Simmel, G., & Levine, D. (1972). *Georg Simmel on individuality and social forms*. Chicago: University of Chicago Press.

Toner, J., & Tu, Y. (1998). Flocks, herds, and schools: A quantitative theory of flocking. *Physical Review E: Statistical Physics, Plasmas, Fluids, and Related Interdisciplinary Topics*, 58(4), 4828–4858. doi:10.1103/PhysRevE.58.4828

Weick, K. E., Sutcliffe, K. M., & Obstfeld, D. (2005). Organizing and the process of sensemaking. *Organization Science*, 16(4), 409–421. doi:10.1287/orsc.1050.0133

Wilensky, U. (1999). *NetLogo*. Evanston, IL: Center for Connected Learning and Computer-Based Modeling, Northwestern University. Retrieved February 11, 2010, from http://ccl.northwestern.edu/netlogo/

This work was previously published in the International Journal of e-Collaboration, Volume 7, Issue 1, edited by Ned Kock, pp. 47-61, copyright 2011 by IGI Publishing (an imprint of IGI Global).

Chapter 5

Using WarpPLS in E-Collaboration Studies:
Descriptive Statistics, Settings, and Key Analysis Results

Ned Kock

Texas A&M International University, USA

ABSTRACT

This is a follow-up on a previous article (Kock, 2010b) discussing the five main steps through which a nonlinear structural equation modeling analysis could be conducted with the software WarpPLS (warppls.com). Both this and the previous article use data from the same E-collaboration study as a basis for the discussion of important WarpPLS features. The focus of this article is on specific features related to saving and analyzing grouped descriptive statistics, viewing and changing analysis algorithm and resampling settings, and viewing and saving the various minor and major results of the analysis. Even though its focus is on an E-collaboration study, this article contributes to the broad literature on multivariate analysis methods, in addition to the more specific research literature on E-collaboration. The vast majority of relationships between variables, in investigations of both natural and behavioral phenomena, are nonlinear; usually taking the form of U and S curves. Structural equation modeling software tools, whether variancE- or covariancE-based, typically do not estimate coefficients of association based on nonlinear analysis algorithms. WarpPLS is an exception in this respect. Without taking nonlinearity into consideration, the results can be misleading; especially in complex and multi-factorial situations such as those stemming from E-collaboration in virtual teams.

DOI: 10.4018/978-1-4666-2020-9.ch005

INTRODUCTION

The vast majority of the statistical methods used in the behavioral sciences, and many of those used in the natural sciences, can be seen as special cases of structural equation modeling (SEM). This applies to both univariate (a.k.a. bivariate) and multivariate statistical analysis methods (Hair et al., 1987). This can be demonstrated through a sequential logical inference process. In short, it can be shown that most of these methods are instances of multiple regression analysis, which is itself an instance of path analysis, which in turn is an instance of SEM.

Methods like ANOVA, ANCOVA, MANOVA and MANCOVA can be shown to be special cases of multiple regression analysis (Hair et al., 1987; Rencher, 1998). In multiple regression analysis, hypothesis testing is typically conducted through the calculation of coefficients of association between multiple independent variables and one main dependent variable. These coefficients of association normally take the form of standardized partial regression coefficients (Rencher, 1998; Rosenthal & Rosnow, 1991). The corresponding P values are the probabilities that the relationships reflected in the coefficients are "real".

Path analysis is a method developed by Sewall Wright in the 1930s (Wolfle, 1999; Wright, 1934) and later "rediscovered" by statisticians and social scientists. Sewall Wright was an evolutionary biologist and animal breeder. He was also one of the founders of the field of population genetics. Population genetics unified Darwin's theory of evolution with Mendel's theory of genetics. Another co-founder of the field of population genetics was Ronald A. Fisher, who also has made many contributions to the field of statistics (Hair et al., 1987; Kock, 2009).

Any path analysis model can be decomposed into one or more multiple regression models (Gefen et al., 2000; Kline, 1998). Each of the multiple regression models can then be solved separately, and the solution combined into one main solution to the path analysis model. In this sense, multiple regression analysis can be seen as a special case of path analysis. Since SEM is essentially path analysis with latent variables (LVs), then path analysis can be seen as a special case of SEM (Maruyama, 1998). As a corollary, all of the methods discussed above can also be seen as special cases of the SEM.

In SEM, LV scores are calculated as weighted averages of their respective indicators. Usually there are two or more indicators for each LV, although that is not always the case. Once LV scores are calculated, the SEM solution problem is reduced to the solution of a path analysis model. That is achieved through the calculation of path coefficients and respective P values, as well as several other ancillary statistical coefficients. The path coefficients are standardized partial regression coefficients, which are mathematically identical to those obtained through multiple regression analyses.

The calculation of weights linking indicators to LVs is one of the key aspects that differentiate SEM approaches. Those approaches can be divided into two with main types: variancE- and covariancE-based (Chin et al., 2003; Gefen et al., 2000; Haenlein & Kaplan, 2004; Kline, 1998). One of the main advantages of variancE-based SEM is that it employs robust statistics to calculate P values, and thus can be seen as a nonparametric equivalent to covariancE-based SEM. That is, unlike covariancE-based SEM, variancE-based SEM typically yields robust results even in the presence of small samples and multivariate deviations from normality (Chin et al., 2003; Gefen et al., 2000). VariancE-based SEM is often referred to as PLS-based SEM, where "PLS" stands for "partial least squares" or "projection to latent structures". The term "PLS-based SEM" is actually more commonly found in the literature than the term "variancE-based SEM" (Chin et al., 2003; Haenlein & Kaplan, 2004).

The vast majority of relationships between variables, in investigations of both natural and behavioral phenomena, are nonlinear; usually taking the form of U and S curves. In spite of this, SEM software tools do not usually take nonlinear relationships between LVs into consideration in the calculation of path coefficients, respective P values, or other related statistical coefficients (e.g., R-squared coefficients). The SEM software WarpPLS (warppls.com), released as version 1.0 at the time of this writing, is an exception in this respect (Kock, 2010).

This article is a follow-up on a previous article (Kock, 2010b) discussing the five main steps through which a nonlinear structural equation modeling analysis could be conducted with the software WarpPLS. Both this and the previous article use the same E-collaboration study as a basis for the discussion of important WarpPLS features. Unlike in the previous article, the focus here is on specific features related to saving and analyzing grouped descriptive statistics, viewing and changing analysis algorithm and resampling settings, and viewing and saving the various minor and major results of the analysis.

THE E-COLLABORATION STUDY

In the following sections, several screens are used to illustrate important features of Warp-PLS. Those screens were generated based on an E-collaboration study if virtual teams. A total of 290 teams were studied. The teams were tasked with developing new products, goods or services, in a variety of organizations belonging to multiple industries and sectors (e.g., aerospace and banking; service and manufacturing; respectively). Data related to five LVs were collected as part of the study. The LVs are indicated here as "ECU", "ECUVar", "Proc", "Effi", and "Effe".

"ECU" refers to the extent to which electronic communication media were used by each team. "ECUVar" refers to the variety of different electronic communication media used by each team. "Proc" refers to the degree to which each team employed established project management techniques, referred to in the study as procedural structuring techniques. "Effi" refers to the efficiency of each team, in terms of task completion cost and time. "Effe" refers to the effectiveness of each team, in terms of the actual commercial success of the new goods or services that each team developed.

SAVING AND ANALYZING GROUPED DESCRIPTIVE STATISTICS

Once steps 1 and 2 of an SEM analysis are completed through WarpPLS, you (the user) can then save and analyze grouped descriptive statistics. Through Step 1, you will open or create a project file to save your work. Through Step 2, you will read the raw data used in the SEM analysis.

When the "Save grouped descriptive statistics into a tab-delimited .txt file" option is selected, a data entry window is displayed (Figure 1). There you can choose a grouping variable, number of groups, and the variables to be grouped. This option is useful if one wants to conduct a comparison of means analysis using the software, where one variable (the grouping variable) is the predictor, and one or more variables are the criteria (the variables to be grouped). Arguably the comparison of means is the most common type of analysis used in the natural and behavioral sciences. One of the reasons for this is that this type of analysis is intuitively appealing and its results are easy to understand.

Figure 2 shows the grouped statistics data saved through the window shown in Figure 1. The tab-delimited .txt file was opened with a spreadsheet program, and contained the data on the left part of the figure.

That data on the left part of Figure 2 was organized as shown above the bar chart. The data are the means and standard deviations for each

Figure 1. Save grouped descriptive statistics window

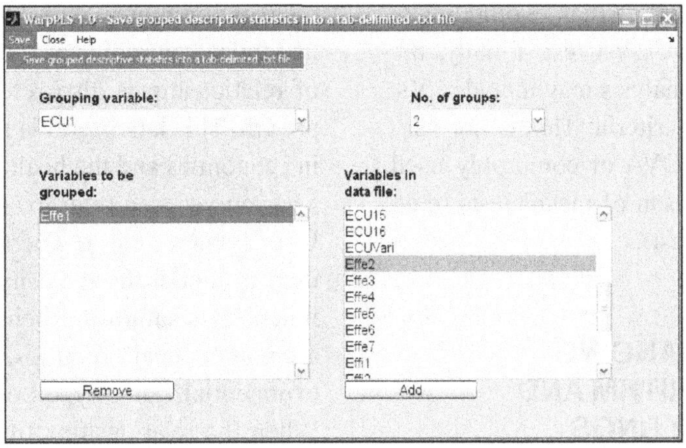

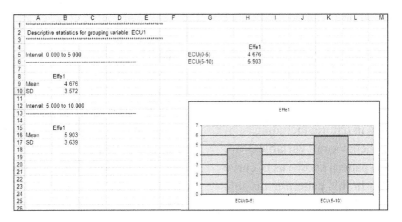

Figure 2. Grouped descriptive statistics bar chart

interval (or group). Next the bar chart was created using the spreadsheet program's charting feature. If a simple comparison of means analysis using this software had been conducted in which the grouping variable (in this case, an indicator called "ECU1") was the predictor, and the criterion was the indicator called "Effe1", those two variables would have been connected through a path in a simple path model with only one path. Assuming that the path coefficient was statistically significant, the bar chart displayed in Figure 2, or a similar bar chart, could be added to a report describing the analysis.

Some may think that it is an overkill to conduct a comparison of means analysis using an SEM software package such as this, but there are advantages in doing so. One of those advantages is that this software calculates P values using a nonparametric class of estimation techniques, namely resampling estimation techniques. (These are sometimes referred to as bootstrapping techniques, which may lead to confusion since bootstrapping is also the name of a type of resampling technique.) Nonparametric estimation techniques do not require the data to be normally distributed, which is a requirement of other comparison of means techniques (e.g., ANOVA).

Another advantage of conducting a comparison of means analysis using this software is that the analysis can be significantly more elaborate.

For example, the analysis may include control variables (or covariates), which would make it equivalent to an ANCOVA test. Finally, the comparison of means analysis may include LVs, as either predictors or criteria. This is not usually possible with ANOVA or commonly used nonparametric comparison of means tests (e.g., the Mann-Whitney U test).

VIEWING AND CHANGING ANALYSIS ALGORITHM AND RESAMPLING SETTINGS

The view or change settings window (Figure 3) allows you to select an algorithm for the SEM analysis, select a resampling method, and select the number of resamples used (this latter option is only useful if the resampling method selected was bootstrapping). The analysis algorithms available are Warp3 PLS Regression, Warp2 PLS Regression, PLS Regression, and Robust Path Analysis.

Many relationships in nature, including relationships involving behavioral variables, are nonlinear and follow a pattern known as U-curve (or inverted U-curve). In this pattern a variable

may affect another in a way that leads to a maximum or minimum value, where the effect is either maximized or minimized, respectively. This type of relationship is also referred to as a J-curve pattern. This latter term is more commonly used in economics and the health sciences.

U curves also refer to sections of a complete U- or J-shaped curve. Therefore U curves can be used to model the majority of the usually seen functions in natural and behavioral studies. These are non-cyclical functions, such as logarithmic, exponential, and hyperbolic decay functions. When the relationships fit well with the forms of these common types of functions, S-curve approximations (which are mono-cyclical) will usually default to U curves.

The Warp2 PLS Regression algorithm tries to identify a U-curve relationship between LVs, and, if that relationship exists, the algorithm transforms (or "warps") the scores of the predictor LVs so as to better reflect the U-curve relationship in the estimated path coefficients in the model.

The Warp3 PLS Regression algorithm, the default algorithm used by the software, tries to identify a relationship defined by a function whose first derivative is a U-curve. This type of relation-

Figure 3. View or change settings window

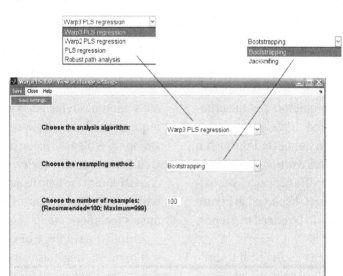

ship follows a pattern that is more similar to an S-curve (or a somewhat distorted S-curve), and can be seen as a combination of two connected U-curves, one of which is inverted.

The PLS Regression algorithm does not perform any warping of relationships. It is essentially a standard PLS regression algorithm (Wold et al., 2001), whereby indicators' weights, loadings and factor scores (a.k.a. LV scores) are calculated based on a least squares minimization sub-algorithm, after which path coefficients are estimated using a robust path analysis algorithm. A key criterion for the calculation of the weights, observed in virtually all PLS-based algorithms, is that the regression equation expressing the relationship between the indicators and the LV scores has an error term that equals zero. In other words, the LV scores are calculated as exact linear combinations of their indicators.

PLS regression (Wold et al., 2001) is the underlying weight calculation algorithm used in both Warp3 and Warp2 PLS Regression. The warping takes place during the estimation of path coefficients, and after the estimation of all weights and loadings in the model. It occurs only if the Warp3 or Warp2 algorithms are used. The weights and loadings of a model with LVs make up what is often referred to as outer model, whereas the path coefficients among LVs make up what is often called the inner model.

Finally, the Robust Path Analysis algorithm is a simplified algorithm in which LV scores are calculated by averaging all of the indicators associated with a LV; that is, in this algorithm weights are not estimated through PLS regression. This algorithm is called "Robust" Path Analysis, because, as with most robust statistics methods, the P values are calculated through resampling. If all LVs are measured with single indicators, the Robust Path Analysis and the PLS Regression algorithms will yield identical results.

One of two resampling methods may be selected: bootstrapping or jackknifing. Bootstrapping, the software's default, is a resampling algorithm that creates a number of resamples (a number that can be selected by the user), by a method known as "resampling with replacement". This means that each resample contains a random arrangement of the rows of the original dataset, where some rows may be repeated. (The commonly used analogy of a deck of cards being reshuffled, leading to many resample decks, is a good one. But it is not entirely correct because in bootstrapping the same card may appear more than once in each of the resample decks.)

Jacknifing, on the other hand, creates a number of resamples that equals the original sample size, and each resample has one row removed. That is, the sample size of each resample is the original sample size minus 1. Thus, the choice of number of resamples has no effect on jackknifing, and is only relevant in the context of bootstrapping.

The default number of resamples is 100, and it can be modified by entering a different number in the appropriate edit box. (Please note that we are talking about the number of resamples here, not the original data sample size.) Leaving the number of resamples for bootstrapping as 100 is recommended because it has been shown that higher numbers of resamples lead to negligible improvements in the reliability of P values; in fact, even setting the number of resamples at 50 is likely to lead to fairly reliable P value estimates (Efron et al., 2004). Conversely, increasing the number of resamples well beyond 100 leads to a higher computation load on the software, making the software look like it is having a hard time coming up with the results. In very complex models, a high number of resamples may make the software run very slowly.

Some researchers have suggested in the past that a large number of resamples can address problems with the data, such as the presence of outliers due to errors in data collection. This opinion is not shared by several researchers, including the original developer of the bootstrapping method, Bradley Efron (Efron et al., 2004).

Arguably jackknifing does a better job at addressing problems associated with the presence of outliers due to errors in data collection. Generally speaking, jackknifing tends to generate more stable resample path coefficients (and thus more reliable P values) with small sample sizes (lower than 100), and with samples containing outliers. In these cases, outlier data points do not appear more than once in the set of resamples, which accounts for the better performance of jackknifing (Chiquoine & Hjalmarsson, 2009).

Bootstrapping tends to generate more stable resample path coefficients (and thus more reliable P values) with larger samples and with samples where the data points are evenly distributed on a scatter plot. The use of bootstrapping with small sample sizes (lower than 100) has been discouraged (Nevitt & Hancock, 2001).

Since the warping algorithms are also sensitive to the presence of outliers, in many cases it is a good idea to estimate P values with both bootstrapping and jackknifing, and use the P values associated with the most stable coefficients. An indication of instability is a high P value (i.e., statistically insignificant) associated with path coefficients that could be reasonably expected to have low P values. For example, with a sample size of 100, a path coefficient of .2 could be reasonably expected to yield a P value that is statistically significant at the .05 level. If that is not the case, there may be a stability problem. Another indication of instability is a marked difference between the P values estimated through bootstrapping and jackknifing.

P values can be easily estimated using both resampling methods, bootstrapping and jackknifing, by following this simple procedure. Run an SEM analysis of the desired model, using one of the resampling methods, and save the project. Then save the project again, this time with a different name, change the resampling method, and run the SEM analysis again. Then save the second project again. Each project file will now have results that refer to one of the two resampling

methods. The P values can then be compared, and the most stable ones used in a research report on the SEM analysis.

VIEWING AND SAVING THE VARIOUS RESULTS OF THE ANALYSIS

As soon as an SEM analysis is completed with WarpPLS, the software shows the results in graphical format on a window, which also contains a number of menu options that allow you to view and save more detailed results. The sections below refer to each of these various menu options.

General Analysis Results

General SEM analysis results (Figure 4) include: project file details, such as the project file name and when the file was last saved; model fit indices, which are discussed in more detail below; and general model elements, such as the algorithm and resampling method used in the SEM analysis.

Under the project file details, both the raw data path and file are provided. Those are provided for completeness, because once the raw data is imported into a project file, it is no longer needed for the analysis. Once a raw data file is read, it can even be deleted without any effect on the project file, or the SEM analysis.

Three model fit indices are provided: average path coefficient (APC), average R-squared (ARS), and average variance inflation factor (VIF). For the APC and ARS, P values are also provided. These P values are calculated through a complex process that involves resampling estimations coupled with Bonferroni-like corrections. This is necessary since both fit indices are calculated as averages of other parameters.

The interpretation of the model fit indices depends on the goal of the SEM analysis. If the goal is to test hypotheses, where each arrow rep-

Figure 4. General SEM analysis results window

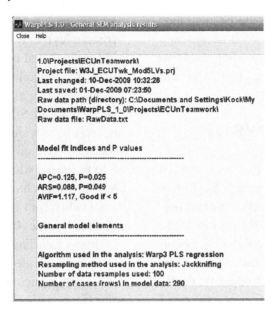

resents a hypothesis, then the model fit indices are of little importance. However, if the goal is to find out whether one model has a better fit with the original data than another, then the model fit indices are a useful set of measures related to model quality.

When assessing the model fit with the data, the following criteria are recommended. First, it is recommended that the P values for the APC and ARS be both lower than .05; that is, significant at the .05 level. Second, it is recommended that the AVIF be lower than 5. When comparing competing models, the ARS index should be given higher importance in terms of model fit than either AVIF or APC. Next in importance comes AVIF. APC comes third. One of the reasons for this is that the APC index may be low simply because there are many changes in path coefficient signs in the model. This is discouraged since it can lead to a phenomenon known as "suppression" (Kline, 1998), where competing path coefficients are distorted due to having different signs. However, different path coefficient signs may not have any significant distorting effect on competing path

coefficients, which warrants placing APC as third in order of importance.

Typically the addition of new LVs into a model will increase the ARS, even if those LVs are weakly associated with the existing LVs in the model. However, that will generally lead to a decrease in APC, since the path coefficients associated with the new LVs will be low. Thus, the APC and ARS will counterbalance each other, and will only increase together if the LVs that are added to the model enhance the overall predictive and explanatory quality of the model. This assumes that all path coefficients have the same sign. Path coefficients can be made to all have the same sign (usually positive) by reversing variables as needed. For example, if a variable D (reflecting dullness) is negatively associated with P (performance), a new variable E (excitement) may be used instead of D. In this case, E is D reversed, and the association between E and P will be positive.

The AVIF index will increase if new LVs are added to the model in such a way as to add multicolinearity to the model, which may result from the inclusion of new LVs that overlap in meaning with existing LVs. It is generally undesirable to have different LVs in the same model that measure the same thing; those should be combined into one single LV. Thus, the AVIF brings in a new dimension that adds to a comprehensive assessment of a model's overall predictive and explanatory quality.

Path Coefficients and P Values

Path coefficients and respective P values are shown together, as can be seen in Figure 5. Each path coefficient is displayed in one cell, where the column refers to the predictor LV and the row to the criterion. For example, let us consider the case in which the cell shows .145, and the column refers to the LV "ECU" and the row to the LV "Proc". This means that the path coefficient associated with the arrow that points from "ECU" to "Proc" is .145. Since the results refer to standardized variables, this means that a 1 standard deviation variation in "ECU" leads to a .145 standard deviation variation in "Proc".

The P values shown are calculated by resampling, and thus are specific to the resampling method and number of resamples selected by the user. As mentioned earlier, the choice of number of resamples is only meaningful for the bootstrapping method, and numbers higher than 100 add little to the reliability of the P value estimates.

One puzzling aspect of many publicly available PLS-based SEM software systems is that they do not provide P values, instead providing standard errors and T values, and leaving the users to figure out what the corresponding P values are. Often users have to resort to tables relating T to P values, or other software (e.g., Excel), to calculate P values based on T values.

This is puzzling because typically research reports will provide P values associated with path coefficients, which are more meaningful than T values for hypothesis testing purposes. This is due to the fact that P values reflect not only the strength of the relationship (which is already provided by the path coefficient itself) but also the power of the test, which increases with sample size. The larger the sample size, the lower a path coefficient has to be to yield a statistically significant P value.

Figure 5. Path coefficients and P values window

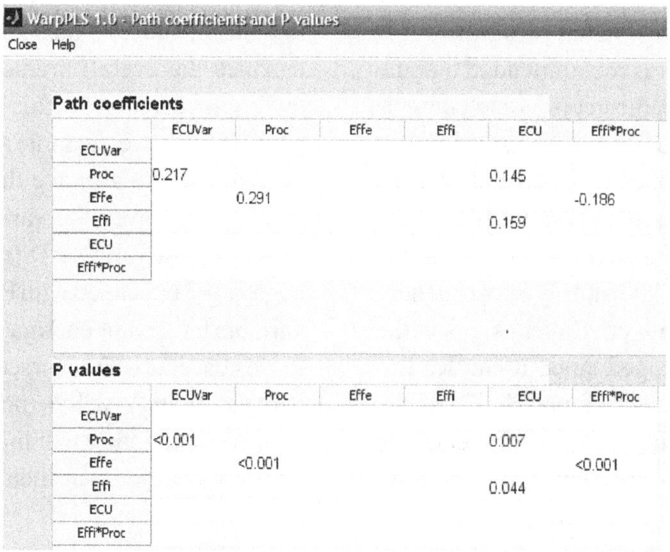
WarpPLS 1.0 - Path coefficients and P values

Close Help

Path coefficients

	ECUVar	Proc	Effe	Effi	ECU	Effi*Proc
ECUVar						
Proc	0.217				0.145	
Effe		0.291				-0.186
Effi					0.159	
ECU						
Effi*Proc						

P values

	ECUVar	Proc	Effe	Effi	ECU	Effi*Proc
ECUVar						
Proc	<0.001				0.007	
Effe		<0.001				<0.001
Effi					0.044	
ECU						
Effi*Proc						

Indicator Loadings and Cross-Loadings

Indicator loadings and cross-loadings are provided in a table with each cell referring to an indicator-LV link (Figure 6). LV names are listed at the top of each column, and indicator names at the beginning of each row.

These indicator loadings and cross-loadings are from a pattern matrix, which is obtained after the transformation of a structure matrix through an oblique rotation. The structure matrix contains the Pearson correlations between indicators and LVs, which are not particularly meaningful prior to rotation in the context of measurement instrument validation. Because an oblique rotation is employed, in some cases loadings may be higher than 1 (Rencher, 1998), which should have no effect on their interpretation. The expectation is that loadings, which are shown within parentheses, will be high; and cross-loadings will be low.

The main difference between oblique and orthogonal rotation methods is that the former assume that there are correlations, some of which may be strong, among LVs. Arguably oblique rotation methods are the most appropriate in PLS-based SEM analysis, because by definition LVs are expected to be correlated in SEM. Otherwise, no path coefficient would be significant. (Technically speaking, it is possible that a research study will hypothesize only neutral relationships between LVs, which could call for an orthogonal rotation. However, this is rarely, if ever, the case.)

P values are also provided, but only for reflective and moderating LVs. These P values are often referred to as validation parameters of a confirmatoty factor analysis, since they result from a test of a model where the relationships between indicators and LVs are defined beforehand. Conversely, in an exploratory factor analysis, relationships between indicators and LVs are not defined beforehand, but inferred based on the results yielded by a factor extraction algorithm; principal components analysis is one of the most popular of these algorithms.

For research reports, users will typically use the table of loadings and cross-loadings provided by this software when describing the convergent validity of their measurement instrument. A measurement instrument has good convergent validity if the question-statements (or other measures) associated with each LV are understood by the respondents in the same way as they were intended by the designers of the question-statements. In this respect, two criteria are recommended as the basis for concluding that a measurement model has acceptable convergent validity: that the P values associated with the loadings be lower than .05; and that the loadings be equal to or greater than .5 (Hair et al., 1987).

Indicators for which these criteria are not satisfied may be removed. This does not apply to formative LV indicators. If the offending indi-

Figure 6. Indicator loadings and cross-loadings window

	ECUVar	Proc	Effe	Effi	ECU	Effi*Proc	P value
ECUVari	(1.000)	0.000	-0.000	0.000	0.000	-0.000	<0.001
Proc1	-0.005	(0.830)	-0.028	0.036	-0.013	-0.027	<0.001
Proc2	-0.035	(0.883)	0.132	-0.083	-0.025	-0.008	<0.001
Proc3	0.044	(0.831)	-0.114	0.063	0.041	0.036	<0.001
Effe1	-0.044	0.060	(0.942)	-0.048	0.004	0.005	<0.001
Effe2	0.028	0.009	(0.978)	-0.055	-0.021	0.030	<0.001
Effe3	0.004	0.016	(0.772)	0.091	0.063	0.019	<0.001
Effe4	0.010	0.020	(0.966)	-0.037	-0.044	-0.002	<0.001
Effe5	0.039	-0.077	(0.932)	0.005	0.024	-0.009	<0.001

cators are part of a moderating effect, then you should consider removing the moderating effect. Moderating effect LV names are displayed on the table as product LVs (e.g., Effi*Proc). Moderating effect indicator names are displayed on the table as product indicators (e.g., "Effi1*Proc1"). Low P values for moderating effects suggest possible multicolinearity problems. This is to be expected with moderating effects, since the corresponding product variables are likely to be correlated with at least their component LVs. Moreover, moderating effects add nonlinearity to models, which can in some cases compound multicolinearity problems. Because of these and other related issues, moderating effects should be used sparingly.

Indicator Weights

Indicator weights are provided in a table, much in the same way as indicator loadings are (Figure 7). All cross-weights are zero, because of the way they are calculated through PLS regression. Each LV score is calculated as an exactly linear combination of its indicators, where the weights are multiple regression coefficients linking the indicators to the LV.

P values are provided for weights associated with formative LVs. These values can also be seen, together with those for loadings associated with reflective and moderating LVs, as the result of a confirmatory factor analysis. In research reports, users may want to report these P values as an indication that formative LV measurement items were properly constructed.

As in multiple regression analysis (Miller & Wichern, 1977; Mueller, 1996), it is recommended that weights with P values lower than .05 be considered valid items in a formative LV measurement item subset. Formative LV indicators whose weights do not satisfy this criterion may be considered for removal.

However, this criterion should not trump other criteria grounded on formative LV theory (Diamantopoulos, 1999; Diamantopoulos & Winklhofer, 2001; Diamantopoulos & Siguaw, 2006). Among other things, formative LVs are expected, often by design, to have many indicators (e.g., 15 or more). Yet, given the nature of multiple regression, indicator weights will normally go down as the number of indicators goes up, as long as those indicators are somewhat correlated. Respective P values will normally go up as well.

Latent Variable Coefficients

Several estimates are provided for each LV that can be used in research reports for discussions on the measurement instrument's reliability and

Figure 7. Indicator weights window

		ECUVar	Proc	Effe	Effi	ECU	Effi*Proc	P value
	Effi3	0.000	0.000	0.000	(0.231)	0.000	0.000	
	Effi4	0.000	0.000	0.000	(0.229)	0.000	0.000	
	Effi5	0.000	0.000	0.000	(0.224)	0.000	0.000	
	ECU1	0.000	0.000	0.000	0.000	(0.401)	0.000	<0.001
	ECU2	0.000	0.000	0.000	0.000	(0.399)	0.000	<0.001
	ECU3	0.000	0.000	0.000	0.000	(0.172)	0.000	0.001
	ECU4	0.000	0.000	0.000	0.000	(0.252)	0.000	<0.001
	ECU5	0.000	0.000	0.000	0.000	(0.217)	0.000	<0.001
	Effi1*Proc1	0.000	0.000	0.000	0.000	0.000	(0.092)	
	Effi1*Proc2	0.000	0.000	0.000	0.000	0.000	(0.094)	
	Effi1*Proc3	0.000	0.000	0.000	0.000	0.000	(0.090)	
	Effi2*Proc1	0.000	0.000	0.000	0.000	0.000	(0.091)	
	Effi2*Proc2	0.000	0.000	0.000	0.000	0.000	(0.093)	
	Effi2*Proc3	0.000	0.000	0.000	0.000	0.000	(0.086)	
	Effi3*Proc1	0.000	0.000	0.000	0.000	0.000	(0.088)	

discriminant validity (Figure 8). R-squared coefficients are provided only for endogenous LVs, and reflect the percentage of explained variance for each of those LVs. Composite reliability and Cronbach alpha coefficients are provided for all LVs; these are measures of reliability. Average variances extracted (AVE) are also provided for all LVs, and are used in the assessment of discriminant validity.

The following criteria, one more conservative and the other two more relaxed, are suggested in the assessment of the reliability of a measurement instrument. These criteria apply only to reflective LV indicators. Reliability is a measure of the quality of a measurement instrument; the instrument itself is typically a set of question-statements. A measurement instrument has good reliability if the question-statements (or other measures) associated with each LV are understood in the same way by different respondents.

More conservatively, both the compositive reliability and the Cronbach alpha coefficients should be equal to or greater than .7 (Fornell & Larcker, 1981; Nunnaly, 1978; Nunnally & Bernstein, 1994). The more relaxed version of this criterion, which is widely used, is that one of the two coefficients should be equal to or greater than

.7. This typically applies to the composite reliability coefficient, which is usually the higher of the two (Fornell & Larcker, 1981). An even more relaxed version sets this threshold at .6 (Nunnally & Bernstein, 1994). If a LV does not satisfy any of these criteria, the reason will often be one or a few indicators that load weakly on the LV. These indicators should be considered for removal.

Average variances extracted are normally used in conjunction with LV correlations in the assessment of a measurement instrument's discriminant validity. This is discussed below, together with the discussion of the table of correlations among LVs.

Correlations Among Latent Variables

Among the results generated by this software are tables containing LV correlations, and the P values associated with those correlations (Figure 9). On the diagonal of the LV correlations table are the square roots of the average variances extracted for each LV. These results are used for the assessment of the measurement instrument's discriminant validity.

In most research reports, users will typically show the table of correlations among LVs, with the square roots of the average variances extracted on the diagonal, to demonstrate that their measurement instrument passes widely accepted criteria for discriminant validity assessment. A measurement instrument has good discriminant validity if the question-statements (or other measures) associated with each LV are not confused by the respondents to the questionnaire with the question-statements associated with other LVs, particularly in terms of the meaning of the question-statements.

The following criterion is recommended for discriminant validity assessment: for each LV, the square root of the average variance extracted should be higher than any of the correlations involving that LV (Fornell & Larcker, 1981). That

Figure 8. Latent variable coefficients window

| | WarpPLS 1.0 - Latent variable coefficients | | | | | |
| Close | Help | | | | | |

R-squared coefficients

ECUVar	Proc	Effe	Effi	ECU	Effi*Proc
	0.072	0.166	0.026		

Composite reliability coefficients

ECUVar	Proc	Effe	Effi	ECU	Effi*Proc
1.000	0.886	0.972	0.926	0.776	0.953

Cronbach alpha coefficients

ECUVar	Proc	Effe	Effi	ECU	Effi*Proc
1.000	0.805	0.966	0.897	0.649	0.947

Average variances extracted

ECUVar	Proc	Effe	Effi	ECU	Effi*Proc
1.000	0.720	0.832	0.711	0.435	0.578

Figure 9. Correlations among latent variables window

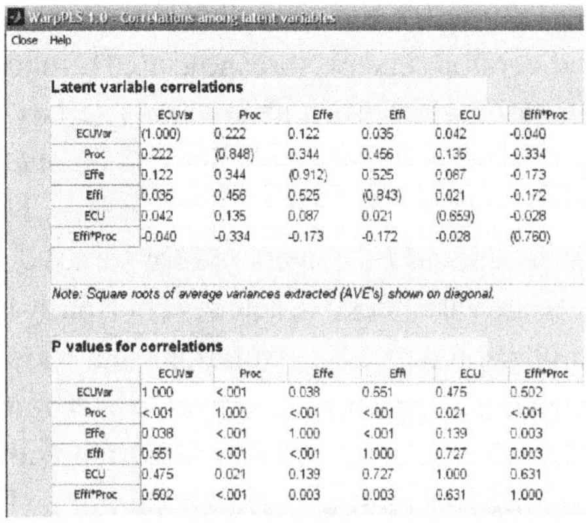

WarpPLS 1.0 - Correlations among latent variables

Close Help

Latent variable correlations

	ECUVar	Proc	Effe	Effi	ECU	Effi*Proc
ECUVar	(1.000)	0.222	0.122	0.035	0.042	-0.040
Proc	0.222	(0.848)	0.344	0.456	0.135	-0.334
Effe	0.122	0.344	(0.912)	0.525	0.087	-0.173
Effi	0.035	0.456	0.525	(0.843)	0.021	-0.172
ECU	0.042	0.135	0.087	0.021	(0.659)	-0.028
Effi*Proc	-0.040	-0.334	-0.173	-0.172	-0.028	(0.760)

Note: Square roots of average variances extracted (AVE's) shown on diagonal.

P values for correlations

	ECUVar	Proc	Effe	Effi	ECU	Effi*Proc
ECUVar	1.000	<.001	0.038	0.551	0.475	0.502
Proc	<.001	1.000	<.001	<.001	0.021	<.001
Effe	0.038	<.001	1.000	<.001	0.139	0.003
Effi	0.551	<.001	<.001	1.000	0.727	0.003
ECU	0.475	0.021	0.139	0.727	1.000	0.631
Effi*Proc	0.502	<.001	0.003	0.003	0.631	1.000

is, the values on the diagonal should be higher than any of the values above or below them, in the same column. Or, the values on the diagonal should be higher than any of the values to their left or right, in the same row; which means the same as the previous statement, given the repeated values of the LV correlations table.

The above criterion applies to reflective and formative LVs, as well as product LVs representing moderating effects. If it is not satisfied, the culprit is usually an indicator that loads strongly on more than one LV. Also, the problem may involve more than one indicator. You should check the loadings and cross-loadings matrix to see if you can identify the offending indicator or indicators, and consider removing it.

Second to LVs involved in moderating effects, formative LVs are the most likely to lead to discriminant validity problems. This is one of the reasons why formative LVs are not used as often as reflective LVs in empirical research. In fact, it is wise to use formative variables sparingly in models that will serve as the basis for SEM analysis. Formative variables can in many cases be decomposed into reflective LVs, which themselves can then be added to the model. Often this provides a better understanding of the empirical phenomena under investigation, in addition to helping avoid discriminant validity problems.

Variance Inflation factors

Variance inflation factors are provided in table format (Figure 10) for each LV that has two or more predictors. Each variance inflation factor is associated with one predictor, and relates to the link between that predictor and its LV criterion. (Or criteria, when one predictor LV points at two or more different LVs in the model).

A variance inflation factor is a measure of the degree of multicolinearity among the LVs that are hypothesized to affect another LV. For example, let us assume that there is a block of LVs in a model, with three LVs: A, B, and C (predictors); pointing at one LV: D. In this case, variance inflation factors are calculated for A, B, and C, and are estimates of the multicolinearity among these predictor LVs.

Two criteria, one more conservative and one more relaxed, are recommended in connection with variance inflation factors. More conservatively, it is recommended that variance inflation factors be lower than 5; a more relaxed criterion is that

Figure 10. Variance inflation factors window

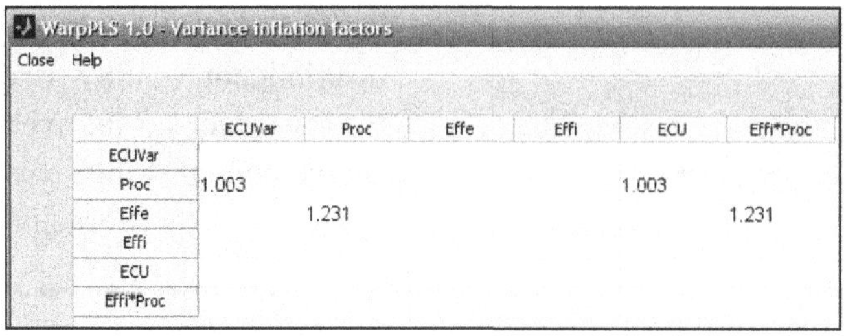

WarpPLS 1.0 - Variance inflation factors

Close Help

	ECUVar	Proc	Effe	Effi	ECU	Effi*Proc
ECUVar						
Proc	1.003				1.003	
Effe		1.231				1.231
Effi						
ECU						
Effi*Proc						

they be lower than 10 (Hair et al., 1987; Kline, 1998). High variance inflation factors usually occur for pairs of predictor LVs, and suggest that the LVs measure the same thing; which calls for the removal of one of the LVs from the block, or the model.

Correlations Among Indicators

The software allows users to view the correlations among all indicators in table format. Only the correlations for indicators included in the model are shown through the menu option "View correlations among indicators", available from the "View and save results" window. This option is useful for users who want to run a quick check on the correlations among indicators while they are trying to identify possible sources of multicolinearity.

The table of correlations among indicators used in the model is usually much larger, with many more columns and rows, than that of the correlations among LVs. For this reason, the P values for the correlations are not shown in the screen view option, but are saved in the related tab-delimited text file.

For correlations among all indicators, including those indicators not included in the model, use the menu option "Save general descriptive statistics into a tab-delimited .txt file". This menu option is available from the main software window, after Step 3 is completed (i.e., the data for the SEM analysis has been prE-processed). This option is generally more appropriate for users who want to include the correlations among indicators in their research reports, as part of a descriptive statistics table. This option also generates means and standard deviations for each of the indicators. Indicators that are not used in the model may simply be deleted prior to the inclusion in a research report.

Linear and Nonlinear Relationships Among Latent Variables

The software shows a table with the types of relationships, warped or linear, between LVs that are linked in the model (Figure 11). The term "warped" is used for relationships that are clearly nonlinear, and the term "linear" for linear or quasi-linear relationships. Quasi-linear relationships are slightly nonlinear relationships, which look linear upon visual inspection on plots of the regression curves that best approximate the relationships.

Plots with the points as well as the regression curves that best approximate the relationships can be viewed by clicking on a cell containing a relationship type description. (These cells are the same as those that contain path coefficients, in the path coefficients table.) See Figure 12 for an example of one of these plots. In this example, the relationship takes the form of a distorted S-curve. The curve may also be seen as a combination of two U-curves, one of which (on the right) is inverted.

Figure 11. Linear and nonlinear ("warped") relationships among latent variables window

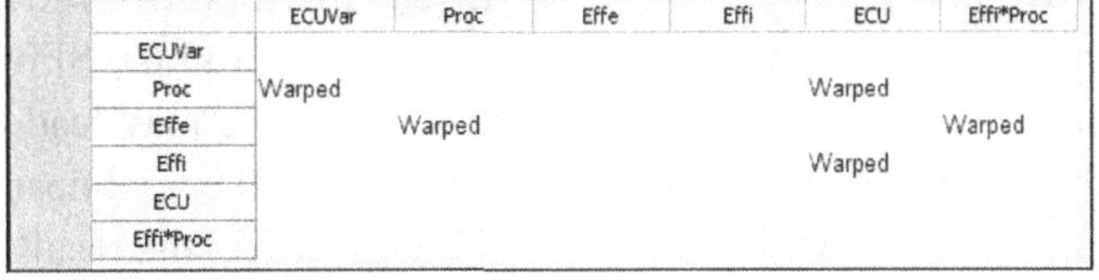

Figure 12. Plot of a relationship between pair of latent variables

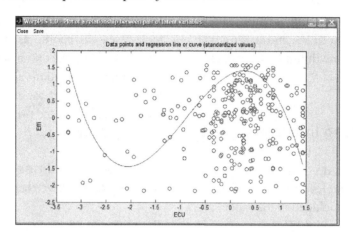

As mentioned earlier, the Warp2 PLS Regression algorithm tries to identify a U-curve relationship between LVs, and, if that relationship exists, the algorithm transforms (or "warps") the scores of the predictor LVs so as to better reflect the U-curve relationship in the estimated path coefficients in the model. The Warp3 PLS Regression algorithm, the default algorithm used by this software, tries to identify a relationship defined by a function whose first derivative is a U-curve. This type of relationship follows a pattern that is more similar to an S-curve (or a somewhat distorted S-curve), and can be seen as a combination of two connected U-curves, one of which is inverted.

Sometimes a Warp3 PLS Regression will lead to results that tell you that a relationship between two LVs has the form of a U-curve or a line, as opposed to an S-curve. Similarly, sometimes a Warp2 PLS Regression's results will tell you that a relationship has the form of a line. This is because the underlying algorithms find the type of relationship that best fits the distribution of points associated with a pair of LVs, and sometimes those types are not S-curves or U-curves.

The plots of relationships between pairs of LVs provide a much more nuanced view of how each pair of LVs is related. However, caution must be taken in the interpretation of these plots,

especially when the distribution of data points is very uneven.

An extreme example would be a warped plot in which all of the data points would be concentrated on the right part of the plot, with only one data point on the far left part of the plot. That single data point, called an outlier, would influence the shape of the nonlinear relationship. In these cases, the researcher must decide whether the outlier is "good" data that should be allowed to shape the relationship, or is simply "bad" data resulting from a data collection error.

If the outlier is found to be "bad" data, it can be removed from the data set by a simple procedure. The user should save the standardized data into a text file, using the menu option "Save standardized prE-processed data into a tab-delimited .txt file". This menu option is available from the main software window, after Step 3 is completed (i.e., the data for the SEM analysis has been prE-processed). Next the user should open the file with spreadsheet software (e.g., Excel). The outlier should be easy to identify, on the dataset, and should be eliminated. Then the user should rE-read this modified file as if it was the original data file, and run the SEM analysis steps again. This procedure may lead to a visible change in the shape of the nonlinear relationship, and significantly affect the results.

REFERENCES

Chin, W. W., Marcolin, B. L., & Newsted, P. R. (2003). A partial least squares latent variable modeling approach for measuring interaction effects: Results from a Monte Carlo simulation study and an electronic-mail emotion/adoption study. *Information Systems Research, 14*(2), 189–218. doi:10.1287/isre.14.2.189.16018

Chiquoine, B., & Hjalmarsson, E. (2009). Jack-knifing stock return predictions. *Journal of Empirical Finance, 16*(5), 793–803. doi:10.1016/j.jempfin.2009.07.003

Diamantopoulos, A. (1999). Export performance measurement: Reflective versus formative indicators. *International Marketing Review, 16*(6), 444–457. doi:10.1108/02651339910300422

Diamantopoulos, A., & Siguaw, J. A. (2006). Formative versus reflective indicators in organizational measure development: A comparison and empirical illustration. *British Journal of Management, 17*(4), 263–282. doi:10.1111/j.1467-8551.2006.00500.x

Diamantopoulos, A., & Winklhofer, H. (2001). Index construction with formative indicators: An alternative scale development. *JMR, Journal of Marketing Research, 37*(1), 269–177. doi:10.1509/jmkr.38.2.269.18845

Efron, B., Rogosa, D., & Tibshirani, R. (2004). Resampling methods of estimation. In Smelser, N. J., & Baltes, P. B. (Eds.), *International Encyclopedia of the Social & Behavioral Sciences* (pp. 13216–13220). New York, NY: Elsevier. doi:10.1016/B0-08-043076-7/00494-0

Fornell, C., & Larcker, D. F. (1981). Evaluating structural equation models with unobservable variables and measurement error. *JMR, Journal of Marketing Research, 18*(1), 39–50. doi:10.2307/3151312

Gefen, D., Straub, D. W., & Boudreau, M.-C. (2000). Structural equation modeling and regression: Guidelines for research practice. *Communications of the AIS, 4*(7), 1–76.

Haenlein, M., & Kaplan, A. M. (2004). A beginner's guide to partial least squares analysis. *Understanding Statistics, 3*(4), 283–297. doi:10.1207/s15328031us0304_4

Hair, J. F., Anderson, R. E., & Tatham, R. L. (1987). *Multivariate data analysis*. New York, NY: Macmillan.

Kline, R. B. (1998). *Principles and practice of structural equation modeling*. New York, NY: The Guilford Press.

Kock, N. (2009). Information systems theorizing based on evolutionary psychology: An interdisciplinary review and theory integration framework. *Management Information Systems Quarterly, 33*(2), 395–418.

Kock, N. (2010a). *WarpPLS 1.0 User Manual*. Laredo, TX: ScriptWarp Systems.

Kock, N. (2010b). Using WarpPLS in E-collaboration studies: An overview of five main analysis steps. *International Journal of E-Collaboration, 6*(4), 1–13. doi:10.4018/jec.2010100101

Maruyama, G. M. (1998). *Basics of structural equation modeling*. Thousand Oaks, CA: Sage.

Miller, R. B., & Wichern, D. W. (1977). *Intermediate business statistics: Analysis of variance, regression and time series*. New York, NY: Holt, Rihehart and Winston.

Mueller, R. O. (1996). *Basic principles of structural equation modeling.* New York, NY: Springer.

Nevitt, J., & Hancock, G. R. (2001). Performance of bootstrapping approaches to model test statistics and parameter standard error estimation in structural equation modeling. *Structural Equation Modeling, 8*(3), 353–377. doi:10.1207/S15328007SEM0803_2

Nunnally, J. C. (1978). *Psychometric theory.* New York, NY: McGrawHill.

Nunnally, J. C., & Bernstein, I. H. (1994). *Psychometric theory.* New York, NY: McGrawHill.

Rencher, A. C. (1998). *Multivariate statistical inference and applications.* New York, NY: John Wiley & Sons.

Rosenthal, R., & Rosnow, R. L. (1991). *Essentials of behavioral research: Methods and data analysis.* New York, NY: McGrawHill.

Wold, S., Trygg, J., Berglund, A., & Antti, H. (2001). Some recent developments in PLS modeling. *Chemometrics and Intelligent Laboratory Systems, 58*(2), 131–150. doi:10.1016/S0169-7439(01)00156-3

Wolfle, L. M. (1999). Sewall Wright on the method of path coefficients: An annotated bibliography. *Structural Equation Modeling, 6*(3), 280–291. doi:10.1080/10705519909540134

Wright, S. (1934). The method of path coefficients. *Annals of Mathematical Statistics, 5*(3), 161–215. doi:10.1214/aoms/1177732676

This work was previously published in the International Journal of e-Collaboration, Volume 7, Issue 2, edited by Ned Kock, pp. 1-18, copyright 2011 by IGI Publishing (an imprint of IGI Global).

Chapter 6
The Influence of Information Technology on Organizational Behavior:
Study of Identity Challenges in Virtual Teams

Babak Sohrabi
University of Tehran, Iran

Aryan Gholipour
University of Tehran, Iran

Behnam Amiri
University of Tehran, Iran

ABSTRACT

This paper attempts to examine the effects of virtual team dimensions on social identities of its members. A review of the literature shows that the geographically dispersed, culturally diverse as well as temporary dimensions of virtual teams do not match with their stability as members have different ethnic, social, or cultural backgrounds. Sources like culture, place, and time seem to continuously acquire social identities. Due to the importance of social identity, an attempt has been made to examine its influence on organizational variables (i.e. job satisfaction, job involvement, job commitment, and organizational citizenship behavior). Questionnaire-based data have been accomplished from 149 members of 44 teams. The hypothesized relationships among the proposed variables are tested via a structural equation model (SEM). Results show that the geographically disperse and culturally diverse variables are negatively related to the social identity as against those of temporary and organizational variables which are related positively.

DOI: 10.4018/978-1-4666-2020-9.ch006

INTRODUCTION

The ever increasing de-centralization and globalization of work processes have caused many organizations to respond to their dynamic environments by introducing virtual teams, in which members are geographically dispersed but coordinate their work via electronic information and communication technologies (Hertel et al., 2005). A virtual team is often consisted of a geographically dispersed, culturally diverse, temporary, electronically communicating work-group (Shin, 2005; Harvey et al., 2004). However, little is known about human resources within these teams, despite the level of research interest and growing of this new work form (Hertel et al., 2005; Lin et al., 2008). In other words, having different human resources challenges, the study of virtual teams with its diverse memberships has become an emerging trend these days.

Team members may have different sexes and racial groups, with different ethnic, social, or cultural backgrounds. Based on the social identity theory, members of a team with heterogeneous characters may find it difficult to integrate their diverse backgrounds, values, and norms and work together (Eckel & Grossman, 2005). Social identity has been defined in many ways; the common element in these definitions is inclusion of group membership as part of one's self-concept (Meyer et al., 2006). However, the virtual teams with geographically dispersed members from different cultures find it difficult to integrate socially.

The social identity involves one as part of a larger whole (Rousseau, 1998; Tajfel, 1978). Since they belong to multiple or collective groups such as an organization, division, and team, employees can form multiple social identities, one or more of which might be prominent at any given time (Meyer et al., 2006).

The present research intends to address the following major questions related to the effects of virtual team on social identity and organizational behavioral variables (satisfaction, job involvement, commitment and organizational citizenship behavior).

1. What are the sources of social identity acquisition and how they affect virtual teams?
2. What is the social identity status in virtual teams?
3. Is there any significant correlation between social identity and organizational behavior variables in virtual team and what is the status of these variables?

Literature review of virtual team and necessary resources for the identity acquisition is given along with the research methodology. Results are discussed with concluding remarks and a brief avenue for future research is highlighted.

DEFINITION OF VIRTUAL TEAMS

Globalization has transformed not only the market structure, rather customers' needs, and technological innovations have made organizations choose a new structure to respond to rapid environmental changes (Harvey et al., 2004; Bauer, 2003; Shin, 2004; Kock, 2008). Virtual organizations are one of the new entities shaped on this basis. The formation of virtual organizations requires information technology and qualified and knowledgeable personnel and leaders (Wickham & Walther, 2007; Kahai, et al., 2007; Hambley et al. 2007; Glückler & Schrott, 2007; Konradt & Hoch, 2007) for inter-organizational group activities (Larser et al., 2002).

The virtual organizations are often defined as the one, constantly interacting with the environment, and whose internal structure is based on virtual teams. In other words, virtual teams constitute the core of virtual organizations (Larser et al., 2002; Lipnack & Stamps, 1997). Researchers have variably defined the virtual organizations and there analysis indicates that the main part of those definitions is highly analogous, except in some cases (Martins et al., 2004).

As such, a virtual team consists of a group of geographically dispersed people utilizing communication and information technologies in order to perform their organizational tasks (Jong, 2008; Kelley & Sankey, 2008; Martin et al., 2004). Most of the definitions introduce the virtual teams as of having the characteristics of temporal structure, cultural variety, geographical dispersion and electronic communications (Hertela et al., 2005; Shine, 2005; Harvey et al., 2004). In other words, they are considered as the combination of distributed specialties in temporal, geographical and cultural domains. Cosequently, their characteristics can generally be defined in four dimensions of spatial, temporal, cultural and organizational dispersion. Spatial dispersion refers to the degree to which the team members' workplaces are dispersed. Temporal dispersion dimension is concerned with the degree to which the team members work at different times. Cultural dispersion is concerned with the extent to which the team members are constituted from various cultures. Organizational dispersion is concerned with the degree to which the team members work between organizational boundaries (in various organizations) (Shin, 2005).

In most of the contemporary organizations, the teams and personnel participate in virtual activities, and organizational processes exist in both the traditional and the virtual forms. Thus, the virtual teams possess different degrees of virtuality depending on the extent to which they use virtual processes to perform their functions. Different definitions apply diverse standard to measure the degree of virtuality. In fact, the degree of virtuality is a function of the magnitude of each of the four factors mentioned above. One of the behavioral dimensions that may be affected by an increase in the team's virtuality as well as a subsequent decrease in face-to-face communications is the identity dimension.

SOCIAL IDENTITY

Individual's self-perception is often shaped by his personal, social and organizational identities. Here the process of perception is a dialectic process between one's own perception and those of others. In other words, the individual's perception is not created in a void, but is affected by the perceptions existing in the group, organization or society (Howard, 2000). Therefore, the theory of social identity is an attempt to explain the interaction between personal perceptions and those of other people (Ashforth & Mael, 1989; Tajfel, 1982; Hogg & Terry, 2000). People's social identity is affected by the groups to which they belong. Possessing organizational and social identity does not mean the individual has no personal identity. In other words, the individual identity refers to ones' personal characteristics and has nothing to do with any particular organization or group; however the organizational identity is defined based on the characteristics of a particular organization. This paper primarily deals with the social identity.

The most famous theoretician of social identity, George Herbert Mead believes that every individual shapes his/her own identity or ego through organizing others' attitudes in the form of an organized social or group attitudes (Mead, 1964). In other words, the image the individual creates or the way he feels about himself, are basically the reflection of other people's attitudes towards him (Jenkins, 2000). The logic of social identity states under what circumstances social contexts cause the organizational identity to gain more significance for the individual. Then, this basis is examined for some important organizational behaviors such as leadership, group's motivation, communications and the organization itself (Haslam, 2001).

Accordingly, the social identity is part of an individual concept originating from the awareness of his membership in a social group (or groups) with having interrelated values and feelings (Turner,

1999). The theory of social identity provides an implicit framework for the understanding of inter-group relationships. This theory tries to identify and analyze motivational processes related to the structural and ideological characteristics of the social environment (Reicher, 2004; Turner, 1999). During the last two decades, the social identity has been developed and organized as one of the most important theoretical frameworks to study inter-group relationships. At the outset, this theory was developed to explain not only inter-group basis but it successfully proposed explanations for these cases in later stages (Ellemers et al., 1999).

The individual's own image is shaped not merely by factors existing in his inner existence; rather some external social entities also play important role in it. Further, the identity is not something given to the individual beforehand rather it is something created through constant interaction with the world (Giddens, 1991). Part of this interaction may be with organizations as individuals define and identify themselves on the basis of their attachment to an organization or involvement to an occupation (Tajfel & Turner, 1986). In other words, people identify themselves with the organization for which they work (worked or will work), and acquire a psychological feeling of possession (Pierce et al., 2001; Shamir & Kark, 2004). Organizational identity consists of establishment of affective-cognitive ties between the organizational definition and the definition of oneself (Dutton, 1994), and means the integration of the self and the organization (Tyler & Blader, 2000). When one unites his identity with beliefs, goals and activities of an organization, he is said to have acquired organizational identity (Albert et al., 2000; Van Dick et al., 2004). Again, when the individual's identity is united with that of an organization he works for, he becomes more loyal, more studious and more committed (Dessler, 1999).

SOURCES OF SOCIAL IDENTITY ACQUISITION

Given the importance of social identity, critics have attempted to identify sources of identity acquisition. As such, components of place, time and culture have been introduced as the primary sources of identity (Golmohammadi, 2007; Goffman, 1959; Jenkins, 2000):

- **Place**: It is one of the important sources of identity acquisition. The feeling of being distinct has always been an essential component of identity, which requires the existence of more or less permanent and impenetrable boundaries. Place not only can be delimited, but it has some degree of permanency. Through creating social solidarity, place also creates the feeling of belonging to the collectivity. In fact, the ability of place to play this particular role is related to its stability and limitability.

- **Time**: If we consider identity as a system of representation, Time and space constitute the principle parts of this system. All identities are based on a representative space and time, and require the imaginary geography of their own (Hall, 1996). Identity is based on continuity, and continuity is defined based on the time factor and every individual or group bases its identity on a historical memory (Jenkins, 2000).

- **Culture**: Culture is the mental software of human beings (Hofsted, 1997). Undoubtedly, it is the richest, and the most important source of identity (Peterson, 1999). It creates both distinction and solidarity. It creates a particular lifestyle. This differentiation not only paves the way for the creation of identities, but also gives meaning to human existence.

Anthropologists, sociologists and many other researchers have defined the culture hence; most of them agree that culture consists of people's particular ways of life. House et al. (2002) in their Globe Research define the culture an entity consisting of values, beliefs, identities and common interpretations and meanings of significant events, originating from the public experience of the members of a society, and handed down to posterity.

SOCIAL IDENTITY CHALLENGES OF HUMAN RESOURCE IN VIRTUAL TEAMS

Given the structure of virtual teams, a research on characteristics and challenges faced by human resource in such teams becomes significant (Harvey et al., 2004). This is also because the main focus of the current article is to focus on identity structure that poses various challenges to the personnel of virtual teams. The most important challenges in such teams seem to be decreasing or lack of face-to-face interactions. Scheduled meetings, face-to-face interactions help create particular situations of bodily and facial postures, nonverbal messages and social impacts, which do not exist among virtual team members using computer-based technologies for their communication (Harvey et al., 2004). This absence of face-to-face interaction and cooperation could create conflicts (Larser et al., 2002) among virtual team members because of their geographical differences or different perceptions (Shin, 2004). Conflicts caused by the absence of common perceptions and the lack of appropriate socialization disrupt communication and cooperation procedures (Harvey et al., 2004). The dynamic environment of virtual teams forces the members into accepting newcomers without sufficient socialization processes. Thus, socialization processes and understanding the norms in

order to mitigate conflicts are disrupted (Haslam, 2001). Given the intense affiliation existing among virtual teams' members, measuring individual and operational efforts of the job will be difficult (Harvey et al., 2004; Lin et al., 2008). The absence of face-to-face interactions also makes the formation of informal norms and regulations, which may be necessary for moderating deviations still more difficult (Harvey et al., 2004).

With regard to the identity concepts, these are believed to be the basic principles in the formation of communications and the requirements of social life (Jenkins, 2000). The identity acquisition requires more or less specific sources, a disruption in each of which would undermine the very foundation of identity acquisition (Goffman, 1959). Since, the structure of identity is based on continuity and differentiation as perceived by individuals (Jenkins, 2000); the formation of a stable identity would be extremely difficult if these requisites are not provided for them through the sources of identity acquisition (Goffman, 1959). As mentioned before, place, time, and culture are the main components of identity acquisition hence; an attempt has been made to investigate each of them in order to assess their ability to create identity under given situations. Some critics however stress on the possibility to define virtual organizations using the four dimensions of space, boundary, time and culture, and to describe their characteristics (Shin, 2004).

- **Place and Space**: This dimension is concerned with the distribution of personnel along various geographical limits. Given the organizational structure, employees while being in different geographical areas are able to communicate with one and another using information technology (Shin, 2004). As such, virtual organizations have wide geographical distributions. Further, the boundary dimension is concerned with the distribution of organizational processes

(Shin, 2004). Since, the virtual activities are often established based on intra-organizational processes, it is not so easy to specify organizational boundaries on the basis of such activities (Vakola, 2004). These two dimensions (space and boundary) in virtual organizations are similar to place and space components in the sources of identity acquisition. Determining more or less permanent boundaries fulfill the need for social solidarity, and contribute to the formation of distinction and continuity (Golmohammadi, 2007). Thanks to the advancement of information technologies, virtual structures have accelerated the process of spatial disintegration, and have increasingly split the living ties of social space with a particular land or place in a way that it is difficult, or sometimes impossible, to determine social boundaries based on geographical and spatial limits (Golmohammadi, 2007).

- **Time Dimension**: This is concerned with temporal dispersion, or in other words, with the degree to which the employees can work together simultaneously (Shin, 2004). Geographical dispersion is one of the factors affecting the temporal dimension, causing some changes in the personnel's working hours in virtual organizations (Larser et al., 2002). Given the fact that different geographical areas may have different working hours depending on ground conditions, the issue of simultaneity gains so much significance that the employees have to develop a regular plan to have simultaneous interactions. Another issue related to the temporal dimension is the nature of temporal relationships in virtual organizations. In such organizations, relationships are often short-term, and the passage of time changes the structures of virtual activities (Chudoba, 2005). The function of time in the identity acquisition,

according to some is "based on continuity, and continuity is defined based on the temporal dimension. Every individual or group bases its own continuity on memory and history (Jenkins, 2000) in a way that all identities are established and developed in their own symbolic time." The concept of time has been changed in virtual organizations as simultaneous communications have been made available to all people. This will eventually overshadow identity distinction and stability among varieties and variations (Golmohammadi, 2007) in a way that due to the rapidity of changes, the connection between the past and present would be broken, and people would no longer be able to base their own identity structures. Temporary communications make people unable to appropriately develop the feeling of solidarity required for the formation of their identities (Giddens, 1991).

- **Culture**: This dimension deals with the cultural distribution of personnel, as the existing cooperation is based on participation of people with diverse organizational and national cultures (Harvey et al., 2004). By definition, virtual teams have common work no matter may possess different organizational and national cultures (Bauer, 2003). People belonging to different cultures communicate in differently and show different behavioral patterns (Shin, 2004). In other words, cultural diversity contributes to complexity, conflict, confusion and ambiguity in communications, making the task of management very difficult. As a matter of fact, the cultural diversity might decrease the real output of such teams (Adler, 1997). Studies have also indicated that the cultural diversity reduces the degree of integration among members of the team, leading to many difficulties in an organizational setup.

As mentioned before, culture is one of the richest as well as the most important sources of identity acquisition. It creates distinction that paves the way for the development of an identity (Jenkins, 2000). In virtual organizations, cultural components and elements inevitably interact with one another and constitute a harmonious whole (Harvey et al., 2004). Through penetrating boundaries and contributing significantly to cultural interactions, the structure of virtual organizations raises people's awareness of other cultural elements such as norms, values and customs. In fact, this awareness is awareness of the relativity of social and cultural world, which indicates that culture is no longer able to fulfill its peculiar function (in creating distinction and solidarity) appropriately. When the most important traditional source of identity becomes so vulnerable and relative, the people relying on that source would also face a crisis of identity and meaning.

A comparison between the characteristics of virtual organizations and the sources of identity shows the lack of actual identity contents and in such organizations hence; this identity crisis is likely to happen. Based on the above discussion, following research hypotheses are formulated.

H1. The culture dimension of virtual team in software producing companies is positively related to social identity.

H2. The place dimension of virtual team in software producing companies is positively related to social identity.

H3. The Time dimension of virtual team in software producing companies is positively related to social identity.

The main function of identity is to develop a framework for social life (Jenkins, 2000). Any change in identity foundations would cause subsequent changes in organizational concepts. Since personnel constitute the main organizational elements at this point, a question arises as how human resource's output is affected by the identity structure and how does any change in identity foundations would change this output?

Identity is one of man's psychological needs, and is the prerequisite for any form of social life. According to Tojfel, social identity is conceptualized for the individual as his awareness of belonging to a particular social group, and the affective importance of this membership for him (Turner, 1999). In recent years, the social identity theory has been examined in a wide range of researches dealing with organizational behavior. This shows that social identity has close connection with organizational issues (Haslam, 2001). Virtual teams are considered as social environments requiring particular identity structures in order to establish and continue communications (Harvey et al., 2004). Regarding the fact that identity contributes to the formation of relationships and creation of meanings in personal and social life (Jenkins, 2000), it influences the personnel's understanding of other organizational variables. Following sections will be investigating the influence of social identity on job satisfaction, job involvement, organizational commitment and organizational citizenship behavior.

SOCIAL IDENTITY IN VIRTUAL TEAMS AND JOB SATISFACTION

Job satisfaction means the extent to which one likes his job i.e. the individual's assessment of his own job. In other words, does the individual have a positive attitude towards his job factors in general? This assessment includes perceived occupational characteristics, job feelings and the workplace as a whole. Due to wide range of aspects, it can be said that the job satisfaction consists of a series of attitudes. Here, one may be satisfied with a series of his job factors or unsatisfied with another. But in the study of organizational behaviors, all of these factors are investigated under a single category of job satisfaction (Weiss 2002; Locke 1976).

Job satisfaction includes satisfaction with the job itself, payment, promotion, colleagues and management (Weiss, 2002). Many social theories state that an increase in the level of organizational identity can contribute to people's satisfaction with the organization. People differentiate between the members of their own group and the others and this creates a feeling of satisfaction among them (Haslam, 2001). People's satisfaction increases once they come across an appropriate definition of themselves and their organization. This satisfaction has great significance in groups. They will reduce their interactions and finally leave the group if the members are unsatisfied and pursue their own private interests, while in organizations active in the area information technologies, much importance is attached to human resource (Tidwell, 2005).

Job satisfaction is the outcome of assessing job characteristics. If an individual is unable to develop his organizational identity by means of which to offer a particular definition about himself and his social relationships in that organization, it will make his task difficult to assess the characteristics of his job hence; this may have negative effects on his job satisfaction. Therefore, yet another research hypothesis may be proposed as follows:

H4. The social identity of virtual team in software producing companies is positively related to job satisfaction of its members.

SOCIAL IDENTITY IN VIRTUAL TEAMS AND JOB-INVOLVEMENT

Job-involvement shows the degree to which an individual is mentally, cognitively and psychologically occupied with his job and attaches a particular importance to his job (Paullay et al., 1994). In other words, the individual takes pleasure doing it and does not get tired once involved with his job. Indeed, making personnel involved with their jobs

is one of the difficult tasks of managers because "self-alienation" and "job-alienation" are among the outcomes of organizational life.

Lodahl and Kenjer (1965) developed a concept of work-involvement to operationalize the Protestant working ethics, in which the value of working is part of the individual's own value. They also differentiated the concepts of "work-involvement" and "job-involvement" where the former is a more general concept, indicating individual's esteem for work and working. But job-involvement is merely concerned with individual's present occupation (Kanungo, 1982). In other words, job-involvement is related to vocational identity and an individual job holder usually identifies himself with it. Such a person does his best to realize the organization's goals (Lawler, 1986; Pfeffer, 1994).

Active participation in groups requires an individual to have feeling of affiliation towards the nature of the job, and appropriately identify himself with the job and actively participate in it. In terms of definition, the function of identity has a close relationship with the development of the concept of job-involvement. Identity enables people to appropriately understand the nature of their jobs, and to formulate the nature of their own personality. Therefore, the study of identity structures and their effect on people's participation in their jobs is crucially important. Thus, the research hypothesis may be stated as follows:

H5. The social identity of virtual team in software producing companies is positively related to job involvement of its members.

SOCIAL IDENTITY IN VIRTUAL TEAMS AND ORGANIZATIONAL CITIZENSHIP BEHAVIOR

In primitive schools of management, people used to be assessed through their behaviors expected from personnel in their job specification.

In the past, based on vocational behaviors of the personnel or their intra-role performance, they were recognized and awarded by the official system. Today, extra-role behaviors are the focus of attention which is concerned with vocational behaviors outside the realm of personnel's formal roles, which are optional and usually thankless (Haslam, 2001).

Researchers have categorized the organizational behaviors with different headings i.e. pro-social behaviors (Brief & Motowildo, 1986; Adebayo, 2005), extra-role behaviors spontaneous behaviors (George & Brief, 1992), Pre-contextual work (Borman & Motowildo, 1993), and generally, organizational citizenship behaviors. However, researchers are disagreed over the aspects of organizational citizenship behaviors. Aspects such as helping behaviors, sportsmanship, organizational loyalty, organizational obedience, individual creativity, conscientiousness, personal development, courtesy, civic virtue, altruism, all have been addressed in various studies.

Studies about social identity and organizational citizenship behavior indicate that people with a high degree of commitment toward group work have a greater tendency to participate in the extra-role activities (organizational citizenship behaviors) (Haslam, 2001). When the vocational behavior of some is determined by individual identities, people are more likely to participate in activities promoting their personal status. But when the vocational behavior is determined by social identities, they are more likely to show greater effort to promote group interests (such as helping new employees and performing other thankless jobs). Studies have indicated that organizational identity can promote organizational citizenship behavior (Dutton et al., 1994; Haslam & Powell, 2000; Van Knippenberg, 2000).

Thus it can be said that the social identity and the organizational citizenship behavior help bring solidarity and stability to teams. Therefore, study of the relationship between these two behavioral variables in virtual teams in which the structures of identity acquisition have not been sufficiently developed is crucially important. Therefore, a research hypothesis statement may be stated as follows:

H6. The social identity of virtual team in software producing companies is positively related to organizational citizenship behavior of its members.

SOCIAL IDENTITY IN VIRTUAL TEAMS AND ORGANIZATIONAL COMMITMENT

Organizational commitment, as a dependent variable, indicates obligation that forces the individual to remain in the organization and studiously work for the realization of its goals (Meyer & Herscovitch, 2001). In other words, organizational commitment is accompanied by a series of productive and constructive behaviors. An individual with a high organizational commitment remains in the organization and puts considerable effort or even self-sacrifice to realize the organizational goals.

Studies show a strong relationship between the concepts of organizational commitment and identity (Haslam, 2001; Van Knippenberg & Sleebos, 2006; Meyer et al., 2006). They are interrelated and the mere difference between these two concepts is that identity is a reflection of the definition of "self", but commitment is not (Van Knippenberg & Sleebos, 2006; Meyer et al., 2006; Brown, 2000).

The identity and organizational commitment have been the focus of attention in recent studies because of their influence on other behavioral variables. Once people promote their knowledge while belonging to a particular group with specific feelings and values, they actually seek to accept a social identity in such groups. Any change in the sources of identity in virtual teams can influence people's identities. Regarding what has been said so far, a research hypothesis can be stated as follows:

H7. The social identity of virtual team (*Figure 1*) in software producing companies is positively related to organizational commitment of its members.

METHODOLOGY

The methodology followed in the current study will be discussed in terms of sampling and data collection, measurement instrument, reliability and construct validity of questionnaire as well as data analysis.

SAMPLING AND DATA COLLECTION

Based on the structured questionnaires from 40 teams, data were collected over a 4-week time frame. These teams which are employed by two software provider companies (System groups, Kishware) work on analyzing, designing and supporting information systems in Iran. These companies were selected for their high-level electronic communication and upgraded services to their customers. Of 85 questionnaires distributed, a total 145 employees completed the question-naire with a response rate of 82.7%. A complete anonymity was guaranteed to all participants. 62 sample (42.8%) were female and 83 male (57.2%). The average age of respondents was 33 years, 60% of whom possessed bachelor degree while 40% had master.

MEASURES

Responses were measured using the same 5-point Likert scale ranging from 1 (strongly disagree) to 5 (strongly agree). The reliability test was done through Cronbach's coefficient alpha (α). An α value of 0.70 or above indicates a reliable measurement instrument.

- **Satisfaction**: The Brayfield and Rothe (1951) measure of satisfaction was adapted to the parameters of the current study. Specifically, respondents came up with statements variably: "I feel fairly satisfied with [organization's name]," "I find real enjoyment when attending functions at [organization's name]," "I am often displeased when at [organization's name]," and "When I go to [organization's name]

Figure 1. Research model

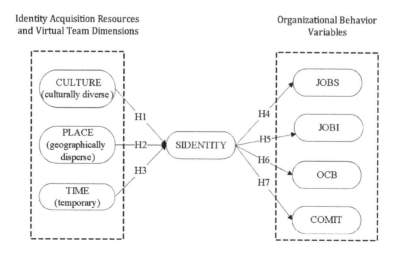

I feel right at home." The alpha level was .86.

- **Commitment**: Commitment was assessed through the Meyer and Allen (1984) affective commitment measure. Participants were asked to respond to the statements such as: "I feel emotionally attached to [organization's name]," "[Organization's name] does not deserve my loyalty (R)," and "I would be happy to participate in [organization's name] for the rest of my life." The alpha coefficient was .85.

- **OCB**: Organization citizenship behavior was assessed by adapting the Podsakoff and MacKenzie (1997) measure. Participants were asked to respond to the following statements: "I help out other [organization's name] member if someone falls behind in his/her works", "I willingly share my expertise with other member of the [organization's name], "I take steps to prevent problems with other [organization's name] member and "I attend and actively participate in [organization's name] meeting." The alpha coefficient was .86.

- **Involvement**: Job-involvement was assessed by adapting the Kanungo (1982) method. Participants were asked to respond to the statements: "The most important things that happen to me involve my present job", "I live, eat and breathe my job", "Most of my interests are centered on my job" and "Most of my personal life goals are job- oriented". The alpha coefficient was .87.

- **Organizational Identification**: Haslam's measure of social identification (2001) was adapted for organizational identification. Participants were asked to respond as: "When someone criticizes [organization's name], it feels like a personal insult," "I am very interested in what others think about [organization's name]," "When I talk about [organization's name] with oth-

ers, I usually say we rather than they," and "[Organization's name] successes are my successes." The alpha level was .84.

- **Culture, Time and Place:** The Chudoba et al., (2005) measure of culture, time and place was adapted to the parameters of identity acquisition resources and virtual team dimensions. Specifically, respondents replied the statements: Place ("I work at home during normal business days", "I work while travelling, e.g. at airports or hotels", "I collaborate with people in different sites or geographies", "I collaborate with people you have never met face to face". The alpha level was .87) Culture ("I collaborate with people who speak different native languages or dialects from your own", "I collaborate with people from different cultural backgrounds", "I collaborate with people from different cultural values". The alpha level was .86) and Time ("My work extended days in order to communicate with remote team members", "I collaborate with people in different time zones", "Participate in real-time online discussions, such as chat or instant messaging",. The alpha level was .85).

DATA ANALYSIS

Structural Equation Modeling (SEM) was applied in this study to estimate direct and indirect effects using LISREL 8.5. Assuming the measurement model meets goodness-of-fit criteria, the hypothesized relationships are tested in a SEM.

The comparative fit index (CFI), the non-normed fit index (NNFI), and the root mean square error of approximation (RMSEA) were used to evaluate the model. Values approaching .95 for the CFI and NNFI and less than .05 for the RMSEA are generally considered indicative of acceptable model fit.

RESULTS

A first exploratory step in the analysis is a correlation analysis that includes all independent and dependent variables (Table 1). Each of the variables in model are shown with the expressions i.e. culture with CULTURE, place with PLACE, time with TIME, social identity with SIDENTITY, job satisfaction with JOBS, job involvement with JOBI, job commitment with COMIT and organizational citizenship behaviors with OCB.

The resulting indexes indicated that the measurement model fitted the data well. Figure 2 shows the results of the Structural Equation Modeling (SEM) for the constructs. The overall fit of the proposed structural model was quite satisfactory (e.g. $\chi 2$=343.86, df=367, ρ<0.001, with Root mean square error of approximation (RMSEA) =0.000, Comparative fit index (CFI)= 0.99, Normed fit index (NFI)=0.86, Goodness-of-fit index (GFI)= 0.86, and Adjusted goodness of fit index (AGFI)=0.84). Although $\chi 2$ is a bit large ($\chi 2$=343.86), the value of (Chi-square/degree of freedom) is less than 2 and the GFI and AGFI are close to 0.90. In addition, the RMSEA value is less than 0.05 (RMSEA=0.000). The above figures imply good model fit. Moreover, the ranges of all factor loadings and the measurement errors were acceptable and significant at alpha=0.001, which provided evidence of convergent validity.

Table 1. Covariance matrix for constructs

Variable	Mean	SD	(1)	(2)	(3)	(4)	(5)	(6)	(7)	(8)
JOBS (1)	2.53	0.57	1							
JOBI(2)	2.31	0.49	0.331	1						
COMIT(3)	2.56	0.57	0.468	0.337	1					
OCB(4)	3.11	0.41	0.316	0.339	0.656	1				
SIDENTITY(5)	2.01	0.599	0.374	0.416	0.767	0.580	1			
TIME(6)	3.27	00	00	00	00	00	00	1		
PLACE(7)	3.46	00	00	00	00	00	00	00	1	
CULTURE(8)	2.98	00	00	00	00	00	00	0000	0000	1
All coefficient are meaningful at 99% level										

Figure 2. Structural Equation Model Results (H1 through H7) $\chi 2$=343.86, ρ<0.001, df=367, RM-SEA=0.000, CFI=0.99, NFI=0.86, GFI=0.86, AGFI=0.84. All solid line path coefficients are significant at ρ<0.001***

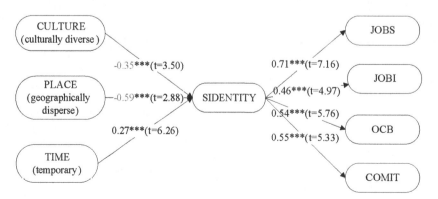

RESEARCH FINDINGS

Hypotheses examination:

Using LISREL, seven significant relationships were accomplished such as: culture and social identity, place and social identity, time and social identity, social identity and job satisfaction, social identity and job involvement, social identity and organizational citizenship behavior and social identity and job commitment (Figure 2). Except hypothesis (H3), all other hypotheses (H1, H2, H4, H5, H6 and H7) were supported (Table 2).

DISCUSSION AND CONCLUSION

As Table 1 indicates, an average sample of the social identity is 2.01. Statistical tests show that this average is low and in is critical situation. The test results find that the identity is a challenge for the virtual teams hence; the first hypothesis is approved.

The influence of the information technology in organizations and emergence of virtual teams along with reduction in the sources of identity acquisition have made identity-building and identity-finding difficult with traditional methods. In such scenario, the individuals in such teams cannot establish meaningful and permanent communication with each other. The identity crisis disturbs the social life, and individual or group need to solve the crisis. Rebuilding the identity is one of the factors that should be considered in such situations that can be considered at three levels i.e. ego, ego and group and intergroup.

Virtual teams continue both to weaken the identity acquisition resource and increase the possibility of rebuilding the individuals' identity. It has a dual feature: it has both opportunity and threat for the organization. On the one hand, individual can take pleasure in building virtual identities (such as male organizational identity instead of female organizational identity) which are desirable to him but on the other hand these

Table 2. Result of hypotheses

Hypotheses		Result
H1	The culture dimension of virtual team is positively related to social identity	Supported
H2	The place dimension of virtual team is positively related to social identity	Supported
H3	The Time dimension of virtual team is positively related to social identity	Not supported
H4	The social identity of virtual team is positively related to job satisfaction of its members	Supported
H5	The social identity of virtual team is positively related to job involvement of its members	Supported
H6	The social identity of virtual team is positively related to organizational citizenship behavior of its members	Supported
H7	The social identity of virtual team is positively related to organizational commitment of its members	Supported

identities affect the organizational identities. In such a situation, employees may be able to select right combinations, create new world for themselves. It must be noted that manager's attempts to establish and create identities are proper in respect to the situation and objectives of organization that can play an important role in establishing identity. Theoretically, the paper has studied comprehensively all the variables affective on social identity of virtual teams. On the other hand it presents organizational variables affected from such identity that is a suitable guide for managers to control and lead virtual teams.

REFERENCES

Adebayo, D. O. (2005). Ethical and attitudes and prosocial behavior in the Nigeria police: Moderator effect of perceived organizational support and public recognition. *Policing: An International Journal of Police Strategies and Management*, *28*(4), 684. doi:10.1108/13639510510628767

Albert, S., Ashforth, B. E., & Dutton, J. E. (2000). Organizational identity and identification: Charting new waters and building new bridges. *Academy of Management Review, 25*(1), 13–18.

Albert, S., & Whetten, D. A. (1985). Organizational identity. In Cummings, L. L., & Staw, B. M. (Eds.), *Research in Organizational Behavior* (*Vol. 7*, pp. 263–295).

Ashforth, B., & Mael, F. (1989). Social identity theory and the organization. *Academy of Management Review, 14*, 20–39. doi:10.2307/258189

Bauer, R., & Koszegi, S. T. (2003). Measuring the degree of virtualization. *Electronic Journal of Organizational Virtualness, 2*, 29–46.

Borman, W. C., & Motowidlo, S. J. (1993). Expanding the criterion domain to include elements of contextual performance. In Schmitt, N., & Borman, W. C. (Eds.), *Personnel selection in organizations* (pp. 71–98). San Francisco, CA: Jossey-Bass.

Brayfield, A. H., & Rothe, H. F. (1951). An index of job satisfaction. *The Journal of Applied Psychology, 35*(5), 307–311. doi:10.1037/h0055617

Brief, A. P., & Motowidlo, S. J. (1986). Prosocial organizational behaviors. *Academy of Management Review, 11*, 710–725. doi:10.2307/258391

Brown, R. (2000). Social identity theory: Past achievements, current problems and future challenges. *European Journal of Social Psychology, 30*, 745–778. doi:10.1002/1099-0992(200011/12)30:6<745::AID-EJSP24>3.0.CO;2-O

Chudoba, K. M., Wynn, E., Lu, M., & Watson-Manheim, M. B. (2005). How virtual are we? Measuring virtuality and understanding its impact in a global organization. *Information Systems Journal, 15*, 279–306. doi:10.1111/j.1365-2575.2005.00200.x

Davis, D., & Bryant, L. (2003). Influence at a distance: Leadership in global virtual teams. *Advances in Global Leadership, 3*, 303–340. doi:10.1016/S1535-1203(02)03015-0

Dessler, G. (1999). How to earn your employee's commitment. *The Academy of Management Executive, 13*(2), 58–67.

Dutton, J. E., Dukerich, J. M., & Harquail, C. V. (1994). Organizational images and member identification. *Administrative Science Quarterly, 39*(2), 239–263. doi:10.2307/2393235

Eckel, C., & Grossman, P. J. (2005). Managing diversity by creating team identity. *Journal of Economic Behavior & Organization, 58*, 371–392. doi:10.1016/j.jebo.2004.01.003

Ellemers, N., Spears, R., & Doosje, B. (Eds.). (1999). *Social identity: Context, commitment, content*. Oxford, UK: Blackwell.

George, J. M., & Brief, A. P. (1992). Feeling good-doing good: A conceptual analysis of the mood at work-organizational spontaneity relationship. *Psychological Bulletin, 112*, 310–329. doi:10.1037/0033-2909.112.2.310

Giddens, A. (1991). *Modernity and self-identity*. Cambridge, UK: Polity Press.

Glückler, J., & Gregor, S. (2007). Leadership and performance in virtual teams: Exploring brokerage in electronic communication. *International Journal of e-Collaboration, 3*, 31–53. doi:10.4018/jec.2007070103

Goffman, E. (1959). *The presentation of self in every day life*. New York, NY: Doubleday.

Golmohammadi, A. (2007). *Globalization, culture and identity*. Skopje, Macedonia: Net Press.

Hall, S. (1996). The question of cultural identity. In Hall, S., Held, D., & McGrew, A. (Eds.), *Modernity and its future*. Cambridge, UK: Polity Press.

Hambley, L. A., O'Neill, T. A., & Kline, T. J. B. (2007). Virtual team leadership: Perspectives from the field. *International Journal of e-Collaboration*, *3*, 40–63. doi:10.4018/jec.2007010103

Harvey, M., Milord, M., & Noveicevic, G. G. (2004). Challenges to staffing global virtual team. *Human Resource Management Review*, *14*, 275–294. doi:10.1016/j.hrmr.2004.06.005

Haslam, S. A. (2001). *Psychology in organizations (the social identity approach)*. London, UK: Sage.

Haslam, S. A., Powell, C., & Turner, J. C. (2000). Social identity, self-categorization and work motivation: Rethinking the contribution of group to positive and sustainable organizational outcomes. *Applied Psychology: An International Review*, *49*, 319–339. doi:10.1111/1464-0597.00018

Hertela, G., Geisterb, T. S., & Konradtb, U. (2005). Managing virtual teams: A review of current empirical research. *Human Resource Management Review*, *15*, 69–95. doi:10.1016/j.hrmr.2005.01.002

Hofsted, G. (1997). *Culture and organizations: Software of the mind*. New York, NY: McGrawHill.

Hogg, M. A., & Terry, D. J. (2000). Social identity and self-categorization processes in organizational contexts. *Academy of Management Review*, *25*, 121–141. doi:10.2307/259266

House, R. J., Javidan, M., Hanges, P. J., & Dorfman, P. W. (2002). Understanding cultures and implicit leadership theories across the globe: An Introduction to Project GLOBE. *Journal of World Business*, *37*, 3–10. doi:10.1016/S1090-9516(01)00069-4

Howard, J. (2000). Social psychology of identities. *Annual Review of Sociology*, *26*, 367–393. doi:10.1146/annurev.soc.26.1.367

Jenkins, R. (2000). *Social identity*. Oxford, UK: Taylor & Francis.

Kahai, S., Jerry, F., Suling, Z., & Bruce, A. (2007). Leadership in virtual teams: Past, present, and future. *International Journal of e-Collaboration*, *3*, 1–10.

Kanungo, R. N. (1982). Measurement of job and work involvement. *The Journal of Applied Psychology*, *67*, 341–349. doi:10.1037/0021-9010.67.3.341

Kelley, L., & Sankey, T. (2008). Global virtual teams for value creation and project success: A case study. *International Journal of Project Management*, *26*, 51–62. doi:10.1016/j.ijproman.2007.08.010

Kock, N. (2008). E-Collaboration and e-commerce in virtual worlds: The potential of second life and world of warcraft. *International Journal of e-Collaboration*, *4*, 114. doi:10.4018/jec.2008070101

Konradt, U., & Julia, E. H. (2007). A work roles and leadership functions of managers in virtual teams. *International Journal of e-Collaboration*, *3*, 16–35. doi:10.4018/jec.2007040102

Larsern, K. R. T., & McInernrey, C. R. (2002). Preparing to work in the virtual organization. *Information & Management*, *39*, 445–456. doi:10.1016/S0378-7206(01)00108-2

Lawler, E. E. (1986). *High involvement management*. San Francisco, CA: Jossey-Bass.

Lin, C., Standing, C., & Liu, Y. C. (2008). A model to develop effective virtual teams. *Journal of Decision Support Systems*, *45*, 1031–1045. doi:10.1016/j.dss.2008.04.002

Lipnack, J., & Stamps, J. (1997). Virtual teams: Reaching across space, time, and organizations with technology. *Strategy and Leadership*, *27*(1), 14–19. doi:10.1108/eb054625

Locke, E. A. (1976). The nature and causes of job satisfaction. In Dunnette, M. D. (Ed.), *Handbook of industrial and organizational psychology* (pp. 1297–1349). Chicago, IL: Rand McNally.

Lodahl, T. M., & Kejner, M. (1965). The definition and a measurement of job involvement. *The Journal of Applied Psychology, 49*, 24–33. doi:10.1037/h0021692

Martins, L. L., Gilson, L. L., & Maynard, M. T. (2004). Virtual teams: What do we know and where do we go from here? *Journal of Management, 30*, 805–835. doi:10.1016/j.jm.2004.05.002

Mead, J. (1964). *On social psychology: Selected papers*. Chicago, IL: University of Chicago Press.

Meyer, A., & Allen, N. (1991). A three-component conceptualization of organizational commitment. *Human Resource Management Review, 1*, 61–89. doi:10.1016/1053-4822(91)90011-Z

Meyer, J. P., Becker, T. E., & Dick, R. V. (2006). Social identities and commitments at work: Toward an integrative model. *Journal of Organizational Behavior, 27*(5), 665–683. doi:10.1002/job.383

Meyer, J. P., Becker, T. E., & Van Dic, R. (2006). Social identities and commitments at work: Toward an integrative model. *Journal of Organizational Behavior, 27*, 665–683. doi:10.1002/job.383

Meyer, J. P., & Herscovitch, L. (2001). Commitment in the workplace: Toward a general model. *Human Resource Management Review, 11*, 299–326. doi:10.1016/S1053-4822(00)00053-X

Morley, D., & Robbins, K. (1996). *Spaces of identity*. London, UK: Rutledge.

Paullay, I. M., Alliger, G. M., & Stone-Romero, E. F. (1994). Construct validation of two instruments designed to measure job involvement and work centrality. *The Journal of Applied Psychology, 79*, 224–228. doi:10.1037/0021-9010.79.2.224

Pfeffer, J. (1994). *Competitive advantage through people: Unleashing the power of the work force*. Boston, MA: Harvard Business School Press.

Pierce, J. L., Kostova, T., & Dirks, K. T. (2001). Toward a theory of psychological ownership. *Academy of Management Review, 26*(2), 298–310. doi:10.2307/259124

Podsakoff, P. M., MacKenzie, S. B., Paine, J. B., & Bachrach, D. G. (2000). Organizational citizenship behaviors: A critical review of the theoretical and empirical literature and suggestions for future research. *Journal of Management, 26*(3), 513–563. doi:10.1177/014920630002600307

Reicher, S. (2004). The context of social identity: Domination, resistance, and change. *Political Psychology, 25*, 921–945. doi:10.1111/j.1467-9221.2004.00403.x

Shamir, B., & Kark, R. (2004). A single-item graphic scale for the measurement of organizational identification. *Journal of Occupational and Organizational Psychology, 77*, 115–124. doi:10.1348/096317904322915946

Shin, Y. (2004). A person-environment fit model for virtual organization. *Journal of Management, 30*(5), 725–743. doi:10.1016/j.jm.2004.03.002

Shin, Y. (2005). Conflict resolution in virtual teams. *Organizational Dynamics, 34*(4), 331–345. doi:10.1016/j.orgdyn.2005.08.002

Smidts, A., van Riel, C. B. M., & Pruyn, A. T. H. (2001). The impact of employee communication and perceived external prestige on organizational identification. *Academy of Management Journal, 44*(5), 1051–1062. doi:10.2307/3069448

Tajfel, H. (1982). *Social identity and intergroup relations*. Cambridge, UK: Cambridge University Press.

Tajfel, H., & Turner, J. C. (1986). *The social identity theory of intergroup behavior: Psychology of intergroup relations* (2nd ed.). Chicago, IL: Nelson-Hall.

Thatcher, S. M. B., & Zhu, X. (2006). Changing identities in a changing workplace: Identification, identity enactment, self-verification, and telecommuting. *Academy of Management Review, 31*(4), 1076–1088.

Tidwell, V. M. (2005). A social identity model of prosocial behaviors within nonprofit organizations. *Nonprofit Management & Leadership, 159*(4), 449–467. doi:10.1002/nml.82

Turner, C. J. (1999). *Some current issue in research on social identity and self – social identity context commitment content*. London, UK: Blackwell.

Tyler, T. R., & Blader, S. (2000). *Cooperation in groups: Procedural justice, social identity and behavioral engagement*. New York, NY: Psychology Press.

Vakola, M., & Wilson, I. E. (2004). The challenge of virtual organization: Critical success factors in dealing with constant change. *Team Performance Management, 10*, 112–120. doi:10.1108/13527590410556836

Van Dick, R., Christ, O., Stellmacher, J., Wagner, U., Ahlswede, O., & Grubba, C. (2004). Should I stay or should I go? Explaining turnover intentions with organizational identification and job satisfaction. *British Journal of Management, 15*, 1–10. doi:10.1111/j.1467-8551.2004.00424.x

Van Knippenberg, D. (2000). Work motivation and performance: A social identity perspective. *Applied Psychology: An International Review, 49*, 357–371. doi:10.1111/1464-0597.00020

Van Knippenberg, D., & Sleebos, E. (2006). Organizational identification versus organizational commitment: Self-definition, social exchange, and job attitudes. *Journal of Organizational Behavior, 27*(5), 571–584. doi:10.1002/job.359

Weiss, H. M. (2002). Deconstructing job satisfaction: Separating evaluations, beliefs and affective experiences. *Human Resource Management Review, 12*, 173–194. doi:10.1016/S1053-4822(02)00045-1

Wickham, K. R., & Joseph, B. W. (2007). Perceived behaviors of emergent and assigned leaders in virtual groups. *International Journal of e-Collaboration, 3*, 1–18. doi:10.4018/jec.2007010101

This work was previously published in the International Journal of e-Collaboration, Volume 7, Issue 2, edited by Ned Kock, pp. 19-34, copyright 2011 by IGI Publishing (an imprint of IGI Global).

Chapter 7
Web Enabled Design Collaboration in India

Shaheli Guha
BigMachines Inc., USA

Biswajit Thakur
Meghnad Saha Institute of Technology, India

Tuhin Subhra Konar
Jadavpur University, India

Shibnath Chakrabarty
Jadavpur University, India

ABSTRACT

Designing large scale real estate projects often requires collaboration between consultants and agencies that are located in different geographical areas. The added constraint of geographical distance to a design approach that already involves multiple participants makes design collaboration a particularly challenging task. This study hypothesizes that design collaboration could benefit from harnessing web technologies. Organizational Risk Analyzer (ORA) software was used to identify the key factors of a collaboration network in a design project located in Kolkata, India. The web enabled internet forum system used was compared with the more traditional system of collaboration using mail. The collaborative network factors like connectedness, density, diffusion, centralization degree, and the node level factors like closeness centrality, eigenvector, betweenness and Burt constraint indicate that internet forums provide a more efficient tool of collaboration than traditional mail network systems. A simulation shows that the forum network operated even in an adverse condition, for example, when the project manager, a key member of the collaboration team, was unavailable.

DOI: 10.4018/978-1-4666-2020-9.ch007

INTRODUCTION

Issues

The building construction industry has been recognized as a project-based business that delivers a one-of-a-kind product. Despite superficial similarity in the end product and the design approach, the detailed engineering of most building projects are uniquely different. The information supplied by the architect and the consultants provide the knowledge based on which the builders and contractors deliver the product.

Jerrard et al. (2002) found that architectural design is a creative service that requires a unique solution and unlike consumer products, it cannot be tried and tested before use. Since it delivers a high value product, stakeholders tend to concentrate more on the quality of the end product rather than the quality of the service. Yet, the construction industry is a knowledge intensive industry and efficient delivery of knowledge among the stake holders is one of the key factors for success of a project. In fact, Fedorowicz, Ballesteros, and Meléndez (2008) studied the opinions of numerous researchers about the tools for collaboration as a part of evaluation of research articles and found it imperative to use only tested tools for creativity and innovation in collaboration. Large building projects in the present globalized business scenario, often deals with multiple consultants, contractors and suppliers from different continents. Proper tools for knowledge management and information technology (IT) play a critical role in managing such projects.

However, small and medium businesses have not yet picked up e-collaboration as a major mode of communication and innovation. Cerdán, Acosta, and Nicolás (2008) found that only 37% out of the 310 numbers surveyed firms had only one type of communication technology within their intranet. Additionally, the web-based knowledge management has found to be dependent upon the role of culture in an organization (Leidner, Alavi,

& Kayworth, 2006) and the construction industry has particularly been reluctant to pick up on new management paradigms. Insiders usually see these as complex forms of established business principles that offer little added business value. Nikas and Poulymenakou (2008) investigated the difficulties of adapting web-based collaboration support in the context of Greek construction industry. They found it impossible to leave the technology intact if the performance goals were to be achieved. The complexity of the construction practice and the lack of established standards and protocols make adoption of new IT tools difficult. It is sometimes argued that the building industry is highly fragmented and smaller firms can not afford to invest adequately for successful implementation of new systems. Shen et al. (2009) found that despite the emergence of IT to assist construction management the industry's productivity has remained low in USA. In the context of the Indian construction industry, the adoption rates of IT tools is even lower. Ahuja et al. (2009) reported a survey of IT use in building project management across India. It was found that external collaborative use of IT was more than the internal use only in about 3% of the surveyed organizations. In fact, comprehensive web based PM solution had not been adopted by any of the respondents.

There is unfortunately no fixed or even widely used tool for knowledge sharing in construction industry. Leiden, Loeh, and Katzy (2010) conducted case studies and compared a project management case with two other types of collaboration. They found extensive additional tool support for project management issues are necessary for effective management. Kittowski and Siegeris (2010) suggested integrated support for different types of collaboration environment in contrast to several individual applications for a seamless transformation of a group from one type to another in a consistent user interface. Fernandez, Alto, and Stewart (2006) studied a web based collaborative decision support tool used by NASA.

The system was considered successful perhaps because it has the flexibility to adopt changes. The biggest barrier of implementation is found to be the attitude of the users. Successful organizations have adapted tools to their own needs. However, they have always ensured easy communications among stake holders. Without such means, knowledge, even if it exists, can not be shared. In this paper, we have studied the design development process for the rejuvenation of a heritage hotel in Kolkata, India. A dedicated project management web site had been developed earlier for managing this project (Guha, 2007). The posts made by the participants of the website had been analyzed to investigate the efficiency and utility of such a tool for project management (Guha et al 2010). In this paper, the nature of collaboration and knowledge sharing among the stakeholders has been studied.

Existing Systems

The search for effective methods of knowledge sharing in building design is not new. Representative literatures would show that researchers are investigating the collaborative architectural design since the proliferation of personal computers. Some of the typical examples over the last 25 years are provided herein. Kalay et al. (1985) reported ALEX (Architectural Learning Expert), a knowledge based architectural design system as early as in 1985. The goal was to integrate various disciplines like architectural design, knowledge representation, information management and human machine interface. However, the authors acknowledged that the systems developed till those times have failed to integrate the advances made in different disciplines resulting in fewer improvements in computer assisted design practice than anticipated.

Catalano (1990) of Harvard School of Design reported a case study of a computerized architectural design firm in 1989. He found that most of the system designers were from computer science discipline which has made the system technically correct but within a strict definition. The designers did not find it as a worthwhile creative media due to inadequate knowledge processing concepts of the system. The actual knowledge processing is more diffused than the strict definitions assumed in the system.

Bottelli and Fogh (1995) reported about Galathea, a case-based planning tool for knowledge navigation in the architectural design process. They assumed the architectural design as a knowledge intensive activity strongly based on memory and experience. They suggested that the planning tool may be viewed as a knowledge navigator, supporting designers to construct a decision making path among recursive and incrementally defined design process based on memory and experience.

Kim (1995) proposed ID'EST, a system that provides the foundations for a seamless and continuous working environment for architects and building engineers. He found that one of the major obstacles was the lack of the evaluation and selection capacity of the computer. Without these key abilities, it is hard for a computer system to employ strategies akin to the mechanisms that a human employs in designing. Proper support of the appropriate knowledge base becomes the most important factor for overcoming this issue.

Rafi and Karboulonis (2001) introduced knowledge management and computer aided visualization as a key in establishing capabilities in the enterprise where dissemination of knowledge and effective sharing of information through collaboration spur creativity and stimulate business practices. They observed that in the present economy, knowledge sharing and management are expected to increasingly play a dominant role in value creation capabilities. Most of these early works in collaborative architectural design have observed that efficient knowledge sharing is the key means for success. The same trend has been found to be continued in later years.

Shiro (2003) presented an actual collaboration network before the introduction of web enabled systems for up gradation of Louvre museum in

Paris, a world class project. A part of the collaboration scheme developed by Shiro (2003) is presented in Figure 1. The 'collaboration triangle' in Figure 1 represents the collaboration between owner, architect and agencies. The collaborative relationships among these members are studied in a quantitative manner in this paper.

Fahdah and Tizani (2006) described a recent architecture for virtual collaborative building design system. The environment helps the design team to work collaboratively and concurrently on a centralized shared model and carries out all necessary communication electronically. The environment has been implemented in a prototype application as server-client model using .NET technologies. Virtual reality is used for visualization and to allow for intuitive interaction with the designers. Software agents are used to carry out communication and design activities. The current implementation has shown the potential of the used technologies to support a practical virtual collaboration. However, appropriate knowledge sharing has still remained as an important issue.

Achten and Beetz (2009) made a comprehensive literature study about collaborative architectural design. They also found that the appropriate knowledge sharing is one of the key ingredients of successful design collaboration.

A few of the literatures of the last two decades stated herein have broadly traced the efforts for

effective development of collaborative schemes in architectural design. In a recent study, Klinc et al. (2009) in the context of project management concluded that it took almost ten years to figure out how to use the Web properly and it will probably take another ten years before decision makers in the traditional industries will realize how to incorporate lessons from Web 2.0 in their core business processes and there are still issues that have to be solved. Beetz (2009) for example studied one of the issues namely, interoperability of tools used by the professionals in architectural design collaboration and identified a number technology related issues for effective development of collaboration platform. Vivacqua and Moreira (2008) found that people often participate in several projects simultaneously dividing their time and attention like in the present case. In such conditions, tools for maintaining awareness among members would be required. They proposed an e-mail based notification tool that requires minimal adoption for notifying the members about the group activities.

Objective

Industry leader construction software firms like Autodesk have started marketing dedicated building information management products like Navisworks (2010), Autodesk (2010) etc for web based collaboration. Remidez, Stam, and Laffey

Figure 1. Collaboration network for Louvre museum

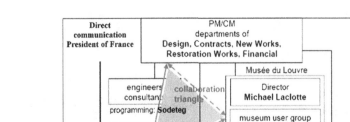

(2007) investigated the interface for communication support systems for virtual teams. They have described the development of a Web-based, template driven communication support tool and how this system can be used to support trust development and performance goals of virtual teams. Such template driven communication systems dedicated to project management forum like Teamwork have been developed. These devices are targeted mainly for the project management and may not be much useful for architectural design development. Beetz (2009) also noted the specific requirements of the architectural collaborations. Web based collaboration systems are relatively new and are not yet common in India. The benefits of such platforms are too early to decide and are expected to evolve rapidly (Becerik & Rice, 2010).

Unhelker et al. (2010) noted potential challenges to collaborative web based system growth in emerging economies and found that solutions providers may aggressively bring to market half-baked products complicating the service. In project management, attention is given to the tangible aspects. However, intangible aspect of designing which has a high failure costs has increased while the systems and methods keep improving Volker (2008). As stated herein there are two major issues identified in the web based architectural collaboration initiation. Firstly, the systems are evolving rapidly and there is no recognized industry leader, which has made system selection difficult for the user. Secondly, the performance measuring methods are inclined towards the project management and intangible benefits like design performance are difficult to conceive and measure.

A quantitative evaluation scheme for objective comparisons among the collaboration platforms will be helpful. The rapidly evolving systems could then be compared in an unbiased and orderly manner. The objective of this study is to propose such a tool that can be used for evaluating the architectural collaboration systems. It will allow the designers as well as the users to compare similar systems for selecting or improving the features of architectural collaboration platforms in an objective manner.

METHODS

Organizational Risk Analyzer

Traditional communication among the design development team is usually in line with the Louvre museum case shown in Figure 1. For example, the relationship between the organizations in this case has been presented in Figures 2 and 3. The collaboration triangle among the owner, architect and agencies are more or less similar to Shiro (2003).

The traditional scheme is replaced in this case with an internet forum for collaborative design development. The collaboration network is composed of postings in a dedicated web forum that were installed for design development of a heritage hotel restoration project in Kolkata (Guha, 2007; Guha et al., 2010). All members of the design development team now post their queries in a common forum. The traditional collaboration triangle shown in Figure 1 and Figure 2 is now modified with a social network as shown in Figure 3.

Figure 2. Organizational network for design

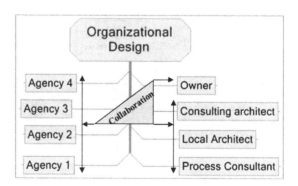

Figure 3. Collaboration network for design Development

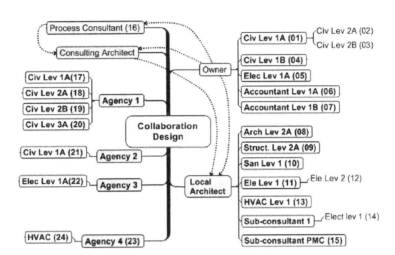

Organizational Risk Analyzer (ORA) is a network analysis tool that detects risks or vulnerabilities of an organization's design structure (Computational Analysis of Social and Organizational Systems, 2009) and its characteristics quantitatively from the point of view of the graph theory. The design structure of an organization is the relationship among its personnel, knowledge, resource, and task entities. These entities and relationships are provided to the software as input. ORA measured the structural properties of these networks of an organization for potential risks. It has tools for graphically visualizing the network for optimizing a network's design structure.

ORA can be used to perform a risk audit for the design development team of its organizational risks. Such risks include issues like group thinking, overlooking information, communication barriers, and critical employees. It has been used to evaluate the potential organizational risks based upon underlying social, knowledge, resource, and task networks. This tool considered the network data at a particular point and calculated a series of metrics assessing the team's design, particularly the command and control structure, and the associated organizational risks.

The organizational network formed under ORA for the present case consists of number of sub groups like tasks, knowledge organizations etc. A list of network data that has been considered is presented in Table 1. The social network showing the participations in the internet forum as depicted in Figure 3 has been formed in ORA. Similarly, the network in an organizational structure as depicted in Figure 2 has been formed in ORA. The organizational network and internet forum network are two different types of operations. However, both the operations are definable in graph theory as graph $G = (V, E)$, consisting of a set of objects vertices V (nodes) and edges E (links) and the ORA software can be used as a tool to compare these two cases. The relationship among the twenty four numbers of design professionals for forty numbers of design development tasks in nine knowledge groups for both forum and organizational set up have been developed in ORA. Views of the network influence diagrams where the links are shown among the factors have been developed. Concise part views for both the internet forum and the organizational structure cases have been presented in Figure 4. A comparison between the influence diagrams would provide a broad idea that

Table 1. List of Factors in the Collaboration Network

Sl	Network Between Factors		Comments
	Factor 1	Factor 2	
1	Agent	Agent	Agents are engineers taking part in the design development forum.
2	Agent	Knowl-edge	The knowledge domain of agents are defined
3	Agent	Task	Agents who have taken part in a particular forum issue (i.e. a task)
4	Knowl-edge	Task	The links between a forum topic and the knowledge domain of it

the internet forum is more densely linked than that of the organizational structure type collaboration network. The links would facilitate the efficiency of the information flow in the internet forum. The observation and findings are investigated in details in the following.

Network Analysis

Detailed study of a network reveals important aspects of an organization. Schreiber (2006) employed network analysis, a methodology that incorporates both social network analysis and multi-agent simulation to represent structure and process of the evolutionary nature of network organizations. Similar process has been used on the present organizational network. Schreiber (2006) identified some of the characteristics in a social network that should be optimized for better performance. In addition, ORA (Computational Analysis of Social and Organizational Systems, 2009) documents were studied for further selections of the factors. These factors are discussed herein.

Connectedness is the degree to which each agent can reach every other agent. The degree of full connectivity is associated with flexibility and the value is one. Density (Wasserman & Faust,

1994) is a standard social network measure of the ratio of existing relations over all possible relations, ranging from 0 to 1. It reflects the social level of organizational cohesion. Diffusion indicates passing of information to immediate contact. In general, its increase would be a positive transformation for a network. Granovetter (1973) suggested that information from people outside a person's immediate circle has a particular value because it is more likely to be novel. Subsequent research has confirmed this, with evidence from a variety of fields. Knowledge diffusion is therefore an important aspect of a network. Global efficiency of a network increases when entities like agents are closely distributed in terms of links across a network. Fragmentation is the proportion of agents in a network that are disconnected on average from other agents in the network. Fragmentation should be reduced for efficient operation of the network.

Betweenness is the extent to which an entity is directly connected to those other entities that are not directly connected. Network centralization betweenness reflects the overall betweenness centrality of all agents that is how an agent connects otherwise disconnected groups. For efficient operation of the network the betweenness should be minimized.

Closeness denotes the entity that is closest to all other entities and has rapid access to all information. Increased closeness centrality denotes agents who can most quickly communicate to the organization at large. Network centralization closeness indicates overall closeness centrality of the network. The closeness should be maximized for efficient operation of the network. Total degree indicates number of links in a network. Total degree centralization computes a value for the centrality that is how an agent has the shortest path to all other agents in the network. Higher value would indicate that the Agent who is most likely to have the most interactions would learn more. It should be maximized. The mathematical details of definitions have been reported by Carley and Reminga (2004).

Figure 4. Network Influence Diagram

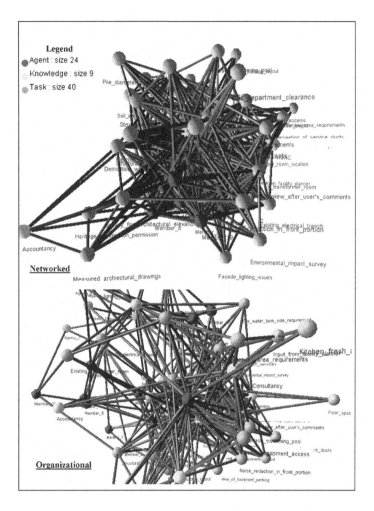

ORA software has been used for optimizing the organizational network by Monte Carlos simulation (MCS). About ten thousand iterations have been used in MCS. The agent to tasks and agent to knowledge networks mentioned in the Table 1 are pre assigned and fixed in character. It has not been simulated in ORA. Parameters of knowledge to task network and agent to agent networks are randomly varied and the resultant effects are noted in ORA. The organizational network is thus optimized by maximizing or minimizing the factors as discussed above. The results are presented in Table 2.

In Table 2, the parameters have been maximized or minimized as already discussed. The existing and optimized values are presented. In addition, the organizational values have been compared with that of networked forum values. It may be noted that the optimized and forum values are close. It indicates that the internet forum established for the architectural design development of the heritage hotel project in Kolkata, India is operating efficiently.

Network Comparisons

A review of the optimized network further reveals the characteristics of the collaborative design forum. Some of the representative network parameters have been presented in Figure 5. The

Table 2. Monte Carlos Simulations in ORA

Parameter	Optimization setting	Organizational value	Optimized value	Forum value
Connectedness	maximize	.2029	1	.9167
Density	maximize	.1522	.1522	.8152
Diffusion	maximize	.2007	.9398	.9123
Efficiency	maximize	.1775	.4940	.8659
Fragmentation	minimize	.7971	0	.0833
Centralization Betweeness	minimize	.0306	.3720	.0041
Centralization Closeness	maximize	.0137	.4411	.0897
Centralization Degree	maximize	.1660	.3557	.6883

frequency diagrams and statistics of network parameters namely Closeness centrality, Eigen vector and Betweenness have been compared for organizational, optimized and networked collaborations in Figure 5. The closeness centrality for the optimized network is much higher than that of the organizational network. The closeness centrality mean for optimized network is close to that of networked forum. For networked forum, high kurtosis, highly negatively skewed distribution with higher mean and lesser standard deviation tend to indicate that the agents have the shortest path length to each other. In other words, the agents can communicate with each other at the earliest in the networked forum.

Eigenvector reflects one's connections to other well-connected agents. In Figure 5, the eigenvector in organizational network is high apparently indicating well connected network. However, a close observation would show that the total degree centrality in organizational network is a low value of only 0.16. In organizational network, all agents are not well connected but only a very few in the network must be highly connected in organizational network to raise the eigenvector values. The frequency distribution of the betweenness in Figure 5 shows that almost all agents have nil values but a few have high values which confirm the proposition

that the collaboration is dependent on a very few highly connected people in organizational case.

In optimized network, the eigenvector distribution in Figure 5 has become uniform indicating dispersion of links among the agents. In networked forum, the mean eigenvector is close to optimized network and the frequency is closer to normal distribution. A Chi-Squared goodness test for normal distribution as derived by Easyfit software (Mathwave Data Analysis and Simulation, 2009) that is presented in Figure 5. The agents in networked forum have similar connections to other agents that indicate a stable network in terms of connections.

Cognitive demand measures the total effort expended by each agent to perform its tasks. The agents with higher cognitive demand vales are emergent leaders and removal of these agents would have a disruptive effect on the network. The agents with higher cognitive values are most likely to induce interactions (Schreiber, 2006) with other agents. In organizational and optimized network the distributions are positively skewed with negative kurtosis which indicates that majority of the agents have lower cognitive demand values. In forum network, the skewness is close to zero indicating symmetric distributions. The chi-squared test is presented in Figure 5 to show the goodness of fit with normal distributions for

Figure 5. Comparisons of the collaborative networks

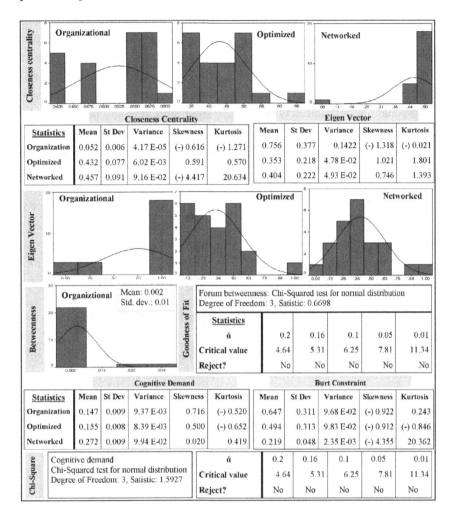

the forum network. The mean value of cognitive demand for the networked forum is about 0.27. It shows that the cognitive demand is dispersed and the disruptive impact upon isolation of any arbitrary agent for a certain period of time is low.

Burt (1992) constraint is a measure of structural hole that indicates the degree of absence of necessary links to perform tasks. For the networked forum, the value is the lowest. It indicates that the network is likely to be operative even after disruption of a few agents compared to that of the organizational network. The finding is affirmative to the observation of Glückler and Schrott

(2007) who has observed supports to structural hole theory that leaders achieve higher values of betweenness and efficiency.

Near Term Simulation

The Near Term Analysis (NTA) is a tool in ORA software (Carley et al., 2009) that allows for the removal of nodes from a given organizational structure to evaluate how the organization will likely to perform as a result. The goal is to provide an answer to the question on how an organization will behave and change after considering a sequence of strategic interventions or personnel loss by way of agent removal. In other words, the system would try to determine the impacts when one removes nodes from an organization, be they people, places, resources, knowledge sets etc.

The NTA were conducted on both networked forum and organizational network datasets with agent by agent, agent by knowledge, agent by task, knowledge by task and task by task networks for different sets of simulation cases in which project management consultant mentioned as PMC (15) in Figure 3 was not present. The NTA was executed to estimate the change in the characteristics of knowledge diffusion and task completion accuracy in absence of PMC. The total time span of the design development forum was divided into 5 time spans (span 0 to span 4). The number of simulation seeds was five for each case. The percentage of time the project consultant was absent were 20 and 40 respectively in different combinations. In a network, knowledge is flowed from agent to agents that are termed as diffusion

(Scott, 2007). The availability of knowledge is easier with more diffusion. In case of the networked forum the knowledge is available on demand to all agents simultaneously. The results of NTA about knowledge diffusion for organizational and networked forum have been presented in Figure 6. The Figure 6 would indicate that the isolation of PMC (15) would decrease knowledge diffusion for both organizational and forum network. However, the diffusion deceases more in forum network than that of organizational collaboration. The bar graphs in Figure 6 would further show that the binary task accuracy has been decreased for isolation of agents in organizational network. However, the binary task accuracy has been increased in most of the cases in the networked forum.

Top Ranked Agents

In order to evaluate the leadership development process Schreiber (2006) suggested estimating several network parameters. He suggested degree

Figure 6. NTA for knowledge diffusion and binary accuracy

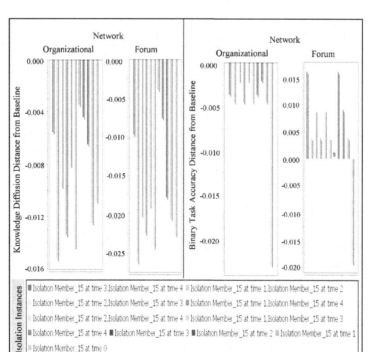

centrality for enhancing knowledge flows, closeness centrality for increasing the speed of learning and effective network size for communicating new knowledge. Each of these measures is presented for both the organizational and internet forum network in Figure 7. The Figure 7 would show that for degree centrality, all agents have a value of around 0.25 indicating same levels of knowledge flows for organizational network. For networked forum, the agents have increased knowledge flows varying from 1 to 0.4. For closeness centrality, the networked forum has much higher values than that of organizational network as evidenced from Figure 7. The effective network size in Figure 7 for organizational network varies from 1 to 3 where as the effective network size internet forum is much higher and varies uniformly from 75 to 175.

The relative measures of total degree, centrality and effective network size have been used as a way to determine the distinctive leaders in the process as suggested by Schreiber (2006). The person corresponding to the outlier points in the plotting of degree centrality versus effective network size represents the distinctive leaders. In Figure 7, the plotting are shown for both the organizational network and the internet forum.

It may be seen in Figure 7 that for organizational network, agent 1 (Civil Engineer Level 1A), agent 11 (Electrical Engineer Level 1) and agent 15 (Project Consultant) as mentioned in Figure 3 correspond to the outlier points in the graph and hence were distinct leaders in the process. The Figure 7 would show that for networked forum, all the points in the plot are well correlated (r^2=0.9989), rendering absence of any outlier and distinct leader in the process. This also indicates that the internet forum is well distributed and robust. Wickham and Walther (2007) studied the

Figure 7. Top rank agents

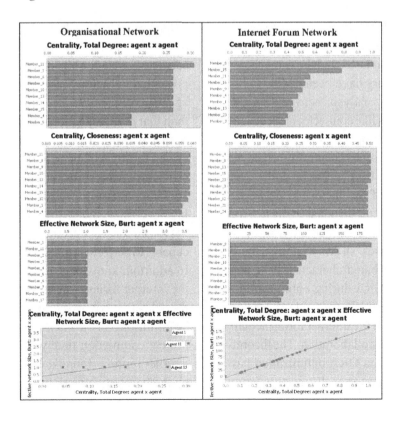

leadership in virtual teams. They found that unlike physical team computer mediated virtual teams may evolve to select multiple leaders or could be even without any distinct leader. The findings of the present study also support such observations.

DISCUSSION

In this study, the collaboration aspects of a network for an architectural design development team of a building restoration project have been studied in the light of graph theory. The traditional collaboration system comprising of the collaboration triangle presented in Figures 1 and 2 has been first analyzed with the help of ORA (Computational Analysis of Social and Organizational Systems, 2009) software. The traditional system has then been optimized by ORA. The software has rearranged the network during optimization according to graph theory for increased efficiency in communication flow. The changes of quantitative factors for optimization in ORA have been recorded and the trend was noted. The internet forum used for collaboration by the design development team has been also analyzed in ORA and the same factors related to graph theory have been noted.

The quantitative analysis between selected network level factors like connectedness, density, diffusion, centralization degree and the node level factors like closeness centrality, eigenvector, betweenness and Burt constraint collectively indicate that most of the factors in networked forum are close or better than that of the network optimized by ORA. For the internet forum, the factors in most cases show well distributed network. Such distributed characters have been also introduced by ORA during optimization of the traditional network. These values have been found to be optimal in the internet forum actually used for architectural collaboration. The theoretical values estimated in ORA optimization have been found to corroborate in the internet forum.

In many cases, the actual values of the factors in the internet forum are found to be more optimal than that of the ORA optimized organizational network. It indicates that the internet forum for architectural collaboration is more effective than even an optimized organizational network.

The NTA was conducted on both organizational and forum network for investigating the adverse impacts of isolation of an agent from the network. In practice, it may take place when an agent is unavailable for some reason. The analysis is intended for investigating the resistive power and the robustness of the network. As a test case, the PMC (15) as shown in Figure 3 is assumed to be absent for several periods of time as presented in Figure 6. The NTA analysis indicates negative impacts on knowledge diffusion for both organizational and network forum cases. The study also shows negative impacts on binary task accuracy for organizational network. However, there are almost no negative impacts on the binary task accuracy for the forum network due to absence of the PMC. The forum network seems to be stable even when one of the key agent's is absent. The existence of well distributed forum network is further confirmed by subsequent leadership determination processes presented in Figure 7. For networked forum, the agents have increased levels of knowledge flows than that of organizational network. On the basis of the analyses, it may be concluded the internet driven forum is likely to perform faster and more efficiently for architectural collaboration.

The comparison of values of different network factors estimated by ORA indicates that the internet forum for architectural design development is capable to perform in a stable and efficient manner. In addition, knowledge diffusion is improved in the internet forum. Therefore, it is expected that the delay that might occur in communication will be minimized in the internet forum and hence the project completion time would be reduced. The internet forum is found to be a sound mechanism on the basis of network theories.

CONCLUSION

The study proposes a quantitative method for analyzing the architectural collaboration network. The leadership characteristics of virtual teams were studied by Hambley, O'Neill, and Kline (2007) through a case study, which was essentially a qualitative method. Nikas and Poulymenakou (2008) observed the difficulties in applying the collaborative technologies in a construction project setting. The present study is proposed as a quantitative complement to such studies. There are numerous commercial and open source platforms for virtual collaboration in the construction industry (Guha, 2007). However, the methodology for comparing the performance of the systems has not been widely reported. The present analysis is a methodology for objective comparison among the collaborative platforms. It can be used as a tool for comparing architectural collaboration platforms.

Virtual collaboration for architectural design development is still viewed with skepticism by stakeholders. Yet, this study shows that there are clear gains experienced by stakeholders when web technologies are harnessed for design management. The proposed method can be extended for comparing similar networks. Additionally, such a comparative study would indicate the points for improvement and the deficiencies in a collaboration scheme.

REFERENCES

Achten, H., & Beetz, J. (2009). What happened to collaborative design? In *Proceedings of the 27th Conference on Education and Research in Computer Aided Architectural Design in Europe*, Istanbul, Turkey (pp. 357-365).

Ahuja, V., Yang, J., & Shankar, R. (2009). Study of ICT adoption for building project management in the Indian construction industry. *Automation in Construction, 18*(4), 415–423. doi:10.1016/j.autcon.2008.10.009

Autodesk (2010) *Autodesk vault products*. Retrieved from http://usa.autodesk.com/adsk/servlet/pc/index?siteID=123112&id=4502718

Becerik, B., & Rice, S. (2010). The perceived value of building information modeling in the U.S. building industry. *Journal of Information Technology in Construction, 15*, 185–201.

Beetz, J. (2009). *Facilitating distributed collaboration in the AEC/FM sector using semantic web technologies*. Berlin, Germany: University of Berlin. Retrieved from http://alexandria.tue.nl/extra2/200911977.pdf

Bottelli, V., & Fogh, C. (1995). Galathea: A case-based planning tool for knowledge navigation in the architectural design process, multimedia and architectural disciplines. In *Proceedings of the 13th European Conference on Education in Computer Aided Architectural Design in Europe*, Palermo, Italy (pp. 427-436).

Burt, R. S. (1992). *Structural holes*. Cambridge, MA: Harvard University Press.

Carley, K., & Reminga, J. (2004). *ORA: Organization risk analyzer* (Tech. Rep. No. CMU-ISRI-04-106). Pittsburgh, PA: Carnegie Mellon University.

Carley, K., Reminga, J., Storrick, J., & DeReno, M. (2009). *ORA user's guide* (Tech. Rep. No. CMU-ISR-09-115). Pittsburgh, PA: Carnegie Mellon University.

Catalano, F. (1989). The computerized design firm. In *Proceedings of the Conference on the Electronic Design Studio: Architectural Knowledge and Media in the Computer Era*, Cambridge, MA (pp. 317-332).

Computational Analysis of Social and Organizational Systems (CASOS). (2009). *ORA*. Pittsburg, PA: Carnegie Mellon University. Retrieved from http://www.casos.cs.cmu.edu/projects/ora/

Fahdah, I., & Tizani, W. (2006). Virtual collaborative building design environment using software agents. In *Proceedings of the 6ᵗʰ International Conference on Construction Applications of Virtual Reality,* Orlando, FL.

Fedorowicz, J., Ballesteros, I., & Meléndez, A. (2008). Creativity, innovation and e-collaboration. *International Journal of e-Collaboration, 4*(4), 1–10. doi:10.4018/jec.2008100101

Fernandez, I., Alto, M., & Stewart, H. (2006). A case study of web-based collaborative decision support at NASA. *International Journal of e-Collaboration, 2*(3), 50–64. doi:10.4018/jec.2006070103

Glückler, J., & Schrott, G. (2007). Leadership and performance in virtual teams: Exploring brokerage in electronic communication. *International Journal of e-Collaboration, 3*(3), 31–52. doi:10.4018/jec.2007070103

Granovetter, M. (1973). The strength of weak ties. *American Journal of Sociology, 78*(6), 1360–1380. doi:10.1086/225469

Guha, S. (2007). Construction management through web services in Calcutta, India. In Helfert, M., Thi, T., & Duncan, H. (Eds.), *Cases and projects in business informatics* (pp. 22–40). Berlin, Germany: Logos-Verlag.

Guha, S., Thakur, B., & Chakrabarty, S. (2010). Collaboration in a web enabled design management system - a case study in Kolkata, India. *Journal of Information Technology in Construction, 15*, 86–107.

Hambley, L., O'Neill, T., & Kline, T. (2007). Virtual team leadership: Perspective from the field. *International Journal of e-Collaboration, 3*(1), 40–64. doi:10.4018/jec.2007010103

Issa, R. R. A., Fllod, I., & Caglasin, G. (2003). A Survey of e-business implementation in the US construction industry. *Journal of Information Technology in Construction, 8*, 15–28.

Jerrard, R., Hands, D., & Ingram, J. (2002). *Design management case studies* (pp. 24–54). London, UK: Routledge.

Kalay, Y. E., Harfmann, A. C., & Swerdloff, L. M. (1985). ALEX: A knowledge-based architectural design system. In *Proceedings of the ACADIA Workshop,* Tempe, AZ (pp. 96-108).

Kazi, A. S. (2005). *Knowledge management in the construction industry-a socio-technical perspective*. Hershey, PA: IGI Global.

Kim, I. (1995). Design tools integration in an integrated design environment. In *Proceedings of the ACADIA Conference on Computing in Design - Enabling, Capturing and Sharing Ideas*, Seattle, WA (pp. 75-95).

Kittowski, F., & Siegeris, E. (2010). An integrated collaboration environment for various types of collaborative knowledge work. *International Journal of e-Collaboration, 6*(2), 45–55. doi:10.4018/jec.2010040103

Klinc, R., Dolenc, M., & Turk, Z. (2009). Engineering collaboration 2.0: Requirements and expectation. *Journal of Information Technology in Construction, 14*, 473–488.

Konradt, U., & Hoch, J. (2007). A work roles and leadership functions of managers in virtual teams. *International Journal of e-Collaboration, 3*(2), 17–35. doi:10.4018/jec.2007040102

Leiden, B., Loeh, H., & Katzy, B. (2010). Emerging collaboration routines in knowledge-intensive work process: Insights from three case studies. *International Journal of e-Collaboration*, *6*(1), 33–52. doi:10.4018/jec.2010091103

Leidner, D., Alavi, M., & Kayworth, T. (2006). The role of culture in knowledge management: A case study of two global firms. *International Journal of e-Collaboration*, *2*(1), 17–40. doi:10.4018/jec.2006010102

Mathwave Data Analysis and Simulation. (2009). *EasyFit: Distribution fitting made easy.* Retrieved from http://mathwave.com/

Matsushima, S. (2003). *The grand Louvre, Paris France*. Retrieved from http://isites.harvard.edu/fs/docs/icb.topic30775.files/3-5_Louvre.pdf

Meroño-Cerdán, A., Soto-Acosta, P., & López-Nicolás, C. (2008). How do collaborative technologies affect innovation in SME's. *International Journal of e-Collaboration*, *4*(4), 34–50. doi:10.4018/jec.2008100103

Navisworks (2010) *Autodesk navisworks products.* Retrieved from http://usa.autodesk.com/adsk/servlet/pc/index?siteID=123112&id=10571060

Nikas, A., & Poulymenakou, A. (2008). Technology adoption: Capturing the appropriate dynamics of web-based collaboration support in a project team. *International Journal of e-Collaboration*, *4*(2), 2–28. doi:10.4018/jec.2008040101

Rafi, A., & Karboulonis, P. (2002). The role of advanced VR interfaces in knowledge management and their relevance to CAD. In *Proceedings of the 7th International Conference on Computer Aided Architectural Design Research in Asia*, Cyberjaya, Malaysia (pp. 277-284).

Remidez, H., Stam, A., & Laffey, J. (2007). Web-based template-driven communication support systems: Using shadow net workspace to support trust development in virtual teams. *International Journal of e-Collaboration*, *3*(1), 65–83. doi:10.4018/jec.2007010104

Schreiber, C. (2006). *Human and organizational risk modeling: critical personnel and leadership in network organizations.* Unpublished doctoral dissertation, Carnegie Mellon University, Pittsburgh.

Scott, J. (2007). *Social network analysis – a handbook*. London, UK: Sage.

Unhelkar, B., Ghanbary, A., & Younessi, H. (2010). *Collaborative business process engineering and global organizations: frameworks for service integration*. Hershey, PA: IGI Global.

Vivacqua, A., & Moreira, J. (2008). The vineyard approach: A computational model for determination of awareness foci in e-mail-based collaboration. *International Journal of e-Collaboration*, *4*(1), 41–59. doi:10.4018/jec.2008010103

Volker, L. (2008). Early design management in architecture. In Smyth, H., & Pryke, S. (Eds.), *Collaborative relationships in construction: Developing frameworks and networks*. London, UK: Blackwell.

Wasserman, S., & Faust, K. (1994). *Social network analysis: Methods and applications*. Cambridge, UK: Cambridge University Press.

Wickham, K., & Walther, J. (2007). Perceived behaviors of emergent and assigned leaders in virtual groups. *International Journal of e-Collaboration*, *3*(1), 1–17. doi:10.4018/jec.2007010101

This work was previously published in the International Journal of e-Collaboration, Volume 7, Issue 2, edited by Ned Kock, pp. 35-51, copyright 2011 by IGI Publishing (an imprint of IGI Global).

Chapter 8
Using WarpPLS in E-Collaboration Studies:
Mediating Effects, Control and Second Order Variables, and Algorithm Choices

Ned Kock
Texas A&M International University, USA

ABSTRACT

This is a follow-up on two previous articles on WarpPLS and E-collaboration. The first discussed the five main steps through which a variancE-based nonlinear structural equation modeling analysis could be conducted with the software WarpPLS (Kock, 2010b). The second covered specific features related to grouped descriptive statistics, viewing and changing analysis algorithm and resampling settings, and viewing and saving various results (Kock, 2011). This and the previous articles use data from the same E-collaboration study as a basis for the discussion of important WarpPLS features. Unlike the previous articles, the focus here is on a brief discussion of more advanced issues, such as: testing the significance of mediating effects, including control variables in an analysis, using second order latent variables, choosing the right warping algorithm, and using bootstrapping and jackknifing in combination.

INTRODUCTION

This article is a follow-up on two previous articles on the use of WarpPLS in E-collaboration studies, and can be seen as the third of a set of related articles. The first article in the series discusses the five main steps through which a nonlinear structural equation modeling (SEM) analysis could be conducted with the software WarpPLS (Kock, 2010b). The second article in the series discusses specific features related to grouped descriptive statistics, viewing and changing analysis algorithm and resampling settings, and viewing and saving various results (Kock, 2011).

DOI: 10.4018/978-1-4666-2020-9.ch008

This and the previous articles focus on version 1.0 of the software, and use data from the same E-collaboration study as a basis for the discussion of important WarpPLS features. While the articles use an E-collaboration study as a basis, the discussions are very generic and apply to areas unrelated to E-collaboration. In fact, the discussions are pertinent to research in many different fields. At the time of this writing, published examples of the use of WarpPLS existed in marketing, management, finance, accounting, anthropology, psychology, and nursing.

Unlike the two previous articles in the three-article set, the focus here is on a brief discussion of more advanced issues, such as: testing the significance of mediating effects, including control variables in an analysis, using second order latent variables, choosing the right warping algorithm, and using bootstrapping and jackknifing in combination.

THE E-COLLABORATION STUDY

Several screen snapshots and composites are used here to illustrate important WarpPLS features. These snapshots and composites were generated based on a study of E-collaboration in virtual teams. Overall, 209 teams were studied. The teams carried out product innovation and development tasks in a variety of economic industries and sectors. The study focused on five main latent variables, referred to here as "ECU", "ECUVar", "Proc", "Effi", and "Effe".

"ECU" and "ECUVar" are technology-related variables. "ECU" refers to the extent to which electronic communication media, in addition to face-to-face communication, were used by each team. "ECUVar" refers to the variety of different electronic communication media used by each team, or the number of electronic communication media with different features (e.g., E-mail, teleconferencing, telephone) used by each team.

"Proc", "Effi", and "Effe" are non-technology-related variables. "Proc" refers to the degree to which each team employed established project management techniques, referred to in the study as "procedural structuring" techniques, hence the name of the variable. "Effi" refers to the efficiency of each team, in terms of task completion cost and time, assessed against previously planned task completion cost and time. "Effe" refers to the effectiveness of each team (a team can be effective but not efficient, and vicE-versa), in terms of the actual commercial success of the new goods or services that each team developed.

TESTING THE SIGNIFICANCE OF MEDIATING EFFECTS

Using WarpPLS, one can test the significance of a mediating effect of a variable M, which is hypothesized to mediate the relationship between two other variables X and Y, by using Baron and Kenny's (1986) criteria. The procedure is outlined below. It can be easily adapted to test multiple mediating effects, and more complex mediating effects (e.g., with multiple mediators). Please note that we are not referring to moderating effects here; these can be tested directly with WarpPLS, by adding moderating links to a model.

First two models must be built. The first model should have X pointing at Y, without M being included in the model. (You can have the variable in the WarpPLS model, but there should be no links from or to it.) The second model should have X pointing at Y, X pointing at M, and M pointing at Y. This is a "triangle"-looking model. A WarpPLS analysis must be conducted with both models, which may be saved in two different project files; this analysis may use linear or nonlinear analysis algorithms. The mediating effect will be significant if the three following criteria are met:

- In the first model, the path between X and Y is significant (e.g., P < 0.05, if this is the significance level used).
- In the second model, the path between X and M is significant.
- In the second model, the path between M and Y is significant.

Note that, in the second model, the path between M and Y controls for the effect of X. That is the way it should be. Also note that the effect of X on Y in the second model is irrelevant for this mediation significance test. Nevertheless, if the effect of X on Y in the second model is insignificant (i.e., indistinguishable from zero, statistically speaking), one can say that the case is one of "perfect" mediation. On the other hand, if the effect of X on Y in the second model is significant, one can say that the case is one of "partial" mediation. This of course assumes that the three criteria are met. Generally, the lower the effect of X on Y in the second model, the more "perfect" the mediation is, if the three criteria for mediating effect significance are met.

Figures 1(a) and 1(b) show two models created for a mediating effect significance test.

The mediating variable is "Proc"; the degree to which each team in our sample E-collaboration study employed established project management techniques. These techniques are referred to in the study as procedural structuring techniques. The effect that is hypothesized to be mediated by "Proc" is that between "ECU" and "Effi". "ECU" refers to the extent to which electronic communication media were used by each team. "Effi" refers to the efficiency of each team, in terms of task completion cost and time.

In this case, the mediating effect of "Proc" is *not* significant, because the first of the three criteria is not met. That is, in the first model, the path between "ECU" and "Effi" is not significant (beta = -.01, P = 0.44).

The conclusion above is reached even though the two other criteria are met. In the second model, the path between "ECU" and "Proc" is significant (beta = .16, P < .01), and the path between "Proc" and "Effi" is also significant (beta = .47, P < .01).

Figure 1. (a) First WarpPLS model in a mediating effect significance test; (b) Second WarpPLS model in a mediating effect significance test

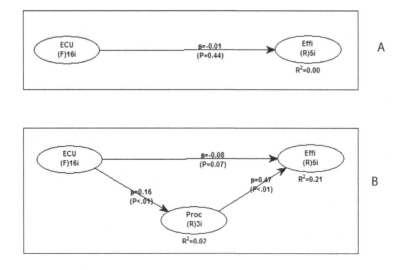

INCLUDING CONTROL VARIABLES IN AN SEM ANALYSIS

As part of an SEM analysis using WarpPLS, a researcher may want to control for the effects of one ore more variables. This is typically the case with what are called "demographic variables", or variables that measure attributes of a given unit of analysis that are (usually) not expected to influence the results of the SEM analysis.

For example, let us assume that one wants to assess the effect of a technology, whose intensity of use is measured by a latent variable T, on a behavioral variable measured by B. The unit of analysis for B is the individual user; that is, each row in the dataset refers to an individual user of the technology. The researcher hypothesizes that the association between T and B is significant, so a direct link between T and B is included in the model.

If the researcher wants to control for age (A) and gender (G), which have also been collected for each individual, in relation to B, all that is needed is to include the variables A and G in the model, with direct links pointing at B. No hypotheses are made. For that to work, gender (G) has to be included in the dataset as a numeric variable. For example, the gender "male" may be replaced with 1 and "female" with 2, in which case the variable G will essentially measure the "degree of femaleness" of each individual.

After the analysis is conducted, let us assume that the path coefficient between T and B is found to be statistically significant, with the variables A and G included in the model as described above. In this case, the researcher can say that the association between T and B is significant, "regardless of A and G" or "when the effects of A and G are controlled for".

In other words, the technology (T) affects behavior (B) in the hypothesized way regardless of age (A) and gender (B). This conclusion would remain the same whether the path coefficients between A and/or G and B were significant, because the focus of the analysis is on B, the main dependent variable of the model.

Some special considerations and related analysis decisions usually have to be made in more complex models, with multiple endogenous latent variables (i.e., variables to which arrows point), and also regarding the fit indices. For example, with multiple endogenous latent variables, you may want to add controls to all of them. Normally this will artificially reduce your APC (the average path coefficient, a model fit index); even thought your ARS (the average R-squared, another model fit index) will most certainly go up.

Figure 2 shows a model created in WarpPLS where the effect of "Proc" on "Effi" is analyzed, controlling for the effects of "ECU" and "ECUVar". Control variables can be latent variables, as is the case here. "ECU" is a latent variable

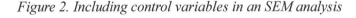

Figure 2. Including control variables in an SEM analysis

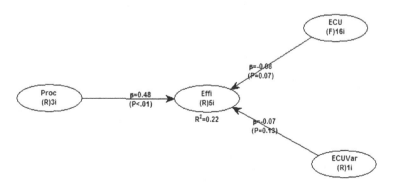

measured formatively through 16 indicators, as indicated by the "(F)16i" notation under the name of the variable.

Based on the results of the analysis we can say that "Proc" is significantly associated with "Effi", regardless of "ECU" and "ECUVar". Again, in this case it does not matter whether the effects associated with control variables are significant or not; in this case they are not. In models like the one above, with one main dependent variable, it is advisable to place the control variables on the right side of the model. This improves the readability of the model.

USING SECOND ORDER LATENT VARIABLES

Second order latent variables can be implemented in WarpPLS through two steps. These steps are referred to as Step 1 and Step 2 in the paragraphs below. Higher order latent variables can also be implemented, following a similar procedure, but with additional steps.

With second order latent variables, a set of latent variables scores are used as indicators of another latent variable. Often second order latent variables are decompositions of a formative latent variable into a few reflective latent variables, but this is not always the case. If this is the case, the scores of the component reflective latent variables are used as indicators of the original formative latent variables.

In Step 1, you will create a model that relates latent variables to their indicators, as in Figure 3(a). Only the latent variables and their indicators should be included. No links between latent variables should be created. This will allow you to calculate the latent variables scores for the latent variables, based on the indicators. You will then

Figure 3(a). Model relating latent variables to indicators (b). Saving latent variable scores

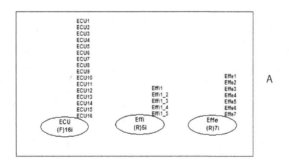

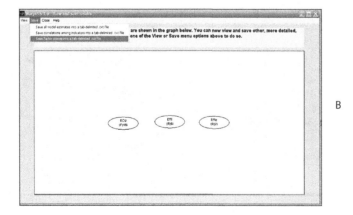

save the latent variables scores using the option "Save factor scores into a tab-delimited .txt file", available from the "Save" option of the "View and save results" window menu, as shown in Figure 3(b).

In Step 2, you will create a new model where the saved latent variables scores are indicators of a new latent variable. This latent variable is usually called the second order latent variable, although sometimes the indicators (component latent variables) are referred to as second order latent variables. The rest of the data will be the same. Note that you will have to create and read the raw data used in the SEM analysis again, for this second step.

CHOOSING THE RIGHT WARPING ALGORITHM: THE ROLE OF THEORY

WarpPLS offers the following analysis algorithms: Warp3 PLS Regression, Warp2 PLS Regression, PLS Regression, and Robust Path Analysis.

Many relationships in nature, including relationships involving behavioral variables, are nonlinear and follow a pattern known as U-curve (or inverted U-curve). In this pattern a variable affects another in a way that leads to a maximum or minimum value, where the effect is either maximized or minimized, respectively. This type of relationship is also referred to as a J-curve pattern; a term that is more commonly used in economics and the health sciences. Other nonlinear patterns that are noncyclical, such as logarithmic and exponential, can be easily modeled as sections of U (or J) curves.

The Warp2 PLS Regression algorithm tries to identify U-curve relationships between latent variables, and, if those relationships exist, the algorithm transforms (or "warps") the scores of the predictor latent variables so as to better reflect the U-curve relationships in the estimated path coefficients in the model. The Warp3 PLS

Regression algorithm, on the other hand, tries to identify a relationship defined by a function whose first derivative is a U-curve. This type of relationship follows a pattern that is more similar to an S-curve (or a somewhat distorted S-curve), and can be seen as a combination of two connected U-curves, one of which is inverted.

The PLS Regression algorithm does not perform any warping of relationships. It is essentially a standard PLS regression algorithm, whereby indicators' weights, loadings and latent variable scores (a.k.a. factor scores) are calculated based on a least squares minimization sub-algorithm, after which path coefficients are estimated using a robust path analysis algorithm. A key criterion for the calculation of the weights, observed in virtually all PLS-based algorithms, is that the regression equation expressing the relationship between the indicators and the latent variable scores has an error term that equals zero. In other words, the latent variable scores are calculated as exact linear combinations of their indicators. PLS regression is the underlying weight calculation algorithm used in both Warp3 and Warp2 PLS Regression. The warping takes place during the estimation of path coefficients, and after the estimation of all weights and loadings in the model. The weights and loadings of a model with latent variables make up what is often referred to as the outer model, whereas the path coefficients among latent variables make up what is often called the inner model.

Finally, the Robust Path Analysis algorithm is a simplified algorithm in which latent variable scores are calculated by averaging all of the indicators associated with a latent variable; that is, in this algorithm weights are not estimated through PLS regression. This algorithm is called "Robust" Path Analysis, because, as with most robust statistics methods, the P values are calculated through resampling. If all latent variables are measured with single indicators, the Robust Path Analysis and the PLS Regression algorithms will yield identical results.

So what algorithm should one use?

Generally it will be one of these: Warp3 PLS Regression, Warp2 PLS Regression, or PLS Regression. Only in a small number of instances, quite rare, will the Robust Path Analysis algorithm be the best choice. An example would be a "pure" path analysis, where all latent variables are measured through one single indicator; in this case, the variables will not be "latent" variables, strictly speaking.

If you analyze your dataset using different algorithms (e.g., Warp3 PLS Regression, Warp2 PLS Regression, and PLS Regression), usually the "best" algorithm will be the one leading to the most stable path coefficients. The most stable path coefficients are the ones with the lowest P values, whether the P values are obtained through bootstrapping or jackknifing. The best algorithm will also be the one leading to the highest average R-squared (ARS).

Another important consideration is theory. Does the theory underlying a hypothesized relationship between latent variables support the expectation of a U-curve or S-curve relationship? If the theory supports the expectation of a U-curve relationship, but not of an S-curve relationship, then you should favor Warp2 PLS Regression over Warp3 PLS Regression, even if the latter leads to the most stable path coefficients (i.e., with the lowest P values).

BOOTSTRAPPING OR JACKKNIFING? MAYBE BOTH

Arguably jackknifing does a better job than bootstrapping at addressing problems associated with the presence of outliers due to errors in data collection. Generally speaking, jackknifing tends to generate more stable resample path coefficients (and thus more reliable P values) with small sample sizes (lower than 100), and with samples containing outliers. With jackknifing, outlier data points do not appear more than once in the

set of resamples, which accounts for the better performance (Chiquoine & Hjalmarsson, 2009).

Bootstrapping tends to generate more stable resample path coefficients (and thus more reliable P values) with larger samples, as well as with samples where the data points are evenly distributed on a scatter plot. Conversely, the use of bootstrapping with small sample sizes (lower than 100) has been discouraged (Nevitt & Hancock, 2001). This makes sense, as it is reasonable to expect an algorithm that performs quite well with large samples not to perform just as well with small samples, particularly when the algorithm features that make it perform well are sensitive to sample size variations.

Given that the warping algorithms are also somewhat sensitive to the presence of outliers, it is frequently a good idea to estimate P values with both bootstrapping and jackknifing. One can then use the P values associated with the most stable coefficients in research reports. There is no valid theoretical reason to assume that all P values must be generated with the same algorithm. An indication of resample set instability is a high P value (i.e., statistically insignificant) associated with path coefficients that could be reasonably expected to have low P values.

For instance, in an analysis of a dataset with a sample size of 100, a path coefficient of .2 or greater could be reasonably expected to yield a P value that would be statistically significant at the .05 level. If that is not the case, there may be a resample set stability problem. Another indication of instability in a resample set is a marked difference between the P values estimated through bootstrapping and jackknifing.

P values can be easily estimated using both resampling methods, bootstrapping and jackknifing, by following this simple procedure. First, run an SEM analysis of the desired model using one of the resampling methods, bootstrapping or jackknifing, and save the project. Then save the project again, this time with a different name. Next change the resampling method, and run the

SEM analysis again, saving the second project again after the analysis is completed. Now each project file will have results that refer to one of the two resampling methods. The resulting P values can then be compared, even side-by-side if model estimates are saved in text files (which can be opened concurrently), and the most stable ones used in a research report on the SEM analysis.

FIELD STUDIES AND SMALL SAMPLES

Let us assume that a researcher wants to evaluate the effectiveness of a new E-collaboration technology by conducting an intervention study in one single organization. In this example, the researcher facilitates the use of the new E-collaboration technology by 20 managers in the organization, and then measures their (i.e., the managers') degree of adoption of the technology and their effectiveness.

The above is an example of a field study. Often field studies will yield small datasets, which will not conform to parametric analysis (e.g., ANOVA and ordinary multiple regression) pre-conditions. For example, the data will not typically be normally distributed. WarpPLS can be very useful in the analysis of this type of data.

One reason is that, with small sample sizes, it may be difficult to identify linear relationships that are strong enough to be statistically significant (at P lower than 0.05, or less). Since WarpPLS implements nonlinear analysis algorithms, it can be very useful in the analysis of small samples.

Another reason is that P values are calculated through resampling, a nonparametric approach to statistical significance estimation. For small samples (i.e., lower than 100), jackknifing is the recommended resampling approach. Bootstrapping is recommended only for sample sizes greater than 100.

PROJECT FILES AND GEOGRAPHICALLY DISTRIBUTED RESEARCH COLLABORATION

A geographically distributed collaborative SEM analysis can be easily conducted using WarpPLS. Let us look at an example of an analysis that involved a few people in different states of the USA, as well as two people outside the country. The collaborators were not only separated by large distances, but also operated in different time zones.

Yet, they had no problems collaborating. The collaboration was asynchronous – one person did some work one day, and shared it with the others, who reviewed the work in the next few days and responded.

Since all of the collaborators had WarpPLS installed on their computers, they exchanged different versions of a WarpPLS project file (extension ".prj") with the same dataset. This way they were able to do analyses in turns, and discuss the results via email.

Each slightly different project file was saved with a different name – e.g., W3J_IO_2010_03_02.prj, W3B_IO_2010_03_02.prj, W2J_IO_2010_03_02.prj etc. In these examples above, the first three letters indicate the SEM algorithm used (W3 = Warp3 PLS Regression; W2 = Warp2 PLS Regression), and the resampling method used (J = jackknifing; B = bootstrapping). The second part of the name describes the dataset, and the final part the date. This is just one way of naming files. It worked for this particular project, but more elaborate file names can be used in more complex collaborative SEM analyses.

This geographically distributed collaborative SEM analysis highlights one of the advantages of WarpPLS over other SEM software: all that is needed for the analysis is contained in one single project file.

119

Moreover, the project file will typically be only a few hundred kilobytes in size. In spite of its small size, the file includes the original data, and all of the results of the analysis. The reason is that all of the SEM analysis results are stored in a format that allows for their rendering every time they are viewed. Plots of nonlinear relationships, for example, are not stored as large bitmaps, but as equations that allow WarpPLS to re-create those plots at the time of viewing.

COMBINING STANDARDIZED AND UNSTANDARDIZED RESULTS

SEM is essentially path analysis with latent variables (Kline, 1998; Maruyama, 1998; Mueller, 1996). Path analysis is method developed by Sewall Wright (Wolfle, 1999; Wright, 1934, 1960), in which path models with multiple variables are analyzed, and where each variable is standardized.

To standardize a variable, one subtracts the variable mean from the values stored by the variable, and divides the resulting values by the variable's standard deviation. Once standardized, a variable becomes dimensionless. The values assumed by a standardized variable are expressed in standard deviations from the mean, where the mean and standard deviation are calculated based on the unstandardized version of the variable. For instance, a standardized value of -0.35 refers to a point on an axis (e.g., the horizontal axis, on a bidimensional graph) that is located -0.35 standard deviations from the mean.

The values stored by a standardized variable can then be compared with the values stored by a different standardized variable. This is impossible with variables measured on different units, if the variables are not standardized. For example, one cannot compare 10 kilograms with 15 dollars, but one can compare the corresponding standardized variables.

Given the above, the values reported by Warp-PLS are standardized values. This is true for the values reported on models and on graphs. The path coefficients shown by WarpPLS on models, after an SEM analysis is completed, are standardized partial regression coefficients. Also, the plots provided by WarpPLS are based on standardized values.

The problem with standardized values is that they cannot be easily interpreted by practitioners, who are more interested in concrete unstandardized values than the more abstract corresponding standardized versions. So what can a researcher do, employing WarpPLS, to overcome this problem?

The solution is to use both standardized and unstandardized values and/or representations in reports. For example, a researcher may show one of the nonlinear plots generated by WarpPLS, where standardized values are shown along the axes; and also a chart created based on the "Save grouped descriptive statistics into a tab-delimited .txt file" option (Kock, 2010a, pp. 3-5). These can be shown next to each other, as in Figures 4(a) and 4(b).

The second graph is much more meaningful to practitioners because it shows the actual number of electronic communication media used on the horizontal axis. Those refer to the number of electronic communication media with different features (e.g., E-mail, teleconferencing, telephone) used by each team. The vertical axis shows the perceived degree to which each team employed established project management techniques, measured on a Likert-type scale going from 0 to 10.

Note that when standardized values are used one can generate and display graphical representations including latent variables measured through multiple indicators (e.g., the latent variable "Proc", which is measured through 3 indicators). This is not possible with unstandardized values, because indicators are standardized prior to being

Figure 4(a). Plot with standardized values (b). Chart with unstandardized values

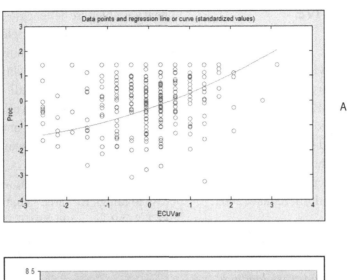

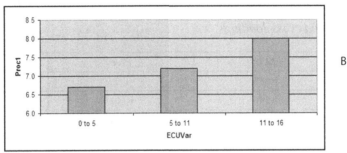

used for the calculation of latent variable scores. Therefore, a chart with unstandardized values can only include single indicators of a latent variable (e.g., "Proc1").

The above leads to an implication, which is that standardized and unstandardized representations are likely to have the same general form when latent variables are measured using: (a) single indicators; or (b) a reflective measurement approach. That is, in these two situations, general association trends (curves or lines) should be the same for standardized and unstandardized representations.

When latent variables are measured using single indicators, standardized and unstandardized representations will have the same form because standardization is a process that does not change the shape of the association between two vari-

ables. The forms will be similar with reflective latent variables because in this case component indicators are expected to be highly correlated with latent variable scores.

However, with formative latent variables, standardized and unstandardized representations may differ significantly. In this case, it would be more appropriate to show multiple unstandardized representations of a relationship between two latent variables (where at least one is formative) in research reports, one for each indicator, together with one standardized representation. This may clutter research reports and make them difficult to read though, because formative latent variables usually have significantly more indicators than reflective latent variables (Diamantopoulos, 1999; Diamantopoulos & Siguaw, 2006).

A NOTE OF CAUTION REGARDING THE USE OF FORMATIVE LATENT VARIABLES

The above discussion provides a solid basis for a warning: one should use formative latent variables with caution in SEM analyses using WarpPLS. It is not uncommon to see formative latent variables being created simply by casually aggregating indicators, without much concern about the indicators being actually facets of the same construct (Diamantopoulos & Siguaw, 2002; Petter et al., 2007).

It is also important to stress that formative latent variables are better assessed when included as part of a model. This is preferable to analyzing formative latent variables individually; that is, as "models" that include one single latent variable. The loadings and cross-loadings table takes into consideration both formative and reflective latent variables in its calculation, and may suggest that some indicators do not "belong" to a formative latent variable.

For example, Table 1 shows the loadings and cross-loadings for three latent variables, namely "ECU", "Proc", and "Effi". The loadings and

Table 1. Indicator loadings and cross-loadings

	ECU	*Proc*	*Effi*
ECU1	0.587	-0.123	0.184
ECU2	0.591	0.001	0.074
ECU3	0.320	0.244	-0.217
ECU4	0.530	-0.022	0.015
ECU5	0.452	0.092	-0.172
ECU6	0.450	-0.045	0.033
ECU7	0.463	-0.155	0.011
ECU8	0.619	-0.092	0.090
ECU9	0.595	-0.062	0.026
ECU10	0.570	-0.101	-0.018
ECU11	0.402	0.119	-0.039
ECU12	0.459	0.154	-0.092
ECU13	0.469	0.074	-0.009
ECU14	0.422	0.026	-0.065
ECU15	0.395	0.100	-0.041
ECU16	0.475	-0.065	0.077
Proc1	-0.010	0.827	0.029
Proc2	0.002	0.896	-0.017
Proc3	0.008	0.821	-0.012
Effi1	0.001	-0.020	0.905
Effi2	0.001	-0.005	0.887
Effi3	-0.007	0.048	0.799
Effi4	-0.032	-0.085	0.852
Effi5	0.037	0.064	0.766

cross-loadings shown are from a pattern matrix, obtained after an oblique rotation of the loadings and cross-loadings from the structure matrix (Hair et al., 2009). The indicators are named starting with the name of the latent variable they refer to, followed by the numbers 1, 2, 3 and so on. One of the three latent variables is measured formatively, namely "ECU", and its loadings are shown in shaded cells.

As it can be seen, the cross-loadings for the formative latent variable "ECU" are all low, which suggests that they do not actually "belong" to any other latent variable in the model. In this case, the model is somewhat simple, including only three latent variables. This check should be complemented with other checks, such as the P values associated with the weights for formative latent variables. The reason is that one cannot use standard tests of convergent validity and reliability with formative latent variables, because the indicators in formative latent variables are expected neither to be highly correlated with the latent variable scores nor with each other (Hair et al., 2009; Kock, 2010a).

Certain model parameters may sometimes become unstable due to collinearity. High collinearity among indicators is to be expected in reflective latent variable measurement, but not in formative latent variable measurement. In the context of formative latent variable assessment, collinearity may be reflected in unstable weights, where unexpected P values (usually statistically insignificant) are associated with weights.

In formative latent variables, indicators are expected to measure different facets of the latent variable, not the same "thing". If two (or more) indicators are collinear in a formative latent variable, it may be a good idea to collapse them into one indicator. This can be done by defining second order latent variables, or creating a new indicator by averaging the collinear indicators. An alternative option is to simply eliminate all but one of the collinear indicators from the latent variable.

REFERENCES

Baron, R. M., & Kenny, D. A. (1986). The moderator–mediator variable distinction in social psychological research: Conceptual, strategic, and statistical considerations. *Journal of Personality and Social Psychology*, *51*(6), 1173–1182. doi:10.1037/0022-3514.51.6.1173

Chiquoine, B., & Hjalmarsson, E. (2009). Jackknifing stock return predictions. *Journal of Empirical Finance*, *16*(5), 793–803. doi:10.1016/j.jempfin.2009.07.003

Diamantopoulos, A. (1999). Export performance measurement: Reflective versus formative indicators. *International Marketing Review*, *16*(6), 444–457. doi:10.1108/02651339910300422

Diamantopoulos, A., & Siguaw, J. A. (2002). *Formative vs. reflective indicators in measure development: Does the choice of indicators matter?* Ithaca, NY: Cornell University.

Diamantopoulos, A., & Siguaw, J. A. (2006). Formative versus reflective indicators in organizational measure development: A comparison and empirical illustration. *British Journal of Management*, *17*(4), 263–282. doi:10.1111/j.1467-8551.2006.00500.x

Hair, J. F., Black, W. C., Babin, B. J., & Anderson, R. E. (2009). *Multivariate data analysis*. Upper Saddle River, NJ: Prentice Hall.

Kline, R. B. (1998). *Principles and practice of structural equation modeling*. New York, NY: The Guilford Press.

Kock, N. (2010a). *WarpPLS 1.0 user manual*. Laredo, TX: ScriptWarp Systems.

Kock, N. (2010b). Using WarpPLS in E-collaboration studies: An overview of five main analysis steps. *International Journal of E-Collaboration*, *6*(4), 1–11. doi:10.4018/jec.2010100101

Kock, N. (2011). Using WarpPLS in E-collaboration studies: Descriptive statistics, settings, and key analysis results. *International Journal of E-Collaboration, 7*(2), 1–17.

Maruyama, G. M. (1998). *Basics of structural equation modeling.* Thousand Oaks, CA: Sage.

Mueller, R. O. (1996). *Basic principles of structural equation modeling.* New York, NY: Springer.

Nevitt, J., & Hancock, G. R. (2001). Performance of bootstrapping approaches to model test statistics and parameter standard error estimation in structural equation modeling. *Structural Equation Modeling, 8*(3), 353–377. doi:10.1207/S15328007SEM0803_2

Petter, S., Straub, D., & Rai, A. (2007). Specifying formative constructs in information systems research. *Management Information Systems Quarterly, 31*(4), 623–656.

Wolfle, L. M. (1999). Sewall Wright on the method of path coefficients: An annotated bibliography. *Structural Equation Modeling, 6*(3), 280–291. doi:10.1080/10705519909540134

Wright, S. (1934). The method of path coefficients. *Annals of Mathematical Statistics, 5*(3), 161–215. doi:10.1214/aoms/1177732676

Wright, S. (1960). Path coefficients and path regressions: Alternative or complementary concepts? *Biometrics, 16*(2), 189–202. doi:10.2307/2527551

This work was previously published in the International Journal of e-Collaboration, Volume 7, Issue 3, edited by Ned Kock, pp. 1-13, copyright 2011 by IGI Publishing (an imprint of IGI Global).

Chapter 9

Shared Mental Model Development During Technology–Mediated Collaboration

Hayward P. Andres
North Carolina A&T State University, USA

ABSTRACT

This study examines how collaboration mode – face-to-face and videoconferencing technology-mediated virtual teams - shapes negotiated shared interpretation of ideas needed for shared mental model construction. Social impact theory and group action theory provide a framework for explaining how technology-mediated collaboration constrains or enhances team shared mental model development. Social impact theory suggests that team member behavior is affected by 1) influential members, 2) number of members, and 3) proximity. Group action theory proposes that team member behavior is guided by 1) assessment of task requirements, 2) adopted task strategy, and 3) evaluation of task solution. This study argues that technology-mediated collaboration will exhibit lower participation rates and intra-team communication deficiencies while developing a shared mental model of task requirements, strategy and status. Partial least squares analysis revealed that technology-mediated collaboration does impact shared mental model development. Observers noted that decision making effectiveness and timeliness regarding task execution strategy and solution content was facilitated by a shared understanding of the task context. The study also confirmed the utility of direct observation for studying communication behaviors and social interaction in the development of shared mental model and teamwork.

DOI: 10.4018/978-1-4666-2020-9.ch009

SHARED MENTAL MODEL DEVELOPMENT DURING TECHNOLOGY-MEDIATED COLLABORATION

Organizations are under constant pressure to leverage expertise both locally and distributed throughout multiple sites (Elsbach & Hargadon, 2006; Williams & Rains, 2007). Consequently, companies are increasingly turning to a new business model where virtual teams are constructed with individuals that 1) are geographical dispersed, 2) are linked via collaboration technologies, and 3) collaborate across time and space (Garton & Wegryn, 2006). In recent virtual team studies, the collaboration technology used to link virtual team members was found to determine the temporal aspect (e.g., asynchronous versus synchronous) of collaboration (DeLuca & Valacich, 2006; Rutkowski, Saunders, & Vogel, 2007), the extent to which team member presence is perceived (Chidambaram & Tung, 2005; Fiol & O'Connor, 2005) and effectiveness of information exchange (Barkhi, Amiri, & James, 2006). A number of studies have also investigated the impact of team member remote distribution on social factors present in virtual team settings such as cultural diversity (Fuller & Davison, 2007; Lim & Zhong, 2006), conflict and cooperation (Hinds & Mortensen, 2005; Kankanhalli, Tan, & Wei, 2007), trust (Boyle, Kacmar, & George, 2008; Thomas & Bostrom, 2008) and leadership (Glückler & Schrott, 2007; Zhang et al., 2009).

A literature review reveals that a gap in technology-mediated collaboration research lies in the limited studies that have investigated the *dynamic* and *emergent* nature of higher order information processing such as team shared mental model development (Hasty, Massey, & Brown, 2006; Kanawattanachal & Yoo, 2007; Majchrzak, Beath, Lim, & Chin, 2005). In this study, a qualitative analysis of group behavior during sense-making of information exchanged and interactions (i.e., direct observation of perceptions, actions, comments,

behaviors of team members) is used to assess their impact on team functioning, productivity and satisfaction. From a theoretical standpoint, such research is necessary promote further construct validity needed to make correct inferences from empirical tests of theoretically derived relationships (Edwards, 2001; MacKenzie, Podsakoff, & Jarvis, 2005). From a practical standpoint, such research is needed for the reason that empirical identification of significant team cognition process behaviors offer more points of leverage for designing prescriptive practices aimed at improving team-based problem solving.

In this study, the following research questions are addressed:

1. What observable behaviors are indicative of shared mental model construction?
2. How does technology-mediated collaboration impact shared mental model construction?
3. How does shared mental model facilitate the quality of team action and ultimately task outcomes?

In what follows, the next section reviews the relevant literature on the role of shared knowledge of task content and task situation awareness on regulating the quality of group action during problem solving. This is followed by the presentation of the research model and hypotheses. The next two sections describe the research methodology and results, respectively. Finally, discussion of the findings, contributions, implications, limitations and suggestions for future research is presented.

LITERATURE REVIEW

Team Cognition and Shared Mental Model

Team cognition refers to the ways in which a team process and use information (He, Butler, & King,

2007; MacMillan, Entin, & Serfaty, 2004). During team cognition, shared information is organized into coherent chunks of causally-related facts which are used to guide behavior and decision-making. These causally-related facts are often referred to in the literature as mental models (Klimoski & Mohammed, 1994; Rentsch & Woehr, 2004). Team mental model content has been argued to be comprised of task-related and team-related knowledge (Cooke et al., 2003; Fiore, Salas, & Cannon-Bowers, 2001). Task-related knowledge refers to knowledge of task procedures, strategies, and constraints. In contrast, team-related knowledge refers to awareness of the knowledge, skills, abilities, and behavioral tendencies of team members. A shared mental model among a team is achieved when behaviors indicate that there is team-wide consensus on interpretation of task-related information and mutual awareness of team-member held knowledge and needs (Cooke et al., 2003; Lewis, 2004; Rentsch & Woehr, 2004).

Social Impact Theory

Social Impact Theory (SIT) is defined as changes in feelings, motivations, and behavior that occur in an individual as a result of the real, implied, or imagined presence or actions of other individuals (Latane, 1981). In a group context, SIT suggests that team member attitude and behavioral outcomes would be a function of three dimensions that influence a group interaction session - *strength, immediacy, and number*. The strength dimension refers to influence that is contingent upon the importance attributed to one or more group members and their ability to induce either positive (e.g., increased motivation, conformance, cooperation) or negative (e.g., disincentive, noncompliance, shirking) behavioral outcomes in others. Immediacy refers to the influence of time lapse between team member exchanges or physical distance between team members. Immediacy suggests that group member contributions and attitudes will take on increasingly negative aspects as greater time and

physical distance is experienced (Chidambaram & Tung, 2005). Immediacy also suggests that information provided by collocated team members would be more influential than information obtained from more distant sources. The numbers dimension expresses the quantity of influential sources on team member behavior. For example, as the number of individuals adopting a specific opinion or perspective greatly increases, others will be influenced to assimilate to the majority consensus. In summary, the tenets of SIT (strength, immediacy, and numbers) can impact team collaboration behaviors by exerting socially derived forces or pressures (e.g., motivational, accountability, influential) on team member behavior. Consequently, SIT offers a potential explanation for sub-optimal performance that may occur during technology-mediated collaboration.

Action Regulation Theory

Hacker's (2003) action regulation theory (ART) provides a framework for explaining self-regulated work behavior. According to the ART framework, there are three mechanisms that regulate task execution behavior - 1) orientation to the task, 2) solution implementation and 3) solution evaluation. *Orientation* focuses on assessing task requirements, goal setting, and defining strategies for goal attainment. The *implementation* process is guided by continuous feedback on team member contribution toward goal achievement, and is followed by *evaluation* of the current form of the task solution. In other words, actions are controlled by goals derived from interpretation of task requirements and status. Furthermore, these goals undergo *redefinition* based on evaluations of work completed. A shared mental model is essential for effective regulation of team member behavior in a group context. Consensus on and shared understanding of task requirements and task execution strategy will promote a collective orientation needed for coordinated effort during task implementation and task redefinition (Banks

& Millward, 2007; Blaskovich, 2008). In other words, by minimizing divergent points of view a shared mental model provides a common ground for effective and efficient regulation of team behavior (Klimoski & Mohammed, 1994).

RESEARCH MODEL AND HYPOTHESES

The research model is depicted in Figure 1. The model suggests that collaboration mode (i.e. face-to-face vs. technology-mediated virtual teams) will impact shared mental model development. It also proposed that that team work quality is a function of the accuracy of and extent of a team-wide shared mental model of the task requirements and appropriate task execution procedures. Finally, teamwork quality impacts task and satisfaction outcomes. The next section discusses how the relationships among the model's variables operate.

Collaboration Mode and Shared Mental Model

Dennis et al. (2008) noted that technology-mediated collaboration can be inferior to face-to-face collaboration because of its ability to facilitate the construction of verbal information or messages that are supplemented with physical gestures or nonverbal cues (e.g., postures, facial expression,

eye gaze, tone of voice, and conversation pauses). These nonverbal cues function as feedback that confirms or disconfirms understanding and controls turn-taking (Cramton, 2001). The resulting coordinated patterns of communication facilitate immediate feedback which minimizes potential disengagement thereby maintaining a shared focus that allows the team to move forward with minimal delays and minimal instances of deadlock or impasse. Miranda and Saunders (2003) noted that such effective face-to-face communication was essential in minimizing misunderstandings and constructing a shared mental model during task execution. In contrast, technology-mediated collaboration more often experienced dysfunctional levels of subjectivity in interpretation and divergent perspectives all of which diminished attainment of team-wide consensus on interpretation of the problem. Kock's (2004) medial naturalness theory suggests that the above stated deficiencies (i.e. cognitive obstacles) associated with technology-mediated collaboration occur because it is an *unnatural* form of human communication and interaction. Shared mental model development would be hampered by extra cognitive effort needed to adapt and overcome the lack of naturalness of technology-mediated collaboration Nikas & Poulymenakou, 2008).

SIT suggests that lack of team member proximity associated with technology-mediated collaboration can limit motivation for team member

Figure 1. Research model

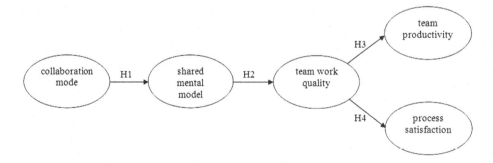

participation needed to offer and evaluate ideas that could otherwise be used in shared mental model development. The diminished motivation can lead to team member disengagement tendencies (Blaskovich, 2008; Chidambaram & Tung, 2005). In summary, technology-mediated collaboration settings should experience lower team-wide contribution of ideas and a greater need for confirmation of mutual understanding (e.g., questioning, rate of explanations and clarifications, rate of acknowledgements) as compared to face-to-face interaction. Thus the following hypothesis is proposed.

Hypothesis 1. Groups collaborating in the face-to-face settings will develop a more accurate shared mental model of the task requirements and task status than the technology-mediated groups.

Shared Mental Model and Teamwork Quality

Bonito (2004) showed that when the degree of shared mental model was low among team members, contribution and participation was limited to and dominated by those with more similar ideas and perspectives. Alternatively, a high degree of shared mental model similarity resulted in greater team-wide contribution and discussions of alternative solutions. In addition to regulating participation, shared understanding has also been linked to the quality of ideas suggested and thoroughness of team discussions (Banks & Millward, 2007; Van Ginkel & Van Knippenberg, 2008). Lewis (2004) noted that a shared understanding of specific expertise possessed by team members enabled them to better anticipate how other members will behave, which in turn lead to coordinated and harmonious group action. Group action regulation theory suggests that the key mechanism by which a shared mental model helps to facilitate coordinated effort is via

shared or common redefinitions of the problem and consistent evaluations of the appropriateness of the current solution and strategy (Hacker, 2003).

Finally, social impact theory suggests that as the number of team members with shared similar opinions and ideas increase (via strength and number effects), others are influenced to seek and attain convergence by submitting contributions complementary and synergistic to the current majority-held shared task mental model (Blaskovich, 2008). Team-wide contribution and discussions of alternative solutions, coordinated and harmonious group action, and cooperative behaviors are all facets of teamwork quality as defined by Hogel and Gemuenden (2001). Thus, the following hypothesis is proposed.

Hypothesis 2. Greater accuracy in shared mental model development will be associated with greater team work quality.

Teamwork Quality and Task Outcomes

According to ART, goal redefinition based on shared mental model will induce cooperative and synergistic behaviors that facilitate effective and efficient teamwork (Hoegl, Weinkauf, & Gemuenden, 2004; Kolbe & Boos, 2009; Rico, Sanchez-Manzanares, Gil, & Gibson, 2008). Using implicit coordination which is enacted tacitly through anticipation and adjustment based on shared mental models, team members can minimize duplication of effort and work in a co-ordinated manner without the need for extensive communication. In this study, it argued that team work quality derived from a shared mental model essentially results in cooperative goals and shared expectations that affect team process satisfaction (i.e. satisfaction with task execution effectiveness, interpersonal interactions, and team solution). Cooperative team level goals have been shown to result in increased team member satisfaction with interpersonal interaction and satisfaction with task solution (Hoegl & Gemuenden, 2001; Hoegl et al., 2004). Reinig (2003) noted that process satisfaction can be defined as the degree to which group members are happy with the way (i.e. team work quality) they arrived at a solution outcome.

Thus, the tendency for technology-mediated collaboration settings to experience relatively lower participation rates, inconsistent interpretation of meaning, and diminished shared task focus will limit realization of optimal teamwork quality which in turn will diminish task performance and satisfaction outcomes. Hence, the following hypotheses are proposed.

Hypothesis 3. Greater teamwork quality will be associated with greater team productivity.
Hypothesis 4. Greater teamwork quality will be associated with greater process satisfaction.

RESEARCH METHODOLOGY

Experimental Design

To test the research model and hypotheses, a laboratory experiment was conducted to examine the effects of two different modes of team collaboration – face-to-face and technology-mediated collaboration. Four person teams were used throughout both conditions. The technology-mediated collaboration setting was configured as a pair of dispersed collocated dyads seated at a table at two different locations. Communication between the pair of dyads occurred via a videoconferencing system (i.e. a fully integrated microphone, speaker and large video display system). In the face-to-face collaboration mode, all four subjects sat across from each other at a conference table. No content sharing technology options (e.g., shared whiteboard or shared desktop) were needed to complete the experimental task by either of the collaboration modes.

Participants

In this study, 48 participants were drawn from a population of Management Information Systems undergraduate students familiar with the Systems Development Life Cycle approach to software design and knowledge of structured programming. Previous research has noted that novice programmers exhibit skills that are comparative to expert programmers, when the program functional requirements are of moderate complexity and when the problem domain is well understood (Balijepally, Mahapatra, Nerur, & Price, 2009; Yoo & Alavi, 2001). For their participation, extra credit was awarded and each design team was eligible to receive a $100 award for the highest team productivity score under each of the experimental conditions (i.e., face-to-face and technology-mediated).

Task and Procedure

The teams were required to enhance the functionality of a hypothetical university information system. The experimental task required each team to construct software design documentation that included (1) a hierarchy chart, (2) a list of function prototypes, and (3) pseudocode for each function identified as part of a solution to the problem. These activities are typical of software design and coding activities conducted within organizations and exhibit the same form of team collaboration and decision-making requirements (Khatri, Vessey, Ram, & Ramesh, 2006; Kumar & Benbasat, 2004). The experimental task duration was 2.5 hours. The teams were given a handout detailing the task objective and required design deliverables and were instructed to complete the task in a timely manner. In order to ensure the manipulation of a demand for team-wide communication, each subteam possessed a unique set of half of the task instructions and was required to share their unique instruction set with the other subteam.

Measures

The behavioral observation approach was used in assessing shared mental model and teamwork quality by using three trained observer ratings of task-related and affect-related behaviors. The observers/raters underwent a 2-hour training session that reviewed construct definitions and relevant behavioral indicators used to provide a rating (Bakeman, 2000). Observer training was concluded with two practice rating sessions. Overall team ratings were comprised of the sum of ratings of one twenty-minute interval at the midpoint and the last twenty minute interval of the overall 2.5 hour session.

Mitchell and James (2001) noted that decisions about when to measure and how frequently to measure a phenomenon of interest require consideration of when events occur, when they change, and how quickly they change. In this study, face-to-face collaboration is hypothesized to more quickly derive accurate shared mental models as compared to the technology-mediated collaboration. Thus, if a lag or delay in measurement intervals to assess behavioral indicators of share mental model and accompanying teamwork quality behaviors is too long, significant differences between collaboration modes at an earlier point in time will be missed. If the measurement interval is started too early, the effect of collaboration mode may not have begun and could result in erroneous assumption of no differences in collaboration mode during the early phase to the task. In addition, assessment too soon could observe initial reactivity unrelated to the treatment resulting in mistakenly associating initial reactivity behaviors with the treatment. Consequently, the timing and duration of the two measurement intervals were chosen to address the lag issues discussed above as well as affording assessment of timeliness (via the first interval measure) and accuracy that develops over time (via the second interval measure). Further, more than two assessment intervals were deemed unnecessary because

rate of change was not of interest (Mitchell & James, 2001). Finally, to control for rater drift (i.e., tendency for change in interpretation of constructs and behavioral indicator identification), constructs and relevant behaviors were reviewed by the observers between rating sessions. Given that the final ratings were averaged among the raters, the *Average Measure Intraclass Correlation* was used to assess inter-rater reliability (Shrout & Fleiss, 1979).

- **Treatment Variable: Collaboration Mode:** The collaboration modes utilized to form the experimental conditions were face-to-face collaboration and technology-mediated collaboration via videoconferencing. Recent research has shown that both collaboration modes differ in the capacity to which they impact communication efficiency, shared understanding and team interactions (Blaskovich, 2008; Chidambaram & Tung, 2005; Fiol & O'Connor, 2005; Furumo, 2009; Kanawattanachal & Yoo, 2007).

- **Shared Mental Model:** The shared mental model rating scale was comprised of four items that assessed behaviors that reflected the degree of 1) shared understanding of task requirements, 2) solution consensus, 3) confusion of task requirements and status, and 4) extent of needed explanations and clarifications (Banks & Millward, 2007; He et al., 2007; Kankanhalli et al., 2007; Van Ginkel & Van Knippenberg, 2008). Three trained raters rated shared mental model development in real time using a 7-point scale ranging from 1 (very low) to 7 (very high). The inter-rater reliability for the shared mental model scale was 0.818 ($p < .001$) indicating very good inter-rater agreement (Cicchetti, 1994). The three shared mental model ratings were averaged to compute a final score.

- **Teamwork Quality:** Teamwork quality was assessed using items that provided observer ratings of 1) active participation, communication, and interaction among all of its members, 2) constructive discussions of team member ideas and suggestions, and 3) maintenance of an encouraging and supportive climate (Hoegl et al., 2004). In providing their ratings, three trained observers used a rating scale that ranged from 1 (very low) to 7 (very high). The inter-rater reliability for the shared mental model scale was 0.873 (p < .001) indicating very good inter-rater agreement. The three team work quality ratings were averaged to compute a final score.

- **Team Productivity:** The team productivity measure was determined by assessing the completeness of the required design documentation against a defined rubric. A research assistant, unaware of the study's objectives, computed the team productivity as a combined score on the completeness of file design (i.e. appropriate data fields), specification of function prototypes (i.e. function name, parameters and return type), and pseudocode for each function. A point was awarded for each correct specification of any data value of a specific data file, correct output and input data value of a program module (i.e., function or subroutine), and correct specification of program statement needed in a specific program module.

- **Satisfaction:** After task completion, a satisfaction questionnaire elicited individual team member responses regarding the extent to which, while executing the task, there was frustration with behaviors of other team members, commitment to and confidence in the solution, and satisfaction with the solution outcome. This scale was adapted from the set of scale items developed by Green and Tabor (1980). Because the research model focuses on the team level, aggregation of individual satisfaction responses required demonstration of within group agreement. In order to justify aggregation, an interrater agreement statistic using the r_{wg} procedure (James, Demaree, & Wolf, 1984) was computed to assess the convergence of responses among team members. The r_{wg} values for all teams ranged from 0.72 to 0.99 which conformed to the generally accepted level of .7 as indication of strong within-group agreement. The scale reliability (Cronbach's alpha) for the satisfaction scale was 0.768.

- **Control Variables:** Programming ability is an important variable that can influence a participant's performance. To minimize the influence of this variable on performance, programming ability was measured and used as a covariate in the analysis. The index of programming ability was computed for each group as the average score of a grade received by each team member in an upper level programming course (Balijepally et al., 2009; Quigley, Tekleab, & Tesluk, 2007; Rulke & Galaskiewicz, 2000).

Analysis

Measurement model validation and structural model testing was conducted using PLS (partial least squares, PLS-Graph version 3.00) where regression is performed on only a portion of the model at any one time (Chin, 1998). The research model has no more than one structural path leads into to any one construct. Thus, the sample size of 12 four-person teams conforms to the sample size recommendation of 5 to 10 times the largest number of structural paths leading into to any one construct given the construct is measured with reflective indicators (Chin & Newsted,

1999). Majchrzak et al. (2005) recently attested to the ability of PLS to obtain robust estimates in a study where a sample size of 17 was used. Researchers have been recently cautioned that use of small samples in PLS data analysis should be accompanied with data conformance to a normal distribution, strong psychometric properties (i.e. high factor loadings and average explained variance - AVE), high magnitude of the path coefficients (e.g., ≥ 0.7) and statistical power analysis of path coefficient estimations (Marcoulides, Chin, & Saunders, 2009). Kolmogorov-Smirnov Z tests resulted in asymptotic significance levels ranging from 0.441 to 1.0 indicating the data adequately conformed to a normal distribution. Strong psychometric properties were evidenced by indicator loadings that ranged from 0.695 to 0.963 and average indicator loadings of 0.9 for shared mental model, 0.8 for teamwork quality and 0.8 for satisfaction. In addition, Figure 2 reveals that all path coefficients were ≥ 0.7 with the exception of one at 0.684. Finally, results from PWR package (Champely, 2007) in the "R" statistical software program (R Development Core Team, 2007) revealed the presence of large effect size and adequate power for the estimation of all four dependent variables – shared mental model ($f^2 = 1.50$; $1- \beta = 0.97$), teamwork quality ($f^2 = 1.38$; $1- \beta = 0.95$), productivity ($f^2 = 1.38$; $1- \beta = 0.95$), and satisfaction ($f^2 = 0.89$; $1- \beta = 0.84$).

Consequently, this study's sample conforms to accepted constraints used to assess small sample adequacy (Marcoulides et al., 2009).

RESULTS

Measurement Model

To assess internal consistency reliability, convergent validity and discriminant validity of the construct measurements, the constructs' composite reliabilities (CR) and the average variance extracted (AVE) were calculated. Regarding internal consistency (reliability), composite reliability scores for every construct (ranging from 0.873 to 0.970, as shown in Table 1) are well above 0.70, which is the suggested benchmark for acceptable reliability (Chin, 1998; Majchrzak et al., 2005). Table 1 indicates with the exception of one item-to-construct loading of 0.695 all of the items have loadings at 0.747 or above and the t-statistic for the item to construct loadings are all significant at either $p \leq .05$ or $p \leq .01$. These results indicate that the measurement model has displayed both item internal reliability and item convergent validity.

Discriminant validity is evidenced when all the loadings of the scale items on their assigned latent variables or construct are larger than their loading on any other latent variable. Table 2 pro-

Figure 2. PLS analysis results

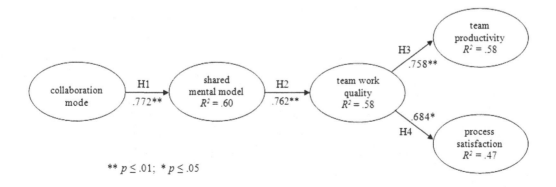

** $p \leq .01$; * $p \leq .05$

Table 1. Composite reliability, AVE, and indicator loadings

Construct and Item Level Values		loading	t-statistic	p-value
Shared Mental Model (Composite Reliability = 0.970; AVE = 0.889)				
smm1	It was clear that everyone developed the same level of understanding of the task requirements.	0.930	47.674	$p \leq .01$
smm2	There was some difference of opinion or concern about the correctness of the proposed solution.	0.963	39.174	$p \leq .01$
smm3	There was significant confusion about what was going on.	0.941	9.005	$p \leq .01$
smm4	Some team members required a lot of explanations about what was going on.	0.936	37.262	$p \leq .01$
Team Work Quality (Composite Reliability = 0.919; AVE = 0.741)				
tmwk1	Team-wide consensus was confirmed before moving forward with an idea.	0.925	40.053	$p \leq .01$
tmwk2	Ideas were thoroughly discussed and evaluated among all team members.	0.901	18.138	$p \leq .01$
tmwk3	Team made an obvious effort to create and maintain a positive climate.	0.747	8.094	$p \leq .01$
tmwk4	Team would clearly enjoy working together on another project.	0.859	7.029	$p \leq .01$
Satisfaction (Composite Reliability = 0.873; AVE = 0.633)				
satisfac1	To what extent did you feel frustrated or tense about another team members' behavior?	0.695	3.964	$p \leq .01$
satisfac2	How satisfied were you with the quality of your team's solution?	0.796	3.689	$p \leq .01$
satisfac3	To what extent do you feel committed to the team's solution?	0.838	4.848	$p \leq .01$
satisfac4	To what extent do you feel confident that the team solution is correct?	0.845	6.943	$p \leq .01$

Note. 2-tailed significance level determination. df = 10.
$p \leq 0.05$ if: $2.763 > |t| \geq 1.812$ $p \leq 0.01$ if: $|t| \geq 2.763$

Table 2. Indicator loadings

Indicator	Latent Variable Item Loadings		
	shared mental model	team work quality	satisfaction
smm1	**.930**	.856	.432
smm2	**.963**	.798	.323
smm3	**.941**	.579	.037
smm4	**.937**	.597	.060
tmwk1	.729	**.925**	.662
tmwk2	.757	**.901**	.540
tmwk3	.532	**.747**	.544
tmwk4	.560	**.859**	.621
satisfac1	.521	.617	**.695**
satisfac2	-.075	.396	**.796**
satisfac3	.229	.646	**.845**
satisfac4	-.125	.388	**.838**

vides the correlations of each item to its intended latent variable (i.e., loadings) and to all other constructs (i.e., cross loadings). Although there is some cross-loading, all items load more highly on their own construct than on other constructs and all constructs share more variance with their measures than with other constructs. It is not uncommon to encounter cross-loading among constructs because behavior and affective responses are rarely partitioned into neatly packaged units that function fully independently of one another (Limayem, Hirt, & Cheung, 2007; Schaupp, Belanger, & Weiguo, 2009; Serenko, Bontis, & Detlor, 2007).

Discriminant validity is further substantiated by using the AVE to assess the variance shared between the construct and its measurement items. A construct is considered to be distinct from other constructs if the square root of the AVE for it is greater than its correlations with other latent constructs. Table 3 indicates that the AVE square roots that appear in the diagonal are larger than any correlation between the associated construct and any other construct (Chin, 1998; Majchrzak et al., 2005). This AVE analysis result and the item to construct loadings discussed above suggest that the measurement model displays discriminant validity.

Structural Model

In PLS analysis, a structural model can be evaluated on the basis of strong indicator to construct loadings, R^2 values, and significance of the structural path coefficients (Chin, 1998). Figure 2 shows that all of the paths are significant at either the 0.05 or 0.01 level. In addition, the model accounts for 47 to 60 percent of the variances (R^2 scores). Tenenhaus et al. (2005) suggested that the geometric mean of the average communality (i.e., variable variance explained by a factor structure) and average R^2 (variable variance explained by model) of latent variables could provide a global fit measure (called GoF) for PLS path modeling.

Table 3. Latent variable correlations and square root of AVE

	shared mental model	team work quality	satisfaction
shared mental model	**0.943**		
team work quality	0.762	**0.861**	
satisfaction	0.242	0.684	**0.796**

Note: square root of the constructs' AVE appear in the diagonal

Three GoF measures in line with effect sizes have been defined as GoF-small = 0.1, GoF-medium = 0.25, and GoF-large = 0.36 (Wetzels, Odekerken-Schröder, & Van Oppen, 2009). A GoF, a value of 0.59 was obtained and it exceeds the cut-off value of 0.36 for large effect sizes of R^2. The resulting R^2 and GoF values suggest that overall the data provides a good fit to the model and also indicates good model predictability. In addition, the hypothesized model provided the best fit to the data (i.e. largest explained variance) compared to all other alternative causal path configurations among the variables.

The PLS analysis results (Figure 2) show that all of the hypotheses were supported. Collaboration mode is shown to increase shared mental model development ($b = 0.772$, $t = 6.230$, $p \leq .01$). Face-to-face groups had a mean shared mental model rating score of 107.25 while the technology-mediated groups had a lower mean score of 70.25. Shared mental model increased teamwork quality ($b = 0.762$, $t = 12.336$, $p \leq .01$). Teamwork quality increased team productivity ($b = 0.758$, $t = 10.875$, $p \leq .01$) and team satisfaction ($b = 0.684$, $t = 2.625$, $p \leq .05$). Mediation was assessed following the procedure recommended by Baron and Kenny (1986). Mediation tests showed that teamwork quality fully mediated the impact of shared mental model on both productivity and team satisfaction. In addition, shared mental model fully mediated the impact of collaboration mode on teamwork quality.

DISCUSSION

Key Findings

Direct observation revealed that the technology-mediated collaboration mode exhibited greater lags between information exchanges, fewer information seeking attempts, greater incoherent exchanges, greater need to repair misunderstandings and diminished team-wide participation all of which limited the extent of shared understanding among all team members. Apparently, lack of co-presence/proximity effects (i.e., strength and immediacy social influences) can diminish team member participation and team members' ability to adequately attend to verbal and nonverbal gestures used in facilitating confirmation of understanding and consensus. Alternatively, the face-to-face groups were better able to maintain a shared focus that resulted in greater frequency of team-wide information seeking and polling for confirmation of mutual understanding and agreement which lead to improved shared mental model development.

As proposed in hypothesis 2, shared mental model was shown to have a positive effect on teamwork quality. Apparently, shared mental models do in fact give rise to implicit coordination which in turn regulates action at the group level through a shared frame of reference that guides individual behavior in a synergistic manner. Decision making effectiveness and timeliness in resolving issues regarding task execution strategy and solution content is also facilitated by a shared understanding of the task context. It is likely that a shared understanding minimized the need to debate divergent contributions making team-wide participation, consensus and mutual support (i.e., teamwork quality) easier to achieve.

Teamwork quality's positive impact on productivity and team satisfaction was consistent with prior research (Hoegl & Gemuenden, 2001; Hoegl et al., 2004). Implicit coordination via a shared mental model helps to maintain a shared focus and coordinated action needed for a more accurate and timely solution. In addition, past research has shown that when team members collectively adopt a prosocial motivation and perceive cooperative outcome interdependence, they respect and value differences of opinion, are better able to arrive at consensus, learn more from each other, perform more effectively and are more satisfied with team process and task outcomes (De Dreu, 2007; Tjosvold et al., 2004).

Contributions to Theory and Research

A contribution of this study involves the integration of social impact theory (Latane, 1981) with action regulation theory (Hacker, 2003) to develop greater insight into both the technology-related and motivational mechanisms that affect team member communication which ultimately impact shared knowledge construction and utilization. A second contribution lies in the extension to the technology-mediated collaboration literature through a test and confirmation of the temporal relationship between shared mental model and teamwork quality. Action regulation theory (Hacker, 2003) provided a good framework for explaining how shared mental model impacts the motivation for and regulation of coordinated group action. A third contribution lies in the demonstration of the utility of direct observation for studying communication behaviors and social interaction in the development of shared mental model and teamwork. It is believed that shared mental model construction is dynamic and emergent rather than purposive and post-task assessment using self-reports would be difficult because it would require a significant amount of reflection to reconstruct an accurate sequence of shared perceptions, understandings, and meanings.

Implications for Research and Practice

This study's results suggest that current technology-mediated collaboration models should consider the inclusion of efficacy-based, motivational, and social influence factors (e.g., perceived efficacy of contribution, perceived salience of team member contribution). Future research should address motivational and social influence factors that may inhibit participation in virtual team settings. In addition, future research should investigate the dynamic interplay between technology-mediated collaboration, team cognition and social interaction processes using a qualitative approach such as direct observation or content analysis of team conversations.

In regard to practical implications, the results suggest that if geographically dispersed technology-mediated collaboration is the only option, distribution of expertise should be strategically managed and/or teamwork facilitation training should be applied. The objective of such interventions would be management of shared understanding by creating a sense of outcome interdependence, mitigating low individual and group efficacy perceptions, encouraging communication and participation and maintenance of shared focus (Okhuysen & Eisenhardt, 2002; Tullar & Kaiser, 2000). For example, a virtual global engineering design team would benefit from facilitation aimed at mitigating cultural differences that lead to miscommunication, diminished trust, and reluctance to contribute or pose controversial ideas. In addition, facilitator awareness expertise loci could help in task allocation and directing contribution. The interventions should also address facilitation of idea negotiation and convergence during team work (Kolbe & Boos, 2009). For example, low participation could be mitigated by encouraging contribution by expressing or promoting the benefits of diverse perspective during team-based problem solving. Knowing the typical communication deficiencies of technology-mediated collaboration, a facilitator could periodically poll all design team members for their interpretation of task requirements, appropriate solution and status of work completed to correct any inconsistencies.

Limitations

One limitation of the study lies in the use of "newly formed" teams. Replication of this study in actual work environments using "intact" teams or where members of temporary virtual teams have a permanent affiliation with an organization is needed. Another potential limitation stems from the use of dispersed collocated dyads. Other configurations such as larger collocated teams and more than two geographical locations are warranted. The use of student subjects presents a potential limitation to the study. However, the use of student subjects in a controlled setting can ensure homogeneous responses, which are critical in theory testing as compared to field settings which can be confounded by unique, unmeasured contextual factors specific to multiple sites. Further, previous studies have demonstrated that there is little difference between using students and using professionals in decision-making situations and problems solving tasks such as software development (Balijepally et al., 2009; Yoo & Alavi, 2001).

CONCLUSION

The overall finding of this study is that technology-mediated collaboration can limit collective contribution from team members, critical analysis of information, and solution consensus needed to construct a shared mental model. The results from this study add to the growing literature on technology-mediated collaboration by providing insight into the motivational and social influence mechanisms associated with shared mental model construction. By integrating social impact and action regulation theories, insights and theoretical contributions that emerge from this study relate to how and why (1) technology-mediated collaboration can diminish participation; (2) collaboration mode can dictate which ideas get incorporated into a team's shared mental model; and (3) shared mental model can regulate both task-related and social-related behaviors. In addition, viability of the direct observation approach as an additional data collection method for use in methodological triangulation (Denzin, 2006) has been demonstrated. Hopefully the study will stimulate more theoretical discussion and empirical research aimed at understanding the cognitive mechanisms (e.g., shared mental model and implicit coordination) underlying team performance and their role in existing models of virtual team phenomena.

REFERENCES

Bakeman, R. (2000). Behavioral observations and coding. In Reis, H. T., & Judd, C. K. (Eds.), *Handbook of research methods in social psychology* (pp. 138–159). Cambridge, UK: Cambridge University Press.

Balijepally, V. G., Mahapatra, R. K., Nerur, S., & Price, K. H. (2009). Are two heads better than one for software development? The productivity paradox of pair programming. *Management Information Systems Quarterly, 33*(1), 91–118.

Banks, A. P., & Millward, L. J. (2007). Differentiating knowledge in teams: The effect of shared declarative and procedural knowledge on team performance. *Group Dynamics, 11*(2), 95–106. doi:10.1037/1089-2699.11.2.95

Barkhi, R., Amiri, A., & James, T. (2006). A study of communication and coordination in collaborative software development. *Journal of Global Information Technology Management, 9*(1), 44–61.

Baron, R. M., & Kenny, D. A. (1986). The moderator-mediator variable distinction in social psychological research: Conceptual, strategic and statistical considerations. *Journal of Personality and Social Psychology, 51*(6), 1173–1182. doi:10.1037/0022-3514.51.6.1173

Blaskovich, J. L. (2008). Exploring the effect of distance: An experimental investigation of virtual collaboration, social loafing, and group decisions. *Journal of Information Systems, 22*(1), 27–46. doi:10.2308/jis.2008.22.1.27

Bonito, J. A. (2004). Shared cognition and participation in small groups: Similarity of member prototypes. *Communication Research, 31*(6), 704–730. doi:10.1177/0093650204269406

Boyle, R., Kacmar, C., & George, J. (2008). Distributed deception: An investigation of the effectiveness of deceptive communication in a computer-mediated environment. *International Journal of e-Collaboration, 4*(3), 14–38. doi:10.4018/jec.2008070102

Champely, S. (2007). *PWR: Basic functions for power analysis, R package version 1.1*. Retrieved from http://www.r-project.org/

Chidambaram, L., & Tung, L. L. (2005). Is out of sight, out of mind? An empirical study of social loafing in technology-supported groups. *Information Systems Research, 16*(2), 149–170. doi:10.1287/isre.1050.0051

Chin, W. W. (1998). Issues and opinions on structural equation modeling. *Management Information Systems Quarterly, 22*(1), 7–16.

Chin, W. W., & Newsted, P. R. (1999). Structural equation modeling analysis with small samples using partial least squares. In Hoyle, R. (Ed.), *Statistical strategies for small sample research* (pp. 307–341). Thousand Oaks, CA: Sage.

Cicchetti, D. V. (1994). Guidelines, criteria, and rules of thumb for evaluating normed and standardized assessment instruments in psychology. *Psychological Assessment, 6*(4), 284–290. doi:10.1037/1040-3590.6.4.284

Cooke, N. J., Kiekel, P. A., Salas, E., Stout, R., Bowers, C., & Cannon-Bowers, J. (2003). Measuring team knowledge: A window to the cognitive underpinnings of team performance. *Group Dynamics*, *7*(3), 179–199. doi:10.1037/1089-2699.7.3.179

Cramton, C. (2001). The mutual knowledge problem and its consequences for dispersed collaboration. *Organization Science*, *12*(3), 346–371. doi:10.1287/orsc.12.3.346.10098

De Dreu, C. K. W. (2007). Cooperative outcome interdependence, task reflexivity and team effectiveness: A motivated information processing approach. *The Journal of Applied Psychology*, *92*(3), 628–638. doi:10.1037/0021-9010.92.3.628

DeLuca, D., & Valacich, J. S. (2006). Virtual teams in and out of synchronicity. *Information Technology & People*, *19*(4), 323–344. doi:10.1108/09593840610718027

Dennis, A., Fuller, R. M., & Valacich, J. S. (2008). Media, tasks and communication processes: A theory of media synchronicity. *Management Information Systems Quarterly*, *32*(3), 575–600.

Denzin, N. (2006). *Sociological methods: A sourcebook* (5th ed.). Piscataway, NJ: Aldine Transaction.

Edwards, J. R. (2001). Multidimensional constructs in organizational behavior research: An integrative analytical framework. *Organizational Research Methods*, *4*(2), 144–192. doi:10.1177/109442810142004

Elsbach, K. D., & Hargadon, A. B. (2006). Enhancing creativity through "mindless" work: A framework of workday design. *Organization Science*, *17*(4), 470–484. doi:10.1287/orsc.1060.0193

Fiol, C. M., & O'Connor, E. J. (2005). Identification in face-to-face, hybrid, and pure virtual teams: Untangling the contradictions. *Organization Science*, *16*(1), 19–32. doi:10.1287/orsc.1040.0101

Fiore, S. M., Salas, E., & Cannon-Bowers, J. A. (2001). Group dynamics and shared mental model development. In London, M. (Ed.), *How people evaluate others in organizations* (pp. 309–336). Mahwah, NJ: Lawrence Erlbaum.

Fuller, M. A., & Davison, R. M. (2007). I know I can, but can we? Culture and efficacy beliefs in global virtual teams. *Small Group Research*, *38*(1), 130–155. doi:10.1177/1046496406297041

Furumo, K. (2009). The impact of conflict and conflict management style on deadbeats and deserters in virtual teams. *Journal of Computer Information Systems*, *49*(4), 66–73.

Garton, C., & Wegryn, K. (2006). *Managing without walls: Maximize success with virtual, global, and cross-cultural teams*. Double Oak, TX: Mc Press Online LP.

Glückler, J., & Schrott, G. (2007). Leadership and performance in virtual teams: Exploring brokerage in electronic communication. *International Journal of e-Collaboration*, *3*(3), 31–52. doi:10.4018/jec.2007070103

Green, S., & Taber, T. (1980). The effects of three social decision schemes in decision group performance. *Organizational Behavior and Human Performance*, *25*(1), 97–106. doi:10.1016/0030-5073(80)90027-6

Hacker, W. (2003). Action regulation theory: A practical tool for the design of modern work processes? *European Journal of Work and Organizational Psychology*, *12*(2), 105–130. doi:10.1080/13594320344000075

Hasty, B. K., Massey, A. P., & Brown, S. A. (2006). Role-based experiences, media perceptions, and knowledge transfer success in virtual dyads. *Group Decision and Negotiation*, *15*(4), 367–387. doi:10.1007/s10726-006-9047-5

He, J., Butler, B., & King, W. R. (2007). Team cognition: Development and evolution in software project teams. *Journal of Management Information Systems, 24*(2), 261–292. doi:10.2753/MIS0742-1222240210

Hinds, P. J., & Mortensen, M. (2005). Understanding conflict in geographically distributed teams: The moderating effects of shared identity, shared context, and spontaneous communication. *Organization Science, 16*(3), 290–309. doi:10.1287/orsc.1050.0122

Hoegl, M., & Gemuenden, H. G. (2001). Teamwork quality and the success of innovative projects: A theoretical concept and empirical evidence. *Organization Science, 12*(4), 435–449. doi:10.1287/orsc.12.4.435.10635

Hoegl, M., Weinkauf, K. H., & Gemuenden, G. (2004). Interteam coordination, project commitment, and teamwork in multiteam R&D projects: A longitudinal study. *Organization Science, 5*(1), 38–55. doi:10.1287/orsc.1030.0053

James, L. R., Demaree, R. G., & Wolf, G. (1984). Estimating within-group interrater reliability with and without response bias. *The Journal of Applied Psychology, 69*(1), 85–98. doi:10.1037/0021-9010.69.1.85

Kanawattanachal, P., & Yoo, Y. (2007). The impact of knowledge coordination on virtual team performance over time. *Management Information Systems Quarterly, 31*(4), 783–808.

Kankanhalli, A., Tan, B. C. Y., & Wei, K. (2007). Conflict and performance in global virtual teams. *Journal of Management Information Systems, 23*(3), 237–274. doi:10.2753/MIS0742-1222230309

Khatri, V., Vessey, I., Ram, S., & Ramesh, V. (2006). Cognitive fit between conceptual schemas and internal problem representations: The case of geospatio-temporal conceptual schema comprehension. *IEEE Transactions on Professional Communication, 49*(2), 109–127. doi:10.1109/TPC.2006.875091

Klimoski, R., & Mohammed, S. (1994). Team mental model: Construct or metaphor? *Journal of Management, 20*(2), 403–437.

Kock, N. (2004). The psychobiological model: Towards a new theory of computer-mediated communication based on Darwinian evolution. *Organization Science, 15*(3), 327–348. doi:10.1287/orsc.1040.0071

Kolbe, M., & Boos, M. (2009). Facilitating group decision-making: Facilitator's subjective theories on group coordination. *Forum Qualitative Sozial Forschung, 10*(1), 1–29.

Kumar, N., & Benbasat, I. (2004). The effect of relationship encoding, task type, and complexity on information representation: An empirical evaluation of 2D and 3D line graphs. *Management Information Systems Quarterly, 28*(2), 255–281.

Latane, B. (1981). The psychology of social impact. *The American Psychologist, 36*(4), 343–356. doi:10.1037/0003-066X.36.4.343

Lewis, K. (2004). Knowledge and performance in knowledge-worker teams: A longitudinal study of transactive memory systems. *Management Science, 50*(11), 1519–1533. doi:10.1287/mnsc.1040.0257

Lim, J., & Zhong, Y. (2006). The interaction and effects of perceived cultural diversity, group size, leadership, and collaborative learning systems: An experimental study. *Information Resources Management Journal, 19*(4), 56–71. doi:10.4018/irmj.2006100104

Limayem, M., Hirt, S. G., & Cheung, C. M. K. (2007). How habit limits the predictive power of intention: The case of information systems continuance. *Management Information Systems Quarterly, 31*(4), 705–737.

MacKenzie, S. B., Podsakoff, P. M., & Jarvis, C. B. (2005). The problem of measurement model misspecification in behavioral and organizational research and some recommended solutions. *The Journal of Applied Psychology, 90*(4), 710–730. doi:10.1037/0021-9010.90.4.710

MacMillan, J., Entin, E. E., & Serfaty, D. (2004). Communication overhead: The hidden cost of team cognition. In Salas, E., & Fiore, S. M. (Eds.), *Team cognition: Understanding the factors that drive process and performance* (pp. 61–82). Washington, DC: American Psychological Association. doi:10.1037/10690-004

Majchrzak, A., Beath, C., Lim, R., & Chin, W. (2005). Managing client dialogues during information systems design to facilitate client learning. *Management Information Systems Quarterly, 29*(4), 653–672.

Marcoulides, G. A., Chin, W. W., & Saunders, C. (2009). A critical look at partial least squares modeling. *Management Information Systems Quarterly, 33*(1), 171–175.

Miranda, S. M., & Saunders, C. S. (2003). The social construction of meaning: An alternative perspective on information sharing. *Information Systems Research, 14*(1), 87–107. doi:10.1287/isre.14.1.87.14765

Mitchell, T. R., & James, L. R. (2001). Building better theory: Time and the specification of when things happen. *Academy of Management Review, 26*(4), 530–547.

Nikas, A., & Poulymenakou, A. (2008). Technology adaptation: Capturing the appropriation dynamics of web-based collaboration support in a project team. *International Journal of e-Collaboration, 4*(2), 1–27. doi:10.4018/jec.2008040101

Okhuysen, G. A., & Eisenhardt, K. M. (2002). Integrating knowledge in groups: How formal interventions enable flexibility. *Organization Science, 13*(4), 370–386. doi:10.1287/orsc.13.4.370.2947

Quigley, N. R., Tekleab, A. G., & Tesluk, P. E. (2007). Comparing consensus- and aggregation-based methods of measuring team-level variables: The role of relationship conflict and conflict management processes. *Organizational Research Methods, 10*(4), 589–606. doi:10.1177/1094428106286853

R Development Core Team. (2007). R: A language and environment for statistical computing. Retrieved from http://www.R-project.org

Reinig, B. A. (2003). Toward an understanding of satisfaction with the process and outcomes of teamwork. *Journal of Management Information Systems, 19*(4), 65–83.

Rentsch, J. R., & Woehr, D. R. (2004). Quantifying congruence in cognition: Social relations modeling and team member schema similarity. In Salas, E., & Fiore, S. M. (Eds.), *Team cognition: Understanding the factors that drive process and performance* (pp. 11–31). Washington, DC: American Psychological Association. doi:10.1037/10690-002

Rico, R., Sánchez-Manzanares, M., Gil, F., & Gibson, C. (2008). Team implicit coordination processes: A team knowledge-based approach. *Academy of Management Review, 33*(1), 163–184. doi:10.5465/AMR.2008.27751276

Rulke, D. L., & Galaskiewicz, J. (2000). Distribution of knowledge, group network structure, and group performance. *Management Science, 46*(5), 612–625. doi:10.1287/mnsc.46.5.612.12052

Rutkowski, A., Saunders, C., & Vogel, D. (2007). Is it already 4 a.m. in your time zone? Focus immersion and temporal dissociation in virtual teams. *Small Group Research*, 38(1), 98–129. doi:10.1177/1046496406297042

Schaupp, L. C., Belanger, F., & Weiguo, F. (2009). Examining the success of websites beyond e-commerce: An extension of the IS success model. *Journal of Computer Information Systems*, 49(4), 42–52.

Serenko, A., Bontis, N., & Detlor, B. (2007). End-user adoption of animated interface agents in everyday work applications. *Behaviour & Information Technology*, 26(2), 119–132. doi:10.1080/01449290500260538

Shrout, P. E., & Fleiss, J. L. (1979). Intraclass correlations: Uses in assessing rater reliability. *Psychological Bulletin*, 86(2), 420–428. doi:10.1037/0033-2909.86.2.420

Tenenhaus, M., Vinzi, V. E., Chatelin, Y. M., & Lauro, C. (2005). PLS path modeling. *Computational Statistics & Data Analysis*, 48(1), 159–205. doi:10.1016/j.csda.2004.03.005

Thomas, D., & Bostrom, R. (2008). Trust and cooperation through technology adaptation in virtual teams: Empirical field evidence. *Information Systems Management*, 25(1), 45–56. doi:10.1080/10580530701777149

Tjosvold, D., Yu, Z., & Chun, H. (2004). Team learning from mistakes: The contribution of cooperative goals and problem-solving. *Journal of Management Studies*, 41(7), 1223–1245. doi:10.1111/j.1467-6486.2004.00473.x

Tullar, W., & Kaiser, P. (2000). The effect of process training on process and outcomes in virtual groups. *Journal of Business Communication*, 37(4), 408–427. doi:10.1177/002194360003700404

Van Ginkel, W. P., & Van Knippenberg, D. (2008). Group information elaboration and group decision making: The role of shared task representations. *Organizational Behavior and Human Decision Processes*, 105(1), 82–97.

Wetzels, M., Odekerken-Schröder, G., & Van Oppen, C. (2009). Using PLS path modeling for assessing hierarchical construct models: Guidelines and empirical illustration. *Management Information Systems Quarterly*, 33(1), 177–195.

Wickham, K. R., & Walther, J. B. (2007). Perceived behaviors of emergent and assigned leaders in virtual groups. *International Journal of e-Collaboration*, 3(1), 1–16. doi:10.4018/jec.2007010101

Williams, T. C., & Rains, J. (2007). Linking strategy to structure: The power of systematic organization design. *Organization Development Journal*, 25(2), 163–170.

Yoo, Y., & Alavi, M. (2001). Media and group cohesion: Relative influences on social presence, task participation, and group consensus. *Management Information Systems Quarterly*, 25(3), 371–391. doi:10.2307/3250922

Zhang, S., Tremaine, M., Egan, R., Milewski, A., O'Sullivan, P., & Fjermestad, J. (2009). Occurrence and effects of leader delegation in virtual software teams. *International Journal of e-Collaboration*, 5(1), 47–68. doi:10.4018/jec.2009010104

This work was previously published in the International Journal of e-Collaboration, Volume 7, Issue 3, edited by Ned Kock, pp. 14-30, copyright 2011 by IGI Publishing (an imprint of IGI Global).

Chapter 10
WikiDesign:
A Semantic Wiki to Evaluate Collaborative Knowledge

Davy Monticolo
National Polytechnic Institute of Lorraine, France

Samuel Gomes
University of Technology of Belfort-Montbéliard, France

ABSTRACT

This paper presents a knowledge evaluation and evolution in a knowledge management system by using a Semantic Wiki approach. The authors describe a Semantic Wiki called WikiDesign which is a component of a Knowledge Management system. Currently WikiDesign is used in engineering departments of companies to emphasize technical knowledge. This study explains how WikiDesign ensures the reliability of the knowledge base thanks to a knowledge evaluation process. After explaining the interest of the use of semantic wikis in knowledge management approach, the architecture of WikiDesign with its semantic functionalities is described. The effectiveness of WikiDesign is proved with a knowledge evaluation example for an industrial project.

1. INTRODUCTION

A wiki is a web site allows collaborative distant creation of information and editing of hypertext content. Leuf and Cunningham (2001) were the first to propose a web site where people could create, modify, transform and link pages all from within their browser and in a very simple way. Indeed Wikis become popular tools for collaboration on the web, and many active online communities employ wikis to exchange information.

Indeed for the most of wikis, public or private, primary goals are to organize the collected information and to share it. Wikis are usually viewed

DOI: 10.4018/978-1-4666-2020-9.ch010

as tools to manage online content in a quick and easy way, by editing some simple syntax known as wikitext (Singh, Wombacher, & Aberer 2007). Schaffert (2006) enumerates the specifications of a wiki system:

- It allows the editing via a browser;
- It has a simplified wiki syntax i.e. simplified hypertext format usable by all the internet users;
- It manages a rollback mechanism i.e. it is able to versioned the changes in the content each time they are stored;
- Its access is unrestricted, everybody can write in the wiki;
- It manages the collaborative editing i.e. if someone create a article, everybody can extend this article;
- It proposes a strong linking, all the pages of the wiki are linked with each other using hyperlinks;
- It has a search function over the content of all pages stored;

It allows the uploading of different content like documents, images or videos. Taking consideration to all these properties, Wikis seem to become a new approach to collaborative knowledge engineering based on social networks of the Web2.0 (Richards, 2009). Indeed new research works (Schaffert, 2006; Vrandecic & Krötzsch, 2006) propose wikis to exchange knowledge. Knowledge is information with a context and value that make it usable. Knowledge is what places someone in the position to perform a particular task by selecting, interpreting and evaluation information depending on the context (Malone, Crowston, & Herman 2003; Volkel Krtozsch, Vrandecic, Haller, & Studer, 2006).

However a serious obstacle for the development of Semantic Web applications is the lack of formal ontologies and knowledge. Indeed, one of the main reasons of this is the rather high technical barrier for using Semantic Web technologies that deters many domain experts from formalizing their knowledge.

In another hand, wiki systems are becoming more and more popular as tools for content and information management. Much information is nowadays available in systems like Wikipedia. Unfortunately, this vast information is not accessible for machines. If a small amount of this information would be formalized to become knowledge, wiki systems could provide improved interfaces and advanced searching and navigation facilities.

Nevertheless, several analyses (Buffa, 2006; Majchrzac, Wagner, & Yates, 2006) of traditional wikis as shown that they are not enough structured, and it's difficult to navigate and to find the relevant information. Besides, the wiki markup language (WikiML) used by most wiki engines makes internet users reluctant to contribute to the wiki.

One solution to perform the knowledge creation, evaluation and navigation inside wikis is to use technologies from the Semantic Web (Aumueller & Auer, 2005) which use the languages like OWL, RDFS and query languages like RDL, SPARQL or annotation languages like RDF to formalized information, content, structures and links in the wiki pages. These Wikis would take consideration of the semantic in their content management and become Semantic Wikis.

"Semantic Wiki" systems aim to combine "traditional" wiki systems with Semantic Technology. This combination bears much potential in many application areas.

Thus we propose to use a Semantic Knowledge Wiki approach to complete our knowledge management system by facilitating the knowledge sharing, updating and evaluation. This article is structured as follows: Section 1 introduces the Semantic Knowledge Wiki concept and describes features which represent advantages for the knowledge management; Section 2 briefly describes the architecture of our Wiki; Section 3 presents a simple application scenario to exploit knowledge and to represent it; Section 4 concludes with some perspectives.

2. WHY USING A SEMANTIC WIKI ON A KM APPROACH

We have developed a Knowledge Management System called StarDesign (Fischer, Gantner, Rendle, Stritt, & Thieme, 2006) allowing capitalizing Knowledge from information shared and used by business actors all along their engineering projects (Figure 1). We use a social and cooperative approach in identifying knowledge needed to be capitalized and reused inside the collaboration between actors in project teams. Indeed the study of the business actors' roles allows getting an organizational model (called OrgaDesign) leading the knowledge capitalization inside professional activities and the knowledge reuse.

From this knowledge identification we have proposed a knowledge typology with six types (Project Context, Project Evolution, Project Vocabulary, Project Process, Project Rule and Project Experience). This knowledge typology is a result of a collaboration work with several companies (Djaiz, Monticolo, & Matta, 2008) where project teams have determinate the information they want to capitalize and to reuse all along a project. Thus this typology defines the structure of a project memory.

This work is completed by the definition of a vocabulary and a semantic i.e. a domain ontology. This ontology (called OntoDesign) (Monticolo, 2007) allows to the knowledge management system to structure the knowledge according to the project memory model and to exploit knowledge in line with the actors' needs. This ontology contains the description of the crucial knowledge identified by several project teams, and which have to be capitalized to buid a project memory.

Figure 1. StarDesign: A knowledge management approach

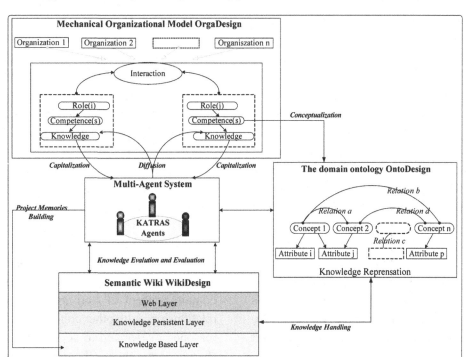

The Knowledge Management System is animated by a Multi Agent System called KATRAS (Monticolo, Hilaire, Koukam, & Gomes, 2008) capables to lead the knowledge management through the 3 components presented below (OrgaDesign and OntoDesign). Agents are used to manage heterogeneous and distributed information. Moreover they perceive the social structure inside projects with the organizational model. Thus they are able to:

- Identify knowledge to capitalize during the professional activities thanks to OrgaDesign;
- Ensure an aided knowledge capitalization all along engineering projects;
- Anticipate knowledge requirements according to the professional roles inside activities.

Therefore the Knowledge Management System create Project Memories where are stored relevant information of a project. This memory is built according to the ontology and is consultable by the business actors.

StarDesign is used since two years in companies but we have observed that the lack of this Knowledge Management System is that business actors can read project memories (in html or pdf format) but are not able to modify it. Indeed the system is capable to capture new knowledge during project but not allow the creation of new knowledge from information already stored in project memories. So we have to think about a system which helps business actors to evaluate, to make evolution or delete knowledge stored from past or current projects. This system will ensure the knowledge evolution in the KM approach.

Thus we propose to use a Semantic Wiki to complete our Knowledge Management Approach in allowing the knowledge evolution. This Wiki is used by the business actors i.e. the engineers who work on a project. Thus, these actors can consult the knowledge capatilized in past projects and update the knowledge based.

The next section describes the Semantic Wiki Architecture called WikiDesign.

3. WIKIDESIGN ARCHITECTURE

In this section we detail the architecture of WikiDesign with three layers (Figure 2): Web Layer, Knowledge Persistent Layer and the Knowledge Base Layer. Each layer communicates with the others through a RDF flow making easy the knowledge diffusion.

3.2. The Knowledge Persistent Layer

The Knowledge Persistent Layer is based on the domain ontology OntoDesign which define a vocabulary and a semantic of the knowledge used in engineering projects. Up to now this layer accept a unique ontology "OntoDesign". In a future work we will consider the addition of external ontologies. OntoDesign is developed in OWL-DL. This language is based on Description Logics (hence the suffix DL). Description Logics are a decidable fragment of First Order Logic and are therefore amenable to automated reasoning. It is therefore possible to automatically compute the classification hierarchy and check for inconsistencies in an ontology that conforms to OWL-DL.

Consequently, OntoDesign provides an integrated conceptual model for sharing information related to a mechanical design project. An OWL property is a binary relation to relate an OWL Class (Concept in OntoDesign) to another one, or to RDF literals and XML Schema datatypes. For example, the "infoInput" property relates the Document class to the Activity class. Described by these formal, explicit and rich semantics, the domain concept of Activity, its properties and relationships with other concepts can be queried, reasoned or mapped to support the Knowledge sharing across the mechanical design projects.

Figure 2. WikiDesign architecture

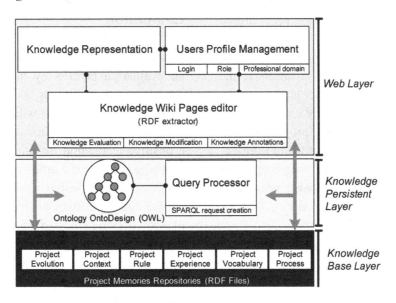

The Knowledge Persistent Layer is also composed by a Query Processor which allows formulating queries to exploit the knowledge based according to the structure of the ontology. The Query Processor builds queries with the SPARQL language (Seaborne & Prud'hommeaux, 2006) in order to exploit the RDF files which composed the knowledge base. We will describe the query process in section 3.

3.3. The Web Layer

WikiDesign allows to relaying semantic tags and navigating functionalities in the wikipages. We have seen that the Knowledge Persistent Layer is composed by a domain ontology OntoDesign which defined a vocabulary and a semantic of the knowledge used in engineering projects. Thanks to the relations in the ontology, WikiDesign is able to automatically tagging keywords in the wikipages. Thus these tags provide to the users, not only a link to wikipages defining the term associated to the tag but also a links to the six types of knowledge associated to this term. Figure 3 shows three knowledge links (Project process, Project Experience and Project Rule) related to the term "hood".

In addition WikiDesign has a Knowledge Wiki Pages editor. A wikipage creator chooses a type of knowledge to classify this article. Each created page is automatically annotated according to its knowledge type. Thus a wikipage is annotated "Project Vocabulary" for the definition of a term or the "Project Process" for the description of a process.

When the wikipage creator has chosen the knowledge type, the Knowledge Wiki Page editor proposes a structuring of the article according to the concepts and sub concepts of the ontology. For example an article describing a project experience is organizing with the tags "Failure, Success or Difficulty", "Description", "cause", "led actions", "consequences", "recommendation".

Figure 3. Example of Knowledge Links from a Term in WikiDesign

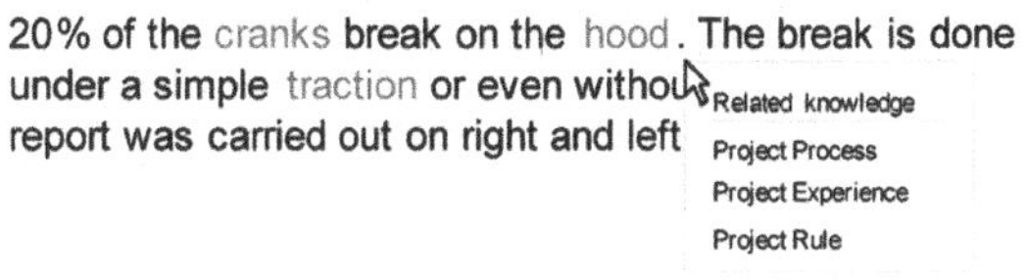

20% of the cranks break on the hood. The break is done under a simple traction or even without. Related knowledge report was carried out on right and left   Project Process
                                                                                Project Experience
                                                                                Project Rule

The structure and the content of the wikipages allow creating the knowledge base according to OntoDesign.

The Web Layer has also a Users Profile Management module where user can create and refine their profile. To be a creator user has to create a new profile. In this profile they can define the different roles they have in a project or their professional domains. According to this information, WikiDesign proposes to a user, when he is connected, a selection of wikipages created by other users and related to his profile.

3.4. Interface

WikiDesign uses a browser based interface. A search page view is shown in Figure 4. From keywords the users request the knowledge base. The users have the possibility in this interface to orient their search by knowledge types or projects. The list of articles (wikipages) is generated in the same page. Each result corresponds to a wikipage and has a evaluation according to its maturity (number of stars describing the number of evaluations) and its percent of positive evaluation.

3.5. Collaborative Knowledge Evaluation

Inside WikiDesign, knowledge is subjected to an evaluation process by the business actors. An actor can modify or accept an article i.e. knowledge related to the wikipage. Thus, when a user approves or modifies an article, he assigns a positive evaluation for this article. Moreover when he refuses, the article obtains a negative evaluation. WikiDesign allows calculating the knowledge maturity by positioning a percentage of positive evaluation and a number of stars. Thus knowledge which has just been created has one hundred percent of positive evaluation. Progressively with the evaluations attributed by users, the percentage can decrease if the article obtains negative evaluations. In addition knowledge which has a score in lower than twenty five percent of positive evaluation, it is deleted in the knowledge base. Indeed the system is able to automatically delete knowledge which is become obsolete or is not a consensus inside the community of experts. Thus the knowledge evaluation ensures the reliability of the shared information in the company.

Figure 4. WikiDesign Interface

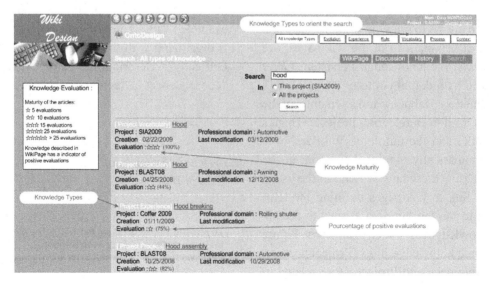

4. EXPLOITING SEMANTICS AND KNOWLEDGE REPRESENTATION

4.1. Browsing

There are two types of Wikis users; the readers and the creators. The first one use the elements stored in the knowledge base to search pertinent information and the second one creates new wikipages.

The readers have access to the knowledge of a project or from several projects. The knowledge representation is structured according to the six different knowledge types. A reader uses a keyword to apply a research. He has the possibility to choose answers from knowledge stored in the current project or for all the projects. The navigation in WikiDesign is made by a click on a term which takes along the reader to the wikipage related to this term (knowledge of the type Project Vocabulary). The other way to navigate in WikiDesign is to use a right click on a term which presents the knowledge types related to the term. Each associated knowledge type leads to one or several wikipages. For example in Figure 2, we have a knowledge type 'Project Experience' related to the term 'Hood' and this type leads to four wikipages describing four project experiences implying a hood.

4.2. Querying

As shown in Figure 1, WikiDesign has a semantic search engine for querying and reasoning on the knowledge base. This query processor used the Jena API. Jena allows loading ontological models in OWL or RDFS format and manages the SPARQL language. SPARQL may become a W3C recommendation to query RDF. It is based on a boolean combination of triples that can be constrained by evaluable expressions. It is also processes datatyped RDF literals, optional properties, alternatives and the named graph scheme of SPARQL using a source statement. It returns an RDF/XML graph or an XML binding format. The bindings are available through an API. SPARQL provides the select, distinct, sort and an equivalent of limit statements.

The Knowledge Persistent Layer module allows building queries according to the keywords posted by the wiki readers. The readers can oriented his requests on the knowledge stored in the current project or in all the projects. Figure 5 describes a classical query to research knowledge associated to the keyword "Hood" in the current project "SIA".

The readers have the possibility to refine their requests according to the names of the projects, the roles of the business actors or the knowledge types.

5. WIKIDESIGN FUNCTIONALITIES

All the knowledge inside the wikipages of WikiDesign is annotated in RDF according to the ontology OntoDesign. These annotations bring information about the type of knowledge, the authors or the project. Thus the ontology makes the inherent

Figure 5. Example of request generated by the knowledge persistent layer

```
PREFIX OntoDesign: <http://acsp.utbm.fr/OntoDesign.owl>
SELECT xml?Vocabulary, ?Experience, ?Rule, ?Process, ?Context, ?Evolution
WHERE
{ ?Terme  rdf:Type OntoDesign:Vocabulary "Hood"
            Union
   ?Projet  rdf:Type OntoDesign:Projet "SIA"
}
```

structure of the wiki. Moreover the annotations facilitate the navigation between wikipages thanks to the links defined in the ontology. We describe in this section the advantages of WikiDesign.

5.1. Typing/Annotating of Links

Like we have seen below, WikiDesign allows annotating links by giving them certain types defined in the ontology OntoDesign. Thus a link created by a user almost always carries meaning beyond mere navigation. WikiDesign manages annotations in its Web Layer. Each WikiPage is annotated as soon as a user (creator) as defined the content related to a knowledge type.

5.2. Context Aware Presentation

WikiDesign can change the way content is presented based on semantic annotations. This includes enriching pages by displaying of semantically related pages in a separate link box, displaying of information that can be derived from the underlying knowledge base. Thus a wikipage defining a professional term i.e. knowledge related to the type 'Project Vocabulary' is automatically associated to others wikipages corresponding to others knowledge types (Project Experience, Project Process, ProjectContext, ProjectRule, ProjectTerm, ProjectEvolution). For example the wikipage defining the term 'Hood' is automatically associated to wikipages describing the experiences associated to a hood. These relations are deduced from the ontology.

5.3. Enhanced Navigation

Knowledge types facilitate annotated links and provide more information for navigation. Whereas a traditional wiki only allows following a link, WikiDesign offers additional information about the relation the link describes.

For example WikiDesign propose to the creator of the wikipages to define the semantic links with the relation defined in the ontology. For example a wikipage about a assembly process of a hood can have some links categorised by "has synonymous" or "has design rule".

Such information can be used to offer additional or more efficient navigation.

5.4. Semantic Search

WikiDesign allows a "semantic search" on the underlying RDF knowledge base. As described above, queries are expressed in the language SPARQL, a query language recently proposed as W3C recommendation for RDF querying. Using "semantic search", users can ask queries like "retrieve all component composed a hood" or "retrieve all Processes and experiences associated to a hood".

5.5. Reasoning Support

Reasoning means deriving additional, implicit knowledge from the facts entered into the system using predefined or userdefined rules in the knowledge base. For example, from the fact that "a hood" is a part of a "rolling shutter", WikiDesign is capable of reasoning and could deduce that "hood" is a "Component" of the assembly processes of a rulling shutter. Reasoning is an important feature which helps readers to understand the links between knowledge in the wikipages.

6. PERFORMANCE ASSESSMENT

6.1. Adhesion of the Business Actors

Since 2002 the managers of the Zurfluh-Feller company have tried to set up a knowledge management program. The first tool to share and reuse information was a document management platform, giving access to project information and the ability to easily structure and share content in using repertories by professional fields. In each repertory, actors were able to add comments corresponding to a document. The comments explain the origin of the document (authors, aims) After several projects engineers don't take time to put and arrange documents of their projects and the majority of the comments were empty. After several debates with the business actors, we have concluded that they don't use this system because they were sure that the documents and their comments were not read by others. Indeed the system doesn't give them a feedback or an interaction with the others. In conclusion the system didn't allow managing information in a collaborative way.

After using our knowledge management system (Star Design with WikiDesign) since almost two years and during several projects, the project teams explain that this new system has two advantages:

- The capability to capitalize knowledge in semi-automatic way (thanks to the multi-agent system of StarDesign) and to make reusable it in a easy way (thanks to a research based on the six knowledge types) inside WiIkiDesign;
- The possibility to make evolve knowledge in collaborative way, inside the wiki, by interacting with all the experts of the company.

In exploiting the indicators of WikiDesign (number of connected people) and after a survey in the Research and Development department of the company (42 engineers and technicians) we have observed that 96% of the business actors take time to research information in WikiDesign and 82% use to create or modify articles.

In the case of the SIA2009 project (Figure 6), we have noted that 56 articles was created automatically in WikiDesign by the software agents. Among these 56 pages, 28 were evaluated and\ or modified to enrich the information by business actors and 17 new articles were posted for this project.

7. RELATED SEMANTIC WIKIS

Since 2004 with the development of *Platypus* Wiki (Campanini Castagna, & Tazzoli 2004), many semantic wikis have been created (Rhizonne Wiki, SweetWiki, MaknaWiki (Dello, Paslaru, Simperl, & Tolksdorf, 2006), IkeWiki (Schaffert, 2006), OntoWiki (Aumueller & Auer, 2005), Shawn, Rise (Decker, Ras, Rech, Klein, & Hoecht, 2005), Semantic MediaWiki (Krotsch, Vrandecic, Volkel, Haller, &, Studer, 2007), WikSar provide the capability to edit RDF content like WikiDesign. All the semantic wikis quoted above are built according

Figure 6. Performance indicators for WikiDesign

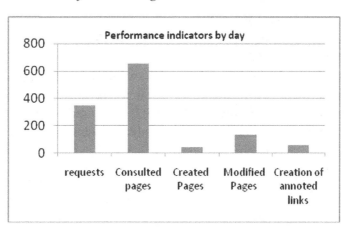

151

to the "wikitology" model i.e. they consider wiki pages as concepts and typed links (in the page content). In these approaches the architecture of the wiki composed the ontology.

All the semantic wikis quoted above aim to manage and to create new Information in using semantic links to facilitate the navigation inside the wiki. WikiDesign brings the innovation in proposing a Knowledge Management approach with broadcasting the Knowledge capitalized in the knowledge based and by diffusing the knowledge indicators (maturity, evaluation, type).

Moreover, WikiDesign was designed differently comparing to the others existing semantic wikis. It use a ontology to the editing of page content and metadata as well as page tagging like only SweetWiki and IkeWiki make it. Nevertheless, differently of these two semantic wikis, WikiDesign was created to be complementary to a knowledge management system and to facilitate the evaluation and the creation of new knowledge from existing project memories. WikiDesign uses a domain ontology (OntoDesign) to edit its pages. Indeed each wiki page is editing according to the relation defined in the ontology. Moreover WikiDesign provides a navigation between its pages in proposing tags (Figure 3) according to the knowledge typology described in OntoDesign.

WikiDesign also provide a framework based on the Jena Api to manage the OWL ontology language and a system uses a reasoning engine in its knowledge persistent layer (Figure 2). Even if WikiDesign does not employ a complete OWL reasoner, it provides partial reasoning support to structure wiki content and to browse data. Finally, semantic WikiDesign appears to be the only wiki which proposes a knowledge evaluation to users to ensure the reliability of the information content. Moreover WikiDesign are associated to a knowledge management system to enrich and initialize its knowledge base.

8. PERSPECTIVES AND CONCLUSION

In this article, we have presented WikiDesign, a feature rich semantic wiki system which complete our knowledge management approach by evaluating and creating new knowledge with pertinent links.

The StarDesign knowledge management approach with WikiDesign is currently used in several engineering design departments in different companies. This approach gives good results because business actors appreciate to use WikiDesign to share information. WikiDesign seems to provide a good framework to evaluate and to create knowledge in an easy way.

Now, future directions for the evolution of WikiDesign might be to provide more support to knowledge creation in using several ontologies. The system has to provide support for inferencing or ontology import i.e. it has to allow users to import data from external ontologies and exploits schema data to provide editing support.

Another work will be to map the competences of the business actors in the ontology to give the possibility to find a knowledge item according to a skill in WikiDesign.

We are currently working on how to merge several domain ontologies to propose more possibilities to create semantic links or to perform the semantic search engine of WikiDesign.

ACKNOWLEDGMENT

We would like to thank all the engineers of the research department of the Zurfluh Feller Company (SOMFY Corporation). Their uses of WikiDesign and their reviews, comments and suggestions have helped us to improve our system.

REFERENCES

Auer, S., Dietzold, S., & Riechert, T. (2006). OntoWiki—a tool for social, semantic collaboration. In *Proceedings of the 5th International Semantic Web Conference*, Toronto, ON, Canada (pp. 18-23).

Aumueller, D. (2005). SHAWN: Structure helps a wiki navigate. In *Proceedings of the BTW-Workshop WebDB Meets IR*, Karlsruhe, Germany (pp. 23-36).

Aumueller, D., & Auer, S. (2005). Towards a semantic wiki experience, desktop integration and interactivity in WikSAR. In *Proceedings of the Workshop on Semantic Desktop*, Galway, Ireland (pp. 10-21).

Berners-Lee, T., Hendler, J., & Lassila, O. (2001). The semantic web. *Scientific American*, 35–43.

Buffa, M. (2006), Intranet wikis. In *Proceedings of the Intraweb 15th International Conference on World Wide Web*, Edinburgh, UK (pp. 231-251).

Buffa, M., Gandon, F., Ereteo, G., Sander, P., & Faron, C. (2008). SweetWiki: A semantic wiki. *Journal of Web Semantics*, 6(1), 84–97. doi:10.1016/j.websem.2007.11.003

Campanini, S. E., Castagna, P., & Tazzoli, R. (2004). Platypus wiki: A semantic wiki wiki web. In *Proceedings of 1st Italian Semantic Web Workshop on Semantic Web Applications and Perspectives*, Freiburg, Germany (pp. 105-121).

Decker, B., Ras, E., Rech, J., Klein, B., & Hoecht, C. (2005). Self-organized reuse of software engineering knowledge supported by semantic wikis. In *Proceedings of the Workshop on Semantic Web Enabled Software Engineering*, Galway, Ireland (pp. 65-78).

Dello, K., Paslaru, E., Simperl, B., & Tolksdorf, R. (2006). Creating and using Semantic Web information with Makna. In *Proceedings of the First Workshop on Semantic Wikis: From Wiki to Semantics*, Budva, Montenegro (pp. 313-352).

Djaiz, C., Monticolo, D., & Matta, N. (2008). Project memory decision making. *International Journal of e-Collaboration on Creativity, Innovation and e-Collaboration, 2*, 12-28.

Fischer, J., Gantner, Z., Rendle, S., Stritt, M., & Thieme, T. (2006). Ideas and improvements for semantic wikis. In Y. Sure & J. Domingue (Eds.), *Proceedings of the 3rd European Semantic Web Conference on the Semantic Web: Research and Applications* (LNCS 4011, pp. 650-663).

Ignat, G. L., Oster, G., Molli, P., Cart, M., Ferrie, J., Kermarrec, A.-M., et al. (2007). A comparison of optimistic approaches to collaborative editing of wiki pages. In *Proceedings of the International Conference on Collaborative Computing: Networking, Applications and Worksharing*, New York, NY (pp. 10-15).

Krotsch, M., Vrandecic, D., & Volkel, M. (2005). Wikipedia and the Semantic Web—the missing links. *WikiMania Journal*, 53-65.

Krotzsch, M., Vrandecic, V., Volkel, M., Haller, H., & Studer, R. (2007). Semantic Wikipedia. *Journal of Web Semantics: Science. Services and Agents on World Wide Web, 5*, 251–261. doi:10.1016/j.websem.2007.09.001

Leuf, B., & Cunningham, W. (2001). *The Wiki way: Quick collaboration on the Web* (pp. 45–59). Reading, MA: Addison-Wesley.

Majchrzac, A., Wagner, C., & Yates, D. (2006). Corporate wiki users: Results of a survey. In *Proceedings of the ACM International Symposium on Wikis*, Odense, Denmark (pp. 452-476).

Malone, T. W., Crowston, K., & Herman, G. A. (2003). *Organizing business knowledge: The MIT process handbook* (pp. 23–36). Cambridge, MA: MIT Press.

Monticolo, D., Hilaire, V., Gomes, S., & Koukam, A. (2008). A multi agents systems for building project memories to facilitate design process. *International Journal in Integrated Computer Aided Engineering, 15*(1), 3–20.

Monticolo, D., Hilaire, V., Koukam, A., & Gomes, S. (2007). OntoDesign: A domain ontology for building and exploiting project memories in product design projects. In *Proceeding of the 2nd International Conference in Knowledge Management in Organizations*, Lecce, Italy (pp. 34-47).

Richards, D. (2009). A social software/Web2.0 approach to collaborative knowledge engineering. *International Journal of Information Sciences, 5*, 34–42.

Schaffert, S. (2006). IkeWiki: A semantic wiki for collaborative knowledge management. In *Proceedings of the 1st International Workshop on Semantic Technologies in Collaborative Applications*, Stanford, CA (pp. 34-45).

Seaborne, A., & Prud'hommeaux, E. (2006). *SPARQL query language for RDF.* Retrieved from http://www.w3.org/TR/2006/CR-rdf-sparql-query-20060406/

Singh, A. V., Wombacher, A., & Aberer, K. (2007). Personalized information access in a wiki using structured tagging. In *Proceedings of the Workshop On the Move to Meaningful Internet Systems*, Toronto, ON, Canada (pp. 427-436).

Souzy, A. (2005). Building a semantic wiki. *IEEE Intelligent Systems, 20*, 87–91. doi:10.1109/MIS.2005.83

Volkel, M., Krtozsch, M., Vrandecic, D., Haller, H., & Studer, R. (2006). Semantic wikipedia. In *Proceedings of the 15th International Conference on World Wide Web*, New York, NY (pp. 54-67).

Vrandecic, D., & Krötzsch, M. (2006). Reusing ontological background knowledge in semantic wikis. In *Proceedings of the First Workshop on Semantic Wiki: From Wikis to Semantics*, Nice, France (pp. 162-174).

This work was previously published in the International Journal of e-Collaboration, Volume 7, Issue 3, edited by Ned Kock, pp. 31-42, copyright 2011 by IGI Publishing (an imprint of IGI Global).

Chapter 11
Industry Perspective–Collaborating from a Distance:
Success Factors of Top-Performing Virtual Teams

Darleen DeRosa
OnPoint Consulting, USA

ABSTRACT

Rising travel costs, coupled with the global dispersion of talent, are two of the reasons that organizations have migrated toward virtual teamwork. While numerous organizations have made significant investments in virtual teams and the technology to support them, a surprising number of virtual teams are not reaching their full potential. A new study conducted by OnPoint surveyed 48 virtual teams across industries and found that there are specific practices that are the key ingredients for optimal virtual team performance. If organizations want to maximize their return on investment, they should ensure that these core practices are in place and continually assess the performance of their virtual teams against these factors over time.

A lot of organizations create virtual teams with almost no understanding of the unique implications of that decision. Margaret A. Neale, Professor, Stanford Graduate School of Business

INTRODUCTION

Rising travel costs, global dispersion of talent, and advances in technology are some of the reasons organizations have migrated toward virtual teams whose members must collaborate from a distance. While numerous organizations have made significant investments in virtual teams (sometimes

DOI: 10.4018/978-1-4666-2020-9.ch011

referred to as geographically dispersed teams) and the technology to support them, a surprising number of these teams are not reaching their full potential.

While there are numerous books and articles about best practices in virtual teamwork, many are not research-based and there are opportunities to further develop targeted recommendations for virtual teams. To address this problem, a new study conducted by OnPoint surveyed 48 virtual teams across industries to identify specific practices associated with the most successful virtual teams. The focus of this study was not to compare face-to-face teams with virtual teams but to understand what factors differentiate high-performing virtual teams so companies can implement high-impact strategies to make virtual teams more productive.

This report highlights the factors that are associated with increased virtual team effectiveness by focusing on the success profile of virtual teams, the key differentiators of virtual team performance, and performance enhancers that teams might leverage.

Study Methodology

For the purposes of this research we defined a virtual team as one that has between three and 35 members who are geographically dispersed (i.e., at least 1/3 of team members work in different locations) but have to collaborate with one another to achieve results.

Forty-eight virtual teams from 16 organizations spanning a variety of industries participated in the study. The following companies participated in the study and are included in the findings:

- American Heart Association
- Barclays Global Investors
- Deloitte
- HSBC
- Kraft
- Merck
- New York Life

- Oppenheimer Funds
- Saint-Gobain
- Schering-Plough
- State Street Investments
- Source Refrigeration
- Sun Microsystems
- TTC Group
- Vail Resorts
- Verizon Wireless

The primary method of data collection was a virtual team inventory that was administered to 427 team members and leaders between May and August 2008. In addition, third party data were collected from 99 key stakeholders (individuals who are very familiar with the teams such as internal customers or the team leader's manager) to objectively assess team performance. Finally, we conducted 45 telephone interviews with team members and team leaders to better understand their experiences and challenges.

The online virtual team inventory assessed six dimensions of virtual team performance, including: Results, Communication, Team Motivation, Interpersonal Relationships, Collaboration, and Purpose & Roles. The overall reliability of the virtual team inventory was very high ($\alpha = .95$). The team performance assessment, completed by stakeholders, contained selected items from the team assessment primarily focused on outcomes, including an overall assessment of team and leader effectiveness.

Team Demographics

Team size and tenure varied:

- The majority of teams (52%) had six to 12 members. One quarter of teams had 13 to 20 members, suggesting that team size was relatively large overall.
- Just under half of those studied had been working together for one to three years,

whereas roughly the same percentage of teams had less than one year of tenure.

- Nearly half of team members reported being on only one virtual team, another third reporting being on two or three virtual teams and the remaining team members were on more than three virtual teams.
- About half of the teams participating were cross-functional in nature.

Team members reported meeting frequently but meetings appeared to be phone-based rather than face-to-face and they did not consistently leverage collaborative tools or video conferencing:

- Half of team members reported meeting once a week or more often, while another 18% met several times a month; the remaining teams met once per month or less frequently.
- The vast majority of team members felt they had the proper technology to work together; however, most relied frequently on email and the telephone.
- Forty-three percent of team members reported meeting face-to-face only once or twice a year. Approximately 20% reported never having a face-to-face meeting.

Criteria for Identifying Top-Performing Teams

In order to identify differences between high- and lower-performing teams, we used the following approach to objectively define team performance and develop a Performance Index by classifying teams as Highly Effective, Effective, and Less Effective:

1. Team members, leaders, and stakeholders were asked to rate overall team effectiveness. For each team, ratings were averaged to produce one score representing overall team effectiveness. This overall average is a more representative measure of effectiveness than any one data point because preliminary

analyses suggested that team leader data were somewhat inflated and stakeholder data were inconsistent across teams.

2. To create a more robust measure of performance for each team, the overall average of the Team Results Dimension (Figure 1) were combined with the overall team effectiveness score to assess each team on specific outcomes related to performance. Regression analysis showed that the items in the Team Results Dimension were most predictive of overall performance which supported this approach.

3. Based on these data points, a Performance Index was created, and all 48 teams were classified into three groups according to their level of effectiveness. Figure 2 illustrates the overall performance differences (which were statistically significant) between less effective, moderately effective, and highly effective teams:

Key Challenges Facing Virtual Teams

We asked team members and team leaders to select the top three challenges that hinder their teams' performance shown in Table 1:

All of the teams in the study, regardless of performance, reported the lack of face-to-face contact, a lack of resources, and time zone differences as top challenges. A higher percentage of team members on lower-performing teams reported an additional challenge—team members are on too many virtual teams.

There were several challenges that were consistently mentioned in the interviews as well as those that were observed anecdotally:

- Surprisingly, team members, and in some cases team leaders, lacked clarity about who was on the team and the size of the team. This may be attributed to the fact that many people are often invited to par-

Figure 1. Team results dimension

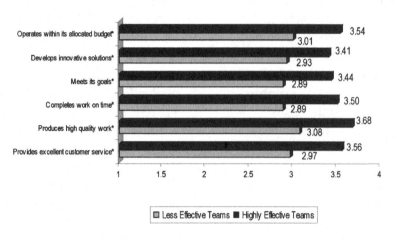

Figure 2. Overall performance differences

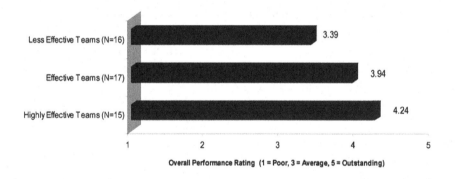

ticipate on a team, even though they may not have a clear role. As such, this leads to having very large virtual teams that may not be effective. Moreover, the membership of some of the teams changed quite frequently, which made it difficult for team members to communicate effectively and build relationships.

• In addition, in numerous instances, there was ambiguity over who led the team, which was also a surprising finding. As previously discussed, this may also be attributed to the large team size and frequency of team membership changes.

As noted above, 20% of team members and team leaders selected lack of skill training as a specific challenge faced by virtual teams. When asked what skill development was needed, team members cited communication/interpersonal skills and collaboration as the top need. Other areas identified most frequently as development needs are listed in Table 2:

The Bottom Line

With multiple demands for resources, limited time, and the lack of face-to-face contact, skill building can decrease the time required for teams to begin performing at their maximum level of effectiveness.

Table 1. Top Challenges from each team

Challenges	Percentage of Responses
Lack of face-to-face contact with team members	46%
Lack of resources	37%
Time zone differences hinder our ability to collaborate	29%
Team members are on more than one team and cannot devote enough time to the team	27%
Team members do not share relevant information with one another	21%
Lack of skill training	20%

THE PROFILE OF TOP-PERFORMING VIRTUAL TEAMS

Based on the research findings, higher-performing teams were profiled to determine what factors differentiate them from teams that were less effective.

Team Composition

- **Stable and consistent team membership:** With less frequent changes in team membership, high-performing teams had greater stability and more time for members to focus on building lasting relationships.
- **Fewer team members:** Teams that were less effective were disproportionately larger such that 37% had 13 or more members compared to 24% for top-performing teams.
- **Members are from the same function:** Fewer high-performing teams were cross-functional, whereas the majority of lower-performing teams were cross-functional. This suggests that cross-functional teams may face unique challenges and greater levels of complexity that inhibit performance in a virtual environment.
- **Members are on fewer teams:** A greater number of team members (42%) on lower-performing teams reported team members'

lack of time due to participating on multiple teams as a key challenge.
- **Members have longer tenure:** Teams with more than three years tenure performed better than those with shorter tenure which suggests that they have been able to improve many of their communication and execution practices.

Communication and Training

- **Face-to-face kick off meeting:** Teams who held an in person initial meeting achieved better performance than those who never met face-to-face. The results indicate that holding the initial meeting within the first 90 days is associated with enhanced team effectiveness.
- **More frequent meetings:** Sixty-three percent of higher-performing teams met at least once a week, compared to 29% of the less effective teams. Interestingly, higher-performing teams also cite communication as a top training need despite their effectiveness, demonstrating their commitment to continuous improvement in this area.
- **Leverage technology:** Members of higher-performing teams were more likely to report that they had the proper technology to facilitate working together effectively. Higher-performing teams also reported us-

Table 2. Identified areas of skill development needs

Skill Development Area	Percentage of Responses
Communication and Interpersonal Skills	45%
Collaboration	42%
Action Planning	35%
Problem Solving	28%
Decision Making	27%
Managing Change	27%

ing video conferencing slightly more often than their counterparts.

- **Provide skill training:** Our results indicated that teams who had more than four training or skill development sessions performed significantly better than those who had one or fewer sessions.

Leadership

- **Team leaders who are able to lead from a distance:** Although leaders of high-performing teams reported facing challenges such as a lack of resources and time to focus on leading the team, they compensate well. They appear to struggle less with building collaboration virtually, which was a key challenge reported by the lower-performing teams.

- **Have more members reporting directly to the team leader:** Leaders of higher-performing teams often had direct reporting relationships with their team members. This facilitates communication, increases the likelihood of team members having shared goals and clear roles and enhances

the ability of the leader to follow through and hold people accountable.

The Bottom Line

Organizations should be more deliberate when forming virtual teams by considering team composition, communication and training needs, as well as the characteristics required for the leader to successfully manage from a distance.

BENCHMARKS OF HIGHLY EFFECTIVE TEAMS

Dimensions and item level benchmarks are provided in Figure 3 which compare the 15 highest-performing teams to the 16 lower-performing teams. Differences on all dimensions were statistically significant, which means that high-performing teams scored significantly higher than lower-performing teams. On a four point scale with 1 being strongly disagree and 4 strongly agree, Team Motivation was the highest-rated dimension followed by Interpersonal Relationships

High-performing teams proactively communicate with one another (Figure 4), sharing infor-

Figure 3. Dimensions of the 15 highest-performing teams and the 16 lowest-performing teams

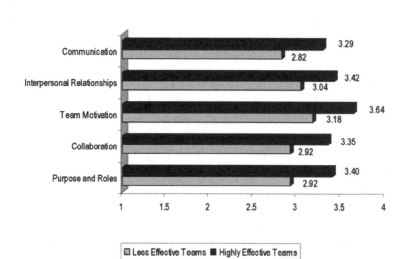

mation and responding quickly when problems arise (asterisks indicate items that were statistically different between highly effective and less effective teams).

A well defined purpose and clear roles differentiates high-performing virtual teams (Figure 5). Less effective virtual teams are less likely to have these elements in place

Interpersonal Relationships (Figure 6) was one of the highest-scoring dimensions for the most effective virtual teams. Higher-performing teams trust one another to get work done and work effectively with team members from other cultures.

Collaboration (Figure 7), evidenced by team members' willingness to help one another achieve goals and the ability to work together effectively, was characteristic of high-performing virtual teams.

Motivation (Figure 8) was the top scoring dimension among the higher-performing virtual teams. Members on these teams report that they are willing to put in extra effort and demonstrated initiative.

VIRTUAL TEAM DIFFERENTIATORS

We identified nine practices that differentiate the highest- and lowest-performing virtual teams which, in our opinion, make these the most important ingredients for optimal team performance.

1. **Demonstrate a high level of initiative:** Members of high-performing virtual teams seem to be more proactive and engaged and they demonstrate high levels of initiative. High-performing virtual teams place greater emphasis on role clarity and are motivated by team success.

2. **Willing to assume leadership responsibility:** Even though the majority of virtual teams had dedicated team leaders, team members on high-performing virtual teams proactively took on leadership responsibilities as required. In contrast, less effective virtual teams were less likely to do this.

3. **Shared process for decision making and problem solving:** While this may seem like a fundamental practice, higher-performing virtual teams had more established processes to facilitate decision making. Effective vir-

Figure 4. Comparison of team communication

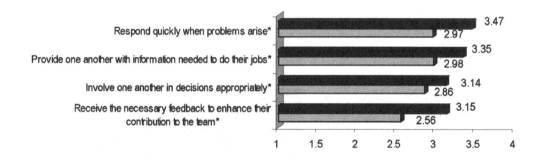

Figure 5. Comparison of purpose and roles

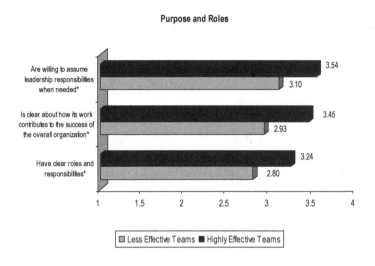

Figure 6. Comparison of interpersonal relationships

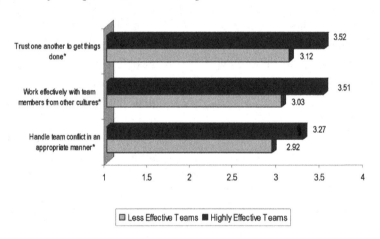

Figure 7. Comparison of team collaboration

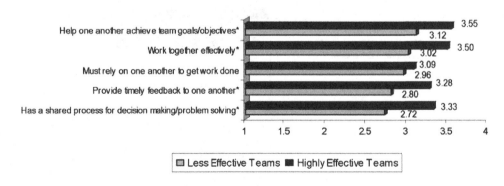

Figure 8. Comparison of team motivation

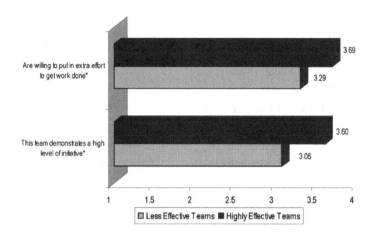

tual team leaders ensure that communication processes are established early on and revisit them over time.

4. **Clarity about how their work contributes to the success of the organization:** High-performing virtual teams have an understanding of how their work aligns with the strategy of their organization. This is extremely important in a virtual environment where it is easy for team members to become disengaged.

5. **Provide timely feedback to one another:** Communication challenges are more pronounced in virtual teams, especially when there is a lack of face-to-face contact and time zone differences. However, high-performing virtual teams are able to overcome these communication challenges.

6. **Trust one another to get things done:** Trust is a top factor for virtual team success, but task-based trust (a belief that team members will do their job) is especially important in a virtual setting. Specifically, trust builds when virtual team members follow through on commitments and take accountability for results.

7. **Willing to put in extra effort to get things done:** Members of high-performing virtual teams were willing to go above and beyond what is required to accomplish team goals. Effective virtual team leaders inspire team members and regularly monitor members' level of motivation.

8. **Work together effectively:** Successful virtual teams have determined how to collaborate effectively and work together to achieve their collective goals.

9. **Help one another achieve team goals:** In high-performing virtual teams, team members support each other in goal achievement rather than independently executing tasks and objectives.

VIRTUAL TEAM PERFORMANCE ENHANCERS

Nearly all of the virtual team survey items differentiated teams along the performance continuum. However, the team practices had a greater impact on enhancing team effectiveness depending on the team's current level of performance (Figure 9).

Our research showed that lower-performing teams should focus on communication, responding to problems, feedback, information sharing, working with people of different cultures, and having clear roles/responsibilities. These practices most differentiated the effective teams when compared to those that had a lower level of performance. In contrast, once teams have achieved a moderate level of effectiveness, focusing on managing conflict is likely to enable them to reach the next level of performance.

The Bottom Line

To compensate for the lack of face-to-face contact, successful virtual teams emphasize the interpersonal dynamics of virtual collaboration and set up practices to build trust, increase transparency, and help build interpersonal relationships.

SUMMARY AND RECOMMENDATIONS

Developing High-performing Virtual Teams: Implications for Organizations

- **Ensure the right fit of skill and character traits to task when selecting virtual team leaders:** Not surprisingly, team leadership is critical to team success. The most effective virtual team leaders are able to balance both the execution-oriented practices and the interpersonal, communication, and cultural factors that are prevalent in virtual teaming. This has important implications for team member and team leader selection. Organizations should select team leaders based on the key characteristics required to manage from a distance and periodically assess the effectiveness of virtual team leaders to provide targeted feedback

Figure 9. Performance enhancers

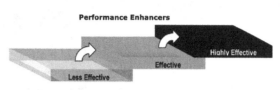

about how these leaders can enhance their performance.

- **Don't take the team launch for granted—set teams up for success:** Organizations need to be thoughtful about team membership, team size, and ensure that teams have the appropriate resources to work together virtually. The following six steps will help ensure virtual teams are set up for success:

1. Use criteria for virtual team member selection and consider who needs to be on the team to make high quality decisions and ensure buy-in. If the size of the team becomes too large, consider having sub-teams work on specific issues and report back to the larger team. This increases role clarity and helps enhance the level of accountability of team members.

2. Participation on multiple virtual teams should be limited so team members can dedicate the time required to fulfill their role successfully. Team members often participate on virtual teams in addition to their day-to-day responsibilities. As such, organizations need to be thoughtful about team membership to better encourage commitment and initiative.

3. Conduct a face-to-face start-up meeting to orient members to the scope of

work, team membership, timelines, and team structure. This meeting should allow time to discuss team purpose, goals, and individual roles, learn more about each team member, develop team norms (e.g., attendance requirements), plan a communication strategy, and conduct team development activities.

4. Help teams compensate for the lack of face-to-face interaction. For example, to help increase engagement and social interaction, some organizations have created "virtual water coolers" and team websites to encourage team communication.

5. Invest in targeted skill training for virtual teams and team leaders (e.g., decision making, communication, giving feedback). Many of the successful teams in the study had skill development during their initial kick-off meeting and subsequent training over time.

6. Develop operating guidelines to help structure team communication and decision making. If organizations invest time and resources in virtual teams, then it is important to capitalize on this and ensure that team members understand how to work together to achieve their goals.

- **Develop strategies to reward virtual teams:** It is important for organizations to implement programs that reward and recognize virtual teams for their collective performance. For example, find opportunities to "spotlight" team members or create mechanisms to virtually celebrate successes as a team.

- **Foster more accountability:** What gets measured is what is likely to get done. Therefore, it is advisable to require both leaders and members of virtual teams to incorporate one or more activities related to their role on the team into their annual objectives/goals or personal development plan. Not only will this ensure individuals are motivated for team success, but it will also encourage them to use team participation as a growth and development mechanism to improve their skills.

- **Assess team progress over time:** Review virtual team processes regularly (e.g., collaboration, decision making, and problem solving) to assess what things are working well and what might be improved. Continually monitor, assess, and improve communication, as this is both the top skill development need reported by team members and the top characteristic needed to lead from a distance. Most importantly, periodically examine the level of team performance by collecting feedback from various stakeholders to assess the team's performance. Based on the outcomes, identify barriers to high performance, as well as steps that can be taken to overcome these barriers.

THE BOTTOM LINE

Virtual teams need to compensate for the inherent lack of human contact in virtual teaming and find ways to enhance trust, engagement, and productivity.

Chapter 12
The Level Paradox of E–Collaboration:
Dangers and Solutions

Ana Ortiz de Guinea
HEC Montréal, Canada

ABSTRACT

Although e-collaboration phenomena are multilevel in nature, research to date has been conducted from an exclusively single-level focus. This has lead to the level paradox. The dangers of the level paradox are discussed, including the potential that apparent cumulative knowledge may actually be spurious. Solutions to the level paradox are proposed in the form of future opportunities of research from several mixed-level approaches, and the benefits and barriers to mixed-level research are discussed. The article ends with a discussion on the necessity of finding a balance between single-level and mixed-level research, as well as on the necessity of single-level studies explicitly specifying the levels of theory, measurement, and data in their research.

INTRODUCTION

In the foundational issue of the International Journal of e-Collaboration (IJeC), founder and editor-in-chief Ned Kock provided the following operational definition of e-collaboration: "col-laboration using electronic technologies among different individuals to accomplish a common task" (Kock, 2005, p. i). Such a broad definition of e-collaboration entails a basic insight into the nature of collaboration that has been for the most part ignored: its multilevel nature. Within this definition we have different concepts that work

DOI: 10.4018/978-1-4666-2020-9.ch012

together in a hierarchical system: the electronic technologies, different individuals, different environments, and a common task. Each of these elements is attached to a different hierarchical level and all together defines what e-collaboration is.

Such a hierarchy implies that e-collaboration includes phenomena at different levels and that the relation between higher and lower levels of the hierarchy should be theoretically specified and empirically examined. Despite this, we find that the vast majority of research in e-collaboration, especially quantitative research, entails single-level models; that is, models that specify relationships among constructs at one level of theory and analysis (Klein & Kozlowski, 2000).

The purpose of this essay is to draw attention to this level paradox of e-collaboration research. In doing so, the intention is not to criticize single-level research, as single-level research has been an essential tool for establishing the legitimacy our field. What is worrisome, though, is the *almost exclusive focus* on single-level research. Such exclusive focus can lead to an incomplete view of the phenomenon of interest (Goodman, 2000) and an impression of cumulative knowledge that might be spurious. Thus, this article hopes to spark some debate and add an additional voice to those of other researchers who have drawn attention to issues of level in e-collaboration research (e.g., Gallivan & Benbunan-Fich, 2005; Walczuch & Watson, 2001).

The above definition of e-collaboration also shows that the e-collaboration field spans multiple disciplines, from technical issues to social aspects. As a result, I would like to point out that when I refer to 'our field' I mean the e-collaboration research that has been done from a social science perspective, including virtual team and communication media choice research, thus excluding technical research on e-collaboration technologies.

This article is organized as follows. First, I explain the level paradox of e-collaboration by describing the multilevel nature of e-collaboration phenomena and the almost exclusive focus on single-level research. Second, I outline the potential dangers of the level paradox for the e-collaboration field. Third, I propose some solutions to the e-collaboration paradox, identify opportunities for research, and explain the barriers and benefits of the proposed solutions. Finally, I end the article with a discussion of the appropriateness of single-level and mixed-level research as well as acknowledge the limitations of this article. The hope is that this paper will give researchers in our field ideas to contribute to a deeper understanding of e-collaboration, its antecedents, its consequences, as well as the different elements that constitute it.

THE LEVEL PARADOX IN E-COLLABORATION RESEARCH

The *level paradox* points to the mismatch between the multilevel nature of e-collaboration phenomena and the fact that most research on it is single-level. Before exposing this contradiction, it is important to define the terms that are going to guide the discussion. When we build theories we should specify which entities need to be considered and are involved in the explanation of the phenomenon of interest (Whetten, 1989). Such entities to which research wishes to generalize are the focal units or level of theory (Hitt, Beamish, Jackson, & Mathieu, 2007; Rousseau, 1985). According to Rousseau (1985), two types of levels exist for research on a focal unit: the level of measurement and the level of analysis. The level of measurement represents the unit to which the data are directly attached (Hitt et al., 2007; Rousseau, 1985). In contrast, the level of analysis "is the unit to which the data are assigned for hypothesis testing and statistical analysis" (Rousseau, 1985, p. 4).

E-Collaboration is Intrinsically a Multilevel Phenomenon

According to Kock (2005), e-collaboration has six main conceptual elements: the collaborative task, the e-collaboration technology, the individuals involved in the collaborative task, the mental schemas possessed by the individuals, and the physical and social environments surrounding the individuals. All these elements take place at different levels. For example, mental schemas belong to the individual level, while the collaborative task belongs to the group level. The other elements of e-collaboration also have important multilevel connotations. The physical and social surroundings of the e-collaboration phenomenon might be the same for some members in a collaborative task but not for others, creating an intermediate level between the collaborative task (at the group level) and the individuals engaged in it (individual level).

A key theoretical concept surrounding all these e-collaboration elements is the concept of technology use (Kock & Nosek, 2005). It has been shown how such use of technology belongs to multiple levels and represents a multilevel concept (Burton-Jones & Gallivan, 2007). The most common levels of technology use are the individual, the group, and the organization (Burton-Jones & Gallivan, 2007). At the organization level, use can be conceptualized as an intra-organizational behavior (e.g., Masetti & Zmud, 1996). At the group level, use can be conceptualized as an aggregation of the individuals' behaviors belonging to the group (e.g., Easley, Devaraj, & Crant, 2003). And, at the individual level, use might represent an individual behavior (e.g., Davis, Bagozzi, & Warshaw, 1989). Use, however, can also belong to further levels such as that of the less intuitive experience level. The experience level (e.g., Rodell & Judge, 2009) is a level nested within individuals. Activities such as an employee browsing several websites, searching for specific information, and/or completing a web form, all belong to the experience level because they represent specific experiences occurring within individuals. The examination of such activities can tell us important information about how and why individuals modify their behaviors with specific technologies as well as how individual patterns of use and mental schemas are formed.

Past papers awarded best article status at IJeC also point to the multilevel nature of e-collaboration. Information warfare threatening commercial and government computing systems (Baskerville, 2006), the different effects of technology within and across individuals and groups (Markus, 2005), the effectiveness of deceptive communication in e-collaboration environments (Boyle, Kacmanr, & George, 2008), gender based cultural patterns through the use of information technology and communications (Gefen, Geri, & Paravatsu, 2007), the impacts of e-collaboration interactions and information capability on firm performance (Ko, Olfman, & Choi, 2009; Kristensen & Kijl, 2010), all point to the fact that e-collaboration is intrinsically multilevel.

In summary, the theoretical underpinnings of an e-collaboration episode, the data collected to examine it, and the analysis conducted in order to evaluate such data, have a hierarchical structure. The experiences with technology (experience level), the characteristics of individuals (individual level), and the dynamics and characteristics of each collaborating group (group level) belonging to one or more organizations (organizational level) in the same or different societies (country level) have multilevel connotations that need to be taken into consideration theoretically and empirically for the advancement of e-collaboration research.

The Single-Level Tradition of E-Collaboration Research

Apart from a few notable exceptions (e.g., de Leede, Kraan, den Hengst, & van Hooff, 2008; Short, Piccolo, Powell, & Ives, 2005), the overwhelming majority of research on e-collaboration is single-level. An informal search within IJeC with the words "multi-level" or "multilevel" renders no results. When this search is extended to databases such ABI/INFORM, similar results are obtained with the exception for the aforementioned studies. Thus, when one reviews the literature on e-collaboration at large, one finds that most of the published articles are single-level (Gallivan & Benbunan-Fich, 2005); that is, papers specify theory at a single-level, they collect data at a single-level, and they conduct analyses at a single-level. Furthermore, as Gallivan and Benbunan-Fich (2005) show, many of these papers, as explained later, have important inconsistencies between the levels of theory, measurement, and analysis that provide threats to the validity of their results.

Equally worrisome is that extensive and comprehensive literature reviews on e-collaboration, such as those conducted on virtual teams, lack discussions about the level of theory, measurement, and analysis of the reviewed papers when synthesising such research (e.g., Martins, 2004; Powell, Piccoli, & Ives, 2004; Webster & Staples, 2006). As a result, we could be discussing the effects of virtuality on communication effectiveness and overlook whether such effects generalize at the individual (e.g., Chidambaram & Jones, 1993) or group (e.g., Benbunan-Fich, Hiltz, & Turoff, 2002) levels and/or whether the studies manifested inconsistencies between the level of theory, analysis, and data (e.g., Burke & Chidambaram, 1999). Consistent with this is the fact that quantitative reviews (meta-analysis) of research on virtual teams have discovered important differences in results when the same relations are examined at the individual or group levels (Ortiz de Guinea, Webster, & Staples, 2005).

Summary

An overwhelming majority of studies of e-collaboration, although studying a multilevel phenomenon, are conducted theoretically and empirically at a single-level. This mismatch between the multilevel structure of the actual phenomenon under study and the single-level ways in which research is theoretically specified and empirically conducted represents a paradox. Such a level paradox has important consequences for our field.

THE DANGERS OF THE LEVEL PARADOX

Studying a multilevel phenomenon from a single-level perspective is worrisome. It can lead to an understanding of the subject under study that may suffer from several fallacies. Such fallacies can be responsible for some of the inconsistent results in our field and can threaten the validity of what we think we know about e-collaboration (Gallivan & Benbunan-Fich, 2005). By overlooking this single-level focus, we may be making erroneous inferences from research that is not comparable (e.g., individual and group levels).

These potential misleading inferences can be classified under the grand umbrella of ecological and atomistic fallacies. An ecological fallacy involves making inferences from aggregated data to a lower level of analysis (Rousseau, 1985). An atomistic fallacy is the opposite: drawing inferences from lower level information to higher level units (Luke, 2004). I will examine each of these fallacies in their most prevalent and specific forms to better illustrate the numerous ways in which they can develop.

Issues Associated with Misalignments Between Levels of Theory, Analysis, and Measurement

A recent review of the empirical literature on e-collaboration shows two thirds of single-level papers (published between 1999 and 2004 in six leading IS journals) have inconsistencies with respect to the level at which theory is specified, the level at which data are collected, and the level at which analyses are conducted (Gallivan & Benbunan-Fich, 2005). Such inconsistencies raise serious questions about the validity of such studies (Gallivan & Benbunan-Fich, 2005).

The first set of problematic studies represent articles in which the focal unit was the group; the data were collected at the individual level and aggregated to the group level without appropriately conducting analyses justifying such aggregation. The aggregation or the combination of data at one level to a higher level (Klein, Danserau, & Hall, 1994; Rousseau, 1985) must be justified by showing that there is enough homogeneity within the higher level unit to which the data is to be aggregated (James, 1982; Klein et al., 2000). If this is not done, as was the case with the studies identified by Gallivan and Benfunan-Fich (2005), there is a threat to the validity of results because of the potential for aggregation bias. The results of such studies might not be valid to the extent that they can be "an artifact of the data combination method" (Rousseau, 1985, p. 6). For example, Limayem and DeSanctis (2000), when studying some constructs at the group level (such as decision confidence) aggregated data based on individual-level responses without conducting statistical tests of within-group homogeneity in order to justify the aggregation of data to the group-level.

A second set of problematic studies identified by Gallivan and Benbunan-Fich (2005) represented articles in which the focal unit was the group but the level of measurement and analysis was the individual. Such studies fail in what is known as misspecification or the fallacy of the wrong level (Rousseau, 1985). The fallacy of the wrong level occurs when we use, for example, individual-level data and analysis to make theoretical inferences about the group level (Rousseau, 1985). For example, Burke and Chidambaram (1999) specified relations at the group level in the hypotheses, such as different perceptions of communication interface between groups using different media; however, when reading their results, it appears

that the analyses on such perceptions were carried out at the individual-level.

Even if the level of analysis and the level of theory are congruent and the aggregation of data to higher levels is justified, there might still be some potential issues. Some authorities in multilevel research have argued that it is the level at which data are analyzed that needs to be congruent with the level of theory and, thus, that the level of data does not need to match the level of theory and analysis (Klein et al., 1994). Accordingly, many ways in which to aggregate individual level data to the group level have been proposed (e.g., Klein et al., 2000; Walczuch & Watson, 2001). However, others have argued that such aggregation of data to the group level to perform analyses has the potential for meaningful individual level variance to be ignored (Hofmann, 1997). These authors explain that if you have individuals working on groups, and you collect data at the individual level, the data should be tested using multilevel approaches rather than aggregating data to the group level; otherwise, there is always variance on the variables of interest within groups that can be meaningful but is ignored (Hofmann, 1997).

Other Issues Associated With Single-Level Research on Multilevel Phenomena

The potential for problematic issues is also high even when we do not have a mismatch between levels of theory, analysis, and data. Potential issues might exist when the theory, data, and analysis are conducted at the individual level but the individuals work in groups (Gallivan & Benbunan-Fich, 2005). For example, when we study the individual learning outcomes of two different distributed environments of individuals working in groups (e.g., Alavi, Marakas, & Yoo, 2002), we need to account for the fact that those individuals are not independent of each other. That is, when we fail to account for the dependencies of those individuals within their groups, the independence of the observations assumption when conducting statistical analysis techniques is violated (Bryk & Raudenbush, 1992; Hofmann, 1997)[1].

Related to this are contextual fallacies. Contextual fallacies occur when we fail to include the potential effects that higher-level factors can have in a relationship between two constructs at a lower level (Rousseau, 1985). If such factors are ignored, the relationship between the two constructs at the lower level might be spurious (Rousseau, 1985). For example, some research on e-collaboration at the individual level has shown that individuals communicating in more virtual ways participate more in their group tasks (Valacich, Sarker, Pratt, & Groomer, 2002). In contrast, other research has found a negative relation between virtuality and participation (Mathieu, 2007). In this case, properties at the group level could be playing a role in moderating the relation between virtualness and participation. For example, a positive relation between virtualness and participation might only hold if certain group norms are in place (e.g., communication anonymity). Such a contextual fallacy points to the fact that when we conduct e-collaboration research, we might be falling in what has been characterized as errors of exclusion (Benbasat & Zmud, 2003), or the failure of including important core properties of e-collaboration in our research models.

Cross-level fallacies can take place when the "same construct is used to characterize phenomena at different levels" (Rousseau, 1985, p. 8). Cross-level fallacies occur when we use constructs in the same content domain but that operate at different levels (Chan, 1998). For example, in e-collaboration we often talk about individual perceived conflict (e.g., Wakefield, Leidner, & Garrison, 2008) and group conflict (e.g., Hobman, Bordia, Irmer, & Chang, 2002). When doing so, we often fail to specify whether these two constructs at different levels mean the same thing across the two levels or are only weakly related to each other (Rousseau, 1985). That is, we need to state how the two constructs relate across levels (Rousseau, 1985) and failure to do so increases the likelihood

of making erroneous inferences from one level to a higher or lower unit. Of special interest is the potential for 'anthropomorphizing' collective activities (Rousseau, 1985). This occurs, for example, if we attribute personality traits, such as extraversion, to the group (e.g., Balthazard, Potter, & Warren, 2002) without specifying how individual extraversion relates to group extraversion or how group extraversion emerges. As a result, we might end with a list of construct names spanning multiple levels that offer little insight into their true meaning (Chan, 1998).

Summary

The level paradox raises some important concerns about research on e-collaboration to date. It might be at the heart of the abundant inconsistent results found in our field (Gallivan & Benbunan-Fich, 2005). It also yields concerns about the validity of some of our research (Gallivan & Benbunan-Fich, 2005). Perhaps most importantly, the level paradox might be offering us a spurious impression of cumulated knowledge based on research that is not comparable to each other. An exclusive focus on single-level research might lead to errors of exclusion and, thus, leave some important core properties of e-collaboration unexplored.

POTENTIAL SOLUTIONS TO THE LEVEL PARADOX

Mixed-level research on e-collaboration can address some of the concerns exposed previously. This idea has been summarized in the words of Luke (2004, p. 7): "Because so much of what we study is multilevel in nature, we should use theories and analytic techniques that are also multilevel". This section explores some mixed-level opportunities for future research on e-collaboration, including composition models, cross-level models, and multilevel models. A summary of these models and opportunities for future research is provided in Figure 1.

Figure 1. Summary of opportunities for mixed-level research on e-collaboration

Mixed-Level Models		Characteristics	Summarized Form[1]	Examples of Possible Research Questions on E-Collaboration
Composition models		Specify the functional relation between constructs at different levels that tap into the same content but might be qualitatively similar, strongly or weakly related.	$X_{level-3}$ $X_{level-2}$ $X_{level-1}$	In communication media choice: what is the relation between individual-level perceived social norms, and actual explicit social norms at the group (and/or organizational) levels? In virtual teams: what is the relation between patterns of individual technology use and patterns of group technology use?
Cross-level	Direct effects models	Specify the influence of a variable at one level on a variable at a different level	$X_{level-2}$ $Y_{level-1}$	In communication media choice: What is the influence of different social factors (e.g., social influence) on individual-level media choice? In virtual team: what is the relation between group-level climate on individuals' commitment to the group?
	Moderator models	Specify the interaction of two variables at a different level in predicting a variable at a lower (or higher) level	$X_{level-2}$ $Z_{level-1}$ $Y_{level-1}$	In communication media choice: How do different social factors influence the relation between individual-level perceived media richness and individual-level media use? In virtual teams: how does group climate influence the relation between individual-personality and individual performance?

Mixed-Level Models		Characteristics	Summarized Form[1]	Examples of Possible Research Questions on E-Collaboration
Cross-level	Frog-pond models	Specify the influence of the relative standing of a lower level unit within a higher level unit on a variable at the lower level	$(X_{L1} - \bar{X}_{L2}) \rightarrow Y_{L1}$	In communication media choice: what is the relation between a person status on a group and his/her choice of media use when treating delicate issues? In virtual teams: what is the relation between an individuals' relative performance in a group on his/her self-efficacy beliefs?
	Mediational models	Specify the interaction of two variables at a different level in predicting a variable at a lower (or higher) level	$Z_{level-2}$ $X_{level-1}$ $Y_{level-1}$	In communication media choice: do social factors mediate the relation between individuals' perceived richness of media and media use? In virtual teams: does group conflict mediate the relation between individuals' attitudes to the group and their commitment to the group?
Multilevel (or homologous) models		Specify relations among independent and dependent variables that are generalizable across levels	$X_{level-3} \rightarrow Y_{level-3}$ $X_{level-2} \rightarrow Y_{level-2}$ $X_{level-1} \rightarrow Y_{level-1}$	In communication media choice: Does the relation between perceived media richness and media choice holds across individuals and groups? In virtual teams: does the relation between perceived task conflict and performance holds across individuals and groups?
Note: The above models can also be combined to examine more complex research questions				

COMPOSITION MODELS

Compositional models represent an opportunity to start differentiating between constructs at different levels. They specify the "the functional relationships between variables at different levels presumed to be functionally similar" (Rousseau, 1985, pp. 11-12). That is, a composition model specifies "the functional relationships among phenomena or constructs at different levels of analysis (e.g., individual level, team level, organizational level) that reference essentially the same content" but may be qualitatively similar or

different at different levels (Chan, 1998, p. 234). Compositional models specify whether constructs at different levels are parallel, identical or weakly related (Hitt et al., 2007; Rousseau, 1985).

A compositional model can be characterized by a functional relation of isomorphism or the fact that constructs mean the same thing across levels (Rousseau, 1985). Other research, although not directly building isomorphic models, provides insights onto the nature of isomorphism (e.g., Klein, Tosi, & Cannella, 1999; Morgeson & Hofmann, 1999) and the different types of group level constructs that might arise (e.g., Klein &

Kozlowski, 2000). Apart from isomorphism, various other composition models exist. Chan (1998) has proposed several compositional models based on different functional relationships between constructs at different levels. The most employed when aggregating data to the group level from individual level information have been the additive and direct consensus models (Chan, 1998). The additive model states that the higher level unit construct is a summation or average of the lower level units' scores (Chan, 1998). In contrast, the direct consensus model state that the meaning of the higher level construct is the consensus among the lower-level units in the subject matter under consideration (Chan, 1998).

Other less intuitive models exist that are characterized by compilation or the fact that the higher level construct reflects a complex nonlinear combination of a lower level property (Kozlowski & Klein, 2000). For example, the dispersion model specifies that the meaning of the higher-level construct resides in the dispersion or variance among lower-level units (Chan, 1998). Such a dispersion model characterizes the functional relation between psychological climate (individual level) and climate strength (group level) (Chan, 1998).

Composition models provide trustworthy research for two main reasons: they provide a strong theoretical argument for justifying different forms of aggregation (Chan, 1998; Rousseau, 1985) and, perhaps most importantly, they increase the validity of the constructs under study (Chan, 1998). As a result, many opportunities for research exist in specifying how constructs at the individual level (e.g., individual-level satisfaction) relate to those same constructs at the group level (e.g., group-level satisfaction). A notable example in virtual team research of such a theoretical specification between an individual-level construct and its group-level counterpart is given by Kirkman, Rosen, Tesluk, and Gibson (2004) in their elegant discussion of how group-level empowerment differs from individual-level empowerment.

CROSS-LEVEL MODELS

As the name indicates, cross-level models include those models that specify relations between variables at different levels (Klein & Kozlowski, 2000; Rousseau, 1985). The following section discusses the different types of cross-level models that can be applied to e-collaboration research.

Cross-Level Direct Effects Models

The first types of cross-level models are those of direct effects. Direct effects models explore the influence of a variable at one level on another variable at a different level (Rousseau, 1985). The most common are those specifying the impact of a variable at one level on another variable at a lower-level (Klein & Kozlowski, 2000). Although such effects have been rarely explored in the Information Systems (IS) field, a domain in which some e-collaboration research is conducted, Cenfetelli and Schwarz (in press) show how different websites (higher-level) have significant effects on individuals' intentions to use those websites in the future (lower-level). More specifically, in the e-collaboration field we could study the effects of group climate on individuals' commitment to the group in virtualized contexts, or the effects that certain organizational and/or group norms might have on individuals' perceived self-efficacy beliefs. Furthermore, the literature on communication media has included social factors, such as social influence (e.g., Treviño & Stein, 2000; Webster & Treviño, 1995), that have been specified at the individual-level. As a result, future research could specify such social factors at a higher level and examine their influence on individual-level media choice.

Although less common, direct effects models can also specify the relations between a variable at a lower level to a variable at a higher level. This possibility appears to be critical for the advancement of knowledge in e-collaboration because such models can answer important research questions. For example, we could study the relationship between individual-level characteristics (e.g. experience, skills, personality traits, or self-efficacy with the task and the technology) and group-level performance (e.g., quality and productivity) in virtualized contexts. This aligns with recent calls for research on individuals' cognitions and emotions in virtual team research (Martins, 2004).

Cross-Level Moderator Models

The second group of cross-level models are moderator models. These models specify that a variable at one level moderates the relationship between two other variables at a lower level (Klein & Kozlowski, 2000; Rousseau, 1985). That is, these models state that two variables at different levels (e.g., group and individual) interact in predicting another variable at the lower level (e.g., individual) (Klein & Kozlowski, 2000). These models are characterized by what Firebaugh (1978) called comparative functions: the effect of a characteristic of a higher unit on the relationship between two variables at a lower unit. Moderator models have the potential to address the contextual fallacy concern explained in the previous section and prevent some of the errors of exclusion from which our research might suffer. Important gaps in our literature can be filled with these models: we could study potential moderators (e.g., group norms about communication) on the relation between the level of perceived virtualness and individual participation, we could see if group climate interacts with individual personality to predict individual performance within groups, we could also study how certain social processes (such as sponsorship) interact with individual-level attitudes in the choice of a specific communication media, as suggested by Markus (1994).

Although less common, cross-level moderator models might also include moderators at a lower level (e.g., individual) on the relation between two variables at a higher level (e.g., group) (Rousseau, 1985). In this case, we could study whether personality characteristics of individuals in the group interact with group cohesion when predicting group performance.

As a note of caution, it is important to stress that these models have been criticized for being empirically driven and thus lacking an appropriate theoretical base (Rousseau, 1985); however, this might not always be the case. One important part of theory construction is the specification of its boundaries (Bacharach, 1989; Bamberger, 2008). Situational, contextual, spatial, and temporal assumptions give us important insights by telling us under which circumstances a theory 'works' (Bacharach, 1989; Bamberger, 2008).

Cross-Level Frog-Pond Models

The third types of cross-level models are the frog-pond models. These uncommon models study normative functions (Firebaugh, 1980) or the relative standing of a lower level unit (e.g., individual) within a higher level one (e.g., group)[2] (Klein et al., 1994; Rousseau, 1985). The idea is that the relative standing of an individual in a group can play an important role in determining his/her behavior because, as Davis (1966, p. 21) explains, individuals "can choose to be big frogs in little ponds or little frogs in big ponds". Although such models are more often pursued in the sociological field, they open interesting opportunities for e-collaboration research. For example, an individual relative performance within an e-collaboration group can have important consequences for his/her self-efficacy beliefs. That is, an individual whose true performance is mediocre, might increase his self-efficacy beliefs when e-collaborating with others whose performance is even lower (Klein & Kozlowski, 2000). Likewise, an individual status position within a group can very well determine his/her leadership behavior in the group.

Cross-Level Meditational Models

Although cross-level mediational models, also called meso-mediational models, have been traditionally ignored when explaining cross-level models[3] (Klein & Kozlowski, 2000; Rousseau, 1985), they represent another possibility for cross-level research. Thus, cross-level models can take complex forms, including meditational relationships across different levels (MacKinnon, 2008; Mathieu, Maybard, Taylor, Gibson, & Ruddy, 2007; Mathieu & Taylor, 2007). These meso-meditational designs follow the same logic for specifying and testing mediational effects as single-level research (Baron & Kenny, 1996) but do so by proposing mediators that can traverse across levels (Mathieu & Taylor, 2007). Mediators play a key role in the advancement of theory and research because they clarify the process by which an antecedent influences the output of interest (Baron & Kenny, 1996; Mathieu & Taylor, 2007). When we include the possibility of characterizing such underlying processes across different levels, the potential for explanation is substantially enhanced. For example, management research has shown that individuals' role clarity mediates the relationship between group level leadership and individuals' self-efficacy (Chen & Bliese, 2002). Likewise, Seibert, Silbert, and Randolph (2004), after explaining that psychological empowerment (individual-level) is different than empowerment climate (group-level), show how psychological empowerment mediates the relation between empowerment climate and individual job satisfaction and performance. As a result, cross-level mediational models provide substantial opportunities for future research on e-collaboration which aligns with calls for research in the socio-emotional and task processes involved in mediating the relations between input and outputs in virtual teams (Martins, 2004; Powell et al., 2004).

MULTILEVEL MODELS

Multilevel models, also called homologous models, specify relations among independent and dependent variables that are generalizable across levels (Chen, Bliese, & Mathieu, 2005; Klein & Kozlowski, 2000; Rousseau, 1985). Such models specify that "a relationship between two variables holds at multiple levels of analysis" (Klein & Kozlowski, 2000, p. 219). An important requirement for drawing such models is that a composition model with such constructs at different levels needs to be specified beforehand because these models assume that constructs at different levels are equivalent (Rousseau, 1985). Before stating and arguing that a positive relation between self-efficacy and performance at both individual and group levels exist, such models need to specify that the self-efficacy and performance constructs are functionally similar across the two levels. Various statistical procedures for testing homologous models have been recently proposed (e.g., Chen et al., 2005). In this case, further research could study the processes by which both individuals and groups decide on which communication media to use and if those relations hold across levels.

The main advantage of these types of models is that they provide theories that are highly generalizable as well as provide integration between different levels (Klein & Kozlowski, 2000). However, such models risk over-simplifying the phenomena under study when finding constructs that are functionally similar across levels (Klein & Kozlowski, 2000). Such models hold two promises for the field of e-collaboration. First, they can specify which relationships are likely to hold across individual and group levels and, thus, provide explanations for the inconsistencies found between levels of analysis (Ortiz de Guinea et al., 2005). For example, such models could specify why the relation between knowledge sharing and performance in virtualized contexts is expected to hold (or not hold) across individual and group levels. Second, if these models are pursued the e-collaboration field might become an important reference discipline for other fields from which to generalize our theoretical insights and empirical findings.

SUMMARY

Mixed-level models represent a potential solution from which to start addressing the level paradox of e-collaboration research. Many mixed-level models exist, from composition models through different types of cross-level models to multilevel ones. Such models represent future opportunities for research on e-collaboration. Of course, these models can be combined with one another to provide more complex explanations of e-collaboration phenomena.

STEPS FOR MIXED-LEVEL RESEARCH ON E-COLLABORATION THROUGH AN EXAMPLE

To better illustrate how the above ideas can be put into practice, I will develop a very brief and simple

example of a possible research project in virtual teams. Imagine we are interested in exploring the extent to which individual's self-efficacy, team's self-efficacy, communication mode (either face to face or electronic), and team leadership influence team performance and whether such relations are moderated by team size (Figure 2). Please note that I am not trying to develop a theoretical sound model; instead, the objective is to provide a *brief example with variables of different types and levels* in order to show the steps that mixed-level research should follow. The recommendations in the next section draw from examples provided by the multilevel literature (e.g., Klein & Kozlowski, 2000; Rousseau, 1985).

Theoretical Development and Construct Specification

With any cross-level research endeavors, we need to follow some steps during theoretical development. Our research model is a cross-level model with both direct and moderator effects and constructs at the individual and team levels. One of the most important steps in the theoretical development is to specify the composition (or compilation) models of how our high level constructs (e.g., team) come to be (Rousseau, 1985).

Figure 2. Example of a cross-level model for virtual team research

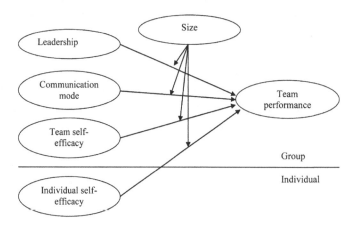

Thus, the first challenge with such research will be to define each of the constructs at their focal unit. Before getting into the team-level constructs, we can define individual's self-efficacy based on past research at the individual level (e.g., Ortiz de Guinea & Webster, 2011).

Now, we turn to the team-level constructs. There are three basic types of team-level constructs: global team properties, shared team properties, and configural team properties (Klein & Kozlowski, 2000). Global team properties are characteristics of teams that are objective and easily observable (Klein & Kozlowski, 2000); such properties do not emerge from the characteristics of the individual team members but they exist apart from them (Klein & Kozlowski, 2000). For example, team size and team communication mode can be thought of as global team properties. Size is an objective characteristic of the team and we do not need to collect data from each individual team member in order to measure it. The same occurs with team communication mode if we are going to characterize it as either face to face or virtual (electronic communication).

Unlike global team properties, shared team properties emerge from individuals team members' attitudes, experience or beliefs (Klein & Kozlowski, 2000). Team self-efficacy and team leadership can be seen as shared team properties for various reasons (Klein & Kozlowski, 2000). Some literature on leadership suggests that team members are likely to have homogeneous perceptions about their leader (Danserau & Yammarino, 1998) because interaction among team members (e.g. discussion) is likely to make individuals' opinions about the leader more alike. Thus team leadership appears to follow the direct consensus composition model (Chan, 1998), explained earlier, where the meaning of team leadership stems from consensus among team members.

Team self-efficacy can also be conceptualized as a shared team property (Klein & Kozlowski, 2000). If we define team self-efficacy as stemming from individuals' self-efficacy belief then team self-efficacy will be characterized by a composition model in which the team self-efficacy variable should be a summation (or average) of individuals' self-efficacy. Our theory, however, might indicate that the team self-efficacy construct is different from a combination of individuals' self-efficacies: it may be that an individual has lower self-efficacy beliefs about himself but still strongly believes in the capabilities of his/her team (Klein et al., 2000). This would be characterized by a reference shift consensus model in which a change in meaning of the construct appears when the reference of such beliefs is shifted from the individual to the team (Chan, 1998). In this case, individuals should be explicitly asked about their team self-efficacy and then the consensus among them can be analyzed to justify the aggregation of individuals' responses about the team to the team level (Chan, 1998). One of the two possibilities for the team self-efficacy construct needs to then be chosen depending on the theory that is guiding our research.

The third type of team constructs are configural team properties. Like shared properties, configural team properties stem from team member's beliefs, attitudes, and behaviors (Klein & Kozlowski, 2000). However, unlike shared properties, configural properties capture the variability of individuals within a team (Klein & Kozlowski, 2000). It can be argued that team performance is a configural team property because it emerges from "the complex conglomeration of individual team members' performance" (Klein & Kozlowski, 2000, p. 217). Depending on the task or the dimension more important for our theory, team level performance might be concerned with the sum of individuals' performance or, instead, might reflect the best member's performance or the variability in performance among team members (Klein & Kozlowski, 2000), thus forming a compilation model. As a result, we should determine and explain which of these reflects team performance for our project while taking into consideration past literature and our theory.

The specification and definition of constructs at their focal unit will help in attaining acceptable construct validity. Furthermore, we should develop the logical arguments (or theory) that provide the justification for the predicted relations between constructs (Whetten, 1989). The process of developing our hypotheses is no different than that done in single-level research. The idea is to state "why" a relation between the constructs of interest exist in a coherent manner (Webster & Watson, 2002) given the theoretical definition of our constructs.

Research Design and Data Analyses

The research design is of paramount importance in establishing the adequate conditions for testing a research model. This requirement is exacerbated in cross-level research because we need to assure variability at different levels (Rousseau, 1985). In our example we need to assure that the sample has sufficient variability at the individual and team levels (Klein et al., 2000). In order to do this for any N individuals we need to maximize the number of teams (Rousseau, 1985). If the number of teams is small compared to the number of individuals, variability in team level variables will be small and thus problematic for testing cross-level hypotheses (Rousseau, 1985). Ideally, measures of shared team properties, such as team self-efficacy, should show variability across teams but at the same time homogeneity within teams (Klein et al., 2000). In contrast, with respect to configural constructs such as team performance, data needs to vary from team to team as well as within teams: "one can only test the correlates of within-unit variability (a configural construct), for example, if units vary in their within-unit variability" (Klein et al., 2000, p. 221). In summary, to test our research model the ideal sample would be as follows: 1) performance varies between and within teams, 2) team self-efficacy and leadership vary between teams but not within teams, 3) individual self-efficacy varies across individuals,

and iv) size and communication mode vary across teams (no variation within teams since they are global constructs).

In terms of data manipulation, it is indispensable to be able to match individuals' responses to the team to which they belong (Rousseau, 1985). Furthermore, if individual level perceptual data is going to be aggregated to the team level (such is the case with team self-efficacy or leadership) we would need to establish the level of agreement of team members in such perceptual measures (Rousseau, 1985). That is, we need to test if perceptions of leadership and team self-efficacy are in fact homogeneous within teams (Klein & Kozlowski, 2000). Numerous statistics, such as the intraclass correlation and the r_{wg} index, exist in order to do so (Klein et al., 2000; Klein & Kozlowski, 2000). The homogeneity of configural properties within units, such as team performance, should also be analyzed in order to see if, in fact, such constructs represent non-homogeneous properties.

In order to be able to perform analyses, the data should be maintained at the lowest level possible: for example, we should have a line (or a case) in our data file for each individual. The global, aggregated, and configural variables of each team should be repeated in the individual line for each individual in the team. This is generally how the data need to be organized in order to perform analyses (e.g., SPSS). Before performing analyses we need to check if data are missing at random and this is done in the same way as testing for missing data in single-level research (Tabachnick & Fidell, 2007). Some techniques for dealing with missing data that are not missing at random exist (Enders, in press; Muthén, Asparouhov, Hunter, & Leuchter, in press). Once we have checked for the occurrence of missing data, we can proceed with analyses. Analyses can be performed with different statistical procedures: SPSS, SAS, and HLM can be used to test direct as well as moderator cross-level effects models. Numerous examples of how to do these analyses exist and can be followed (e.g., Bickel, 2007; Otondo, Barnett,

Kellermans, Pearson, & Pearson, 2009; Peugh & Enders, 2005). Finally, it is important to note that if complex models need to be tested using path analysis techniques then there is the possibility of employing MPlus or other structural equation modeling techniques such as LISREL.

An important implication worth mentioning is that mixed-level techniques for construct specification can inform single-level research, especially at the group or higher levels. The mixed-level literature on construct specification offers a good approach for the definition of constructs at higher levels and single-level research (e.g., research conducted at the group level) can benefit from such literature when theoretically developing concepts and models.

Summary

A simple and brief example of cross-level research in virtual teams is provided here in order to offer specific and practical steps for researchers when approaching cross-level research. During theoretical development, the constructs need to be defined and specified at their appropriate levels. Also, the theory needs to explain how such constructs emerge (e.g., global properties, shared properties, or configural properties). A justification of the hypothesized relations between constructs is also needed as it is done with single-level research. For research design purposes, it is critical to draw samples for which the number of high level units is maximized. For some variables we might need variability within and across units while for other constructs we need homogeneity within units but variability across them. Techniques for assessing homogeneity and consensus within units exist as well as statistical packages that allow for multi-level regression techniques to be used to test the relations of interest.

BARRIERS AND BENEFITS OF MIXED-LEVEL RESEARCH ON E-COLLABORATION

Although mixed-level research on e-collaboration can be beneficial, there are some barriers to conducting mixed-level research on e-collaboration. Likewise, although some benefits of e-collaboration were outlined in the earlier sections, less intuitive benefits need to be discussed.

Barriers to Mixed-Level Research

A barrier to mixed-level research has been statistical packages (Bamberger, 2008). However, with the appearance of multiple statistical packages that include the possibility of multilevel modeling and mixed-level analyses (e.g., HML, SAS, SPSS, MPlus) that are well suited for answering different research questions, this appears to be less of a concern. A related issue is the traditional lack of training of researchers in mixed-level analytical techniques and multilevel development theory (Klein et al., 1999). Thus (micro and macro) researchers need to be open minded when studying a phenomenon and ready to look up or down to different levels in order to better study the e-collaboration phenomenon.

This point has an important consequence as well for the review process. The institutional pressures of our academic lives dictate that we need to 'publish or perish'. If we construct mixed-level theory and research, micro reviewers might not see the necessity of including higher-level elements and/or macro reviewers might not see the relevance of the lower-level components of our research (Klein et al., 1999). More importantly, our lack of training on multilevel research might trigger difficult reviews of mixed-level research with important consequences for our research careers.

Another barrier for mixed-level research is in determining the scope of such research (Klein et al., 1999). If e-collaboration is a phenomenon that occurs at the experience, individual, group, organizational, inter-organizational, and societal levels, then the volume of research and theory available and relevant to researchers is too vast and problems concerning the scope of the proposed theory and research might arise (Klein et al., 1999). If one decides to shift levels from relations and constructs at the individual level to the group, one might end up with a too simplistic view of the phenomenon under study. On the contrary, if one decides to study cross-level theories spanning different constructs and diverse levels, one might end up with very complex systems that compromise the parsimony of theory and research. As Klein et al. (1999, p. 244) put it "The appropriate middle ground – not too simple, yet not too complex – may be difficult to find".

Multilevel data are difficult to collect as well. If gathering samples for our single-level research is already a challenging task, having to do so from multiple individuals across multiple groups and organizations might be appalling (Klein et al., 1999), not to mention time consuming and expensive. Furthermore, the required sample size at each different level to yield powerful results is difficult to determine (Klein & Kozlowski, 2000). For example, if samples do not contain enough variability, our results might result in range restriction biases (Klein & Kozlowski, 2000).

Related to this is the fact that conducting mixed-level analyses is also a difficult task. Not only because of the lack of training but, more importantly, because the appropriate ways in which to conduct analyses of mixed-level data have been at the core of many debates (e.g., Klein et al., 2000; Kozlowski & Klein, 2000; Yammarino & Markham, 1992). These debates include discussions about appropriate ways to specify multilevel theory, multilevel techniques for conducting analyses, and the combination methods for appropriately aggregating data from one level

to the next. For example, ongoing debates exist on the ways in which construct validity of multilevel constructs can be tested (e.g., Chen, Mathieu, & Bliese, 2004; Hofmann & Jones, 2004). As a result these debates on the core properties of multilevel research leave a sense of confusion for the researcher willing to pursue mixed-level endeavors.

BENEFITS OF MIXED-LEVEL RESEARCH

Some benefits of mixed-level research can be drawn from earlier sections of this paper and do not need to be repeated. Others however, because less intuitive, warrant explicit attention. For example, the goal of e-collaboration research, as of any other scientific discipline, is to build a cumulative set of knowledge about the phenomena under inquiry (Keen, 1980). Single-level research in our field might have given a spurious sensation of cumulative knowledge resulting from reviewing articles that are not comparable or that include inconsistencies between levels of analysis, data, and theory. Thus mixed-level research approaches in e-collaboration can very much contribute to the research goal of cumulative knowledge by overcoming the limitations of single-level research. Although these approaches can generate complex theories and results, they can also provide much of the clarification, synthesis and synergy of knowledge needed in our field (Klein et al., 1999).

Mixed-level approaches can provide a richer and more realistic understanding of e-collaboration (Klein et al., 1999). Because such approaches are parallel to the multilevel nature of actual e-collaboration practices, they will also tackle relevant issues with important practical implications for individuals, groups, organizations, and society (Hitt et al., 2007).

Another benefit of mixed-level research on e-collaboration is that it might bring collaboration across disciplines (Hitt et al., 2007). Because e-collaboration episodes are composed of elements occurring at multiple levels (Kock, 2005), research into these different levels will benefit from experts on psychology and micro research issues, researchers on group and organizational issues, and researchers concerned with sociological issues. It is important to note, however, that such multidisciplinary collaborations represent a double-edge sword; although multidisciplinary research might provide deeper and comprehensive understandings of e-collaboration practices, it can entail some risks as well. As Klein et al. (1999, p. 244) explain that "an interdisciplinary and multilevel work may paradoxically be at home everywhere and nowhere: of some interest and appeal to numerous disciplines and journals but of central interest and appeal to none".

DISCUSSION

After having argued that e-collaboration is intrinsically a multilevel phenomenon, it might seem counterintuitive to still emphasize the importance for single-level research on e-collaboration. However, the goal of this article is not to criticize single-level research or censure its pursuit; the goal is to expose the level paradox of *exclusively conducting single-level research* on a multilevel phenomenon and the dangers associated with it. This is very different from stating that single-level research is not desirable or of interest to our discipline. In fact the opposite is true; single-level research has been critical for our understanding of e-collaboration. And it still is important. For example, single-level research has given us important insights into how processes and outcomes in e-collaboration are substantially different from those in face-to-face collaborative contexts (Webster & Staples, 2006). Furthermore, because mixed-level theories can "lack prediction accuracy in specific contexts" (Burton-Jones & Gallivan, 2007, p. 673), it is

appropriate to conduct single-level research when more accuracy is needed over generalization.

Likewise, the scientific method of theory testing coupled with the scarcity of multi-level theories (Goodman, 2000) points to the necessity of conducting single-level research to empirically examine our theories. Equally important is the fact that, from a practical standpoint, it is neither realistic nor desirable for researchers to exclusively commit and engage in more costly, complex, and larger in scope, mixed-level programs of research. Therefore, what might be needed when conducting single-level research is a careful justification of its appropriateness as well as explicit discussion of its generalizability (Klein et al., 1994).

What is important is that the mixed-level research is relevant for conducting single-level research. The mixed-level literature provides actionable ways in which constructs at higher levels (e.g., group) can be theoretically specified and empirically tested regardless of whether the research is single-level. Furthermore, it provides an adequate vocabulary for single-level researchers to explicitly and clearly state the levels of theory, measurement, and analyses in their studies.

It is worth noting that the level paradox, or the exclusivity of single-level research on e-collaboration, might be a consequence of the state of maturity of our field. E-collaboration, when compared other disciplines, is still in its infancy (Martins, 2004). For example, organizational behaviour is a much older field in which multilevel studies are only now flourishing (Bamberger, 2008). It is possible that as our field matures, the theories, analytical techniques, and data collected to answer research questions become more complex and thus include mixed-level possibilities.

The view of the field portrayed in this article is not free of limitations. One obvious shortcoming is that much of the review and discussion has been done from a positivistic and quantitative view of e-collaboration research to date. Thus important work carried out from interpretivist and qualitative approaches[4] that has included multilevel explanations of technology use and collaboration by individuals, groups, and organizations has been ignored (Orlikowski, 2000; Sarker, Valacich, & Sarker, 2005).

All in all, this article aims to draw attention to the single-level paradox of e-collaboration research, its potential dangers to build a cumulative knowledge tradition, and possible research opportunities from which to start the laborious task of building multilevel theories and research. Its purpose is not to advocate for the disappearance of single-level research but to find common ground in balancing our single-level view of e-collaboration by also conducting cross-level research. Such balance has the promise to close the gap that exists between issues of level in the e-collaboration field.

ACKNOWLEDGMENT

I gratefully acknowledge the helpful and encouraging comments of Jane Webster and Xiaojun Zhang, in addition of those of Ned Kock and the anonymous reviewers, in earlier versions of this manuscript.

REFERENCES

Alavi, M., Marakas, G. M., & Yoo, Y. (2002). A comparative study of distributed learning environments on learning outcomes. *Information Systems Research, 13*(4), 404–415. doi:10.1287/isre.13.4.404.72

Bacharach, S. B. (1989). Organizational theories: Some criteria for evaluation. *Academy of Management Review, 14*(3), 496–515.

Balthazard, P. E., Potter, R. E., & Warren, J. (2002). The effects of extraversion and expertise on virtual team interaction and performance. In *Proceedings of the 34th Hawaii International Conference on System Sciences*, Hawaii, HI (pp. 1-10).

Bamberger, P. (2008). Beyond contextualization: Using context theories to narrow the micro-macro grap in management research. *Academy of Management Journal, 51*(5), 839–846. doi:10.5465/AMJ.2008.34789630

Baron, R. M., & Kenny, D. A. (1996). The moderator-mediatior variable distinction in social psychological research: Conceptual, strategic, and statistical considerations. *Journal of Personality and Social Psychology, 51*, 1173–1182. doi:10.1037/0022-3514.51.6.1173

Baskerville, R. (2006). Hacker wars: E-collaboration by vandals and warriors. *International Journal of e-Collaboration, 2*(1), 1–16. doi:10.4018/jec.2006010101

Benbasat, I., & Zmud, R. W. (2003). The identity crisis within the IS discipline: Defining and communicating the discipline's core properties. *Management Information Systems Quarterly, 27*(2), 183–194.

Benbunan-Fich, R., Hiltz, S. R., & Turoff, M. (2002). A comparative content analysis of face-to-face vs. Asynchronous group decision making. *Decision Support Systems, 34*, 457–469. doi:10.1016/S0167-9236(02)00072-6

Bickel, R. (2007). *Multilevel analysis for applied research: It's just regression!* New York, NY: Guilford Press.

Boyle, R. J., Kacmanr, C., & George, J. F. (2008). Distributed deception: An investigation of the effectiveness of deceptive communication in a computer-mediated environment. *International Journal of e-Collaboration, 4*(3), 14–39. doi:10.4018/jec.2008070102

Bryk, A. S., & Raudenbush, S. W. (1992). *Hierarchical linear models*. Newbury Park, CA: Sage.

Burke, K., & Chidambaram, L. (1999). How much bandwidth is enough? A longitudinal examination of media characteristics and group outcomes. *Management Information Systems Quarterly*, *23*(4), 233–246. doi:10.2307/249489

Burton-Jones, A., & Gallivan, M. J. (2007). Towards a deeper understanding of system usage in organizations: A multilevel perspective. *Management Information Systems Quarterly*, *31*(4), 657–679.

Cenfetelli, R., & Schwarz, A. (in press). Identifying and testing inhibitors of technology usage intentions. *Information Systems Research*.

Chan, D. (1998). Functional relations among constructs in the same content domain at different levels of analysis: A typology of composition models. *The Journal of Applied Psychology*, *83*(2), 234–246. doi:10.1037/0021-9010.83.2.234

Chen, G., & Bliese, P. D. (2002). The role of different levels of leadership in predicting self- and collective efficacy: Evidence for discontinuity. *The Journal of Applied Psychology*, *87*(3), 549–556. doi:10.1037/0021-9010.87.3.549

Chen, G., Bliese, P. D., & Mathieu, J. E. (2005). Conceptual framework and statistical procedures for delineating and testing multilevel theories of homology. *Organizational Research Methods*, *8*(4), 375–409. doi:10.1177/1094428105280056

Chen, G., Mathieu, J. E., & Bliese, P. D. (2004). A framework for conducting multi-level construct validation. In Yammarino, F. J., & Danserau, F. (Eds.), *Multi-level issues in organizational behavior and processes* (pp. 273–303). Amsterdam, The Netherlands: Elsevier Science. doi:10.1016/S1475-9144(04)03013-9

Chidambaram, L., & Jones, B. (1993). Impact of communication medium and computer support on group perceptions and performance: A comparison of face-to-face and dispersed meetings. *Management Information Systems Quarterly*, *17*, 465–491. doi:10.2307/249588

Danserau, F., & Yammarino, F. J. (1998). Introduction and overview. In Danserau, F., & Yammarino, F. J. (Eds.), *Leadership: The multiple-level approaches* (pp. xxv–xliii). Greenwich, CT: JAI Press.

Davis, F. D., Bagozzi, R. P., & Warshaw, P. R. (1989). User acceptance of computer technology: A comparison of two theoretical models. *Management Science*, *35*(8), 982–1003. doi:10.1287/mnsc.35.8.982

Davis, J. A. (1966). The campus as a frog pond: An application of the theory of relative deprivation to career decisions of college men. *American Journal of Sociology*, *72*(1), 17–31. doi:10.1086/224257

de Leede, J., Kraan, K. O., den Hengst, M., & van Hooff, M. L. M. (2008). Conditions for innovation behaviour of virtual team members: A 'high road' for internationally dispersed virtual teams. *Journal of E-Working*, *2*, 22–46.

Easley, R. F., Devaraj, S., & Crant, J. M. (2003). Relating collaborative technology use to teamwork quality and performance: An empirical study. *Journal of Management Information Systems*, *19*(4), 249–270.

Enders, C. K. (in press). Missing not at random models for latent growth curve analyses. *Psychological Methods*.

Firebaugh, G. A. (1978). A rule for inferring individual-level relationships from aggregate data. *American Sociological Review*, *43*(4), 557–572. doi:10.2307/2094779

Firebaugh, G. A. (1980). Groups as contexts and frog ponds. In Roberts, K. H., & Burstein, L. (Eds.), *New directions for methodology of social and behavioral science* (*Vol. 6*, pp. 43–52). San Francisco, CA: Jossey-Bass.

Gallivan, M. J., & Benbunan-Fich, R. (2005). A framework for analyzing levels of analysis: Issues in studies of e-collaboration. *IEEE Transactions on Professional Communication, 48*(1), 87–104.

Gefen, D., Geri, N., & Paravatsu, N. (2007). Vive la différence: The cross-cultural differences within us. *International Journal of e-Collaboration, 3*(3), 1–15. doi:10.4018/jec.2007070101

Goodman, P. S. (2000). *Missing organizational linkages: Tools for cross-level research*. Thousand Oaks, CA: Sage.

Hitt, M. A., Beamish, P. W., Jackson, S. E., & Mathieu, J. E. (2007). Building theoretical and empirical bridges across levels: Multilevel research in management. *Academy of Management Journal, 50*(6), 1385–1399. doi:10.5465/AMJ.2007.28166219

Hobman, E. V., Bordia, P., Irmer, B., & Chang, A. (2002). The expression of conflict in computer-mediated and face-to-face groups. *Small Group Research, 33*(33), 4.

Hofmann, D. A. (1997). An overview of the logic and rationale of hierarchical linear models. *Journal of Management, 23*(6), 723–744. doi:10.1177/014920639702300602

Hofmann, D. A., & Jones, L. M. (2004). Some foundational and guiding questions for multilevel construct validation. In Dansereay, F., & Yammarino, F. J. (Eds.), *Multi-level issues in organizational behavior and processes* (pp. 305–317). Amsterdam, The Netherlands: Elsevier Science. doi:10.1016/S1475-9144(04)03014-0

James, L. R. (1982). Aggregation bias in estimates of perceptual agreement. *The Journal of Applied Psychology, 67*(2), 219–229. doi:10.1037/0021-9010.67.2.219

Keen, P. G. W. (1980). MIS research: Reference disciplines and a cumulative tradition. In *Proceedings of the First International Conference on Information Systems*, Philadelphia, PA.

Kirkman, B. L., Rosen, B., Tesluk, P. E., & Gibson, C. B. (2004). The impact of team empowerment on virtual team performance: The moderating role of face-to-face interaction. *Academy of Management Journal, 47*(2), 175–192. doi:10.2307/20159571

Klein, K. J., Bliese, P. D., Kozlowski, S. W. J., Dansareay, F., Gavin, M. B., & Griffin, M. A. (2000). Multilevel analytical techniques: Commonalitites, differences, and continuing questions. In Klein, K. J., & Kozlowski, S. W. J. (Eds.), *Multilevel theory, research, and methods in organizations* (pp. 512–553). San Francisco, CA: Jossey-Bass.

Klein, K. J., Danserau, F., & Hall, R. J. (1994). Levels issues in theory development, data collection, and analysis. *Academy of Management Review, 19*(2), 195–229.

Klein, K. J., & Kozlowski, S. W. (2000). From micro to meso: Critical steps in conceptualizing and conducting multilevel research. *Organizational Research Methods, 3*(3), 211–236. doi:10.1177/109442810033001

Klein, K. J., Tosi, H., & Cannella, A. A. J. (1999). Multilevel theory building: Benefits, barriers, and new developments. *Academy of Management Review, 24*(2), 243–248. doi:10.5465/AMR.1999.1893934

Ko, I., Olfman, L., & Choi, S. (2009). The impacts of electronic collaboration and information exploitation capability on firm performance: Focusing on suppliers using buyer-dominated interorganizational systems. *International Journal of e-Collaboration, 5*(2), 1–17. doi:10.4018/jec.2009040101

Kock, N. & Nosek, J. (2005). Expanding the boundaries of e-collaboration. *IEEE Transactions on Professional Communication, 48*(1), 1–9. doi:10.1109/TPC.2004.843272

Kock, N. (2005). What is e-collaboration? *International Journal of e-Collaboration, 1*(1), i–vii.

Kozlowski, S. W., & Klein, K. J. (2000). *Multilevel theory, research and methods in organizations: Foundations, extensions, and new directions.* San Francisco, CA: Jossey-Bass.

Kristensen, K., & Kijl, B. (2010). Collaborative performance: Addressing the ROI of collaboration. *International Journal of e-Collaboration, 6*(1), 53–69. doi:10.4018/jec.2010091104

Limayem, M., & DeSanctis, G. (2000). Providing decisional guidance for multicriteria decision making in groups. *Information Systems Research, 11*(4), 386–401. doi:10.1287/isre.11.4.386.11874

Luke, D. A. (2004). *Multilevel modeling.* Thousand Oaks, CA: Sage.

MacKinnon, D. P. (2008). Multilevel mediation models. In McKinnon, D. P. (Ed.), *Introduction to statistical mediation analysis* (pp. 237–274). New York, NY: Routledge.

Markus, M. L. (1994). Electronic mail as the medium of managerial choice. *Organization Science, 5*(4), 502–527. doi:10.1287/orsc.5.4.502

Markus, M. L. (2005). Technology-shaping effects of e-collaboration technologies: Bugs and features. *International Journal of e-Collaboration, 1*(1), 1–23. doi:10.4018/jec.2005010101

Martins, L. L. (2004). Virtual teams: What do we know and where do we go from here? *Journal of Management, 30*(6), 805–835. doi:10.1016/j.jm.2004.05.002

Masetti, B., & Zmud, R. W. (1996). Measuring the extend of EDI usage in complex organizations: Strategies and illustrative examples. *Management Information Systems Quarterly, 4*(1), 95–105.

Mathieu, J. E. (2007). The effects of leader empowering behavior, members' experience, and virtuality on sales team processes and performance. In *Proceedings of the Academy of Management,* Philadelphia, PA.

Mathieu, J. E., Maybard, M. T., Taylor, S. R., Gibson, L. L., & Ruddy, T. M. (2007). An examination of the effects of organizational district and team contexts on team processes and performance: A meso-mediational model. *Journal of Organizational Behavior, 28*(7), 891–910. doi:10.1002/job.480

Mathieu, J. E., & Taylor, S. R. (2007). A framework for testing meso-mediational relationships in organizational behavior. *Journal of Organizational Behavior, 28,* 141–172. doi:10.1002/job.436

Morgeson, F. P., & Hofmann, D. A. (1999). The structure and function of collective constructs: Implications for multilevel research and theory development. *Academy of Management Review, 24*(2), 249–265.

Muthén, B., Asparouhov, T., Hunter, A., & Leuchter, A. (in press). Growth modeling with non-ignorable dropout: Alternative analyses of the STAR*D antidepressant trial. *Psychological Methods.*

Orlikowski, W. J. (2000). Using technology and constituting structures: A practice lens for studying technology in organizations. *Organization Science, 11*(4), 404–428. doi:10.1287/orsc.11.4.404.14600

Ortiz de Guinea, A., & Webster, J. (2011). Are we talking about the task or the computer? An examination of the associated domains of task-specific and computer self-efficacies. *Computers in Human Behavior, 27*(2), 978–987. doi:10.1016/j.chb.2010.12.002

Ortiz de Guinea, A., Webster, J., & Staples, D. S. (2005). *A meta-analysis of the virtual team literature.* Paper presented at the High Performance Professional Teams Symposium, Industrial Relations Centre, School of Policy Studies, Queen's University, Kingston, ON, Canada.

Otondo, R. F., Barnett, T., Kellermans, F. W., Pearson, A. W., & Pearson, R. A. (2009). Assessing information technology use over time with growth modeling and hierarchical linear modeling: A tutorial. *Communications of the Association for Information Systems, 25*(1), 45.

Peugh, J. L., & Enders, C. K. (2005). Using the spss mixed procedure to fit cross-sectional and longitudinal multilevel models. *Educational and Psychological Measurement, 65*(5), 717–741. doi:10.1177/0013164405278558

Powell, A., Piccoli, G., & Ives, B. (2004). Virtual teams: A review of current literature and directions for future research. *The Data Base for Advances in Information Systems, 35*(1), 6–36.

Rodell, J. B., & Judge, T. A. (2009). Can "good" stressors spark "bad" behaviors? The mediating role of emotions in links of challenge and hindrance stressors with citizenship and counterproductive behaviors. *The Journal of Applied Psychology, 94*(6), 1438–1451. doi:10.1037/a0016752

Rousseau, D. M. (1985). Issues of level in organizational research: Multi-level and cross-level perspectives. In Staw, B. M., & Cummings, L. L. (Eds.), *Research in organizational behavior* (*Vol. 7*, pp. 1–37). Greenwich, CT: JAI Press.

Sarker, S., Valacich, J. S., & Sarker, S. (2005). Technology adoption by groups: A valence perspective. *Journal of the Association for Information Systems, 6*(2), 37–71.

Seibert, S. E., Silvert, S. R., & Randolph, W. A. (2004). Taking empowerment to the next level: A multiple-leveled model of empowerment, performance, and satisfaction. *Academy of Management Journal, 47*(3), 332–349. doi:10.2307/20159585

Short, J. S., Piccolo, G., Powell, A., & Ives, B. (2005). Investigating multilevel relationships in information systems research: An application to virtual teams research using hierarchical linear modeling. *Journal of Information Technology Theory and Application, 7*(3), 1–17.

Tabachnick, B. G., & Fidell, L. S. (2007). *Using multivariate statistics* (5th ed.). Boston, MA: Pearson Education.

Treviño, L. K. W., J., & Stein, E. W. (2000). Making connections: Complementary influences on communication media choices, attitudes, and use. *Organization Science, 11*(2), 163–182. doi:10.1287/orsc.11.2.163.12510

Valacich, J. S., Sarker, S., Pratt, J., & Groomer, M. (2002). Computer-mediated and face-to-face groups: Who makes riskier decisions? In *Proceedings of the 35th Hawaii International Conference on System Sciences*, Hawaii, HI (pp. 133-142).

Wakefield, R. L., Leidner, D. E., & Garrison, G. (2008). A model of conflict, leadership, and performance in virtual teams. *Information Systems Research, 19*(4), 434–455. doi:10.1287/isre.1070.0149

Walczuch, R. M., & Watson, R. T. (2001). Analyzing group data in mis research: Including the effect of the group. *Group Decision and Negotiation, 10*, 83–94. doi:10.1023/A:1008765029795

Webster, J., & Staples, D. S. (2006). Comparing virtual teams to traditional teams: An identification of new research opportunities. In Martocchio, J. J. (Ed.), *Research in personnel and human resources management* (*Vol. 25*, pp. 181–215). Oxford, UK: Elsevier.

Webster, J., & Treviño, L. K. (1995). Rational and social theories as complementary explanations of communication media choices: Two policy capturing studies. *Academy of Management Journal, 38*, 1544–1572. doi:10.2307/256843

Webster, J., & Watson, R. T. (2002). Analyzing the past to prepare for the future: Writing a literature review. *Management Information Systems Quarterly, 26*(2), xiii–xxiii.

Whetten, D. A. (1989). What constitutes a theoretical contribution. *Academy of Management Review, 14*(4), 490–495.

Yammarino, F. J., & Markham, S. E. (1992). On the application of within and between analysis: Are absence and affect really group-based phenomena? *The Journal of Applied Psychology, 77*, 168–176. doi:10.1037/0021-9010.77.2.168

ENDNOTES

[1] A related issue worth mentioning is the disaggregation of data or the "breaking down of information at one level by assigning its component parts to individual units at a lower level" (Rousseau, 1985, p. 5). One problematic issue of these data is the violation of the independence of observation assumption, explained earlier (Hofmann, 1997). Another problematic issue of disaggregated data is that biases can arise when calculating statistical estimates because such estimates are based on the total number of lower-level units (Hofmann, 1997).

[2] It is important to note that normative functions and comparative functions – explained earlier – can cancel each other (Firebaugh, 1980). The difference between normative and comparative functions is explained as follows by Rousseau (1985, p. 10): "Generally, normative effects result from appraisal or evaluation of one's relative standing in a group. Unlike comparative functions which assume that all individuals in a unit are equally affected by some composite unit characteristic, normative effects assume differences in individual responses according to one's relative standing".

[3] Perhaps because they can be thought of as an extension of cross-level direct effects models.

[4] This paragraph points only to the fact that much of the positivist research uses quantitative methodologies and that much of interpretivist research employs qualitative data. This does not mean, however, that philosophical approaches to science and theory have a one-to-one relation with method. For example, it is possible to conduct positivist research with qualitative data.

This work was previously published in the International Journal of e-Collaboration, Volume 7, Issue 4, edited by Ned Kock, pp. 1-21, copyright 2011 by IGI Publishing (an imprint of IGI Global).

Chapter 13
E–Collaboration Within, Between, and Without Institutions:
Towards Better Functioning of Online Groups Through Networks

Ina Blau
Open University of Israel, Israel

ABSTRACT

This paper discusses different ways for the exchange of knowledge in networks - within, between, and without institutions, as well as their implication on networks in economy and society. Network systems based on technologies and architectures of participation offer a new model of online knowledge sharing, cooperation, and collaboration, that are different from the traditional institutional framework. This paper suggests that this model opens new horizons for both companies and non-profit organizations. By developing an e-networked business model, companies can make as much or even more money in the long tail of power low distribution than they were making at the head of the curve in the traditional business model. This opens to everyone the possibility of participating and contributing content, non-profit organization and online communities, including Communities of Practice and online learning communities, which can ensure reaching the "critical mass" of contributors and involvement level that will keep these communities active. This paper concludes with an example illustrating how the ideas discussed could facilitate knowledge exchange in companies, organizations or educational institutions.

DOI: 10.4018/978-1-4666-2020-9.ch013

INTRODUCTION

The clear boundary between creators and consumers of online content has blurred in the past decade because of the enormous expansion of a new culture - the participatory culture. Jenkins et al. (2006b) define the participatory culture as one in which members believe their contributions matter, and feel some degree of social connection with one another. Community and knowledge management are two features that online environment can do much better than its physical counterpart (Chen & Tsai, 2009). The Web 2.0 is an information space through which people can communicate by sharing their knowledge and ideas in a common pool and find items shared by others. Network technologies allow geographically dispersed users in companies, organizations, and communities of practice to communicate, share their knowledge, cooperate, and collaborate online in order to work or learn together (Bouras, Giannaka, & Tsiatsos, 2009).

As a response to a key social value of participatory literacy at the 21st century workplace, educational practitioners, and researchers have demonstrated a growing interest in developing pedagogical practices enhancing a participatory culture in all levels of education (Coiro, Knobel, Lankshear, & Leu, 2008). Differing from the traditional whereby compulsory and higher education are based on lectures and individual assignments; the emergence of a participatory culture at schools, colleges, and universities changes the focus of literacy from individual expression to collaboration and community involvement (Jenkins, 2006a).

Mediated collaboration is not limited to computer mediated communication (CMC). Kock, Davison, Ocker, and Wazlawick (2001) suggested a broad definition of e-collaboration as "a process of collaboration among individuals engaged in a common task using electronic technologies". According to Kock and Nosek (2005), not only computers, but many other electronic technologies can be used to support collaboration among individuals engaged in a common task.

A variety of electronic technologies now enable different types of coordination and knowledge exchange. First this paper will make the distinction between the different forms of knowledge exchange through information technologies. Following that, different ways of exchanging knowledge in networks - within, between, and without institutions, as well as their implication on networked economy and society will be discussed. Motivation for contributions will be presented and e-collaboration through networked systems which will be examined from different perspectives - synchronous versus asynchronous knowledge exchange, continuous versus one-time contribution, active community involvement and content contribution versus lurking. The paper concludes with an example illustrating how the ideas discussed could facilitate knowledge exchange in companies, organization or educational institutions.

SHARING, COOPERATION, AND COLLABORATION

Some authors use the term "knowledge sharing" in a broad sense – as the process of mutually exchanging knowledge and jointly creating new knowledge (van den Hooff & de Ridder, 2004). However, exchange and creating knowledge through information technology have different forms and it is important to make a distinction between the processes of knowledge sharing, cooperation, and collaboration. Knowledge sharing is the provision or receipt of task information, know-how, and feedback regarding a product or procedure (Hansen, 1999), "an activity where agents - individuals, communities, or organizations - exchange their knowledge - information, skills, or expertise" (Ireson & Burel, 2010, p. 351). Examples of knowledge sharing through information technology are Flikr and YouTube where participants contribute pictures or video clips to the system and other users can retrieve their output. Cooperation described as working on a task that is accomplished by dividing it among participants, where "each person is responsible for a *portion* of the problem solving" [*emphasis added*] (Roschelle & Teasley, 1995, p. 70). An example of online cooperation is the development of Linux, in which different programmers around the world improve the *same* open-source system by contributing *different* patches or fixing *different* bugs. Collaboration, in contrast, is defined as "a method that implies working in a group of two or more to achieve a common goal, while respecting each individual's contribution to the *whole*" [*emphasis added*] (McInnerney & Robert, 2004, p. 205). An example of e-collaboration process is the Wikipedia project in which groups of users write and edit the *same entries* improving their quality and correcting errors.

The results of collaborative production tend to be more profound compared to sharing or cooperation (Caspi & Blau, in press; Ingram & Hathorn, 2004). Shirky (2009) pointed to the fact that collaborative production, where people have to coordinate with one another to get anything done, is considerably harder than simple knowledge sharing and cooperation. The author argued that compared to more passive cooperative activities, working collaboratively on the same task places more cognitive and interpersonal demands on participants.

In learning settings, working collaboratively, participants build a new knowledge by defending their ideas and by challenging other learners. According to Ingram and Hathorn (2004), the outcomes of successful collaborative learning process are qualitatively different from what any individual could produce alone.

However, collaboration often does not come naturally to participants, especially in cultures that cultivate individual accountability and responsibility. In most companies, it is difficult to encourage employees to collaborate and even cooperate with others; they avoid sharing resources

or customers on tasks with little recognition of individual input (Hansen, 2009). Similarly, many learners prefer using a "divide and conquer" cooperative strategy to prepare their part of the group project (Blau & Caspi, 2009). This strategy can be useful working on assignment, but it tends to lose most of the advantages of collaborating throughout the entire learning process (Ingram & Hathorn, 2004).

Blau and Caspi (2009) argued that discussing the preferences for knowledge sharing, cooperation, and collaboration is important when taking into consideration the sense of psychological ownership. Psychological ownership is "the state in which individuals feel as though the target of ownership or a piece of that target is 'theirs'" (Pierce, Kostova, & Dirks, 2003, p. 86). This sense of possession is not restricted to physical objects, but may be felt toward information (Raban & Rafaeli, 2007), words, ideas, creations, or academic products (Pierce et al., 2003). Compare to knowledge sharing and cooperation, editing collaborative documents has the higher level of intrusion and decreases the sense of psychological ownership (Caspi & Blau, in press). Thus, participants may avoid collaboration partly because they do not want to lose a sense of personal ownership or to reduce the ownership of others.

Knowledge Exchange in Networks: Within, Between, and Without Institutions

The knowledge sharing research and practice using information and communication technologies (ICT) traditionally has been focused on the knowledge exchange within and between professional organizations (Ireson & Burel, 2010). The Web 2.0 applications extended these possibilities promoting online interactions and knowledge exchange in three ways: (1) between employees *within* organization or group of organizations, (2) *between* the organization and users of its products or services, and (3) between users themselves, creating a network based on user-to-user coordination, *without* forming an institution.

Online interactions and knowledge exchange *within* organizations often happened in the form of online projects. Deepwell and King (2009) defined online project management as "processes employing a virtual infrastructure to plan, manage, and control the activities of a project team which may be geographically and/or temporally dispersed" (p. 12). Online collaboration tools help teams to build virtual workspaces where the group members can work on projects, collectively author, edit, and review materials (Fichter, 2005). These virtual workspaces can include member profiles, online discussion groups, file-sharing areas, integrated calendaring, and collaborative authoring tools. For example, providing commentaries on a particular subject in interactive format through a blog can increase information sharing in organizations (Bouras, Giannaka, & Tsiatsos, 2009). Some organizations encourage executives or experts posting their preliminary thoughts and ideas in blogs in order to start discussion and information exchange both inside and outside the organization.

Using network technologies for online interactions and knowledge exchange *between* the organization and users of its products or services, institutions strengthen connections with their potential target audience and in some cases encourage active participation and/or content contribution by users. This model of audience involvement can be adapted whether by economic institutions such as firms, cooperatives, unions, by political organization such as parties, governing bodies, agencies, or by social institutions such as religious organizations, associations, and clubs (Ulieru & Verdon, 2009). In the traditional version of this model, organizations broadcast to all users regardless of the individual user needs, while users just provide a reaction to the organization activities (Ireson & Burel, 2010). This process based on

two-way communication: Providing relevant information by organization to individuals or groups of users, and receiving user feedback on the products or services provided by the organization. Ireson and Burel however argued that some organizations realized the potential benefits offered through harnessing the power of the potential customers of their products and services. Thus, in an advanced version of this model, users can be pro-actively engaged in the decision-making process determining the nature, importance, extent of issues and opportunities faced by organizations, as well as the mode in which activities of organizations are carried out. Ireson and Burel (2010) give an example of "Johnson & Johnson" company setting up the Baby Center - global interactive parenting network, where the company consumers are actively engaged in conversations to solicit information on given topics. Ulieru and Verdon (2008) argued that embracing the power of decentralized user-generated content supported by network technologies, institutions are shifting from the 'command economy' to the 'e-networked industrial ecosystem'. However, the connections and interdependencies between people and institutions give rise to new patterns of interaction and challenge the hierarchical top-down management business model (Shirky, 2009).

There is a relatively new trend of pushing the processes of knowledge sharing, cooperation, and collaboration into the infrastructure (Coleman & Levine, 2008). In this model technologies create online networks based on user-to-user coordination, *without* forming institutions and shift the world from the industrial to the networked society and economy (Ulieru & Verdon, 2009). A network system coordinates the output of the group as a byproduct of operating the system, avoiding difficulties and costs related to running an institution. According to Shirky (2009), additional advantages of this collaboration mode are: Including all the participants in the process of knowledge exchange and collaboration instead of hire professionals only in institutional model, taking a problems to the participants around the world rather then moving them to the institution for solving the problems, and replacing long-term planning and the necessity of deciding in advance with point-to-point coordination.

User-generated content networks such as You-Tube, Flikr, and Wikipedia are examples of this growing trend of using a network infrastructure for knowledge sharing, cooperation, and collaboration, without forming an institution. YouTube.com is a way of upload, share, and tag videos worldwide, with more than 100 million videos being watched every day (Cheng, Dale, & Liu, 2008). YouTube has been online since 2005 and by the time of this writing, according to the three-month traffic rankings (Alexa.com), the website is ranked as number 3 in the world. Weinberger (2007) mentioned that Flickr.com - user-generated picture platform - have approximately 225 million images uploaded by users with almost one million being added every day. The platform contains picture galleries available with chat, groups, tag, and photo ratings (Alexa.com). Wikipedia project started in 2001 and now it is the world's largest encyclopedia with about 15 millions of articles in 250 languages and over 3.5 million articles in the largest English version. The website is ranked as number 8 in the world according to the three-month Alexa.com traffic rankings. Ulieru and Verdon (2009) explained the fast growing and updating of the Wikipedia by relatively costless coordination and self-organization, as well as by editing history transparency of the wiki technology. Wikipedia contains features that enable co-authoring and collaboration (Rafaeli, Hayat, & Ariel, 2009). Thus, the system allows anyone (registered as well as anonymous and occasional users) to add, change or delete content in any of the articles and saves a detailed history of changes. Instead of professional editors, visitors are collectively monitoring the content. Participants, who have interest in

specific topics, may purposefully follow recent changes and traffic in articles related to this topic. The quality of outcomes after the collaboration in networks is high and explained in the literature by "wisdom of crowds" (Surowiecki, 2004).

User-generated tags is the answer of online networks to the problem of classification in file-sharing areas, the way in which the infrastructure coordinates contributions of users and make possible to find and retrieve them (Shirky, 2009). For example, Flickr has not only almost one million pictures being added every day, but also 5.7 million tags applied (Weinberger, 2007). YouTube platform uses tags, titles, and descriptions of the videos to find related clips (Cheng et al., 2008). Allowing the users to upload and characterize their content is an especially effective way to access the needed content in cases when only a small fraction of people possess the output we are interested it (Shirky, 2009).

E-Collaboration in a Networked Economy: Using the Long Tail of Peer-Production

The future of business is selling more of less (Anderson, 2008).

As mentioned earlier, network systems based on technologies and architectures of participation offer a new model of e-collaboration, which is completely different from the existing institutional framework (Shirky, 2009; Ulieru & Verdon, 2009). This new model can be coined within the power-law distribution known as 80-20 rule (Pennock et al., 2002). According to the rule, for some natural phenomena about 80% of the effects come from approximately 20% of the causes.

Productivity in networked systems follows the same type of power-low distribution (Ulieru & Verdon, 2009). While sales are decreasing and costs increasing, traditional hierarchic institutions can no longer be viable. Therefore organizations using traditional business model hire the most talented and productive people available within the constraints of the cost-value threshold.

The model based on network technologies adapts a different approach and tend to capitalize the whole curve of potential productivity by reaping the aggregated value of the many people, including many participants who make only one contribution (Shirky, 2009). This new mode of production rooted in network technologies as platforms of near costless coordination, maximizes organizational capability and uses a long tail of peer-production as a synergetic 'force multiplier' (Ulieru & Verdon, 2009).

However, researchers predict (Shirky, 2009; Ulieru & Verdon, 2009) that the traditional hierarchic organizations will not be completely displaced by the model based on network technologies and user participation only, instead of forming an institution. Rather online networks offer the traditional business model a new platform for coordinating efforts of contributors, using a long tail of peer-production and building networked economy. These mixed companies may *coexist* with online communities based on user-to-user coordination, without forming institutions.

E-Collaboration in Networked Society

E-collaboration in networked society is primarily concerned with facilitating e-government and knowledge exchange process in Communities of Practice (CoP) - "normally professional, social grouping whose members work actively on a shared interest, solving shared problems, sharing and constructing knowledge over time" (Deepwell & King, 2009, p. 12). Considering e-government, the majority of the research focuses on either intra- and inter-organizational knowledge exchange using ICT, or explores how different technologies can improve the communication from organizations to citizens (Vitvar et al., 2010). Thus, investigating networked society, it seems

that research still focuses on two traditional forms of online interactions, knowledge exchange, and e-collaboration mentioned above: between employees *within* organization, as well as *between* the organization and users of its products or services.

Taking advantage of users and adapting a model based on network technologies, knowledge become a property of CoP - groups of people with shared interests, who benefit from knowledge exchange and collaboration (Ireson & Burel, 2010). Technological tools are used by members of CoP on order to identify specific information and experts, share successes and develop best practices, exchange thoughts and replicate ideas. These communities function as informal networks of individuals who share a common set of information needs or problems. Thus, CoP can be characterized as the third model presented above- a network based on user-to-user coordination, *without* forming institutions. Ireson and Burel argued that to support CoP and make them effective it is important to choose knowledge management tools that allow efficacious interactions and intuitive access to the shared knowledge database. An example of community with effective technological platform is Wikipedia, which fit into the category of CoP by forming a social collective of individuals that deal with similar problems that matter to them (Rafaeli, Hayat, & Ariel, 2009). These characteristics of CoP, as well as the sense of community that the participants share, foster the process of e-collaboration and knowledge building taking place in the Wikipedia.

CoP function in networked society as engines for development of social capital (Lesser & Storck, 2001). *Social capital* is "the actual and potential resources individuals obtain from knowing others, being part of a social network with them, or merely being known to them and having a good reputation" (Baron & Markman, 2000, p. 107). Findings of Ardichvili, Page, and Wentling (2003) suggest that online CoP strengthen the social capital by enhancing the ties between people who have met earlier face-to-face, but due to geographical distance or other reasons would not have kept in touch. Lesser and Storck (2001) identify performance outcomes associated with CoP they studied and link these outcomes to the basic dimensions of social capital. These dimensions include: connections among practitioners who may or may not be co-located, relationships that build a mutual obligation and sense of trust, as well as a common language and context that can be shared by community members. The authors argue that the social capital that is present in CoP leads to behavioral changes, which in turn improve organizational performance and create organizational value.

However, the model based on network infrastructure is value neutral; in some cases this may lead to negative consequences and even contradict rules of society (Shirky, 2009). For example, network infrastructure equally supports programmers improving open source software code, as well as hackers who share tips on how to program a computer virus or break into security networks. It allows online support for people having different health problems, as well as for groups like ProAna, a community of teenage girls that try to maintain their anorexia by choice and use the network for "thinspiration" - sharing diets, tips, and pictures of thin models. It is important to be aware not only of the advantages, but also the disadvantages and downsides of technological infrastructures in an e-network society.

Synchronous Versus Asynchronous E-Collaboration

Information exchange is not only held within documents and networked systems, but also in inter-personal and group dialogues among people (Ireson & Burel, 2010). During these dialogues via electronic technologies, different communication channels are used: Synchronous communication that supports real-time interactions (e.g., video conferencing, audio conferencing, textual chat), as well as asynchronous communication that sup-

ports 24/7 interactions (e.g., email, SMS, forum, blog, wiki, twitter). Kock (2010) argued that e-collaboration technologies based on textual interactions without supporting oral speech leads to two negative consequences when knowledge exchange is attempted: (1) a decrease in communication fluency and (2) an increase in communication ambiguity. Kock claimed that the negative effects of absence oral speech are particularly strong in short-term collaborative tasks and need to be taken into consideration when choosing collaborative technology. Consistent with this claim, Blau and Barak (2010) found lower communication fluency in short-term knowledge exchange in groups interacting through textual chat compared to groups communicating through audio conferencing.

Some networked systems support both synchronous and asynchronous form of sharing knowledge and/or collaboration. For example, the Google Docs application allows access from any computer and eases sharing documents with specific participants or publishing them on the web were everyone can find and retrieve them (Conner, 2008). In addition to the file-sharing function, Google Docs affords synchronous as well as asynchronous cooperation and collaboration by supporting easy editing, comment writing, and saving versions of the document (Blau & Caspi, 2009). Flexible systems supporting synchronous as well as asynchronous communication are prominent for both work and learning purposes, since using the same network the participants can choose the most convenient form of interaction and collaboration for each task.

Continuous Versus One-Time Contribution

As mentioned above, the model of collaboration in a networked economy can be coined within the power-law distribution. Therefore a very large number of participants in a networked economy model make only one-time contributions to their communities, while the traditional institutional model is based exclusively on continuous contribution (Shirky, 2009). For example, exploring the efforts behind the development of Linux, Microsoft discovered that the majority of programmers made only one contribution to the system. Commenting on this fact, Ulieru and Verdon (2009) pointed out that the long tail of Linux's e-networked productivity model makes possible the contribution of millions of programmers, without significant additional transaction and coordination costs. Moreover, the potential of including every programmer around the world in its development of Linux, leads in some cases to really essential one-time improvements, such as contributing important security patches or fixing serious bugs. Traditional organizational business models give up this value because it cannot tolerate workers that contribute once in several years, even if their contribution is priceless (Ulieru & Verdon, 2009; Shirky, 2009).

Similarly, the capacity of the Wikipedia project to grow, keep articles up to date, and correct errors far exceeds the capacity of Encyclopedia Britannica to do the same. The most recent 15th edition of Encyclopedia Britannica was published in 1985; the Wikipedia project started in 2001 and its growth in terms of volume, number of articles, and percentage of contributors has been very impressive. By the time of this writing, the largest English version of Wikipedia contains more than 3.5 million articles, the German version- 1.5 million articles, French versions more than a million articles and Spanish, Italian, Portuguese, Chinese, Dutch, Polish, and Russian versions - over half a million articles each. For comparison, only a few years ago Rafaeli and Ariel (2008) reported about significantly less content in Wikipedia: Two million articles in English, more than half a million articles in German, and more than 100,000 in other languages mentioned above. Benkler (2006) explained the rapid growth of the Wikipedia project by adapting the networked model: "The shift in strategy toward an open, peer-produced model proved enormously successful. The site

saw tremendous growth both in the number of contributors, which included the number of active and very active contributors, and the number of articles included in the encyclopedia" (p. 71). However, despite the fact that number of active and very active contributors of Wikipedia is growing rapidly, similarly to other social phenomena with power-law distribution, the ratio of contributors that keep the community active is low. About 2.5% of Wikipedia users contribute 80% of all the content and only 1% of the users generated 50% of the content (Tapscott & Williams, 2007).

The model of networked collaboration using a one-time contribution of many participants works not only for open-source development communities or non-profit projects and organization. For example, developing an e-networked business model, Amazon.com discovered that they were able to make as much or even more money in the long tail of their book sales than they were making in the head of the curve (Ulieru & Verdon, 2009). The Amazon.com website has been online since 1994. By the time of this writing, according to Alexa.com, Amazon's three-month global traffic rank is 14 and 5 in US. It turns out that once the network was built, coordination costs of Amazon decreased significantly and as the network business grew, they totally collapsed (Ulieru & Verdon, 2009). Amazon has numerous personalization features and services including one-click buying, extensive customer and editorial product reviews, seeking to be the most customer-centric company, where customers can find and discover anything they might want to buy online by the lowest possible prices (Alexa.com).

These examples of open-source program development such as Linux, community of practice writing online encyclopedia such as Wikipedia, and company developing an e-networked business model such as Amazon, show the possibility of success based on the long tail – a very large number of participants' one-time contribution through the networked infrastructure.

Content Contribution and Involvement: Expectations and Explanations

Ingram and Hathorn (2009) claimed that in learning settings, an indispensible element of collaboration is that all learners involved in a collaborative task must contribute more or less *equally*. However, due to the lack of content contributors, online communities have serious problems in sustaining the community active (Rafaeli & Ariel, 2008). Adar and Huberman (2000) argued that the cyberspace is overloaded with empty communities and with communities where many of the participants are "free riders" or "lurkers". Moreover, according to these researchers, free riding leads to degradation of the community performance and may collapse such a networked system. Indicating the disproportion of content contribution and community involvement, Peddibhotla and Subramani (2007) claim that a "critical mass" of contributors is needed to maintain a community active.

Other researchers (Rafaely & Ariel, 2008; Shirky, 2009), however, pointed to the fact that in networked systems the participation is non-mandatory and people contribute as much as they like. Therefore in communities with user-generated content typically is observed a *power low distribution* of participation and content contribution. For example, studying the temporal evolution of two online communities and the changes in the communication activity of their users on a longitudinal basis, Schoberth, Heinzl, and Rafaeli (2011) found that a small portion of participants possess a large number of connections, while the majority of the community members hold only very few connections. The distribution of content contribution is extremely skewed also among writers of articles in the open community around the world such as Wikipedia (Ravid, 2007). Similarly, a power low distribution was find in relatively small learning community of undergraduates in three Universities collaboratively writing and updating Wiki-books,

instead of using traditional text-books written by others (Ravid, Kalman, & Rafaeli, 2008). Skewed distribution was also found among the "digital generation" of elementary school students when interacting, sharing, and collaborating with other children in a small online learning community preparing Scratch programming media projects (Zuckerman, Blau, & Monroy-Hernández, 2009). It seems that the power low distribution is neither restricted to the text medium nor to the participant age.

Schoberth, Heinzl, and Rafaeli (2011) tried to identify an analytical model able to fit power low distributions in online communities and explain their causes. They found that the theoretical model by Pennock et al. (2002) which unites two approaches - Scale-free Networks and Random Network Theory, allows the operationalization of member activity distribution. Moreover, the Pennock et al.'s model explain functions of the communication activity in communities with only one free parameter- the mixing factor α, which represents the ratio between the antagonists- homogeneity and heterogeneity. Authors found that in both larger and smaller communities the mixing factor α and therefore the level of heterogeneity, were relatively stable over time (Schoberth et al., 2011). However, they also discovered that participants in both communities prefer to interact and collaborate with members having many communication partners, while members with low activity are less attractive for interaction. This finding is consistent with general striking "rich get richer" behavior observed on the Internet, e.g., when a relatively small number of websites receiving a disproportionately large share of traffic and hyperlink references (Pennock et al., 2002). According to Schoberth et al. (2011), this phenomenon was stronger in a large online community - it members had almost twice as many connections as those of a small community. Authors concluded that compared to the large network, the tighter community might lead to the more homogeneous distribution of its activity.

Motivation for E-Collaboration

To develop an effective networked system it is essential to consider the motivation of the users for sharing their knowledge and collaborating with others (Ireson & Burel, 2010). However, Rafaeli and Ariel (2008) noted that studies of incentives for participation and content contribution are limited. Describing motivation of the Wikipedia contributors, Ciffolilli (2003) distinguished between personal and social motivation. *Personal* motivation factors involve satisfaction, self-efficacy, and intrinsic drive to acquire knowledge. *Social* motivation factors include a desire to participate in producing collective good, a need for support, and a need for belonging to the group. *Uses and Gratifications* approach is a theoretical framework for examining media users and investigating how people use the media to gratify their needs. Rubin's uses and gratification approach (1994) suggested five generic motivation clusters of needs that media could fulfill: cognitive, affective, personal integrative, social integrative, and diversion needs. Rafaeli and Ariel (2008) and Rafaeli, Hayat, and Ariel (2009) expanded uses and gratification approach for analyzing online environments, attempting to identify the cognitive and social-integrative motivators for active participation in Wikipedia. Based on uses and gratification approach, Zuckerman, Blau, and Monroy-Hernández (2009) explored *cognitive versus social* motivators for content contribution among children and youth producing programming media in the Scratch online community. Stafford, Stafford and Schkade (2004) emphasized the role of cognitive gratification of online communities - the desire for information acquisition – and argued that it is one of the principal motivators for participation and content contribution. In contrast, Blau, Zuckerman, and Monroy-Hernández (2009) found that children in Scratch community gratify different forms of social participation, but not a cognitive contribution.

Other researchers suggest a different perspective grounded on their empirical data. Joyce and Kraut (2006) suggested that newcomers' interaction with a group through initial postings followed by responses of other community members will be a first step in building their commitment to the group. This claim was empirically proved by Burke, Marlow, and Lento (2009) through log analysis of approximately 140,000 newcomers on Facebook, a social networking website. Their findings on Facebook indicate that receiving feedback on a newcomer's contribution was a significant predictor of subsequent content contribution.

Although there are different type of motivation for different users of an e-collaboration system, generally, in organizations there is an expectation of some *extrinsic* reward (external-oriented motives, e.g., enhance reputation, social ranking, competition, social affiliation, reciprocity, expected economic and organizational rewards) for any knowledge shared (Palmisano, 2008). In community-based systems, incentives become less significant, while the *intrinsic* motivation to participate and share knowledge (self-oriented motives, e.g., self expression, personal development, utilitarian motives, economic motives, and knowledge efficacy) becomes more important. Consistent with this claim, the assessment of Wikipedians' motivation (Rafaeli, Hayat, & Ariel, 2009) indicated that at least two motivators ("sharing my knowledge" and "contributing to others") ranked high in comparison to other motivation descriptors, had a selfless flavor. The researchers concluded that, at least partially, contribution to Wikipedia CoP based on altruistic sharing and collaborative reasons.

Different factors, such as *communication medium, personal traits,* and the *characteristics of the task*, may influence on individual online behavior and motivation for contribution in communities. Blau and Barak (2009) found that participant personality affected their willingness to partake in group interacting online: Extroverts and neurotic participants preferred taking part through a more exposing communication medium such as audio conferencing, while introverts and emotionally stable participants expressed greater readiness to communicate through textual chat. The effect of task characteristic interacted with participant personal traits and type of medium, adding to this trend. In contrast to very low participation and contribution of introverts in face-to-face communication, it seems that asynchronous interactions (Amichai-Hamburger, 2007) as well as synchronous communication through textual chat (Blau & Barak, 2010) empowers introverts by releasing inhibitions of their anxiety of interpersonal interactions ("the poor get richer" phenomenon).

Studies into group dynamics indicate that self-efficacy, or *belief* that one's actions have an effect, seem to motivate sharing in online environments. Participants believed that she or he can "make a difference" contributed to the group regardless of other members' activity (Benbunan-Fich & Koufaris, 2008; Chen, Chen, & Kinshuk, 2009).

Implementing the Model of Network Systems with Google Apps

In order to illustrate how the ideas discussed in this paper could be implemented in companies, organizations or educational institutions, an example of Google Apps is used. There are versions of Google Apps for business, governmental and nonprofit organizations, as well as an educational edition. This system is a cloud workspace whereby, using the same username and password, members can share files, work on projects, collectively author, edit, and review materials, communicate and organize their efforts.

The system is flexible and includes components for different tasks and for different employee or learner needs. Providing commentaries in interactive format through a Blogger application can be recommended to increase dialogue and information exchange both inside and outside the organization. Google Documents allow all the forms of online knowledge exchange: sharing, cooperation,

and collaboration of documents, spreadsheets or presentations – across the organization or with specific people. Depending on the task features, editing Google Documents can be asynchronous and in real-time, supported if necessarily by instant communication. Integrating Google Calendar and/or Task function is recommended for coordination between the participants of collaborative projects. The final version of Google Documents can be published directly on the net or easily embedded in shared or public Google Sites. All versions of the documents are saved and allow exploration of the contribution made by an individual employee or learner. The use of this function of Google Documents is highly recommended for enhancing the willingness to participate and contribute content. In addition, transparency of individual contribution might enhance the willingness of employees or learners to collaborate and co-authoring by diminish the feel of losing a sense of personal ownership or reducing the ownership of others.

Opening worldwide the possibility to edit Google Documents and Sites can help companies receive value in the long tail of power low distribution as well as help CoP and learning communities reach the "critical mass" of content contributors and community involvement. User-generated tags enable the classification of documents and correspondence; internal find function allows easy retrieve of participant contribution. For tracking silent participation (lurking) in Site pages monitoring by administrators through Google Analytics application is recommended.

During the collaboration process, it is important that employees or learners choose an appropriate form of communication. According to the characteristics of the task and personal traits, participants can choose asynchronous communication (interpersonal interaction via email or group discussion through Google Groups application) as well as synchronous interactions based on textual chat, voice, and video interpersonal or group communication. Asynchronous communication is recommended for discussions and reflection. Textual chat is embedded in Google email and documents, providing instant support for group members working on collaborative outcomes. Google Talk opens the possibility for audio and video conferencing, avoiding negative consequences, such as a decrease in communication fluency and an increase in communication ambiguity, when knowledge exchange is attempted. Leaders may recommend to employees or learners avoiding these negative effects of oral speech absence by communicating through audio and video conferencing during short-term collaborative tasks and brainstorming.

CONCLUSION AND IMPLICATIONS

Network systems based on technologies and architectures of participation offer a new model of online knowledge sharing, cooperation, and collaboration, that are different from the traditional institutional framework. This model opens new horizons for both companies and non-profit organizations. Developing an e-networked business model, companies can make as much or even more money in the long tail of power low distribution than they were making on the head of the curve in the traditional business model. Opening to everyone the possibility of participating and contributing content, non-profit organization and online communities, including CoP and online learning communities, can ensure reaching the "critical mass" of contributors and involvement level that will keep these communities active. However, in both institutional e-collaboration and e-learning projects with non-mandatory participation it is unrealistic to expect more or less equal content contribution among the participants described as a goal in the literature. It seems that small online groups have a more homogeneous contribution compared to the large networks, but it is still an extremely skewed distribution of activity, very different from the equal participation and content contribution.

Using the trend of pushing the knowledge exchange into the infrastructure it is important to choose flexible technological platforms that supports groups working and learning online on tasks involving the processes of knowledge sharing, cooperation, and collaboration. Similarly, it is important to choose flexible communication technology that opens the possibilities for synchronous and asynchronous group interactions, video, audio, and textual communication- depending on participant personal traits and task characteristics. In addition, practitioners should consider the potential negative effects of e-collaboration accompanied by interactions through communication channels not supporting oral speech.

In future investigations it would be interesting not only on to explore different positive aspects of online communities of practice and open-source development projects, but also to investigate companies adapting the e-networked business model and making profit on the long tail of power low distribution, as well as the new downsides of a networked society as mentioned above. Additional empirical testing of analytical models, such as Pennock et al. (2002), that are able to fit low power distributions and explain their causes, are needed. In such investigations, it would be interesting to explore the influence of different platforms and user interests / company goals on the distribution of member / employee activity and content contribution in the community or company.

REFERENCES

Adar, E., & Huberman, B. A. (2000). Free riding on Gnutella. *First Monday*, 5.

Amichai-Hamburger, Y. (2007). Personality, individual differences and Internet use. In Joinson, A., McKenna, K. Y. A., Postmes, T., & Reips, U. D. (Eds.), *Oxford handbook of Internet psychology* (pp. 187–204). Oxford, UK: Oxford University Press.

Anderson, C. (2008). *The long tail: The future of business is selling more of less*. New York, NY: Hyperion.

Ardichvili, A., Page, V., & Wentling, T. (2003). Motivation and barriers to participation in virtual knowledge-sharing communities of practice. *Journal of Knowledge Management*, *7*(1), 64–77. doi:10.1108/13673270310463626

Baron, R. A., & Markman, G. D. (2000). Beyond social capital: How social skills can enhance entrepreneurs' success. *The Academy of Management Executive*, *14*(1), 106–116. doi:10.5465/AME.2000.2909843

Benbunan-Fich, R., & Koufaris, M. (2008). Motivations and contribution behaviour in social bookmarking systems: An empirical investigation. *Electronic Markets*, *18*(2), 150–160. doi:10.1080/10196780802044933

Blau, I., & Barak, A. (2009). Synchronous online discussion: Participation in a group audio conferencing and textual chat as affected by communicator's personality characteristics and discussion topics. In *Proceedings of the International Conference on Computer Supported Education*, Lisbon, Portugal (pp. 19-24).

Blau, I., & Barak, A. (2010, October). *Synchronous online participation: The effects of participant's personality and discussion topic on participation in face-to-face versus voice chat, and textual group discussions*. Paper presented at the 11th Annual Conference of the Association of Internet Researchers: Sustainability, Participation, Action, Gothenburg, Sweden.

Blau, I., & Caspi, A. (2009). Sharing and collaborating with Google Docs: The influence of psychological ownership, responsibility, and student's attitudes on outcome quality. In *Proceedings of the E-Learn World Conference on E-Learning in Corporate, Government, Healthcare, & Higher Education*, Vancouver, BC, Canada (pp. 3329-3335).

Blau, I., Zuckerman, O., & Monroy-Hernández, A. (2009). Children participation in media content creation community: Israelis learners in Scratch programming environment. In Y. Eshet-Alkalai, A. Caspi, S. Eden, N. Geri, & Y. Yair (Eds.), *Learning in the technological era* (pp.65-72). Ra'anana, Israel: Open University of Israel.

Bouras, C., Giannaka, E., & Tsiatsos, T. (2009). E-collaboration concepts, systems, and applications. In Kock, N. (Ed.), *E-collaboration: Concepts, methodologies, tools, and applications* (pp. 8–16). Hershey, PA: IGI Global. doi:10.4018/978-1-60566-652-5.ch002

Burke, M., Marlow, C., & Lento, T. (2009). Feed me: Motivating newcomer contribution in social network sites. In *Proceedings of the 27th International Conference of Human Factors in Computing Systems* (pp. 945-954).

Caspi, A., & Blau, I. (in press). Collaboration and psychological ownership: How does the tension between the two influence perceived learning? *Social Psychology of Education: An International Journal*.

Chen, I. Y. L., & Chen, N. S., & Kinshuk. (2009). Examining the factors influencing participants' knowledge sharing behavior in virtual learning communities. *Journal of Educational Technology & Society*, *12*(1), 134–148.

Chen, N.-S., & Tsai, C.-C. (2009). Knowledge infrastructure of the future. *Journal of Educational Technology & Society*, *12*(1), 1–4.

Cheng, X., Dale, C., & Liu, J. (2008). Statistics and social network of YouTube videos. In *Proceedings of the 16th International Workshop on Quality of Service*, Enschede, The Netherlands (pp. 229-238).

Ciffolilli, A. (2003). Phantom authority, self-selective recruitment and retention of members in virtual communities: The case of Wikipedia. *First Monday*, 8.

Coiro, J., Knobel, M., Lankshear, C., & Leu, D. (Eds.). (2008). *The handbook of research on new literacies*. Mahwah, NJ: Lawrence Erlbaum.

Coleman, D., & Levine, S. (2008). *Collaboration 2.0: Technology and best practices for successful collaboration in a Web 2.0 world*. Silicon Valley, CA: Happy About Info.

Conner, N. (2008). *Google Apps: The missing manual*. Sebastopol, CA: O'Reilly Media.

Deepwell, F., & King, V. (2009). E-research collaboration, conflict and compromise. In Salmons, J., & Wilson, L. (Eds.), *Handbook of research on electronic collaboration and organizational synergy* (pp. 1–15). Hershey, PA: IGI Global.

Fichter, D. (2005). The many forms of e-collaboration: Blogs, wikis, portals, groupware, discussion boards, and instant messaging. *Online, 29*(5).

Hansen, M. T. (1999). The search-transfer problem: The role of weak ties in sharing knowledge across organization subunits. *Administrative Science Quarterly, 44*(1), 82–111. doi:10.2307/2667032

Hansen, M. T. (2009). When internal collaboration is bad for your company. *Harvard Business Review, 87*(4), 82–88.

Ingram, A. L., & Hathorn, L. G. (2004). Methods for analyzing collaboration in online communications. In Roberts, T. S. (Ed.), *Online collaborative learning: Theory and practice* (pp. 215–241). Hershey, PA: IGI Global.

Ingram, A. L., & Hathorn, L. G. (2009). Collaboration in online communications. In Howard, C., Boettcher, J., Justice, L., Schenk, K., Berg, G., & Rogers, P. (Eds.), *Encyclopedia of distance learning* (2nd ed., *Vol. 1*, pp. 314–318). Hershey, PA: IGI Global. doi:10.4018/978-1-60566-198-8.ch045

Ireson, N., & Burel, G. (2010). Knowledge sharing in e-collaboration. In M. A. Wimmer, J.-L. Chappelet, M. Janssen, & H. J. Scholl (Eds.), *Proceedings of the 9th IFIP WG 8.5 International Conference on Electronic Government* (LNCS 6228, pp. 351-362).

Jenkins, H. (2006a). *Confronting the challenges of participatory culture*. Chicago, IL: MacArthur Foundation.

Jenkins, H. (2006b). *Convergence culture: Where old and new media collide*. New York, NY: NYU Press.

Joyce, E., & Kraut, R. E. (2006). Predicting continued participation in newsgroups. *Journal of Computer-Mediated Communication, 11*(3), 723–747. doi:10.1111/j.1083-6101.2006.00033.x

Kock, N. (2010). Costly traits and e-collaboration: The importance of oral speech in electronic knowledge communication. In Kock, N. (Ed.), *Evolutionary psychology and information systems research: A new approach to studying the effects of modern technologies on human behavior* (pp. 289–303). New York, NY: Springer.

Kock, N., Davison, R., Ocker, R., & Wazlawick, R. (2001). E-collaboration: A look at past research and future challenges. *Journal of System Information Technology, 5*(1), 1–9. doi:10.1108/13287260180001059

Kock, N., & Nosek, J. (2005). Expanding the boundaries of e-collaboration. *IEEE Transactions on Professional Communication, 48*(1), 1–9. doi:10.1109/TPC.2004.843272

Lesser, E. L., & Storck, J. (2001). Communities of practice and organizational performance. *IBM Systems Journal, 40*(4), 831–841. doi:10.1147/sj.404.0831

McInnerney, J., & Robert, T. S. (2004). Collaborative or cooperative learning? In Roberts, T. S. (Ed.), *Online collaborative learning: Theory and practice* (pp. 203–214). Hershey, PA: IGI Global.

Nelson, R. (2008). *Learning and working in the collaborative age: A new model for the workplace.* Video of presentation at the Apple Education Leadership Summit, San Francisco, CA.

Palmisano, J. (2008). A motivational model of knowledge sharing. In Burstein, F., & Holsapple, C. W. (Eds.), *Handbook on decision support systems* (*Vol. 1*, pp. 355–370). Berlin, Germany: Springer-Verlag. doi:10.1007/978-3-540-48713-5_18

Peddibhotla, N. B., & Subramani, M. R. (2007). Contributing to public document repositories: A critical mass theory perspective. *Organization Studies*, *28*(3), 327–346. doi:10.1177/0170840607076002

Pennock, D. M., Flake, G. W., Lawrence, S., Glover, E. J., & Giles, C. L. (2002). Winners don't take all: Characterizing the competition for links on the web. *Proceedings of the National Academy of Sciences of the United States of America*, *99*(8), 5207–5211. doi:10.1073/pnas.032085699

Pierce, J. L., Kostova, T., & Dirks, K. T. (2003). The state of psychological ownership: Integrating and extending a century of research. *Review of General Psychology*, *7*(1), 84–107. doi:10.1037/1089-2680.7.1.84

Raban, D. R., & Rafaeli, S. (2007). Investigating ownership and the willingness to share information online. *Computers in Human Behavior*, *23*(5), 2367–2382. doi:10.1016/j.chb.2006.03.013

Rafaeli, S., & Ariel, Y. (2008). Online motivational factors: Incentives for participation and contribution in Wikipedia. In Barak, A. (Ed.), *Psychological aspects of cyberspace: Theory, research, applications* (pp. 243–267). Cambridge, UK: Cambridge University Press.

Rafaeli, S., Hayat, T., & Ariel, Y. (2009). Knowledge building and motivations in Wikipedia: Participation as "Ba". In Ricardo, F. J. (Ed.), *Cyberculture and new media* (pp. 52–69). New York, NY: Rodopi.

Ravid, G. (2007, August). *Open large shared knowledge construction systems' dominance: The Wikipedia social structure.* Paper presented at the Academy of Management Annual Meeting, Philadelphia, PA.

Ravid, G., Kalman, Y. M., & Rafaeli, S. (2008). Wikibooks in higher education: Empowerment through online distributed collaboration. *Computers in Human Behavior*, *24*(5), 1913–1928. doi:10.1016/j.chb.2008.02.010

Roschelle, J., & Teasley, S. (1995). The construction of shared knowledge in collaborative problem solving. In O'Malley, C. E. (Ed.), *Computer supported collaborative learning* (pp. 69–97). Heidelberg, Germany: Springer-Verlag.

Rubin, A. M. (1994). Media uses and effects: A uses-and-gratifications perspective. J. Bryant & D. Zillmann (Eds.), *Media effects: Advances in theory and research* (pp. 417-436). Mahwah, NJ: Lawrence Erlbaum.

Schoberth, T., Heinzl, A., & Rafaeli, S. (2011). *Quantifying the skewed distribution of activity in virtual communities within a longitudinal study.* Retrieved from http://wifo1.bwl.uni-mannheim.de/fileadmin/files/publications/Working%20Paper%203_2009.pdf

Shirky, C. (2009). *Here comes everybody: The power of organizing without organizations.* New York, NY: Penguin Press.

Stafford, T., Stafford, M., & Schkade, L. (2004). Determining uses and gratifications for the Internet. *Decision Sciences Atlanta*, *35*(2), 259–288. doi:10.1111/j.00117315.2004.02524.x

Surowiecki, J. (2004). *The wisdom of crowds: Why the many are smarter than the few and how collective wisdom shapes business, economies, societies, and nations.* New York, NY: Doubleday.

Tapscott, D., & Williams, A. D. (2007). *Wikinomics: How mass collaboration changes everything.* New York, NY: Portfolio.

Ulieru, M., & Verdon, J. (2008). IT revolutions in the industry: From the command economy to the e-networked industrial ecosystem. In *Proceedings of the 6ᵗʰ IEEE International Conference of Industrial Informatics*, Daejoen, Korea (pp. 1315-1320).

Ulieru, M., & Verdon, J. (2009). Organizational transformation in the digital economy. In *Proceedings of the 7ᵗʰ IEEE International Conference of Industrial Informatics*, Cardiff, Wales (pp. 17-24).

van den Hooff, B., & de Ridder, J. A. (2004). Knowledge sharing in context: The influence of organizational commitment, communication climate, and CMC use on knowledge sharing. *Journal of Knowledge Management, 8*(6), 117–130. doi:10.1108/13673270410567675

Vitvar, T., Peristeras, V., & Tarabanis, K. (Eds.). (2010). *Semantic technologies for e-government.* Berlin, Germany: Springer-Verlag. doi:10.1007/978-3-642-03507-4

Weinberger, D. (2007). *Everything is miscellaneous: The power of the new digital disorder.* New York, NY: Times Books.

Zuckerman, O., Blau, I., & Monroy-Hernández, A. (2009). Children's participation patterns in online communities: An analysis of Israeli learners in the Scratch online community. *Interdisciplinary Journal of E-Learning and Learning Objects, 5*(1), 263–274.

This work was previously published in the International Journal of e-Collaboration, Volume 7, Issue 4, edited by Ned Kock, pp. 22-36, copyright 2011 by IGI Publishing (an imprint of IGI Global).

Chapter 14
Towards an Affordance-Based Theory of Collaborative Action (CoAct)

John Teofil Paul Nosek
Temple University, USA

ABSTRACT

<u>C</u>ollaborative <u>A</u>ction provides a novel approach to modeling interaction among users and machines and IT-mediated collaboration among people to solve problems. CoAct extends the notions of affordance and moves away from idiosyncratic, subjective mental models of the world to the notion that actors with similar capacities to act can potentially discern similar action possibilities in the world. It changes the direction from discovery and alignment of internal representations to mutual attunement of collaborators to build sufficient capabilities, share informational structures, and calibrate selectivity to achieve shared affordances. CoAct has the potential to influence such diverse areas as usability engineering, information overload, and group decision making. CoAct can be used at multiple levels of granularity, from fine granularity of a single interaction to tracking intermediate progress and results of a set of interactions. Propositions based on CoAct are presented. An initial experiment provides some support for an affordance-based approach to information sharing/design.

INTRODUCTION

In complex environments, where not all variables and relationships are known, i.e., where data are uncertain and incomplete, humans create rather than discover their future (Nosek, 2005). They create the future by perceiving affordances within their environment and acting. The subsequent actions, including probing of the environment, lead to changes in the environment that must provide meaningful affordances for other actors, both human and non-human. These behaviors can be immediately perceived by other actors or they can

DOI: 10.4018/978-1-4666-2020-9.ch014

modify the environment, such as the creation of a report, to provide affordances at some later time. Human and non-human actors must be attuned to relevant affordances, to act based on them, and to probe for additional relevant affordances. The more important the action, the more dynamic, equivocal the task, the more unreliable the data, the more important group sensemaking (Gephart, 1993; Weick, 1979) to the emergence of socially-constructed capacities to act, sufficiently coordinated to engender effective action (Nosek, 2005).

The Theory of Collaboration Action (CoAct) has grown out of the desire to provide more theory-based direction in information system development, especially in development of collaboration technology to enable creative solutions to wicked problems (Farooq, Carroll, & Ganoe, 2008). Relying on the assumption of the existence of idiosyncratic, intermediary internal representations, such as mental models, to filter sense-data limits practical, theory-based guidance. Extending this assumption so that collaboration technology must support the creation and maintenance of shared mental models within teams exacerbates the problem. "This all-absorbing concern for the internal, mental model unfortunately led to a neglect of other aspects, of which the most important was the flexibility and variability of human performance (Hollnagel & Woods, 2005, p. 41)." Hollnagel and Woods question derivative folk models, which are based on consensus and "privileged knowledge' about how the mind works (Morick in Hollnagel & Woods, 2005, p. 51)." Examples of folk models include fatigue; workload (Stassen, Johannsen & Moray, 1990) and situation awareness (Endsley, 1995, 2001). Many folk models purport to measure intervening variables representing intermediate mental states rather than performance. Folk models may not be incorrect but are hard to disprove, i.e., they are not falsifiable. Others (Bloor, 1983; Brand, 1979; Heft, 2001; Wilson, 1998) have argued that there are no intermediary internal representations, i.e., no "proverbial little men in the mind," such as mental

models (Cannon-Bowers, Sala, & Converse, 1993; Gentner & Stevens, 1983; Johnson-Laird, 1983), beliefs, cognitive constructs (Adams-Webber, 1979; Fransella & Bannister, 1977), or scripts that are invoked to take-in sensory information and process it. They argue that there is no mind/body dichotomy (Heft, 2001). This view is supported by recent findings in brain research (Yufik & Georgopoulos, 2002).

The purpose of this paper is not to disparage folk models, but to introduce a theory of collaborative action that does not rely on sharing internal, mental models and extend Gibson's ecological theory of affordance to provide guidance in understanding collaborative acts and developing technology that supports them. The paper provides the following: background for the development of an affordance-based theory of collaboration; explication of Individual Action (IAct) and Collaborative Action (CoAct) Models; propositions and research questions based on these models; results of an initial experiment to test some of these propositions and research questions; followed by examples of how CoAct can be used in design of information systems.

BACKGROUND FOR AFFORDANCE-BASED THEORIES

As actors move within an environment, they discern available informational structures that afford action possibilities. These action possibilities, affordances, are available for the class of actors who have the same potential to discern informational structures that provide these affordances from the same observation point (Gibson, 1979). While an affordance is potentially available for the class of actors with certain capabilities, a perceived affordance is what emerges or surfaces for a given member of the class at a specific moment in time as the member moves through the environment to achieve some goal, i.e., while affordances are available to all actors with similar capabilities and can be defined statically, perceived affordances are a subset of available affordances that emerge dynamically based on what the actor is engaged in at the time and what the goal of the actor is. Also, actors can perceive affordances, but not be self-aware of this perception. The critical difference between available affordances and perceived affordances is often overlooked and may be the cause of some confusion. This may stem from researchers who have been introduced to Gibson's work on affordances through Norman and Draper's (1986) work in design of Human-computer Interaction. Affordances, as used in human interface design, are usually inferred to be available to all humans and not dependent on individual differences. Norman is associated with the idea that interfaces should be "user friendly," i.e., so clear that they intuitively afford any human user what to do with the interface at any time.

However, affordances only make sense when actor capabilities are coupled with available informational structures within an environment, i.e., actor and environment are inexorably linked and affordances exist at the intersection of actor capabilities and the environment (Gibson, 1979) (Figure 1).

For a given environment, a change in an actor's capabilities can change available action possibilities within the environment (affordances). Figure 2a depicts an example where actor capabilities increase and the environment remains the same as in Figure 1. Available affordances increase for the actor to most of what actions can be available in this environment. Similarly, for a given class of actors, a change in the environment can change the available action possibilities (affordances). Figure 2b depicts one example where actor capabilities remain the same as in Figure 1, but where the environment increases in informational structures. In this case, available action possibilities remain the same as in Figure 1, but the available action possibilities (affordances) are less than what may be available for an actor with greater capabilities. In another example not de-

Figure 1. Affordances = intersection of actor capabilities and the environment

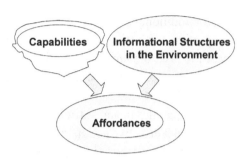

picted, the environment could change by increasing equivocality of the informational structures and the existing capabilities of actors are such that available action possibilities (affordances) are reduced. What this also means is that with respect to affordances, actors can be a member of some classes but not others. It means that actors can join classes and may leave classes based on their changes in capacities to act, for example, they may learn, but then forget certain knowledge, or develop, then lose physical abilities. It also means that actors within the same class do not necessarily share all the same capabilities; they only need to share the same capabilities necessary to pick up informational structures that reveal affordances for those in the class.

As noted previously, perceived affordances are a subset of available affordances that emerge/ surface as an actor moves through the environment to achieve some goal or assuage some need. Figure 3 depicts how perceived affordances are dynamic and change over time given the goal and current activity. For simplicity, in Figure 3 the informational structures within the environment and actor capabilities remain the same through time, which means that the set of affordances remain the same for actors in the class with these capabilities, while what is perceived within this set changes over time.

Figure 2. a. Changed Capabilities (increased) b. Changed Environment (increased)

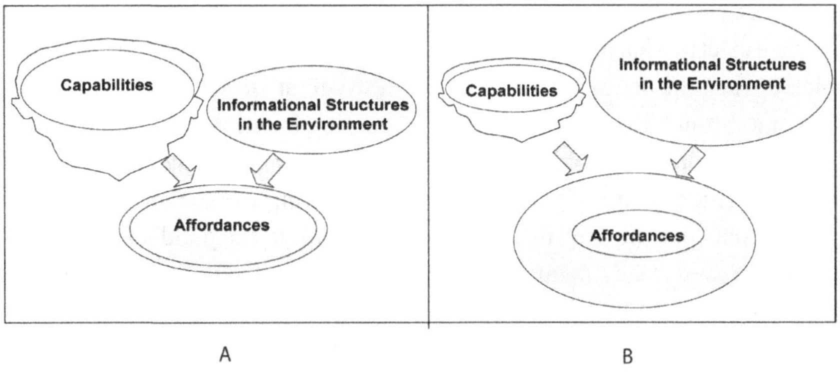

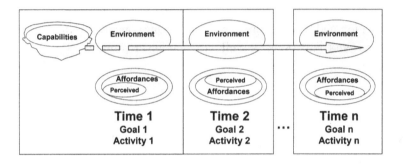

Figure 3. Perceived Affordances = Subset of Affordances based on Goal and Current Activity over Time

For example, a doorknob in its normal position on a door may afford graspability for the class of average humans, but not for a class of one-foot-tall, blind actors with no limbs. This doorknob may be in a room where there are chairs that afford sitability, pens that afford writability, etc. (the set of affordances that are defined at the intersection of an average human actor within this given environment). However, a given actor of the class of average humans may only perceive the doorknob's graspability when the member is confronted with a closed door as he is attempting to enter or exit a space. As noted previously, it is important to remember that perception does not mean that the actor is self-aware of the doorknob's graspability.

Extending Gibson's Affordance-Based Theory Beyond The Physical

While Gibson (1979) focused on affordances that are discernable to a class of actors with certain physical capabilities to act, CoAct extends the notion of capacities/capabilities to include more than just physical attributes. This is consistent with Gibson's view of the potentially broad applicability of his theory. Capacities to act can broadly include capacities to do, think, feel, etc. For example, informational structures in the environment may afford sadness or happiness for one class of actors with certain capabilities, but not another. In addition, the idea of an actor moving through an environment is not restricted to the physical movement of the actor within a physical environment, but includes the notion that actors are active with respect to what informational structures they pick up, i.e., the notion of static is the exception. Moving through the environment can mean the working through a problem, the reading of a book, the engagement in a discussion. The importance of the concept of moving through the environment means that one is continually experiencing one's environment and is forever changed by this experience, i.e., "cognitively rewired" (Pizlo, 2007). Even visual perception to recognize objects in the environment appears to be dependent on prior experience and/or genetic encoding (Pizlo, 2001, 2007). "Cognitive systems do not passively react to events; they rather actively look for information and their actions are determined by purposes and intentions as well as externally available information and events (Hollnagel & Woods, 2005, p. 16)."

Reinterpreting Existing Research from an Affordance-Based Perspective

As noted earlier, the purpose of this paper is to provide an alternate view of collaborative action that does not rely on hidden, internal representations, such as, mental models, and not necessarily to dismiss previous non affordance-based work. There are constructs from non affordance-based theories that can be useful when reinterpreted from an affordance-based perspective.

Osgood (1969), in his Theory of Meaning, attempted to identify the objective meanings of words. Coincidentally, Osgood started publishing this work about the time of the death of Wittgenstein, a philosopher whose earlier philosophy would be in complete agreement with Osgood's, but who rejected this objective reality in his later philosophy where he passionately proselytized that the meaning of words can only be ascertained through their use. However, Osgood's contribution is that he could explain about 50% of the

variability in the meaning of words. Of the 50% he could explain, most of it could be explained as (1) judgment (70%), followed by (2) potency, how great or small, and (3) action (direction), moving in one direction or another. For example, something is bad (judgment), very bad (potency), and getting worse (action/direction).

Applying Osgood's Theory of Meaning to Gibson's Ecological Theory of Affordance, one can see the correspondence, in that some affordances can be described as a judgment (inference) of a certain potency and direction. However, Gibson and Wittgenstein would say that an actor is not necessarily self-aware of the judgment, potency and direction in acting on available affordances with these properties.

One conceives rather than perceives of a thing having a property (Brand, 1979). It would be consistent with Wittgenstein to say that an actor can perceive and then act without self-awareness (Bloor, 1983; Boland & Tenkasi, 1995). Self-reflection (conception) may cause the actor to project onto the available informational structures the judgment that these informational structures afford some action opportunities, but self-awareness is not necessary for perception to occur. In fact, perception, and not conception, is the norm and only through self-reflection by the actor or observation of the actor's action could one ascertain the affordance that was perceived. For example, in the previous example with the doorknob, only upon self-reflection by the actor or observation of the actor grasping the doorknob as he was leaving could one ascertain that the doorknob's affordance of graspability was perceived.

Kelly's Cognitive Construct Theory proposes that each individual uses a limited, personal set of "cognitive" constructs to make sense of a situation (Adams-Webber, 1979). Although Kelly did not use the term judgment, it appears that these so-called cognitive constructs are actually elicited judgments that individuals project onto the situation when queried about it. These judgments have bi-polar values, e.g., jumpability only makes sense with respect to the opposite pole of non-jumpability. This projection of a judgment onto a situation when queried is similar to the use of self-reflection to project onto available informational structures the judgment that they afford action possibilities.

The value of Osgood's and Kelly's work to affordance-based theories comes from the fact that self-reflection on informational structures provided to actors, elicits a judgment, and this is similar to what occurs in self-reflection by actors, or observation of actors, acting on available affordances. Osgood also provides useful dimensions of potency and direction. For actors with sufficient capabilities, informational structures afford action opportunities, of a certain potency and direction.

What this affordance-based reinterpretation of Osgood's and Kelly's work points out, and which may apply to much of folk theories that purport to have "privileged knowledge" about the internal workings of the mind, is that self-reflection is the less-frequent way that one acts. When one is self-reflecting, perception of action possibilities within externally available informational structures (perceived affordances) declines. One interpretation may be that self-reflection causes something like "conceived affordances" to emerge within internally available informational structures in a similar way the subset of perceived affordances emerge from the set of affordances available in external informational structures for actors with similar capabilities. The problem occurs when proponents of folk theories interpret these elicited "conceived affordances" as internal representations, such as cognitive constructs or mental models that "process" stimuli. To further clarify, these "conceived affordances" are a result or snapshot of the intersection of existing actor capabilities and informational structures that become available upon reflection, i.e., the actor projects onto an elicited, self-reflection at a given moment of time these "conceived affordances." Conceived affordances are not the cognitive constructs or mental models that actors use to process information.

In fact, because much of folk-theory research on internal representations demands actors to reflect and project meaning onto these reflections, their results may still be valid, but not their interpretation, i.e., not why the researchers think. These projections of "conceived affordances" may be used to align other actors so that the projections of collaborating actors elicit similar "conceived affordances." However, what is occurring is not the alignment of internal representations, such as cognitive constructs and mental models, but the building of sufficient, similar capacities in actors, sharing informational structures, and calibrating selectivity of relevant informational structures at the appropriate time.

One may interpret the above arguments as "no big deal." Ecological psychologists use affordances to explain phenomena and cognitive psychologists use such things as mental models and cognitive constructs. However, affordance-based interpretations do not rely on knowing and sharing internal representations. Conceptualizing phenomena from an affordance-based perspective may expand current boundaries that exist (Kock & Nosek, 2005) when restricted to consensus-based, folk theories that purport to have "privileged knowledge" about the internal workings of the mind. The following section explores affordance-based models and theories.

AFFORDANCE-BASED MODELS

We first model an affordance-based theory of individual action (IAct). This model will then be expanded to include actors in collaborative action (CoAct).

Individual Action (IAct)

Referring to Figure 4, as an actor with a certain capacity to act (Gibson, 1979; Heft, 2001) actively engages within his environment (current activity) (Gibson, 1979; Heft, 2001) for some purpose (achieve goal or fulfill need) (Heft, 2001), the actor actively selects from available informational structures that afford action opportunities (affordances) (Gibson, 1979; Heft, 2001; Osgood, 1969). Behavior includes intended and unintended, explicit and implied, verbal and non-verbal. Behavior of the actor becomes part of the informational structures available within the environment "insofar as they are tangible, audible, odorous, tastable, or visible" (Gibson, 1979, p. 135). This behavior may also provide informational structures to observers as to affordances perceived by the actor. As noted previously, self-reflection or observation of behavior may indicate what affordances were perceived by the actor.

<u>Co</u>llaborative <u>Act</u>ion Theory (CoAct)

In this section, IAcT is expanded to build a model of <u>Co</u>llaborative <u>Act</u>ion (CoAct). CoAct can be used at multiple levels of granularity, from fine granularity of understanding a single interaction, to tracking intermediate progress and final results of interactions. For effective collaborative action, actors, whether human or non-human, must perceive shared, relevant affordances at the appropriate time (Figure 5). A shared affordance is an affordance that is shared by more than one actor. To achieve a shared, perceived affordance: 1. the actors must share sufficient capabilities so that a given environment affords the same action opportunity for the actors; and 2. this affordance or action opportunity is available (or perceived) at the appropriate time, i.e., an affordance that is available to an actor, but is not perceived when it is suppose to be, is not considered a shared, perceived affordance. A shared, perceived affordance may occur at the same time among actors, but it may also occur asynchronously, as long as this is considered an appropriate time to support collaborative action.

Figure 4. <u>I</u>ndividual <u>Ac</u>tion (IAct)

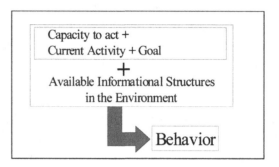

The process to achieve and the end-state of achieving shared, perceived affordances use the same label, "attunement." Attunement means "being or bringing into harmony; a feeling of being "at one" with another" (Dictionary.com's 21st Century Lexicon). For example, one can say that collaborators attune each other, i.e., undergo mutually attunement (bringing into harmony) to achieve attunement (being in harmony) of perceiving shared relevant affordances at the appropriate time. Context determines which form of the word is meant.

Actors engaged in collaborative action must take responsibility for mutual attunement by 1. sharing relevant informational structures, 2. bringing each other up to the sufficient capabilities of the class of actors for whom the environment affords the desired, relevant action opportunities (affordances), and 3. assisting each other in perceiving the subset of relevant affordances at the appropriate time (Selectivity Calibration).

In Figure 5, we identify the actor who is actively attuning as the Source Actor, and the actor who is the target of this attunement effort as the Target Actor. However, as noted previously, these roles alternate as collaborators engage in mutual attunement. Initially, at Time 1, the actors do not share the relevant informational structures within the environment and sufficient capabilities. Therefore, they cannot perceive relevant affordances. This is depicted by the actor at the bottom (the

Figure 5. Attunement to Perceive Shared, Relevant Affordances at the Right Time

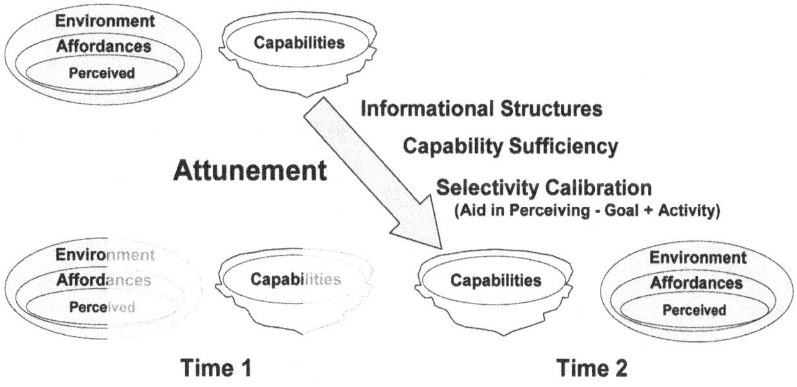

Target Actor) only sharing half of what the actor on the top (Source Actor) has available.

In Time 2, the Source Actor attunes the Target Actor by sharing relevant informational structures in the environment, assisting the Target Actor to achieve sufficient capabilities (this is shown by the capabilities of the Target Actor are now the same as the Source Actor), and assisting the Target Actor in perceiving relevant informational structures at the appropriate time (Selectivity Calibration). At the end of Time 2, both actors perceive similar, relevant affordances. For simplicity sake, although we only depict one Target Actor in Figure 5, there could be more than one Target Actor in a given collaborative act.

In Gibsonian terms, actors attune each other to perceive relevant affordances by building sufficient capabilities in each other, exchanging informational structures so they are available to both, and bringing each other to a common observation point within the environment of available informational structures at the appropriate time (Figure 6).

Examples of Achieving Shared Affordance

The following examples use the shared affordance of stream-jumpability. Consider the scenario where actors are running for their lives when they come upon a stream, although not necessarily at the same time. For simplicity, only two actors are presented, however, in actuality there could be more than two.

Example with No Self-Reflection and No Conscious Attunement

1. Actor 1 jumps the stream. Actor 1 perceived the jumpability of the stream (perceived affordance) from the available informational structures. He may have further perceived that the stream was very jumpable (potency), and increasingly jumpable (direction), i.e., increasing strength of the affordance due to the immediate threat, but there is no way to know.
2. Actor 2 observes Actor 1's jumping of the stream which attunes Actor 2.
3. Actor 2 attempts to jump the stream.

Example with Self-Reflection and Conscious Attunement

1. Actor 1 perceives the stream, but does not jump.
2. Actor 1 becomes self-aware of the perceived stream and conceives the affordance of

Figure 6. Gibsonian Mutual Attunement

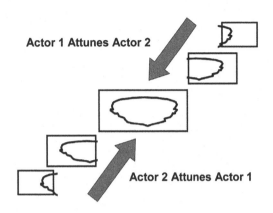

stream-jumpability, i.e., he reflects on the circumstances and projects onto available informational structures that the stream is jumpable, very jumpable (potency), and increasingly jumpable (direction).

3. Actor 1 consciously attunes Actor 2 so that Actor 2 will share his affordance of stream-jumpability by exposing behavior.
4. Actors 1 and 2 attempt to jump the stream.

Attunement

The above examples illustrate the affordance-based notions of attunement, which is both conscious and unconscious, to effect collaborative action among actors. Although the very act of participating in a collaborative act may increase the likelihood of self-awareness; it is also possible that conception (self-awareness) may not occur, as in Example 1.

Attunement can be intended and unintended, explicit and implied, verbal and non-verbal. For example, an actor may explicitly expose his/her identity intending to imply positive informational structures as to status, however, the receiving actor may not treat this datum as positive. As noted earlier, actors attune each other by sharing relevant informational structures in the environment, assisting each other to achieve sufficient capabilities,

and assisting each other in perceiving relevant informational structures at the appropriate time. Table 1 summarizes components of attunement. Note, not all components exist in every act of attunement. Attunement related to Selectivity Calibration aligns the goals and activities of actors. As noted earlier, this relates to Gibson's idea that an actor moves within the environment picking up informational structures to achieve some goal and affects what affordances are perceived at a given moment in time.

CoAct

Figure 7 depicts CoAct, an affordance-based model of collaborative acts. As noted earlier, this model can be used at multiple levels of granularity, from fine granularity of understanding a single interaction, to tracking intermediate progress and final results of interactions. In a collaborative act, there can be more than one Target Actor, but the Source Actor should be considered a single entity (Nosek, 2005). As noted earlier, actors interchangeably take on the roles of Source and Target as they attune each other to achieve shared affordances. Overall, the model shows that the Source Actor, with certain capabilities, moves through a given environment and perceives affordances available to actors with those capabilities (upon self-reflection these perceived affordances become

Table 1. Summary of attunement components

Informational Structures: Relevant aspects of the environment/situation.
Capability Sufficiency Building: Building sufficient, similar capability needed so that affordances needed for collaboration are available to the actors.
Perceived Affordances: Perceived action opportunities in the environment (inferred through observation).
Conceived Affordances: Conceived action opportunities in the environment (explicit through self-aware reflection).
Selectivity Calibration: Assistance in perceiving the relevant affordances at the appropriate time. **Achieve goal or fulfill need** - Align goals; **Current activity** - Align current activity.

Figure 7. Model of Collaborative Action (CoAct)

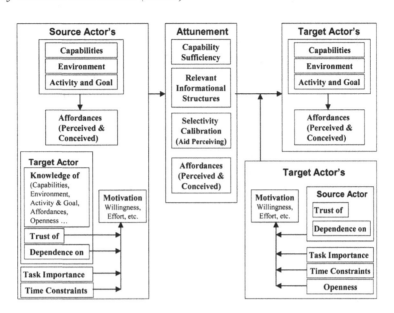

conceived affordances). The Source Actor attunes the Target Actor by building sufficient capabilities, sharing relevant informational structures, calibrating selection of relevant informational structures, and exposing affordances (perceived are inferred by the Target Actor and conceived are relayed to the Target Actor). The Attunement Process changes capabilities, available informational structures, and selectivity which results in changes to the Target Actor's affordances.

Factors which affect the Source Actor's attunement of the Target Actor include such things as the Source Actor's knowledge of (Vivacqua & Moreira de Souza, 2008), trust of (Remidez, Stam, & Laffey, 2010), and dependence on (Pick, Romano, & Roxtocki, 2009) the Target Actor. Other variables such as task importance and time constraints can affect the attunement process. These variables should not be considered complete and there may be other variables, not specifically identified in the model, such as collaborative distance (Fallot, Martinez-Carreras, & Prinz, 2010) that affect attunement. Some of these variables affect attunement by affecting the Source Actor's motivation. There are similar factors that affect the effectiveness of the attunement on the

Target Actor. Variables such as task importance and time constraints can vary from actor to actor and even from time to time, for example, the Source Actor may view the task as important and urgent, although the Target Actor may not.

One aspect of the model may not be adequately depicted, but deserves special mention. Target Actors may accept the affordances of the Source Actor without being brought up to sufficient capabilities and having shared informational structures so that these affordances are available for Target Actors themselves. For example, Source Actors, who are trusted, may be able to transfer their affordance, but the Target Actors do not have sufficient capabilities so that they can perceive the affordances for themselves. Does this affordance fade easily?

If Source Actors expose their affordances (perceived and conceived) as part of their attunement for a given shared environment, is this a form of learning, i.e., does this teach the Target Actor, either explicitly through conceived affordances transmitted or implicitly through perceived affordances ascertained through observation, that these and future, similar informational structures afford these action possibilities? Does repetition reinforce building sufficient capabilities? Is learning-by-example a form of this process?

Note, attunement is neither inherently good nor correct and can result in building sufficient capabilities so that Target Actors perceive good, correct affordances or warped, incorrect affordances (Boyle, Kacmar, & George, 2008). For example, Source Actors who enjoy very high trust, such as some fanatical religious leaders, may be able to transfer their affordances of world events in a continuously, warped manner such that Target Actors will perceive affordances within current and future environments that will result in unwarranted and apparently irrational actions, but consistent with CoAct.

Propositions

This section discusses some CoAct propositions. Please refer to Figure 7.

Proposition 1. Relevant exposed behavior will consist of components of attunement. CoAct provides a way to differentiate behavior and predicts the categories of behavior which actors will expose to achieve shared affordances. This proposition does not deal with the quality of the exposed behavior of the actors or the success of achieving shared affordances, but does provide a boundary on what is expected in the behavior exposed to achieve shared affordances.

Proposition 2. Better attunement will lead to more shared affordances. For a given situation, actors who do a better job in attunement should be more successful in achieving shared affordances.

Propositions 3 through 6 relate to the Source Actor's knowledge of the Target Actor. The better this is, then all other things being equal, the better the attunement. If the Source Actor exposes behavior relevant just for his or her class and the Target Actor is not part of this class, then the

Source Actor will be less successful in achieving shared affordances. The Target Actor may be from a different class than the Source Actor where attunement is not possible and exposed behavior may focus on achieving shared affordances that are not available to the Target Actor. The Target Actor may not understand or pay attention to such exposed behavior and shared affordances cannot be achieved.

Proposition 3. The better the Source Actor's knowledge of the Target Actor's capabilities, informational structures available to the Target Actor, current activity and goal, etc., the better the attunement.

Proposition 4. The better the Source Actor's knowledge of the Target Actor's capabilities, the better the attunement in building capability sufficiency.

Corollary 4a. The more the Target Actor shares capabilities with the Source Actor, the less the Source Actor will expose behavior related to building capabilities. If an actor is aware that actors, with whom collaboration must occur, are from the same class, then actors will expect greater shared background. Therefore, less effort will be expended to attune these actors so that they have sufficient shared capabilities to pick up relevant informational structures to achieve shared affordances.

This brings us to **Corollary 4b.** The less the Target Actor shares capabilities with the Source Actor, the more the Source Actor will expose behavior related to achieving sufficient shared capabilities. If an actor is aware that actors, with whom collaboration must occur, are from other classes, then more effort will be expended to attune these actors so that they have sufficient shared capabilities to pick up relevant informational structures to achieve shared affordances.

However, as noted previously, the gap between the Source-Actor and Target-Actor classes may be too high to achieve affordances available to the Source Actor's class. This brings us to **Corollary 4c:** The Source Actor, who is aware that the gap of the Target Actor is too great to achieve shared affordances of the Source Actor's class, will expose behavior to achieve shared affordances at some intersection of the classes.

Habermas (1984) offers the concept of lifeworlds to explain the difficulty in achieving shared affordances among actors from different lifeworlds. Borrowing loosely from Habermas, actors of dissimilar backgrounds may be able to find some common elements of lifeworlds that can be shared. Figure 8 provides a schematic of an example of stratifying the shared social world of an individual actor. The unshared subjective world can only be contained within the shared social world. An actor living in the world is part of and helps to create a shared social world.

For example, the Target Actor may be an integral part of the decision making process, but is not experiencing the situation for himself or herself, and may not have the ability to understand the relevancy of facts of the situation at hand. In this case, actors must find a common aspect of a lifeworld to share, for example, the capabilities of actors from the two different classes may intersect on similar cultural or human capabilities to pick up informational structures to share that the situation affords danger. Two examples are offered to illustrate this.

Example 1: Command and Control

In this military situation, a commander on the ground feels threatened, perceives the attackability of the enemy, but must obtain permission to engage from a distant political leader with no military background. In this case, the Source Actor from the class of experienced warfighters must obtain permission from this politician, the Target Actor, who is not within the class of experienced warfighters, and may not be attunable within limited time requirements, to perceive the affordance of

Figure 8. Stratification of Social and Subjective Worlds

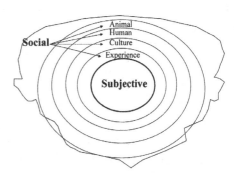

attackability of the enemy. However, the Source Actor (warfighter) can then expose behavior that will permit the political decision maker to perceive that the situation affords danger The decision maker at headquarters would then trust the local on-scene commander to make the best decision (including attacking) and implicitly trust the advancement system (shared culture) that puts commanders in this position of responsibility.

Example 2: Medical Emergency Surgery

In emergency exploratory surgery, family members and patients, may share decision-making responsibility with surgeons but do not have the capabilities of the surgeon to pick up informational structures that afford necessary surgery. It may be even more difficult for family members than for patients, who may be experiencing pain, to perceive affordances available to the class of surgeons. Surgeons should, and the best most likely do, focus on selectivity calibration and informational structure sharing to achieve the shared affordance of imminent danger among surgeon, patient and family members. Patients and family members must then trust the surgeon to make the best decision and implicitly trust the medical system (shared culture) that puts surgeons in this position of responsibility.

Proposition 5. The better the Source Actor's knowledge of the Target Actor's Selectivity Calibration (current activity and goal), the better the attunement in Selectivity Calibration. **Corollary 5a.** The more the Target Actor is aligned with the Source Actor's Selectivity Calibration (activity and goal), the less the Source Actor will expose behavior related to Selectivity Calibration. **Corollary 5b:** The less the Target Actor is aligned with the Source Actor's activity and goal, the more the Source Actor will expose behavior aiding in perception.

Proposition 6. The better the Source Actor's knowledge of the Target Actor's environment, the better the attunement in providing needed, relevant informational structures. **Corollary 6a:** The more the Target Actor shares the Source Actor's environment, the less the Source Actor will expose behavior providing informational structures. **Corollary 6b:** The less the Target Actor shares the Source Actor's environment, the more the Source Actor will expose behavior providing informational structures.

Proposition 7. Perceived affordances will change with changes in Selectivity Calibration. Assuming actor capabilities and informational structures available in the environment remain the same, then changing Selectivity Calibration should change what subset of informational structures are picked up within the environment, i.e., perceived affordances should change.

Proposition 8. For a class of actors, informational structures in the environment can be altered to achieve the desired affordances.

Additional Research Questions

There are several interesting related research questions related to CoAct which may help refine CoAct and which will be addressed.

Research Question 1. In the collaborative act to achieve shared affordance, do some categories of exposed behavior with respect to Selectivity Calibration and informational structures available in the environment provide more informational value than others?

Currently CoAct does not predict what parts of the exposed behavior may be more important than others in achieving shared affordances. This question deals with the efficiency in achieving shared affordances and extending CoAct to incorporate these aspects. In some sense this is a novel extension of the ideas of Shannon and Weaver (1969) when they showed the decreasing informational value of letters in transmitting a word. It may be possible to extend CoAct to provide guidance as to what aspects of exposed behavior to prioritize when transmitting, and/or receiving exposed behavior. It may provide ways to reduce information overload and/or make use of limited bandwidth while still achieving sufficient shared affordances to act effectively. A few responses in the preliminary experiments seem to indicate that perhaps this may be the case. For example, it may be that exposed behavior related to goals provides more informational power than other categories of exposed behavior to more quickly achieve shared affordances. If this is true, then the actor exposing the behavior may choose to transmit this first or only this portion. Likewise, the receiving actor may choose to receive this portion of the exposed behavior first, or only receive this portion.

Research Question 2. Do the perceived characteristics of informational structures change with changes in Selectivity Calibration?

This question relates to how informational structures that do not change in any physical way may be perceived to be different with changes in Selectivity Calibration. For example, let's say an actor is running through the woods for fun and comes upon a stream versus the same actor running through the woods to escape from imminent death and comes upon the same stream that he must cross to survive. Would the actor who is running for fun perceive the same exact stream as being wider and deeper than the actor who is running for his life?

INITIAL EXPERIMENTS

The next sections describe early investigations in testing CoAct.

Operational Hypotheses

The following three null hypotheses were tested. For the first two hypotheses, subjects are not discerning what the environment affords for themselves. Subjects must act as observers of an actor within a scene and indicate what they think the environment affords for the actor.

Hypothesis 1. In trying to achieve shared affordance, the exposed behavior of subjects will not be able to be categorized as Selection Calibration, building capability sufficiency, or informational structure sharing. This hypothesis partially operationalizes Proposition 1. There is a further requirement for this hypothesis in that the subject must describe in words to an assumed other actor, who cannot see the picture, what aspects of the picture this other actor would need to know to describe, in a similar manner as the subject, what the environment affords.

Hypothesis 2. Changing informational structures will not change affordances. This operationalizes Proposition 8. Using CoAcT, different scenes can be constructed to provide different affordances.

Hypothesis 3. Subjects will indicate that the same informational structure, within two different situations that alter Selectivity Calibration (goal and current activity), as being the same. This explores Research Question 2.

Design

The experiment was designed so that subjects from a wide variety of ages and background could participate. It was a web-based, within-group experiment, i.e., one group received Treatment 1 first, followed by Treatment 2, while the other group received Treatment 2 first, followed by Treatment 1.

Pilot Tests

Several pilot tests were conducted to refine the experimental design and the interface. Some of these pilot tests were pen and paper tests and one was a test of the web-based interface that was used in the actual experiment.

Subjects

There were 48 subjects who participated in the web-based test. Subjects were of convenience and were randomly assigned to one of the groups automatically through the web-based system when they began the experiment. The treatments were designed so that participating human subjects would have sufficient capacities to complete the treatments.

Treatments

There were two treatments that followed a modified general allegory scenario previously used in explicating affordance by ecological researchers (Clancey, 1997). Treatment 1 was a picture of a deer standing near a stream. Treatment 2 was a picture of a running deer heading towards the same-sized stream, followed by a lion. For each treatment, there was the same set of questions. The subject viewed the picture while he or she answered the questions. However, after the question was answered, the subject was not allowed to return to the question. After a subject received the first treatment, there was displayed a screen with no picture and a notification that the experiment would continue with a new treatment. Since the subject could not go back, once a subject started the next treatment, the subject had no access to the picture or questions with the previous treatment. For each picture, subjects were required to

1. Indicate the state afforded by the environment as depicted in the pictures from great safety to great danger;
2. Describe in words to an assumed other actor, who does not see the picture, what aspects of the picture this other actor would need to know to indicate in a similar manner as to what state the environment affords;
3. Indicate the next action that the actor in the picture could take, i.e., what affordance to act is immediately available;
4. Similar to 2 above, describe in words to another actor, who does not see the picture, those aspects of the picture that would have this actor answer in the same way as in 3;
5. Indicate the depth and width of the stream in the picture. (Note: the depth and width of the stream were exactly the same in both pictures and all other aspects of the pictures were of similar scale. As noted earlier, the idea here was to ascertain whether manipulation of the

Selectivity Calibration components, goal and current activity (grazing to assuage hunger versus running to escape death), can influence the perception of the depth and width of identical streams).

Results

The evaluation of requirements 2, 3, and 4 is incomplete. The descriptive statistics for questions related to requirements 1 and 5 are presented below in two separate tables. Table 2 is for the group who received Treatment 1, deer standing near a stream, first followed by Treatment 2, deer running towards a stream followed by a lion. Table 3 is for the group who received Treatment 2, followed by Treatment 1. Table 4 presents the results of a One Way ANOVA for two groups. This is similar to a student t-test because there are only two groups, but is considered more powerful. Since there are only two groups, there is no need for post hoc tests.

Discussion

The results of 48 subjects were used in the analysis. With respect to Hypothesis 1, fewer subjects completed these sections with valid answers. Most likely this was because it required more effort and

Table 2. Descriptive Statistics: Treatment 1 First

Question	N	Min	Max	Mean	SD
Deer by the stream:					
Q1a: Great danger (1) to great safety (5)	28	1	5	3.25	1.076
Q3a: Very deep (1) to very shallow (5)	23	2	5	3.39	.988
Q3b: Very wide (1) to very narrow (5)	23	2	4	3.43	.843
Running deer followed by a lion:					
Q4a: Great danger (1) to great safety (5)	22	1	5	1.68	1.086
Q6a: Very deep (1) to very shallow (5)	22	2	4	3.55	.739
Q6b: Very wide (1) to very narrow (5)	22	2	4	3.59	.734

Notes: Q1a, Q4a: what the environment affords the deer from great danger (1) to great safety (5);
Q3a, Q6a: The water in the picture is very deep (1) to very shallow (5);
Q3b, Q6b: The water in the picture is very wide to (1) to very narrow (5).

Table 3. Descriptive Statistics: Treatment 2 First

Question	N	Min	Max	Mean	SD
Deer by the stream:					
Q1a: Great danger (1) to great safety (5)	20	2	5	3.90	.912
Q3a: Very deep (1) to very shallow (5)	19	1	5	3.42	1.071
Q3b: Very wide (1) to very narrow (5)	19	2	5	3.26	.933
Running deer followed by a lion:					
Q4a: Great danger (1) to great safety (5)	21	1	5	2.81	1.289
Q6a: Very deep (1) to very shallow (5)	21	2	5	3.67	.856
Q6b: Very wide (1) to very narrow (5)	22	1	5	3.29	1.056

Notes: Q1a, Q4a: what the environment affords the deer from great danger (1) to great safety (5);

Q3a, Q6a: The water in the picture is very deep (1) to very shallow (5);

Q3b, Q6b: The water in the picture is very wide to (1) to very narrow (5).

Table 4. ANOVA Results

Question	Sum of Squares	df	Mean Squares	F	Significance
Q1a BG WG Total	4.929 47.050 51.979	1 46 47	4.929 1.023	4.819	.033
Q3a BG WG Total	.009 42.110 42.119	1 40 41	.009 1.053	.009	.926
Q3b BG WG Total	.306 31.336 31.643	1 40 41	.306 .783	.391	.535
Q4a BG WG Total	13.664 58.011 71.674	1 41 42	13.664 1.415	9.657	.003
Q6a BG WG Total	.158 26.121 26.279	1 41 42	.158 .637	.248	.621
Q6b BG WG Total	1.001 33.604 34.605	1 41 42	1.001 .820	1.221	.276

Note: BG: Between Groups; WG: Within Groups

subjects were not adequately motivated. Although a small sample, a few observations can be made:

1. The null hypothesis is rejected. CoAcT provides a valid means to categorize exposed behavior. Content of their descriptions to other actors could be categorized according to CoAcT: Selectivity Calibration (goals, current activity), building capability sufficiency; and sharing relevant informational structures.

2. Although there are not sufficient data points for statistical analysis, several observations can be made with regards to effort to categorize and inter-rater reliability:

   a. It is fairly easy to learn to categorize exposed behavior, however, more training will be needed to increase inter-rater reliability;

   b. Some behavior is easier to rate than others. For example, Selectivy Calibration, building capability sufficiency and affordances seem to be very clear and there is higher inter-rater reliability, while what constitutes informational structures seems to be less clear.

   c. There is a need to develop a process where perhaps a third rater is used when inter-rater reliability is not close enough. If the third rater does not resolve the discrepancy than that portion of the response should not be used.

   d. There is a need to develop a protocol to handle words that provide little informational value as to affordance but are used to make sense grammatically.

   e. Although not tested, anecdotally raters were able to judge a difference in the quality of descriptions. Those subjects who provided better Selectivity Calibration, capability sufficiency-building behavior and more precise informational structures were judged

to be of higher quality and more likely to achieve shared affordance. Testing of other propositions require evaluation of the quality of the exposed behavior. Metrics to measure quality appears to be achievable.

3. Although subjects were directed to not provide the actual affordance in getting other actors to perceive the same affordance, some found it difficult to provide descriptions without including words that could be considered similar to the affordance they identified.

4. Although not tested, some parts of the descriptions seem to provide more informational value than others. See Research Question 1.

Null Hypothesis 3 is not rejected. There is no statistically significant finding for changes in the perceptions of the width and depth of the river under different treatments; however, there was a small change of means for the subjects who had Treatment 1 first. They perceived that the river was less deep (3.39 versus 3.55) and less wide (3.43 versus 3.59) for Treatment 2 where the deer was running, followed by a lion.

Null Hypothesis 2 is rejected. Without resorting to internal representations, treatments were modified to afford different actions. Subjects perceived that one treatment afforded more danger than another and afforded different physical actions for the actor. This demonstrates that subjects clearly viewed that the environments in Treatments 1 and 2 afforded different actions. In Treatment 1, where the deer is standing by a stream, subjects perceived that the environment afforded the deer the action opportunities to eat, drink, play, or do nothing. However, in Treatment 2, subjects perceived that the environment afforded running (fleeing, escaping) or jumping. This reinforces that changes in the environment, including Selectivity Calibration (in this case goals and current activity), changes available and perceived affordances.

What was also interesting and is deserving of more study is the finding that groups differed in the evaluation of how much danger the environment afforded depending on what treatment they first received. Subjects who received Treatment 1 first, i.e., the picture of the deer by the stream, indicated that this environment afforded less safety as compared to subjects who received Treatment 1 second, i.e., after the treatment with the deer followed by the lion (statistical significance .033). Also, subjects that received Treatment 1 first, found that the environment in Treatment 2 (deer being chased by the lion) afforded more danger as compared to subjects when presented Treatment 2 first (statistical significance .003) It appears that the experience of the first treatment has "cognitively rewired" the subjects (Pizlo, 2005). According to CoAcT, these experiences attuned the subjects, i.e., calibrated the selection of informational structures within the environment so that they now perceive the environment providing more or less safety.

Limitations

Two hypotheses tested the most basic research objectives which were of a binary nature. Does CoAcT provide a means to categorize exposed behavior and can the environment be manipulated to alter affordances? These are important questions, but do not lend themselves to sophisticated statistics. Although these are preliminary experiments with crude experimental materials, they demonstrate that CoAcT can provide a potentially powerful model of collaborative interaction not dependent on eliciting internal representations that filter sense data. However, the major limitation of the study was the inadequate test bed. Comprehensive testing of propositions and research questions demands the development of a more powerful, flexible test bed, capturing better metrics. Testing will require first person scenarios where subjects

interact directly with the environment and their success depends on exposing behavior to other collaborators to achieve shared affordance. In addition, subject motivation was an issue. More engaging testing interaction and some minimal reward structure may improve subject motivation.

IMPACT AND APPLICATION OF CoACT

There are a number of areas where CoAct can have an impact. A few are described below.

Usability Engineering

Usability Engineering is emerging as a parallel process to software engineering, where software engineering focuses on system functionality and usability engineering focuses on methods and processes to design appropriate system usability (Leventhal & Barnes, 2007). In usability engineering, users are characterized along several dimensions, such as age, gender, nationality, etc. and tasks can be categorized along several dimensions including complexity and frequency of task completion (Leventhal & Barnes, 2007; Rosson & Carroll, 2002). It has been accepted practice to reduce these dimensions by broadly describing users as novice, infrequent knowledgeable, and expert (Leventhal & Barnes, 2008; Rosson & Carroll, 2002). It has also been accepted practice to characterize the artifacts, with which users interact, separately from the user, i.e., it is common to describe an interface as easy-to-use or not easy-to-use without referring to the capabilities of the user. Along with this, there exists the unspoken assumption that more usability is always better. However, providing unnecessary usability may cost more and delay system release.

Humans, using computers to complete their work, progress through a sequence of cycles of interaction steps and information displays, where the last information display provides affordances for the next interaction step (Preece, 1994), as the user takes action to achieve some goal. For each step in the cycle, the usability engineer's design assumes an envisioned user, i.e., the design will provide appropriate affordances at the appropriate time for a user with certain capabilities engaged in an activity to achieve some goal. In a sense this describes a CoAct-valid collaborative act, where effective design must provide that future users will share the same affordances at the appropriate time as the envisioned class of users with sufficient, similar capabilities. The difference between the envisioned user and the actual user equals design quality and attunement needed, such as training.

In interface development, theoretical analysis is more efficient than empirical testing (Preece, 1994). Iact and CoAct provides the basis for more precise theoretical analysis that can be used in creating and evaluating designs. For example, does the usability engineer's design achieve effectiveness, efficiently? Analysis may indicate what attunement, in the form of training, will be required to bring expected users to the level of the envisioned user. If judged too much, the usability engineer may be able to alter the design to reduce attunement (training) needs. On the other hand, analysis may reveal a simpler, less user-friendly, but adequate, design that is faster and less-costly to develop. This process helps to prioritize features and fits well with agile development processes (Larman & Vodde, 2009).

Reducing Data Overload/More Effective Use of Bandwidth

Data overload, sometimes referred to as information overload, is growing exponentially worse as the amount of data increases. Having some theory related to what data provides more informational value than others or having informational structures become available as one is performing a certain activity in achieving a goal would be enormously helpful. In times of reduced bandwidth,

CoAct may provide guidance on what exposed behavior should be transmitted or received.

Improving Group Decision Making

Moving away from shared mental models to shared affordance could help improve decision making. When group decision making involves members of different classes, for example, in politician-directed military action and emergency surgery, then decision processes could move towards finding affordances at the intersection of classes or through the process of attunement to bring actors to a sufficient common capacity to act effectively.

EXAMPLE OF APPLYING CoACT TO USABILITY DESIGN

As noted earlier, providing theory-based guidance that does not rely on idiosyncratic, internal representations motivated development of CoAct, an affordance-based theory. This section illustrates the application of CoAct within usability engineering. First, categorization of user capabilities with respect to interface design are discussed, including the concept of multi-level affordances enabled by learning. Next, CoAct is used to evaluate a feature of a common interface.

In usability engineering, it is useful to identify user capabilities with respect to semantic and syntactic knowledge. Semantic knowledge deals with conceptual knowledge, while syntactic knowl-

Figure 9. Part of a job contracting screen

Customized

edge deals with the specific rules. For example, in programming, semantic knowledge of loops would include the understanding of initial value, condition, and increment; syntactic knowledge would be the rules of implementation within a given programming language.

Figure 9 shows a small part of a screen in an actual application to support estimating contracting jobs. There are levels of understanding with the checkbox and accompanying label, "Installation." The lowest level affordance deals with the checkbox and the "checkability" of the box.

The semantic and syntactic knowledge needed for this "lower level affordance" of checkability is as follows:

Semantic knowledge. a checkbox allows Boolean values; when checked, the characteristic of the associated labeled value is applied, when not, the characteristic is not applied (Note, this is for computerized and non-computerized checkboxes - for example, a printed form with the checkbox would require this same knowledge)

Syntactic knowledge. This is variable. One can press (by hand or with a stylus) the checkbox or label to add or remove a check in the box; one can bring the cursor over the box and left click; one can tab over to the control and select. Even this simple example illustrates a broad range of applicable syntactic knowledge, some of which are more intuitive to use than others. The goal of usability design is for syntactic knowledge requirements to disappear, i.e., one relies on the user's semantic understanding as much as possible - I think this is what people mean when they say that an interface is intuitive. For a given class of users with semantic knowledge, the interface allows them to naturally perform their work without too much effort to learn how to use the system.

However, there are higher levels of affordance that come with learning. As Gibson (1979) noted, a mailbox affords "insertability" but a human can learn that it also affords "mailability." The designer hopes this label and checkbox affords the user the action possibility of indicating that this is a "customized" installation, in affordance-like terms, the label and checkbox affords "customizability characterizing" for a given contract. Users would have to have semantic knowledge about what a customized installation is and syntactic knowledge that this label and checkbox would provide a way to record this.

Example - Illustrating CoAct with "Save As" Command

A client uses MS Word on a frequent basis, but only needs to use the "Save As" command once every six months when the new brochure is created from the old one. The user gets confused and is afraid that this command will overwrite the existing file and she will lose the contents of this document. Every six months this user needs to confirm that this command will make a copy and not overwrite the existing file.

Figure 10 depicts a CoAct-based analysis of the "Save As" command. Although this command is second-nature to people who frequently use this command in MS Word, there is a heavy burden of what capabilities are needed for users to be in the same class for this command to afford everything that is does.

In addition to the "Save As" command for experienced users, it may make sense to have another command, such as "Save Copy" that reduces the capability requirements for users who infrequently copy files (Figure 11). Users could select "Save Copy" and an interactive session could ensue that provides the infrequent user "locus of control" (Preece, 1994), where the user is allowed to close the existing document without changes and to make the new copy of the active document. Informally, when students enrolled in

Figure 10. CoAct-based analysis of the "save as" command

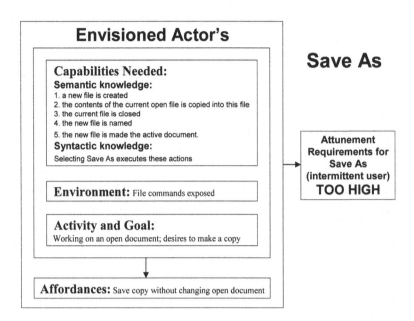

Figure 11. CoAct-based analysis of the "save copy" command

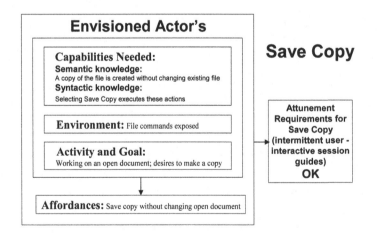

a usability engineering class are asked to step back and identify the problems with "Save As," they can readily identify the problems for the infrequent user of this command. CoAct provides an affordance-based model to guide such evaluation without needing to rely on internal representations, such as mental models.

This example also illustrates the case where actors can move in and out of classes of actors with capacities to act. Actors can learn new capacities for which the environment affords desired action opportunities, but then they can forget and the same environment no longer affords the same action opportunities. For example, the infrequent user is attuned every six months and the "Save As" command within the list of file commands affords her the opportunity to create a copy without modifying the original. However, six months later, when she forgets, the same list of commands no longer affords her the same action opportunity.

SUMMARY

Models of collaboration that rely on internal representations, such as mental models, to filter sense-data are problematic. Folk theories that purport to have "privileged knowledge" about the internal workings of the mind may be true, but they are not falsifiable. In line with Gibson's view of the potentially broad application of his ecological theory of affordance, CoAct extends the notions of affordance and moves away from idiosyncratic, subjective mental models of the world to the notion that actors with similar capacities to act can potentially discern similar action possibilities in the world. It changes the direction from discovery and alignment of internal representations to mutual attunement of collaborators to build sufficient capabilities, share informational structures, and calibrate selectivity to achieve shared affordances.

Preliminary results of initial experiments to test CoAct were presented and provide some support for CoAct. Two interface design examples were presented to demonstrate the applicability of CoAct to usability design. More research is needed, but this work has the potential to impact the design and teaching of human-machine interfaces, provide guidance on reducing data overload among classes of users with different capacities to act, and improve collaborative decision making.

ACKNOWLEDGMENT

This paper has evolved over the last decade. I was originally funded to explore team cognitive constructs. When I reported that I did not think they existed, my funding ceased. This work has benefited from many people who commented, supported, criticized, offered suggestions, and took the time to discuss. Some of these include Alan Dennis, Tom Gradel, Jane Klobas, Ned Kock, George Mathew, John Venable and anonymous reviewers. I especially want to thank the School of Information Systems, Curtin University of Technology, where I was a Research Fellow in July 2010, for providing financial support and the opportunity to reflect, present, and discuss these ideas in such a positive, collegial atmosphere. I apologize in advance if I have missed acknowledging someone. Of course, I own all errors of thinking and limitations.

REFERENCES

Adams-Webber, J. R. (1979). *Personal construct theory: Concepts and applications*. New York, NY: John Wiley & Sons.

Bloor, D. (1983). *Wittgenstein: A social theory of knowledge*. London, UK: Macmillan.

Boland, R. J., & Tenkasi, R. V. (1995). Perspective making and perspective taking in communities of knowing. *Organization Science, 6*(4), 350–372.

Boyle, R. J., Kacmar, C. J., & George, J. F. (2008). Distributed deception: an investigation of the effectiveness of deceptive communication in a computer-mediated environment. *International Journal of e-Collaboration, 4*(3), 14–39.

Brand, G. (1979). *The essential Wittgenstein.* New York, NY: Basic Books.

Cannon-Bowers, J. A., Sala, E., & Converse, S. A. (1993). Shared mental models in expert team decision making. In Castellan, N. J. Jr., (Ed.), *Individual and group decision-making: Current issues* (pp. 221–246). Mahwah, NJ: Lawrence Erlbaum.

Clancey, W. J. (1997). *Situated cognition: On human knowledge and computer representations.* Cambridge, UK: Cambridge University Press.

Dictionary.com. (n. d.). *Attunement.* Retrieved from http://dictionary.reference.com/browse/attunement

Endsley, M. R. (1995). Toward a theory of situation awareness in dynamic systems. *Human Factors, 37*(1), 32–64.

Endsley, M. R. (2001). A model of inter- and intrateam situational awareness: Implications for design, training, and measurement. In McNeese, M., Salas, E., & Endsley, M. (Eds.), *New trends in cooperative activities* (pp. 46–67). Santa Monica, CA: Human Factors and Ergonomics Society.

Fallot, M., Martinez-Carreras, M. A., & Prinz, W. (2010). Collaborative distance: A framework for distance factors affecting the performance of distributed collaboration. *International Journal of e-Collaboration, 6*(2), 1–32.

Farooq, U., Carroll, J. M., & Ganoe, C. H. (2008). Designing for creativity in computer-supported cooperative work. *International Journal of e-Collaboration, 4*(4), 51–75.

Fransella, F., & Bannister, D. (1977). *A manual for repertory grid technique.* New York, NY: Academic Press.

Gentner, D., & Stevens, A. L. (Eds.). (1983). *Mental models.* Mahwah, NJ: Lawrence Erlbaum.

Gephart, R. P. (1993). The textual approach: Risk and blame in disaster sensemaking. *Academy of Management Journal, 36*(6), 1465–1514.

Gibson, J. J. (1979). *The ecological approach to visual perception.* Boston, MA: Houghton-Mifflin.

Habermas, J. (1984). *The theory of communicative action: Reason and the rationalization of society.* Boston, MA: Beacon Press.

Heft, H. (2001). *Ecological psychology in context.* Mahwah, NJ: Laurence Erlbaum.

Hollnagel, E., & Woods, D. D. (2005). *Joint cognitive systems.* Boca Raton, FL: CRC Press.

Johnson-Laird, P. (1983). *Mental models.* Cambridge, MA: Harvard University Press.

Kock, N., & Nosek, J. T. (2005). Expanding the boundaries of e-collaboration. *IEEE Journal of Professional Communication, 48*(1), 1–9.

Larman, C., & Vodde, B. (2009). *Scaling lean & agile development: Thinking and organizational tools for large-scale Scrum.* Reading, MA: Addison-Wesley.

Leventhal, L., & Barnes, J. (2007). *Usability engineering: Process, products, and examples.* Upper Saddle River, NJ: Prentice Hall.

Norman, D. A., & Draper, S. W. (1986). *User centered system design.* Mahwah, NJ: Lawrence Erlbaum.

Nosek, J. T. (2005). Collaborative sensemaking support: Progressing from portals and tools to Collaboration Envelopes™. *International Journal of e-Collaboration, 1*(2), 25–39.

Osgood, C. E. (1969). The nature and measurement of meaning. In Snider, J. G., & Osgood, C. E. (Eds.), *Semantic differential technique*. Chicago, IL: Aldine Publishing.

Pick, J. B., Romano, N. C. Jr, & Roztocki, N. (2009). Synthesizing the research advances in electronic collaboration: Theoretical frameworks. *International Journal of e-Collaboration, 5*(1), 1–12.

Pizlo, Z. (2001). Perception viewed as an inverse problem. *Vision Research, 41*(24), 3145–3161.

Pizlo, Z. (2007). Human perception of 3D shapes. In W. G. Kropatsch, M. Kampel, & A. Hanbury (Eds.), *Proceedings of the 12th International Conference on Computer Analysis of Images and Patterns* (LNCS 4673, pp. 1-12).

Preece, J. (1994). *Human-computer interaction*. Reading, MA: Addison-Wesley.

Remidez, H. Jr, Stam, A., & Laffey, J. M. (2010). Scaffolding solutions to business problems: Trust development as a learning process. *International Journal of e-Collaboration, 6*(4), 12–31.

Rosson, M. B., & Carroll, J. M. (2002). *Usability engineering: Scenario-based development of human computer interaction*. San Francisco, CA: Morgan Kaufmann.

Shannon, C. E., & Weaver, W. (1969). *The mathematical theory of communication*. Urbana, IL: University of Illinois Press.

Stassen, H. G., Johannsen, G., & Moray, N. (1990). Internal representation, internal model, human performance model and mental workload. *Automatica, 26*(4), 811–820.

Vivacqua, A. S., & Moreira de Souza, J. (2008). The vineyard approach: A computational model for determination of awareness foci in e-mail-based collaboration. *International Journal of e-Collaboration, 4*(1), 41–59.

Weick, K. E. (1979). *The social psychology of organizing*. Reading, MA: Addison-Wesley.

Wilson, B. (1998). *Wittgenstein's philosophical investigations: A guide*. Edinburgh, UK: Edinburgh University Press.

Yufik, Y. M., & Georgopoulos, A. P. (2002). Understanding understanding: Modeling cognitive mechanisms of comprehension in complex dynamic tasks. In *Proceedings of the Technology for Command and Control Workshop: Cognitive Elements of Effective Collaboration* (pp. 91-96).

This work was previously published in the International Journal of e-Collaboration, Volume 7, Issue 4, edited by Ned Kock, pp. 37-60, copyright 2011 by IGI Publishing (an imprint of IGI Global).

Chapter 15
Working Effectively in a Matrix:
Building and Sustaining Cooperation

Jennifer Forgie
OnPoint Consulting, USA

ABSTRACT

The complexities of today's organizations have made it increasingly challenging for leaders to encourage and sustain a culture of cooperation. As organizations become flatter and leaner and people are required to do "more with less," the key to success is the ability to coordinate decisions and actions across organizational boundaries and gain the support of people who often have competing priorities or conflicting goals. Further, the increasing prevalence of virtual teamwork and widespread use of e-collaboration tools have additional implications for how leaders encourage cooperation and coordinate work. This article explores the critical organizational factors and leadership skills that are required to build a culture of cooperation in today's highly matrix, and often virtual, organizations.

INTRODUCTION

If you have ever worked in a public or private organization of any size you know that cooperation and coordination are critical for effective execution and organizational success. It is almost impossible to get anything important done without the assistance and joint efforts of others. Yet, despite the fact that there is little argument about the role coordination and cooperation play in the execution of plans and initiatives, it appears that they are elusive and difficult to attain.

In a matrix organization—where people rely on getting work done through others over whom they have no direct authority—maintaining high levels of cooperation and coordination can be a challenge. Added to this is the increasing prevalence of e-collaboration in today's organizations. OnPoint's 2011 study of over 900 leaders across industries found that 53% of their organizations used virtual teams and 57% employ telecommuting, where people work remotely from home. The virtual nature of the work, coupled with the need to work across organizational boundaries, makes it even more difficult for today's organizations

DOI: 10.4018/978-1-4666-2020-9.ch015

and leaders to create and sustain high levels of cooperation and coordination. Our study revealed some surprising findings related to the extent to which organizations struggle with this:

- Only 47% responded favorably to the item, "decisions and actions are well coordinated across departments/functions."
- Only 49% responded favorably to the item, "decisions and actions are well coordinated across levels of management."
- 40% **do not** believe that people cooperate across functions and departments to achieve their organization's strategic objectives.
- 44% **do not** believe that people in different divisions readily share information, ideas, and best practices.

Given the challenges and complexities of today's organizations, what can leaders do to encourage and sustain cooperation? Our research suggests that there are three key elements that need to be in place to build a culture of collaboration, and there are two core skills that are critical for leaders to master in order to effectively cooperate in a global matrix structure.

THE THREE COOPERATION BUILDERS

Encouraging and sustaining cooperation and collaboration with people you depend on to get things done can be a daunting challenge. However, it is not an insurmountable one. There are certain conditions that predict when cooperation is more likely to trump competition—namely, when communication is clear and there is transparency about intent, when people understand what they can expect from others and how they will work together, and when the interests of individuals or groups are aligned. We refer to these elements

as the Cooperation Builders, and they are critical for encouraging high levels of coordination (Lepsinger, 2011).

Cooperation Builder #1: Improve Communication and Transparency

When we communicate our intent to cooperate, we can increase the likelihood the other person will respond in kind. This, of course, assumes that our communication is clear and our intentions are understood. Unfortunately, this is not always the case. Although people often act with good intent and do what they think is right, they are often unable to coordinate their actions because of a breakdown in communications.

The most common mistake is assuming the other person understands what we want or intended. The lesson for leaders is simple: don't make this assumption. Develop the habit of being explicit about *why* you are doing something or making a request. Another mistake is not taking the time to do a "comprehension check" by paraphrasing to ensure understanding and, when appropriate, asking questions to confirm the other person's understanding of actions and next steps.

These two simple actions—not assuming people know what you are thinking and paraphrasing to check for understanding—can go a long way toward making communication clear and transparent and help prevent communication-related missteps. In a virtual organization that relies on significantly more e-collaboration, leaders operate with little face-to-face contact or visual cues which can enhance understanding. In this situation, the effective use of paraphrasing is even more essential. In addition, top performing virtual teams and team leaders leverage technology for communicating (e.g., weekly teleconferences, appropriate use of email, Instant Messaging, webinars) and effectively identify the most appropriate technology to enhance transparency and ensure mutual understanding (DeRosa & Lepsinger, 2011).

Cooperation Builder #2: Agree On When Cooperation Is Needed and What It Looks Like

Lack of clarity about roles and responsibilities is another cooperation-crusher. It results in conflicts among team members or groups. It also allows key responsibilities to "fall through the cracks" because each party believes that someone else is responsible for them. It seems our level of cooperation is generally higher when everyone involved agrees on when it is needed and what it looks like in these situations. When we know what to expect from other people we are more willing to trust them and take the risk of cooperation.

Here is an example: A U.S. based, wholly owned subsidiary of a Japanese pharmaceutical company found its growth objectives threatened because of role ambiguity and the resulting lack of cooperation and coordination among members of its R&D function. When the company was smaller, each therapeutic head had been able to carve out a comfortable niche for his or her area, a practice that continued as the company grew. Each manager acted as if his or her development projects had the highest priority.

Managers frequently ignored requests or decisions they disagreed with and seldom worked with colleagues to coordinate activities that required shared resources (such as clinical trials and the timing of regulatory submissions). As a result, many projects were behind schedule and the leaders in Japan were losing confidence in the teams' ability to deliver on their commitments.

Although individual conversations were held with each member of the R&D team to encourage cooperation, there remained a fundamental difference of opinion about roles and who needed to be involved in key decisions. What was the solution? The team conducted a meeting to list the decisions and activities for which they shared accountability. Using that list as a starting point, the team discussed and agreed on the level of authority and degree of involvement each person needed to have in order to ensure work was done efficiently, on time, and well.

The agreements were then documented and distributed to each manager's department so the behavior of direct reports would be consistent with the agreements reached by the managers. The tool this R&D team used is commonly referred to as the RACIN model. The tool, whose acronym stands for five levels of authority and involvement—*Responsible, Approve, Consult, Inform,* and *Not Involved*—enables individuals and teams to describe what cooperation and collaboration looks like for the most important decisions and activities for which they are responsible.

As we saw in the R&D team example, the team starts by listing the critical decisions and activities for which they are accountable and then discusses and reaches agreement on who has which role. The process takes time but it is well worth the investment. On their own, some teams may eventually come to an understanding about when and how to work together. That journey, however, takes much longer than a RACIN meeting and relationships and trust can be damaged along the way.

The reality is that when left to its own devices, the team is likely to never reach a sustained level of cooperation as its members repeatedly work through misunderstandings and conflicts. Formally and explicitly working out roles at the early stage of a team's formation, or whenever you notice a lack of cooperation, helps accelerate the process and preserve trust.

Clearly articulated goals, roles, and accountabilities are particularly important to success in environments where e-collaboration is prevalent. While e-collaboration tools are not a substitute for face-to-face contact in a virtual setting, leveraging tools such as instant messaging, email, chat rooms, and websites to provide team members with updates and reinforce goals can go a long way in ensuring success. For example, posting a "team handbook" on a shared site with background on each team member and each person's respective role is one way of communicating and reinforcing roles and responsibilities. Periodic e-newsletters are another way to provide team members with updates and create a shared understanding of roles, goals, and priorities.

Clarifying roles and responsibilities not only defines when cooperation is necessary and what it looks like, it also reinforces the norm that cooperation is expected and appropriate. However, to get cooperation you must demonstrate cooperation. If you or members of your team take the first step and model cooperative behavior you will increase the likelihood that the people you depend on to get work done will respond the same way. Through your behavior at work you can signal that cooperation is the expectation, encourage others to reciprocate in kind, and, when they do, demonstrate that they will not be taken advantage of.

Cooperation Builder #3: Align Interests and Establish Common Ground

When the objectives of one person or group are at odds with the objectives of another, cooperation and collaboration suffer.

Picture the potential conflicts and inefficiencies that would result if one group in your department was working toward reducing costs, while another group was focused on bringing state-of-the-art products and services to market. These objectives can coexist, but it most likely won't happen on its own. To facilitate alignment between the two groups, leaders must develop compatible and mutually supportive objectives in a thoughtful and explicit manner.

One approach is to develop a set of broader, collective objectives for a team or work unit, then review the task objectives for specific individuals or groups and ensure that they are consistent with and mutually supportive of the collective objec-

tives. For example: to set the stage at the beginning of the year, the Chief Technology Officer of a large brokerage firm and his boss identify the ten critical objectives for the organization. These are goals that reflect its mission and are necessary for the overall success of the business enterprise. After the extended management team briefly reviews the goals, in-depth work is done to ensure that each will be accomplished.

Cross-functional teams discuss the goals in concurrent sessions to clarify, fine-tune, and determine what it will take to accomplish them, including key deliverables, help required, mileposts, key stakeholders, and so on. Following these discussions, the individual with primary accountability for a particular goal reports on the overall plan, identifies areas that require problem solving, and explains how progress and success will be monitored and communicated throughout the year.

After all the goals have been discussed, possible overlaps, synergies, trade-offs and barriers are highlighted and resolved. The process results in clarity among members of the extended team on priorities, resource allocation, and role expectations.

DISAGREEMENT HAPPENS: HOW TO RESOLVE CONFLICT AND MAINTAIN SUPPORT

Although the cooperation builders set the stage and provide a foundation to encourage cooperation, they won't eliminate disagreements about what and how to do things—and they won't change the fact that people have different priorities, make mistakes, and sometimes, fail to meet others' expectations. In order to sustain cooperation and collaboration, leaders must gain the support of others for their ideas and constructively resolve differences across organizational boundaries.

Eleven Tactics for Influencing Others

Despite having shared goals in place, a leader's success often depends on his or her ability to gain the support and cooperation of people who have competing priorities and/or conflicting goals. The effective use of influence is the most powerful tool a leader has to create alignment and build commitment in these situations.

The most common form of influence behavior is a "simple request": *Please provide me with the report by Friday; Could you please prepare a summary of the results by close of business today?* A simple request is appropriate when compliance is all that is needed and the person being influenced views the request as legitimate, relevant for the work, and something that would be relatively easy to do (i.e., he or she knows how to do it, has the required resources, etc.). However, if the requested action would be unpleasant, inconvenient, or irrelevant, the person's reaction is likely to be resistance. In these situations, a "simple request" would not suffice and it is necessary to use other forms of influence behavior called a "proactive influence tactic." There are 11 proactive influence tactics (Table 1) that are relevant for influencing direct reports, colleagues, and bosses that we categorize based on their effectiveness in gaining commitment (Yukl, 2002):

Four "core tactics" are most effective at gaining commitment. They are *rational persuasion, inspirational appeals, consultation*, and *collaboration*. Following is a description of each.

Rational Persuasion involves the use of explanations, logical arguments, and factual evidence to explain why a request or proposal will benefit the organization or help to achieve an important task objective. This tactic can be effectively used in all directions (with bosses, colleagues, and direct reports) and is particularly powerful when you are seen as an expert or have a track record of success. The key to using rational persuasion is the ability to convert features into benefits—*benefits as seen*

Table 1. The most effective tactics

Most Effective	Moderately Effective	Least Effective
• Rational Persuasion • Inspirational Appeals • Consultation • Collaboration	• Apprising • Ingratiation • Personal Appeals • Exchange	• Legitimating Tactics • Coalition Tactics • Pressure

by the person you are influencing. Following is an example of the use of rational persuasion:

Jim manages a team that generates reports that field personnel depend on to provide effective client service. The system his staff currently uses is old, inefficient, and often malfunctions. Since Charlotte recently left the department, Jim's team has had to put in extra time to keep things running smoothly. Citing budget constraints, management has postponed replacing Charlotte. Jim recently met a programmer who has extensive knowledge of a new system that would require significantly less manual labor. Jim would like to hire this person and needs to convince his boss to approve the hiring decision. Jim says to his boss: "I'd like to talk with you about hiring a programmer to implement a new system in our department. Compared to our existing system, this new system has greater accuracy and requires significantly less manual labor. I recently ran some numbers that I'd like to share with you that indicate the new system would boost our productivity by at least 10%. In addition, the new system would enhance morale and help us retain top performers."

Inspirational Appeals involves an emotional or value-based appeal, in contrast to the logical arguments used in rational persuasion. While rational persuasion appeals to the "head", inspirational appeals focuses on "the heart". It is more effective with direct reports and peers than with bosses and requires an understanding of the other person's values and motivators. A common misconception is that inspirational appeals requires a leader to be "rah rah" and highly charismatic.

This is not the case—in fact, if a leader is effective at using rational persuasion, he or she can be just as effective at using inspirational appeals. The difference is that—with inspirational appeals--benefits are positioned in a more value-oriented manner. Following is an example of the use of inspirational appeals.

Linda is a member of a cross-functional task force charged with developing recommendations to enhance existing project management processes. Recently, Linda was asked by the leader of the task force to head up a new project. One of the key people she will need support from is Joe, a peer of Linda's who is also part of the task force. Linda knows that Joe is very busy with other work for the task force as well as his daily job responsibilities. Linda has worked with Joe for a number of years and knows that he is particularly motivated by achievement and excellence. In her first meeting with Joe she says, "I know it will be a challenge and the goals we've set out are a stretch—but I believe we have what it takes to be successful. The new approach we develop will be much better than anything done in the past and we have the opportunity to build it. When we successfully complete this project there is no question in my mind that we will have a significant and lasting impact on organizational performance."

Consultation involves asking a person to suggest improvements or help plan a proposed activity or change for which his/her support is desired. With this tactic the other person is invited to participate in planning how to carry out a request or implement a proposed change. Following is an example of the use of consultation.

Susan is the manager in charge of developing a new system to process financial transactions that will provide a significant cost savings to the company. She is new to the position and her experience has been in other areas of technical development. John built the current system and is the manager in charge of running and maintaining the system. His expertise will be essential in designing the new system. Susan knows John is

very busy with other priorities, yet without his direct involvement, she can't be sure she is making the best decisions. In her meeting with John she says, "I'd like to get your thoughts on the best approach to developing the new system. Based on conversations with users and my team, I have a beginning idea about how to get started. But I wanted to get your input to help refine the idea and increase the likelihood of success. What are your thoughts on the next steps and from your experience what are some of the pitfalls we need to avoid?"

Collaboration involves offering to provide relevant resources or assistance if the person will carry out a request or approve a proposed change. Like consultation, collaboration is participative, but the focus of collaboration is on reducing difficulty or costs of carrying out a request. This tactic is most effective with peers. Following is an example of the use of collaboration:

Bill is struggling to meet a critical deadline for an important project he is working on for his boss. The deadline is two days away, and Bill knows he won't be able to hit the deadline without help from Andy, one of his colleagues, who is more familiar with the system required to analyze the data Bill needs. Bill approaches Andy and says, "I'm concerned about being able to meet my deadline and I was hoping to get your help." Andy says that he has been working long hours to respond to a request from one of the organization's key clients and taking this on would be difficult. In response, Bill suggests, "What if I identify and organize the relevant data files, which is the most time consuming part of the work. That way you would just have to run the analyses and I can take that and finish the report."

It is more challenging to gain others' support and commitment without face-to-face contact. However, the appropriate use of e-collaboration tools can facilitate a leader's ability to influence from a distance. For example, email or a webinar can be used to make a rational argument by clarifying the benefits of a proposal. Using email to summarize the key features and benefits of your plan or proposal as follow up to a conversation can also be very effective. Instant Messaging can be used to support the tactic of consultation. The immediate, real time exchange of ideas replicates the spontaneity of a face-to-face discussion. Te best virtual leaders are able to effectively match the technology to the influence approach necessary.

The Moderately Effective and Least Effective Tactics

The moderately effective tactics are likely to result in compliance rather than commitment and are more effective for influencing direct reports and peers (they are less effective in an upward influence attempt). They include:

- **Apprising:** Explaining how carrying out a request or supporting a proposal will benefit the person personally or will help to advance the person's career.
- **Ingratiation:** Using praise and flattery before or during an attempt to influence someone to carry out a request or support a proposal.
- **Personal Appeals:** Asking the person to carry out a request or support a proposal out of friendship, or asks for a personal favor before saying what it is.
- **Exchange:** Offering something the person wants, or offering to reciprocate at a later time, if the person will do what you request.

The least effective tactics can be thought of as the "last resort" tactics, since at best, they will result in compliance with a request and, if overused, will erode trust. However, they are legitimate approaches particularly when the stakes are high and other tactics have been used without success. They include:

- **Legitimating:** Establishing the legitimacy of a request or verifying that you have the authority to make it.
- **Coalition:** Enlisting the aid of others, or using the support of others, as a way to influence someone to do something.
- **Pressure:** Using demands, threats, frequent checking, or persistent reminders to influence someone to do something.

Manage Differences and Reach Agreement

In addition to gaining support and commitment, leaders must be able to effectively manage differences and reach agreement to build a culture of collaboration and succeed in a matrix. The word "conflict" often conjures up images of confrontation and anger, but this is frequently not the case. Disagreements occur in even the most positive and productive work relationships—at least, they should. Conflict itself is neither inherently good nor bad—what is positive or negative is how the differences are managed and the outcome that results. Surprisingly, OnPoint's 2011 study found that nearly half of respondents *do not* believe that leaders effectively manage or resolve conflict in their organizations.

What does it take to manage conflict effectively? For one, conflict needs to be acknowledged. When conflict is brought to the surface, problems can be addressed and people can take action to resolve issues. Many people avoid or minimize conflicts in an attempt to maintain harmonious relationships. This is a mistake because the problem may never be resolved. And while not all problems can be resolved to everyone's satisfaction, recognizing that conflict exists and attempting to deal with it is preferable to ignoring the situation. Many a solid long-term relationship is born from the difficult but constructive resolution of a conflict.

Another key to managing conflict is clarifying the source of the conflict. Differences of opinion concerning one or more of the following four issues will cause conflict to occur: facts, methods, goals, and values. Differences of *fact* are the most straightforward conflicts to resolve. Facts are concrete. They can be checked, compared, and tested, and this provides a basis for discussion and the exchange of information. Conflicts over facts can be resolved through dialogue more often than conflicts involving the other basic issues.

Methods are the second issue over which a conflict may arise. People may have similar goals and agree on the facts, but may be unable to agree on ways to achieve their goals. However, the presence of similar goals means that a logical, rational way of choosing among alternative approaches is possible. It's just a matter of convincing everyone that a particular method will achieve the goals at hand.

To illustrate, two production managers are trying to rework an assembly-line process, and they each prefer a different method for accomplishing their goal. At meetings they each promote their preferred method with little progress toward agreement—until, that is, they realize they share the goal of improving assembly line efficiency. Once this common ground is established the two managers are able to look at each method more objectively. It now becomes a matter of reviewing the facts to determine which method does the best job. And because the managers have a shared goal they can focus on finding the method that "is the best" rather than on the one they "like the best."

When the issue is related to *goals*, people have different objectives and may be supporting different courses of action. Information sharing is the key to resolving conflicts over either methods or goals. It helps each person understand what is important to the other person. Occasionally, when differing goals exist, a third person may be needed to determine which goal (or combination of goals) is most appropriate.

For example, a cereal company's marketing group wants a package redesigned in a certain way to make it more attractive and to increase sales. The distribution group feels the new design will lead to breakage problems and will affect their quality standards. Once each group understands the needs and goals of the other they can focus on developing a solution that works for everyone (in this case a redesign that was more attractive and did not create breakage problems). If they are unable to find a solution that meets the goal of both groups they may need to involve the Product Manager to clarify which goal has the higher priority.

Conflicts arising from different values are most difficult to resolve. In fact, they are often not able to be resolved. People's beliefs tend to become inflexible over long periods of time, and are often based on emotion rather than on reason. Finding common ground and separating those that are not solvable from those that are frequently moves such conflicts toward productive action.

For example, the general manager of a manufacturing company feels that it's inappropriate to have alcoholic beverages at the annual picnic. Most of the team members feel that, since it is their picnic, they should have the right to determine the way the picnic fund is used. This conflict is almost impossible to resolve without creating some ill will or resentment because it is based on personal preferences and beliefs. If, however, a conflict is related to the core values of the organization, the organizational core values should override individual preferences.

Neglected conflicts have a tendency to grow. Generally speaking, a conflict left unresolved or unattended will morph from a conflict over facts, methods, or goals into a conflict over values— and in turn will become increasingly difficult to resolve. This underscores the importance of addressing conflict head-on.

Conflict is managed through a combination of assertiveness and cooperativeness. *Assertive-*

ness is defined as behaviors that are used to meet your own needs. *Cooperativeness* is defined as behaviors that are used to meet the needs of others. These two dimensions of behavior are not mutually exclusive—for example, you can work toward getting your needs met and, at the same time, work toward helping the person with whom you have a difference of opinion get her needs met—and yield five distinct conflict management styles. (Thomas & Kilmann, 1974). Finding the right balance between assertiveness and cooperativeness is key to managing conflict effectively—the right balance depends on the situation, what is at stake for the parties involved, position and role, time pressure, quality of the relationship, and the extent to which there are shared goals in place.

In general, to manage differences effectively, your mindset should be that people have the right to think or feel differently than you do and that it is to your benefit to develop solutions that will be acceptable and beneficial to everyone concerned. In a less-than-ideal world, however, people don't always hold that mindset. Here are a few mistakes they commonly make when trying to resolve conflicts:

- Minimizing or ignoring others' concerns
- Pulling power plays
- Attacking the legitimacy of the other person's position or priorities
- Suppressing differences
- Imposing their own goals/priorities
- Refusing to temporarily remove constraints
- Going through the motions of managing the difference, but refusing to carry it through

To avoid these pitfalls, it is best to clarify the situation by identifying the individuals involved in the conflict, identify the specific issues, and gather facts and perceptions of the people involved. A seven-step process for managing conflict can be applied to most situations:

1. Describe what's important to you and why.
2. Check your understanding of what's important to the other person and why.
3. Identify common ground and look for points of interdependence.
4. Invite alternatives that address your needs/goals and those of the other person.
5. Use active listening (paraphrase, questions, balanced response) to evaluate alternatives, resolve concerns, and improve ideas.
6. If an alternative isn't immediately available, temporarily remove constraints to invite and propose new alternatives.
7. End the discussion by summarizing key points and stating next steps.

SUMMARY AND IMPLICATIONS FOR E-COLLABORATION

Organizations are complex structures with many interdependencies. We must rely on others to help get things done and meet our objectives, and that means cooperation and collaboration are often the key to our success. The challenge leaders face in the workplace is to ensure the conditions that create and sustain cooperation and collaboration are in place. This is even more challenging in a virtual environment.

Given the widespread use technology for e-collaboration, leaders must understand how to best leverage technology to help build a culture of collaboration and be aware of situations where a face- to-face or telephone conversation would be beneficial. At times, an over-reliance on one type of technology may cause cooperation and coordination to break down. For example, when using email to solve a problem or make a decision, it can be difficult to check for understanding. Certain influence tactics (e.g., consultation, collaboration) are also difficult to use effectively without having a direct conversation with the other person. However, used appropriately, technology can greatly facilitate and reinforce high levels of collaboration and coordination. For example, e-collaboration tools such as shared intranet sites, e-newsletters, and webinars help to increase role clarity and reinforce goals and objectives.

Cooperation and collaboration are facilitated by clear communication, shared goals, and clearly defined roles. These conditions help encourage and motivate people to focus on the group's best interest without feeling that they are minimizing or trading off their own interests in the process. Once in place, however, cooperation is a delicate state. People will still have disagreements and different points of view about how and when things should happen. Leaders' ability to effectively and constructively influence others and gain their support is critical to maintaining cooperation.

Leaders who focus on these key areas will have much greater success in creating a culture of cooperation and achieving their business objectives in today's highly matrix and virtual organizations.

REFERENCES

DeRosa, D., & Lepsinger, R. (2010). *Virtual team success: A practical guide for working and leading from a distance*. New York, NY: John Wiley & Sons.

Lepsinger, R. (2010). *Closing the execution gap: How great leaders and their companies get results*. New York, NY: John Wiley & Sons.

Thomas, K. W., & Kilmann, R. H. (1974). *The conflict mode instrument*. Tuxedo, NY: Xicom.

Yukl, G., Seifert, C. F., & Chaver, C. (2008). Validation of the extended influence behavior questionnaire. *The Leadership Quarterly*, *19*, 609–621. doi:10.1016/j.leaqua.2008.07.006

This work was previously published in the International Journal of e-Collaboration, Volume 7, Issue 4, edited by Ned Kock, pp. 61-70, copyright 2011 by IGI Publishing (an imprint of IGI Global).

Compilation of References

Achenbach, T. M., Altrichter, H., Posch, P., & Bridget, S. (2003). *Teachers investigate their work*. New York: Routledge.

Achten, H., & Beetz, J. (2009). What happened to collaborative design? In *Proceedings of the 27th Conference on Education and Research in Computer Aided Architectural Design in Europe*, Istanbul, Turkey (pp. 357-365).

Adams-Webber, J. R. (1979). *Personal construct theory: Concepts and applications*. New York, NY: John Wiley & Sons.

Adar, E., & Huberman, B. A. (2000). Free riding on Gnutella. *First Monday*, 5.

Adebayo, D. O. (2005). Ethical and attitudes and prosocial behavior in the Nigeria police: Moderator effect of perceived organizational support and public recognition. *Policing: An International Journal of Police Strategies and Management*, 28(4), 684. doi:10.1108/13639510510628767

Ahuja, V., Yang, J., & Shankar, R. (2009). Study of ICT adoption for building project management in the Indian construction industry. *Automation in Construction*, 18(4), 415–423. doi:10.1016/j.autcon.2008.10.009

Aiken, M., Martin, J., Reithel, B., Shirani, A., & Singleton, T. (1992, November 22-24). Using a group decision support system for multicultural and multilingual communication. In *Proceedings of the 23rd Annual Meeting of the Decision Sciences Institute*, San Francisco (Vol. 2, pp. 792-794).

Aiken, M., Park, M., Simmons, L., & Lindblom, T. (2009). Automatic translation in multilingual electronic meetings. *Translation Journal*, 13(9).

Aiken, M. (2008). Multilingual collaboration in electronic meetings . In Kock, N. (Ed.), *Encyclopedia of E-Collaboration* (pp. 457–462). Hershey, PA: Information Science Publishing.

Aiken, M., Hwang, C., Paolillo, J., & Lu, L. (1994). A group decision support system for the Asian Pacific rim. *Journal of International Information Management*, 3(2), 1–13.

Aiken, M., & Vanjani, M. (2002). A mathematical foundation for group support system research. *Communications of the International Information Management Association*, 2(1), 73–83.

Aiken, M., Vanjani, M., & Paolillo, J., J. (1996). A comparison of two electronic idea generation techniques. *Information & Management*, 30(2), 91–99. doi:10.1016/0378-7206(95)00048-8

Aiken, M., & Waller, B. (2000). Flaming among first-time group support system users. *Information & Management*, 37(2), 95–100. doi:10.1016/S0378-7206(99)00036-1

Alavi, M., Marakas, G. M., & Yoo, Y. (2002). A comparative study of distributed learning environments on learning outcomes. *Information Systems Research*, 13(4), 404–415. doi:10.1287/isre.13.4.404.72

Albert, S., Ashforth, B. E., & Dutton, J. E. (2000). Organizational identity and identification: Charting new waters and building new bridges. *Academy of Management Review*, 25(1), 13–18.

Albert, S., & Whetten, D. A. (1985). Organizational identity . In Cummings, L. L., & Staw, B. M. (Eds.), *Research in Organizational Behavior* (*Vol. 7*, pp. 263–295).

Alonzo, M., & Aiken, M. (2004). Flaming in electronic communication. *Decision Support Systems*, *36*(3), 205–213. doi:10.1016/S0167-9236(02)00190-2

Altrichter, H., Posch, P., & Somekh, B. (1993). *Teachers investigate their work. An introduction to the methods of action research New York*. Routledge.

Amichai-Hamburger, Y. (2007). Personality, individual differences and Internet use . In Joinson, A., McKenna, K. Y. A., Postmes, T., & Reips, U. D. (Eds.), *Oxford handbook of Internet psychology* (pp. 187–204). Oxford, UK: Oxford University Press.

Amirian, P., & Alesheikh, A. A. (2008). Publishing Geospatial Data through Geospatial Web Service and XML Database System. *American Journal of Applied Sciences*, *5*(10), 1358–1368. doi:10.3844/ajassp.2008.1358.1368

Anderson, C. (2008). *The long tail: The future of business is selling more of less*. New York, NY: Hyperion.

Ardichvili, A., Page, V., & Wentling, T. (2003). Motivation and barriers to participation in virtual knowledge-sharing communities of practice. *Journal of Knowledge Management*, *7*(1), 64–77. doi:10.1108/13673270310463626

Ashforth, B., & Mael, F. (1989). Social identity theory and the organization. *Academy of Management Review*, *14*, 20–39. doi:10.2307/258189

Auburn University. (2009). *Auburn University MBA program*. Retrieved November 9, 2009, from http://www.mba.business.auburn.edu/FAQ/OnCampus/oncampus.cfm

Auer, S., Dietzold, S., & Riechert, T. (2006). OntoWiki—a tool for social, semantic collaboration. In *Proceedings of the 5th International Semantic Web Conference*, Toronto, ON, Canada (pp. 18-23).

Aumueller, D. (2005). SHAWN: Structure helps a wiki navigate. In *Proceedings of the BTW-Workshop WebDB Meets IR*, Karlsruhe, Germany (pp. 23-36).

Aumueller, D., & Auer, S. (2005). Towards a semantic wiki experience, desktop integration and interactivity in WikSAR. In *Proceedings of the Workshop on Semantic Desktop*, Galway, Ireland (pp. 10-21).

Autodesk (2010) *Autodesk vault products*. Retrieved from http://usa.autodesk.com/adsk/servlet/pc/index?siteID=123112&id=4502718

Bacharach, S. B. (1989). Organizational theories: Some criteria for evaluation. *Academy of Management Review*, *14*(3), 496–515.

Bakeman, R. (2000). Behavioral observations and coding . In Reis, H. T., & Judd, C. K. (Eds.), *Handbook of research methods in social psychology* (pp. 138–159). Cambridge, UK: Cambridge University Press.

Balasubramanian, S., & Mahajan, V. (2001). The economic leverage of the virtual community. *International Journal of Electronic Commerce*, *5*(3), 103–138.

Balijepally, V. G., Mahapatra, R. K., Nerur, S., & Price, K. H. (2009). Are two heads better than one for software development? The productivity paradox of pair programming. *Management Information Systems Quarterly*, *33*(1), 91–118.

Balthazard, P. E., Potter, R. E., & Warren, J. (2002). The effects of extraversion and expertise on virtual team interaction and performance. In *Proceedings of the 34th Hawaii International Conference on System Sciences*, Hawaii, HI (pp. 1-10).

Bamberger, P. (2008). Beyond contextualization: Using context theories to narrow the micro-macro grap in management research. *Academy of Management Journal*, *51*(5), 839–846. doi:10.5465/AMJ.2008.34789630

Banks, A. P., & Millward, L. J. (2007). Differentiating knowledge in teams: The effect of shared declarative and procedural knowledge on team performance. *Group Dynamics*, *11*(2), 95–106. doi:10.1037/1089-2699.11.2.95

Barkhi, R., Amiri, A., & James, T. (2006). A study of communication and coordination in collaborative software development. *Journal of Global Information Technology Management*, *9*(1), 44–61.

Baron, R. A., & Markman, G. D. (2000). Beyond social capital: How social skills can enhance entrepreneurs' success. *The Academy of Management Executive*, *14*(1), 106–116. doi:10.5465/AME.2000.2909843

Baron, R. M., & Kenny, D. A. (1986). The moderator-mediator variable distinction in social psychological research: Conceptual, strategic and statistical considerations. *Journal of Personality and Social Psychology*, *51*(6), 1173–1182. doi:10.1037/0022-3514.51.6.1173

Barta, R. (2007, October 11-12). Towards a Formal TMQL Semantics. In L. Maicher, A. Sigel, & L. M. Garshol (Eds.), *Leveraging the Semantics of Topic Maps: Second International Conference on Topic Maps Research and Applications, TMRA 2006,* Leipzig, Germany (pp. 90-106). Berlin: Springer.

Baskerville, R. (2006). Hacker wars: E-collaboration by vandals and warriors. *International Journal of e-Collaboration, 2*(1), 1–16. doi:10.4018/jec.2006010101

Bauer, R., & Koszegi, S. T. (2003). Measuring the degree of virtualization. *Electronic Journal of Organizational Virtualness, 2,* 29–46.

Becerik, B., & Rice, S. (2010). The perceived value of building information modeling in the U.S. building industry. *Journal of Information Technology in Construction, 15,* 185–201.

Beetz, J. (2009). *Facilitating distributed collaboration in the AEC/FM sector using semantic web technologies.* Berlin, Germany: University of Berlin. Retrieved from http://alexandria.tue.nl/extra2/200911977.pdf

Benbasat, I., & Zmud, R. W. (2003). The identity crisis within the IS discipline: Defining and communicating the discipline's core properties. *Management Information Systems Quarterly, 27*(2), 183–194.

Benbunan-Fich, R., Hiltz, S. R., & Turoff, M. (2002). A comparative content analysis of face-to-face vs. Asynchronous group decision making. *Decision Support Systems, 34,* 457–469. doi:10.1016/S0167-9236(02)00072-6

Benbunan-Fich, R., & Koufaris, M. (2008). Motivations and contribution behaviour in social bookmarking systems: An empirical investigation. *Electronic Markets, 18*(2), 150–160. doi:10.1080/10196780802044933

Berners-Lee, T., Hendler, J., & Lassila, O. (2001). The semantic web. *Scientific American,* 35–43.

Bickel, R. (2007). *Multilevel analysis for applied research: It's just regression!* New York, NY: Guilford Press.

Bishr, Y. (1998). Overcoming the semantic and other barriers to GIS interoperability. *International Journal of Geographical Information Science, 12*(4), 299–314. doi:10.1080/136588198241806

Blanchard, A. (2004). Virtual behavior settings: An application of behavior setting theories to virtual communities. *Journal of Computer-Mediated Communication, 9*(2).

Blaskovich, J. L. (2008). Exploring the effect of distance: An experimental investigation of virtual collaboration, social loafing, and group decisions. *Journal of Information Systems, 22*(1), 27–46. doi:10.2308/jis.2008.22.1.27

Blau, I., & Barak, A. (2009). Synchronous online discussion: Participation in a group audio conferencing and textual chat as affected by communicator's personality characteristics and discussion topics. In *Proceedings of the International Conference on Computer Supported Education,* Lisbon, Portugal (pp. 19-24).

Blau, I., & Barak, A. (2010, October). *Synchronous online participation: The effects of participant's personality and discussion topic on participation in face-to-face versus voice chat, and textual group discussions.* Paper presented at the 11th Annual Conference of the Association of Internet Researchers: Sustainability, Participation, Action, Gothenburg, Sweden.

Blau, I., & Caspi, A. (2009). Sharing and collaborating with Google Docs: The influence of psychological ownership, responsibility, and student's attitudes on outcome quality. In *Proceedings of the E-Learn World Conference on E-Learning in Corporate, Government, Healthcare, & Higher Education,* Vancouver, BC, Canada (pp. 3329-3335).

Blau, I., Zuckerman, O., & Monroy-Hernández, A. (2009). Children participation in media content creation community: Israelis learners in Scratch programming environment. In Y. Eshet-Alkalai, A. Caspi, S. Eden, N. Geri, & Y. Yair (Eds.), *Learning in the technological era* (pp.65-72). Ra'anana, Israel: Open University of Israel.

Bloor, D. (1983). *Wittgenstein: A social theory of knowledge.* London, UK: Macmillan.

Böhm, K., & Maicher, L. (2006, October 6-7). Real-Time Generation of Topic Maps from Speech Streams. In L. Maicher & J. Park (Eds.), *Charting the Topic Maps Research and Applications Landscape: First International Workshop on Topic Map Research and Applications, TMRA 2005,* Leipzig, Germany (pp. 112-124). Berlin: Springer.

Boland, R. J., & Tenkasi, R. V. (1995). Perspective making and perspective taking in communities of knowing. *Organization Science, 6*(4), 350–372.

Bonabeau, E. (2002). Agent-based modeling: Methods and techniques for simulating human systems. *Proceedings of the National Academy of Sciences of the United States of America, 99*(3), 7280–7287. doi:10.1073/pnas.082080899

Bonito, J. A. (2004). Shared cognition and participation in small groups: Similarity of member prototypes. *Communication Research, 31*(6), 704–730. doi:10.1177/0093650204269406

Borman, W. C., & Motowidlo, S. J. (1993). Expanding the criterion domain to include elements of contextual performance . In Schmitt, N., & Borman, W. C. (Eds.), *Personnel selection in organizations* (pp. 71–98). San Francisco, CA: Jossey-Bass.

Bottelli, V., & Fogh, C. (1995). Galathea: A case-based planning tool for knowledge navigation in the architectural design process, multimedia and architectural disciplines. In *Proceedings of the 13th European Conference on Education in Computer Aided Architectural Design in Europe*, Palermo, Italy (pp. 427-436).

Bouras, C., Giannaka, E., & Tsiatsos, T. (2009). E-collaboration concepts, systems, and applications . In Kock, N. (Ed.), *E-collaboration: Concepts, methodologies, tools, and applications* (pp. 8–16). Hershey, PA: IGI Global. doi:10.4018/978-1-60566-652-5.ch002

Boyle, R. J., Kacmanr, C., & George, J. F. (2008). Distributed deception: An investigation of the effectiveness of deceptive communication in a computer-mediated environment. *International Journal of e-Collaboration, 4*(3), 14–39. doi:10.4018/jec.2008070102

Boyle, R., Kacmar, C., & George, J. (2008). Distributed deception: An investigation of the effectiveness of deceptive communication in a computer-mediated environment. *International Journal of e-Collaboration, 4*(3), 14–38. doi:10.4018/jec.2008070102

Brand, G. (1979). *The essential Wittgenstein*. New York, NY: Basic Books.

Brayfield, A. H., & Rothe, H. F. (1951). An index of job satisfaction. *The Journal of Applied Psychology, 35*(5), 307–311. doi:10.1037/h0055617

Brief, A. P., & Motowidlo, S. J. (1986). Prosocial organizational behaviors. *Academy of Management Review, 11*, 710–725. doi:10.2307/258391

Brownell, M. T., Adams, A., & Sindelar, P. (2006). Learning from collaboration: The role of teacher qualities. *Exceptional Children, 72*(2), 169–185.

Brown, R. (2000). Social identity theory: Past achievements, current problems and future challenges. *European Journal of Social Psychology, 30*, 745–778. doi:10.1002/1099-0992(200011/12)30:6<745::AID-EJSP24>3.0.CO;2-O

Bryk, A. S., & Raudenbush, S. W. (1992). *Hierarchical linear models*. Newbury Park, CA: Sage.

Buffa, M. (2006), Intranet wikis. In *Proceedings of the Intraweb 15th International Conference on World Wide Web*, Edinburgh, UK (pp. 231-251).

Buffa, M., Gandon, F., Ereteo, G., Sander, P., & Faron, C. (2008). SweetWiki: A semantic wiki. *Journal of Web Semantics, 6*(1), 84–97. doi:10.1016/j.websem.2007.11.003

Burke, M., Marlow, C., & Lento, T. (2009). Feed me: Motivating newcomer contribution in social network sites. In *Proceedings of the 27th International Conference of Human Factors in Computing Systems* (pp. 945-954).

Burke, K., & Chidambaram, L. (1999). How much bandwidth is enough? A longitudinal examination of media characteristics and group outcomes. *Management Information Systems Quarterly, 23*(4), 233–246. doi:10.2307/249489

Burton-Jones, A., & Gallivan, M. J. (2007). Towards a deeper understanding of system usage in organizations: A multilevel perspective. *Management Information Systems Quarterly, 31*(4), 657–679.

Burt, R. S. (1992). *Structural holes*. Cambridge, MA: Harvard University Press.

Bybee, R. W. (1997). *Achieving scientific literacy: From purposes to practices*. Portsmouth, NH: Heinemann Educational Books.

Cacioppo, J. T., & Petty, R. E. (1982). The need for cognition. *Journal of Personality and Social Psychology, 42*, 116–131. doi:10.1037/0022-3514.42.1.116

Campanini, S. E., Castagna, P., & Tazzoli, R. (2004). Platypus wiki: A semantic wiki wiki web. In *Proceedings of 1st Italian Semantic Web Workshop on Semantic Web Applications and Perspectives*, Freiburg, Germany (pp. 105-121).

Campbell, P. H., & Halbert, J. (2002). Between research and practice: Provider perspectives in early intervention. *Topics in Early Intervention and Childhood Education, 22*(2), 213–220. doi:10.1177/027112140202200403

Cannon-Bowers, J. A., Sala, E., & Converse, S. A. (1993). Shared mental models in expert team decision making. In Castellan, N. J. Jr., (Ed.), *Individual and group decision-making: Current issues* (pp. 221–246). Mahwah, NJ: Lawrence Erlbaum.

Carley, K. M. (1996). *Validating computational models*. Retrieved July 21, 2010, from http://citeseerx.ist.psu.edu/viewdoc/summary?doi=10.1.1.87.9019

Carley, K., & Reminga, J. (2004). *ORA: Organization risk analyzer* (Tech. Rep. No. CMU-ISRI-04-106). Pittsburgh, PA: Carnegie Mellon University.

Carley, K., Reminga, J., Storrick, J., & DeReno, M. (2009). *ORA user's guide* (Tech. Rep. No. CMU-ISR-09-115). Pittsburgh, PA: Carnegie Mellon University.

Caspi, A., & Blau, I. (in press). Collaboration and psychological ownership: How does the tension between the two influence perceived learning? *Social Psychology of Education: An International Journal*.

Casti, J. (1997). *Would-be worlds: How simulation is changing the world of science*. New York: Wiley.

Catalano, F. (1989). The computerized design firm. In *Proceedings of the Conference on the Electronic Design Studio: Architectural Knowledge and Media in the Computer Era*, Cambridge, MA (pp. 317-332).

Caulfield, H., & Reeder, F. (2001). *Evaluation of endogenous systems*. Retrieved November 9, 2009, from http://www.mitre.org/work/tech_papers/tech_papers_01/reeder_evaluation/index.html

Cenfetelli, R., & Schwarz, A. (in press). Identifying and testing inhibitors of technology usage intentions. *Information Systems Research*.

Champely, S. (2007). *PWR: Basic functions for power analysis, R package version 1.1*. Retrieved from http://www.r-project.org/

Chan, D. (1998). Functional relations among constructs in the same content domain at different levels of analysis: A typology of composition models. *The Journal of Applied Psychology, 83*(2), 234–246. doi:10.1037/0021-9010.83.2.234

Cheng, X., Dale, C., & Liu, J. (2008). Statistics and social network of YouTube videos. In *Proceedings of the 16th International Workshop on Quality of Service*, Enschede, The Netherlands (pp. 229-238).

Chen, G., & Bliese, P. D. (2002). The role of different levels of leadership in predicting self- and collective efficacy: Evidence for discontinuity. *The Journal of Applied Psychology, 87*(3), 549–556. doi:10.1037/0021-9010.87.3.549

Chen, G., Bliese, P. D., & Mathieu, J. E. (2005). Conceptual framework and statistical procedures for delineating and testing multilevel theories of homology. *Organizational Research Methods, 8*(4), 375–409. doi:10.1177/1094428105280056

Chen, G., Mathieu, J. E., & Bliese, P. D. (2004). A framework for conducting multi-level construct validation. In Yammarino, F. J., & Danserau, F. (Eds.), *Multi-level issues in organizational behavior and processes* (pp. 273–303). Amsterdam, The Netherlands: Elsevier Science. doi:10.1016/S1475-9144(04)03013-9

Chen, I. Y. L., & Chen, N. S., & Kinshuk. (2009). Examining the factors influencing participants' knowledge sharing behavior in virtual learning communities. *Journal of Educational Technology & Society, 12*(1), 134–148.

Chen, N.-S., & Tsai, C.-C. (2009). Knowledge infrastructure of the future. *Journal of Educational Technology & Society, 12*(1), 1–4.

Chidambaram, L., & Jones, B. (1993). Impact of communication medium and computer support on group perceptions and performance: A comparison of face-to-face and dispersed meetings. *Management Information Systems Quarterly, 17*, 465–491. doi:10.2307/249588

Chidambaram, L., & Tung, L. L. (2005). Is out of sight, out of mind? An empirical study of social loafing in technology-supported groups. *Information Systems Research, 16*(2), 149–170. doi:10.1287/isre.1050.0051

Chin, W. W. (1998). Issues and opinions on structural equation modeling. *Management Information Systems Quarterly, 22*(1), 7–16.

Chin, W. W., Marcolin, B. L., & Newsted, P. R. (2003). A partial least squares latent variable modeling approach for measuring interaction effects: Results from a Monte Carlo simulation study and an electronic-mail emotion/ adoption study. *Information Systems Research, 14*(2), 189–218. doi:10.1287/isre.14.2.189.16018

Chin, W. W., & Newsted, P. R. (1999). Structural equation modeling analysis with small samples using partial least squares. In Hoyle, R. (Ed.), *Statistical strategies for small sample research* (pp. 307–341). Thousand Oaks, CA: Sage.

Chiquoine, B., & Hjalmarsson, E. (2009). Jackknifing stock return predictions. *Journal of Empirical Finance, 16*(5), 793–803. doi:10.1016/j.jempfin.2009.07.003

Chiu, T., Fang, D. P., Chen, J., Wang, Y., & Jeris, C. (2001). A robust and scalable clustering algorithm for mixed type attributes in large database environments. In *Proceedings of the Seventh ACM SIGKDD International Conference on Knowledge Discovery and Data Mining,* San Francisco (p. 263). New York: ACM Press.

Chudoba, K. M., Wynn, E., Lu, M., & Watson-Manheim, M. B. (2005). How virtual are we? Measuring virtuality and understanding its impact in a global organization. *Information Systems Journal, 15,* 279–306. doi:10.1111/ j.1365-2575.2005.00200.x

Cicchetti, D. V. (1994). Guidelines, criteria, and rules of thumb for evaluating normed and standardized assessment instruments in psychology. *Psychological Assessment, 6*(4), 284–290. doi:10.1037/1040-3590.6.4.284

Ciffolilli, A. (2003). Phantom authority, self-selective recruitment and retention of members in virtual communities: The case of Wikipedia. *First Monday, 8.*

Clancey, W. J. (1997). *Situated cognition: On human knowledge and computer representations.* Cambridge, UK: Cambridge University Press.

Coiro, J., Knobel, M., Lankshear, C., & Leu, D. (Eds.). (2008). *The handbook of research on new literacies.* Mahwah, NJ: Lawrence Erlbaum.

Coleman, D., & Levine, S. (2008). *Collaboration 2.0: Technology and best practices for successful collaboration in a Web 2.0 world.* Silicon Valley, CA: Happy About Info.

Computational Analysis of Social and Organizational Systems (CASOS). (2009). *ORA.* Pittsburg, PA: Carnegie Mellon University. Retrieved from http://www.casos. cs.cmu.edu/projects/ora/

Conner, N. (2008). *Google Apps: The missing manual.* Sebastopol, CA: O'Reilly Media.

Cooke, N. J., Kiekel, P. A., Salas, E., Stout, R., Bowers, C., & Cannon-Bowers, J. (2003). Measuring team knowledge: A window to the cognitive underpinnings of team performance. *Group Dynamics, 7*(3), 179–199. doi:10.1037/1089-2699.7.3.179

Cramton, C. (2001). The mutual knowledge problem and its consequences for dispersed collaboration. *Organization Science, 12*(3), 346–371. doi:10.1287/ orsc.12.3.346.10098

Daily, B., & Steiner, R. (1998). The influence of group decision support systems on contribution and commitment levels in multicultural and culturally homogeneous decision-making groups. *Computers in Human Behavior, 14*(1), 147–162. doi:10.1016/S0747-5632(97)00037-X

Danserau, F., & Yammarino, F. J. (1998). Introduction and overview. In Danserau, F., & Yammarino, F. J. (Eds.), *Leadership: The multiple-level approaches* (pp. xxv–xliii). Greenwich, CT: JAI Press.

Davis, D., & Bryant, L. (2003). Influence at a distance: Leadership in global virtual teams. *Advances in Global Leadership, 3,* 303–340. doi:10.1016/S1535-1203(02)03015-0

Davis, E. S., & Hantula, D. A. (2001). The effects of download delay on performance and end-user satisfaction in an Internet tutorial. *Computers in Human Behavior, 17,* 249–268. doi:10.1016/S0747-5632(01)00007-3

Davis, F. D., Bagozzi, R. P., & Warshaw, P. R. (1989). User acceptance of computer technology: A comparison of two theoretical models. *Management Science, 35*(8), 982–1003. doi:10.1287/mnsc.35.8.982

Davis, J. A. (1966). The campus as a frog pond: An application of the theory of relative deprivation to career decisions of college men. *American Journal of Sociology*, *72*(1), 17–31. doi:10.1086/224257

De Dreu, C. K. W. (2007). Cooperative outcome interdependence, task reflexivity and team effectiveness: A motivated information processing approach. *The Journal of Applied Psychology*, *92*(3), 628–638. doi:10.1037/0021-9010.92.3.628

de Leede, J., Kraan, K. O., den Hengst, M., & van Hooff, M. L. M. (2008). Conditions for innovation behaviour of virtual team members: A 'high road' for internationally dispersed virtual teams. *Journal of E-Working*, *2*, 22–46.

de Vreede, G., Mgaya, R., & Qureshi, S. (2003). Field experiences with collaboration technology: A comparative study in Tanzania and South Africa. *Information Technology for Development*, *10*(3), 201–219. doi:10.1002/itdj.1590100306

Decker, B., Ras, E., Rech, J., Klein, B., & Hoecht, C. (2005). Self-organized reuse of software engineering knowledge supported by semantic wikis. In *Proceedings of the Workshop on Semantic Web Enabled Software Engineering*, Galway, Ireland (pp. 65-78).

Deepwell, F., & King, V. (2009). E-research collaboration, conflict and compromise . In Salmons, J., & Wilson, L. (Eds.), *Handbook of research on electronic collaboration and organizational synergy* (pp. 1–15). Hershey, PA: IGI Global.

Dello, K., Paslaru, E., Simperl, B., & Tolksdorf, R. (2006). Creating and using Semantic Web information with Makna. In *Proceedings of the First Workshop on Semantic Wikis: From Wiki to Semantics*, Budva, Montenegro (pp. 313-352).

DeLuca, D., Gasson, S., & Kock, N. (2006). Adaptations that virtual teams make so that complex tasks can be performed using simple e-collaboration technologies. *International Journal of e-Collaboration*, *2*(3), 64–90.

DeLuca, D., & Valacich, J. S. (2006). Virtual teams in and out of synchronicity. *Information Technology & People*, *19*(4), 323–344. doi:10.1108/09593840610718027

Dennis, A., Fuller, R. M., & Valacich, J. S. (2008). Media, tasks and communication processes: A theory of media synchronicity. *Management Information Systems Quarterly*, *32*(3), 575–600.

Dennis, A., & Valacich, J. S. (1993). Computer brainstorms: More heads are better than one. *The Journal of Applied Psychology*, *78*(4), 531–537. doi:10.1037/0021-9010.78.4.531

Denzin, N. (2006). *Sociological methods: A sourcebook* (5th ed.). Piscataway, NJ: Aldine Transaction.

DeRosa, D. M., Hantula, D. A., Kock, N., & D'Arcy, J. (2004). Trust and leadership in virtual teamwork: A media naturalness perspective. *Human Resource Management*, *43*, 219–232. doi:10.1002/hrm.20016

DeRosa, D. M., Smith, C., & Hantula, D. (2007). The medium matters: Mining the long-promised merit of group interaction in creative idea generation tasks in a meta-analysis of the electronic group brainstorming literature. *Computers in Human Behavior*, *23*(3), 1549–1581. doi:10.1016/j.chb.2005.07.003

DeRosa, D., & Lepsinger, R. (2010). *Virtual team success: A practical guide for working and leading from a distance*. New York, NY: John Wiley & Sons.

Dessler, G. (1999). How to earn your employee's commitment. *The Academy of Management Executive*, *13*(2), 58–67.

DeWert, M. H., Babinski, L. M., & Jones, B. D. (2003). Safe passages: Providing online support to beginning teachers. *Journal of Teacher Education*, *54*(4), 311–320. doi:10.1177/0022487103255008

DeWever, B., Schellens, T., Valcke, M., & Van Keer, H. (2006). Content analysis schemes to analyze transcripts of online asynchronous discussion groups: A review. *Computers & Education*, *46*(1), 6–28. doi:10.1016/j.compedu.2005.04.005

Diamantopoulos, A. (1999). Export performance measurement: Reflective versus formative indicators. *International Marketing Review*, *16*(6), 444–457. doi:10.1108/02651339910300422

Diamantopoulos, A., & Siguaw, J. A. (2002). *Formative vs. reflective indicators in measure development: Does the choice of indicators matter?* Ithaca, NY: Cornell University.

Diamantopoulos, A., & Winklhofer, H. (2001). Index construction with formative indicators: An alternative scale development. *JMR, Journal of Marketing Research*, *37*(1), 269–177. doi:10.1509/jmkr.38.2.269.18845

Dictionary.com. (n. d.). *Attunement.* Retrieved from http://dictionary.reference.com/browse/attunement

Diosteanu, A., & Cotfas, L. (2009). Agent Based Knowledge Management Solution using Ontology, Semantic Web Services and GIS. *Informatica Economica*, *13*(4), 90–98.

Djaiz, C., Monticolo, D., & Matta, N. (2008). Project memory decision making. *International Journal of e-Collaboration on Creativity, Innovation and e-Collaboration, 2*, 12-28.

Doll, W. J., & Torkzadeh, G. (1988). The measurement of end-user computing satisfaction. *Management Information Systems Quarterly*, *12*(2), 259–274. doi:10.2307/248851

Dourish, P., & Bellotti, V. (1992). Awareness and coordination in shared workspaces. In M. Mantel & R. Baecker (Eds.), *Proceedings of the 1992 ACM Conference on Computer-supported Cooperative Work* (pp. 107-114). New York: ACM Press.

Dutton, J. E., Dukerich, J. M., & Harquail, C. V. (1994). Organizational images and member identification. *Administrative Science Quarterly*, *39*(2), 239–263. doi:10.2307/2393235

Easley, R. F., Devaraj, S., & Crant, J. M. (2003). Relating collaborative technology use to teamwork quality and performance: An empirical study. *Journal of Management Information Systems*, *19*(4), 249–270.

Eckel, C., & Grossman, P. J. (2005). Managing diversity by creating team identity. *Journal of Economic Behavior & Organization*, *58*, 371–392. doi:10.1016/j.jebo.2004.01.003

Edwards, J. R. (2001). Multidimensional constructs in organizational behavior research: An integrative analytical framework. *Organizational Research Methods*, *4*(2), 144–192. doi:10.1177/109442810142004

Efron, B., Rogosa, D., & Tibshirani, R. (2004). Resampling methods of estimation . In Smelser, N. J., & Baltes, P. B. (Eds.), *International Encyclopedia of the Social & Behavioral Sciences* (pp. 13216–13220). New York, NY: Elsevier. doi:10.1016/B0-08-043076-7/00494-0

Eisenberg, E. M., & Phillips, S. R. (1990). What is organizational miscommunication? In Wiemann, J., Coupland, N., & Giles, H. (Eds.), *Handbook of miscommunication and problematic talk* (pp. 85–103). Oxford, UK: Multilingual Matters.

Ellemers, N., Spears, R., & Doosje, B. (Eds.). (1999). *Social identity: Context, commitment, content.* Oxford, UK: Blackwell.

Elsbach, K. D., & Hargadon, A. B. (2006). Enhancing creativity through "mindless" work: A framework of workday design. *Organization Science*, *17*(4), 470–484. doi:10.1287/orsc.1060.0193

Emerson, R. M., Fretz, R. I., & Shaw, L. L. (1995). *Writing Ethnographic Fieldnotes.* Chicago: University of Chicago Press.

Enders, C. K. (in press). Missing not at random models for latent growth curve analyses. *Psychological Methods*.

Endsley, M. R. (1995). Toward a theory of situation awareness in dynamic systems. *Human Factors*, *37*(1), 32–64.

Endsley, M. R. (2001). A model of inter- and intrateam situational awareness: Implications for design, training, and measurement . In McNeese, M., Salas, E., & Endsley, M. (Eds.), *New trends in cooperative activities* (pp. 46–67). Santa Monica, CA: Human Factors and Ergonomics Society.

Epstein, J. M., & Axtell, R. L. (1996). *Growing artificial societies: Social science from the bottom up.* Cambridge, MA: MIT Press.

Fahdah, I., & Tizani, W. (2006). Virtual collaborative building design environment using software agents. In *Proceedings of the 6th International Conference on Construction Applications of Virtual Reality,* Orlando, FL.

Fallot, M., Martinez-Carreras, M. A., & Prinz, W. (2010). Collaborative distance: A framework for distance factors affecting the performance of distributed collaboration. *International Journal of e-Collaboration*, *6*(2), 1–32.

Farooq, U., Carroll, J. M., & Ganoe, C. H. (2008). Designing for creativity in computer-supported cooperative work. *International Journal of e-Collaboration, 4*(4), 51–75.

Fedorowicz, J., Ballesteros, I., & Meléndez, A. (2008). Creativity, innovation and e-collaboration. *International Journal of e-Collaboration, 4*(4), 1–10. doi:10.4018/jec.2008100101

Feely, A., & Harzing, A. (2003). Language management in multinational companies. *Cross Cultural Management: An International Journal, 10*(2), 37–52. doi:10.1108/13527600310797586

Fernandez, I., Alto, M., & Stewart, H. (2006). A case study of web-based collaborative decision support at NASA. *International Journal of e-Collaboration, 2*(3), 50–64. doi:10.4018/jec.2006070103

Fichter, D. (2005). The many forms of e-collaboration: Blogs, wikis, portals, groupware, discussion boards, and instant messaging. *Online, 29*(5).

Fiol, C. M., & O'Connor, E. J. (2005). Identification in face-to-face, hybrid, and pure virtual teams: Untangling the contradictions. *Organization Science, 16*(1), 19–32. doi:10.1287/orsc.1040.0101

Fiore, S. M., Salas, E., & Cannon-Bowers, J. A. (2001). Group dynamics and shared mental model development. In London, M. (Ed.), *How people evaluate others in organizations* (pp. 309–336). Mahwah, NJ: Lawrence Erlbaum.

Firebaugh, G. A. (1978). A rule for inferring individual-level relationships from aggregate data. *American Sociological Review, 43*(4), 557–572. doi:10.2307/2094779

Firebaugh, G. A. (1980). Groups as contexts and frog ponds. In Roberts, K. H., & Burstein, L. (Eds.), *New directions for methodology of social and behavioral science* (*Vol. 6*, pp. 43–52). San Francisco, CA: Jossey-Bass.

Fischer, J., Gantner, Z., Rendle, S., Stritt, M., & Thieme, T. (2006). Ideas and improvements for semantic wikis. In Y. Sure & J. Domingue (Eds.), *Proceedings of the 3rd European Semantic Web Conference on the Semantic Web: Research and Applications* (LNCS 4011, pp. 650-663).

Fjermestad, J. (2004). An analysis of communication mode in group support systems research. *Decision Support Systems, 37*(2), 239–263.

Flournoy, R., & Callison-Burch, C. (2000, November 16-17). Reconciling user expectations and translation technology to create a useful real-world application. In *Proceedings of the 22nd International Conference on Translating and the Computer*, London.

Fornell, C., & Larcker, D. F. (1981). Evaluating structural equation models with unobservable variables and measurement error. *JMR, Journal of Marketing Research, 18*(1), 39–50. doi:10.2307/3151312

Fransella, F., & Bannister, D. (1977). *A manual for repertory grid technique*. New York, NY: Academic Press.

Fuchs, L., PankokE-Babatz, U., & Prinz, W. (1995). Supporting Cooperative Awareness with Local Event Mechanisms: The GroupDesk System. In H. Marmolin, Y. Sundblad, & K. Schmidt (Eds.), *Proceedings of the Fourth European Conference on Computer-Supported Cooperative Work* (pp. 247-262). Norwell, MA: Kluwer Academic Publishers.

Fuchs-Kittowski, F., & Faust, D. (2009). Collaborative Enterprise Architecture Design and Development with a Semantic Collaboration Tool. *International Journal of E-Collaboration, 5*(4), 53–66.

Fügen, C., Waibel, A., & Kolss, M. (2007). Simultaneous translation of lectures and speeches. *Machine Translation, 21*, 209–252. doi:10.1007/s10590-008-9047-0

Fuller, M. A., & Davison, R. M. (2007). I know I can, but can we? Culture and efficacy beliefs in global virtual teams. *Small Group Research, 38*(1), 130–155. doi:10.1177/1046496406297041

Funakoshi, K., Yamamoto, A., Nomura, S., & Ishida, T. (2009). *Lessons learned from multilingual collaboration in global virtual teams*. Retrieved November 9, 2009, from http://www.ai.soc.i.kyoto-u.ac.jp/ice/slides/kfHCII2003.pdf

Furumo, K. (2009). The impact of conflict and conflict management style on deadbeats and deserters in virtual teams. *Journal of Computer Information Systems, 49*(4), 66–73.

Gable, G. G., Sedera, D., & Chan, T. (2008). RE-conceptualizing Information System Success: The IS-Impact Measurement Model. *Journal of the Association for Information Systems, 9*(7), 377–408.

Gallivan, M. J., & Benbunan-Fich, R. (2005). A framework for analyzing levels of analysis: Issues in studies of e-collaboration. *IEEE Transactions on Professional Communication, 48*(1), 87–104.

Garshol, L. M. (2006, October 6-7). tolog – A Topic Maps Query Language. In L. Maicher & J. Park (Eds.), *Charting the Topic Maps Research and Applications Landscape: First International Workshop on Topic Map Research and Applications, TMRA 2005,* Leipzig, Germany (pp. 183-196). Berlin: Springer.

Gartin, B., & Murdick, N. (2005). IDEA 2004: The IEP. *Remedial and Special Education, 26*(6), 327–331. doi:10.1177/07419325050260060301

Garton, C., & Wegryn, K. (2006). *Managing without walls: Maximize success with virtual, global, and cross-cultural teams.* Double Oak, TX: Mc Press Online LP.

Gefen, D., Geri, N., & Paravatsu, N. (2007). Vive la différence: The cross-cultural differences within us. *International Journal of e-Collaboration, 3*(3), 1–15. doi:10.4018/jec.2007070101

Gefen, D., Straub, D. W., & Boudreau, M.-C. (2000). Structural equation modeling and regression: Guidelines for research practice. *Communications of the AIS, 4*(7), 1–76.

Genovese, J. E. (2002). Cognitive skills valued by educators: Historical content analysis of testing in Ohio. *The Journal of Educational Research, 96*(2), 101–115. doi:10.1080/00220670209598797

Gentner, D., & Stevens, A. L. (Eds.). (1983). *Mental models.* Mahwah, NJ: Lawrence Erlbaum.

George, J. M., & Brief, A. P. (1992). Feeling good-doing good: A conceptual analysis of the mood at work-organizational spontaneity relationship. *Psychological Bulletin, 112*, 310–329. doi:10.1037/0033-2909.112.2.310

Gephart, R. P. (1993). The textual approach: Risk and blame in disaster sensemaking. *Academy of Management Journal, 36*(6), 1465–1514.

Gibson, J. J. (1979). *The ecological approach to visual perception.* Boston, MA: Houghton-Mifflin.

Giddens, A. (1991). *Modernity and self-identity.* Cambridge, UK: Polity Press.

Gilbert, M., & Masucci, M. (2006). Geographic Perspectives on E-collaboration Research. *International Journal of E-Collaboration, 2*(1), i–v.

Gilder, G. (1993, September 3). Metcalfe's law and legacy. *Forbes ASAP*.

Glazer, E. M., & Hannafin, M. J. (2006). The collaborative apprenticeship model: Situated professional development within school settings. *Teaching and Teacher Education: An International Journal of Research and Studies, 22*(2), 179–193. doi:10.1016/j.tate.2005.09.004

Glückler, J., & Gregor, S. (2007). Leadership and performance in virtual teams: Exploring brokerage in electronic communication. *International Journal of e-Collaboration, 3*, 31–53. doi:10.4018/jec.2007070103

Goffman, E. (1959). *The presentation of self in every day life.* New York, NY: Doubleday.

Golmohammadi, A. (2007). *Globalization, culture and identity.* Skopje, Macedonia: Net Press.

Goodman, P. S. (2000). *Missing organizational linkages: Tools for cross-level research.* Thousand Oaks, CA: Sage.

Granovetter, M. (1973). The strength of weak ties. *American Journal of Sociology, 78*(6), 1360–1380. doi:10.1086/225469

Green, S., & Taber, T. (1980). The effects of three social decision schemes in decision group performance. *Organizational Behavior and Human Performance, 25*(1), 97–106. doi:10.1016/0030-5073(80)90027-6

Grohowski, R., McGoff, C., Vogel, D., Martz, B., & Nunamaker, J. (1990). Implementing electronic meeting systems at IBM: Lessons learned and success factors. *Management Information Systems Quarterly, 14*(4), 369–384. doi:10.2307/249785

Gronau, N., Müller, C., & Korf, R. (2005). KMDL – Capturing, Analysing and Improving KnowledgE-Intensive Business Processes. *Journal of Universal Computer Science, 11*(4), 452–472.

Guha, S. (2007). Construction management through web services in Calcutta, India . In Helfert, M., Thi, T., & Duncan, H. (Eds.), *Cases and projects in business informatics* (pp. 22–40). Berlin, Germany: Logos-Verlag.

Guha, S., Thakur, B., & Chakrabarty, S. (2010). Collaboration in a web enabled design management system - a case study in Kolkata, India. *Journal of Information Technology in Construction*, *15*, 86–107.

Gu, L., Aiken, M., & Wang, J. (2007). Topic effects on process gains and losses in electronic meetings. *Information Resources Management Journal*, *20*(4), 1–11.

Habermas, J. (1984). *The theory of communicative action: Reason and the rationalization of society*. Boston, MA: Beacon Press.

Hacker, W. (2003). Action regulation theory: A practical tool for the design of modern work processes? *European Journal of Work and Organizational Psychology*, *12*(2), 105–130. doi:10.1080/13594320344000075

Haenlein, M., & Kaplan, A. M. (2004). A beginner's guide to partial least squares analysis. *Understanding Statistics*, *3*(4), 283–297. doi:10.1207/s15328031us0304_4

Hair, J. F., Anderson, R. E., & Tatham, R. L. (1987). *Multivariate data analysis*. New York, NY: Macmillan.

Hair, J. F., Black, W. C., Babin, B. J., & Anderson, R. E. (2009). *Multivariate data analysis*. Upper Saddle River, NJ: Prentice Hall.

Häkkinen, P. (2003). Collaborative learning in networked environments: Interaction through shared workspaces and communication tools. *Journal of Education for Teaching*, *29*(3), 279–281. doi:10.1080/0260747032000120178

Hall, S. (1996). The question of cultural identity . In Hall, S., Held, D., & McGrew, A. (Eds.), *Modernity and its future*. Cambridge, UK: Polity Press.

Hambley, L. A., O'Neill, T. A., & Kline, T. J. B. (2007). Virtual team leadership: Perspectives from the field. *International Journal of e-Collaboration*, *3*, 40–63. doi:10.4018/jec.2007010103

Hambley, L., O'Neill, T., & Kline, T. (2007). Virtual team leadership: Perspective from the field. *International Journal of e-Collaboration*, *3*(1), 40–64. doi:10.4018/jec.2007010103

Hansen, M. T. (1999). The search-transfer problem: The role of weak ties in sharing knowledge across organization subunits. *Administrative Science Quarterly*, *44*(1), 82–111. doi:10.2307/2667032

Hansen, M. T. (2009). When internal collaboration is bad for your company. *Harvard Business Review*, *87*(4), 82–88.

Hantula, D. A., Kock, N. F., D'Arcy, J., & DeRosa, D. M. (in press). Media Compensation Theory: A Darwinian perspective on adaptation to electronic communications and collaboration . In Saad, G. (Ed.), *Darwinian theory in the organizational sciences*. New York: Springer.

Hantula, D. A., & Pawlowicz, D. M. (2004). Education mirrors industry: On the not-so surprising rise of Internet distance education . In Monolescu, D., Schifter, C., & Greenwood, L. (Eds.), *The distance education evolution* (pp. 142–162). Hershey, PA: Information Sciences Publishing.

Harfitt, G. J., & Tavares, N. J. (2004). Obstacles as opportunities in the promotion of teachers' learning. *International Journal of Educational Research*, *41*(5), 353–366. doi:10.1016/j.ijer.2005.08.006

Harvey, M., Milord, M., & Noveicevic, G. G. (2004). Challenges to staffing global virtual team. *Human Resource Management Review*, *14*, 275–294. doi:10.1016/j.hrmr.2004.06.005

Haslam, S. A. (2001). *Psychology in organizations (the social identity approach)*. London, UK: Sage.

Haslam, S. A., Powell, C., & Turner, J. C. (2000). Social identity, self-categorization and work motivation: Rethinking the contribution of group to positive and sustainable organizational outcomes. *Applied Psychology: An International Review*, *49*, 319–339. doi:10.1111/1464-0597.00018

Hasty, B. K., Massey, A. P., & Brown, S. A. (2006). Role-based experiences, media perceptions, and knowledge transfer success in virtual dyads. *Group Decision and Negotiation*, *15*(4), 367–387. doi:10.1007/s10726-006-9047-5

Hawkes, M. (2000). Structuring computer-mediated communication for collaborative teacher development. *Journal of Research and Development in Education*, *33*(4), 268–277.

Hawkes, M., & Romiszowski, A. (2001). Examining the reflective outcomes of asynchronous computer-mediated communication on inservice teacher development. *Journal of Technology and Teacher Education*, *9*(2), 285–308.

Haythornthwaite, C. (2005). Introduction: Computer-mediated collaborative practices. *Journal of Computer-Mediated Communication, 10*(4).

Heft, H. (2001). *Ecological psychology in context*. Mahwah, NJ: Laurence Erlbaum.

Heinrich, C. E. (2005). *RFID and Beyond: Growing Your Business Through Real World Awareness*. Indianapolis, IN: Wiley Publishing.

He, J., Butler, B., & King, W. R. (2007). Team cognition: Development and evolution in software project teams. *Journal of Management Information Systems, 24*(2), 261–292. doi:10.2753/MIS0742-1222240210

Hertela, G., Geisterb, T. S., & Konradtb, U. (2005). Managing virtual teams: A review of current empirical research. *Human Resource Management Review, 15*, 69–95. doi:10.1016/j.hrmr.2005.01.002

Hiltz, S., Turoff, M., & Johnson, K. (1989). Experiments in group decision making, 3: Disinhibition, deindividuation, and group process in pen name and real name computer conferences. *Decision Support Systems, 5*, 217–232. doi:10.1016/0167-9236(89)90008-0

Hinds, P. J., & Mortensen, M. (2005). Understanding conflict in geographically distributed teams: The moderating effects of shared identity, shared context, and spontaneous communication. *Organization Science, 16*(3), 290–309. doi:10.1287/orsc.1050.0122

Hitt, M. A., Beamish, P. W., Jackson, S. E., & Mathieu, J. E. (2007). Building theoretical and empirical bridges across levels: Multilevel research in management. *Academy of Management Journal, 50*(6), 1385–1399. doi:10.5465/AMJ.2007.28166219

Hobbs, T., Day, S. L., & Russo, A. (2002). The virtual conference room: Online problem solving for first year teachers. *Teacher Education and Special Education, 25*(4), 352–361. doi:10.1177/088840640202500404

Hobman, E. V., Bordia, P., Irmer, B., & Chang, A. (2002). The expression of conflict in computer-mediated and face-to-face groups. *Small Group Research, 33*(33), 4.

Hoegl, M., & Gemuenden, H. G. (2001). Teamwork quality and the success of innovative projects: A theoretical concept and empirical evidence. *Organization Science, 12*(4), 435–449. doi:10.1287/orsc.12.4.435.10635

Hoegl, M., Weinkauf, K. H., & Gemuenden, G. (2004). Interteam coordination, project commitment, and teamwork in multiteam R&D projects: A longitudinal study. *Organization Science, 5*(1), 38–55. doi:10.1287/orsc.1030.0053

Hoffman, J. D. (2001). *Numerical methods for engineers and scientists*. New York: McGraw-Hill.

Hofmann, D. A. (1997). An overview of the logic and rationale of hierarchical linear models. *Journal of Management, 23*(6), 723–744. doi:10.1177/014920639702300602

Hofmann, D. A., & Jones, L. M. (2004). Some foundational and guiding questions for multilevel construct validation . In Dansereay, F., & Yammarino, F. J. (Eds.), *Multi-level issues in organizational behavior and processes* (pp. 305–317). Amsterdam, The Netherlands: Elsevier Science. doi:10.1016/S1475-9144(04)03014-0

Hofsted, G. (1997). *Culture and organizations: Software of the mind*. New York, NY: McGrawHill.

Hogg, M. A., & Terry, D. J. (2000). Social identity and self-categorization processes in organizational contexts. *Academy of Management Review, 25*, 121–141. doi:10.2307/259266

Hollnagel, E., & Woods, D. D. (2005). *Joint cognitive systems*. Boca Raton, FL: CRC Press.

Hong, I. (1999). Information technology to support any-time, any-place team meetings in Korean organizations. *Industrial Management & Data Systems, 99*(1), 18–24. doi:10.1108/02635579910247145

House, R. J., Javidan, M., Hanges, P. J., & Dorfman, P. W. (2002). Understanding cultures and implicit leadership theories across the globe: An Introduction to Project GLOBE. *Journal of World Business, 37*, 3–10. doi:10.1016/S1090-9516(01)00069-4

Howard, J. (2000). Social psychology of identities. *Annual Review of Sociology, 26*, 367–393. doi:10.1146/annurev.soc.26.1.367

Hutchins, J. (2007). Machine translation: A concise history . In Wai, C. (Ed.), *Computer Aided Translation: Theory and Practice*. Hong Kong: Chinese University of Hong Kong.

Ignat, G. L., Oster, G., Molli, P., Cart, M., Ferrie, J., Kermarrec, A.-M., et al. (2007). A comparison of optimistic approaches to collaborative editing of wiki pages. In *Proceedings of the International Conference on Collaborative Computing: Networking, Applications and Worksharing*, New York, NY (pp. 10-15).

Ingram, A. L., & Hathorn, L. G. (2004). Methods for analyzing collaboration in online communications . In Roberts, T. S. (Ed.), *Online collaborative learning: Theory and practice* (pp. 215–241). Hershey, PA: IGI Global.

Ingram, A. L., & Hathorn, L. G. (2009). Collaboration in online communications . In Howard, C., Boettcher, J., Justice, L., Schenk, K., Berg, G., & Rogers, P. (Eds.), *Encyclopedia of distance learning* (2nd ed., Vol. 1, pp. 314–318). Hershey, PA: IGI Global. doi:10.4018/978-1-60566-198-8.ch045

Ireson, N., & Burel, G. (2010). Knowledge sharing in e-collaboration. In M. A. Wimmer, J.-L. Chappelet, M. Janssen, & H. J. Scholl (Eds.), *Proceedings of the 9th IFIP WG 8.5 International Conference on Electronic Government* (LNCS 6228, pp. 351-362).

Issa, R. R. A., Fllod, I., & Caglasin, G. (2003). A Survey of e-business implementation in the US construction industry. *Journal of Information Technology in Construction, 8*, 15–28.

James, L. R. (1982). Aggregation bias in estimates of perceptual agreement. *The Journal of Applied Psychology, 67*(2), 219–229. doi:10.1037/0021-9010.67.2.219

James, L. R., Demaree, R. G., & Wolf, G. (1984). Estimating within-group interrater reliability with and without response bias. *The Journal of Applied Psychology, 69*(1), 85–98. doi:10.1037/0021-9010.69.1.85

Jenkins, H. (2006). *Fans, bloggers, and gamers: Exploring participatory culture*. New York: New York University Press.

Jenkins, H. (2006a). *Confronting the challenges of participatory culture*. Chicago, IL: MacArthur Foundation.

Jenkins, H. (2006b). *Convergence culture: Where old and new media collide*. New York, NY: NYU Press.

Jenkins, R. (2000). *Social identity*. Oxford, UK: Taylor & Francis.

Jerrard, R., Hands, D., & Ingram, J. (2002). *Design management case studies* (pp. 24–54). London, UK: Routledge.

John, R., Ietto-Gillies, G., Cox, H., & Grimwade, N. (1997). *Global Business Strategy*. London: International Thomson Press.

Johnson-Laird, P. (1983). *Mental models*. Cambridge, MA: Harvard University Press.

Joyce, E., & Kraut, R. E. (2006). Predicting continued participation in newsgroups. *Journal of Computer-Mediated Communication, 11*(3), 723–747. doi:10.1111/j.1083-6101.2006.00033.x

Kahai, S., Jerry, F., Suling, Z., & Bruce, A. (2007). Leadership in virtual teams: Past, present, and future. *International Journal of e-Collaboration, 3*, 1–10.

Kalay, Y. E., Harfmann, A. C., & Swerdloff, L. M. (1985). ALEX: A knowledge-based architectural design system. In *Proceedings of the ACADIA Workshop*, Tempe, AZ (pp. 96-108).

Kanawattanachal, P., & Yoo, Y. (2007). The impact of knowledge coordination on virtual team performance over time. *Management Information Systems Quarterly, 31*(4), 783–808.

Kankanhalli, A., Tan, B. C. Y., & Wei, K. (2007). Conflict and performance in global virtual teams. *Journal of Management Information Systems, 23*(3), 237–274. doi:10.2753/MIS0742-1222230309

Kanungo, R. N. (1982). Measurement of job and work involvement. *The Journal of Applied Psychology, 67*, 341–349. doi:10.1037/0021-9010.67.3.341

Kaufman, L., & Rousseeuw, P. (1990). *Finding Groups in Data: An Introduction to Cluster Analysis*. London: John Wiley & Sons.

Kazi, A. S. (2005). *Knowledge management in the construction industry-a socio-technical perspective*. Hershey, PA: IGI Global.

Keen, P. G. W. (1980). MIS research: Reference disciplines and a cumulative tradition. In *Proceedings of the First International Conference on Information Systems*, Philadelphia, PA.

Kelley, L., & Sankey, T. (2008). Global virtual teams for value creation and project success: A case study. *International Journal of Project Management, 26*, 51–62. doi:10.1016/j.ijproman.2007.08.010

Khatri, V., Vessey, I., Ram, S., & Ramesh, V. (2006). Cognitive fit between conceptual schemas and internal problem representations: The case of geospatio-temporal conceptual schema comprehension. *IEEE Transactions on Professional Communication, 49*(2), 109–127. doi:10.1109/TPC.2006.875091

Kim, I. (1995). Design tools integration in an integrated design environment. In *Proceedings of the ACADIA Conference on Computing in Design - Enabling, Capturing and Sharing Ideas*, Seattle, WA (pp. 75-95).

Kirkman, B. L., Rosen, B., Tesluk, P. E., & Gibson, C. B. (2004). The impact of team empowerment on virtual team performance: The moderating role of face-to-face interaction. *Academy of Management Journal, 47*(2), 175–192. doi:10.2307/20159571

Kitchin, R. (1998). *Cyberspace the world in the wires*. Chichester, UK: Wiley.

Kittowski, F., & Siegeris, E. (2010). An integrated collaboration environment for various types of collaborative knowledge work. *International Journal of e-Collaboration, 6*(2), 45–55. doi:10.4018/jec.2010040103

Klein, K. J., Bliese, P. D., Kozlowski, S. W. J., Dansareay, F., Gavin, M. B., & Griffin, M. A. (2000). Multilevel analytical techniques: Commonalitites, differences, and continuing questions . In Klein, K. J., & Kozlowski, S. W. J. (Eds.), *Multilevel theory, research, and methods in organizations* (pp. 512–553). San Francisco, CA: Jossey-Bass.

Klein, K. J., Danserau, F., & Hall, R. J. (1994). Levels issues in theory development, data collection, and analysis. *Academy of Management Review, 19*(2), 195–229.

Klein, K. J., & Kozlowski, S. W. (2000). From micro to meso: Critical steps in conceptualizing and conducting multilevel research. *Organizational Research Methods, 3*(3), 211–236. doi:10.1177/109442810033001

Klein, K. J., Tosi, H., & Cannella, A. A. J. (1999). Multilevel theory building: Benefits, barriers, and new developments. *Academy of Management Review, 24*(2), 243–248. doi:10.5465/AMR.1999.1893934

Klimoski, R., & Mohammed, S. (1994). Team mental model: Construct or metaphor? *Journal of Management, 20*(2), 403–437.

Klinc, R., Dolenc, M., & Turk, Z. (2009). Engineering collaboration 2.0: Requirements and expectation. *Journal of Information Technology in Construction, 14*, 473–488.

Kline, R. B. (1998). *Principles and practice of structural equation modeling*. New York, NY: The Guilford Press.

Kline, R. B. (1998). *Principles and practice of structural equation modeling*. New York, NY: The Guilford Press.

Kock, N. & Nosek, J. (2005). Expanding the boundaries of e-collaboration. *IEEE Transactions on Professional Communication, 48*(1), 1–9. doi:10.1109/TPC.2004.843272

Kock, N. (2004). The psychobiological model: Towards a new theory of computer-mediated communication based on Darwinian evolution. *Organization Science, 15*(3), 327–348. doi:10.1287/orsc.1040.0071

Kock, N. (2005). What is E-collaboration? *International Journal of E-Collaboration, 1*(1), i–vii.

Kock, N. (2008). E-Collaboration and e-commerce in virtual worlds: The potential of second life and world of warcraft. *International Journal of e-Collaboration, 4*, 114. doi:10.4018/jec.2008070101

Kock, N. (2009). Information systems theorizing based on evolutionary psychology: An interdisciplinary review and theory integration framework. *Management Information Systems Quarterly, 33*(2), 395–418.

Kock, N. (2010). Costly traits and e-collaboration: The importance of oral speech in electronic knowledge communication . In Kock, N. (Ed.), *Evolutionary psychology and information systems research: A new approach to studying the effects of modern technologies on human behavior* (pp. 289–303). New York, NY: Springer.

Kock, N. (2010a). *WarpPLS 1.0 user manual*. Laredo, TX: ScriptWarp Systems.

Kock, N. (2010b). Using WarpPLS in E-collaboration studies: An overview of five main analysis steps. *International Journal of E-Collaboration*, 6(4), 1–11. doi:10.4018/jec.2010100101

Kock, N. (2011). Using WarpPLS in E-collaboration studies: Descriptive statistics, settings, and key analysis results. *International Journal of E-Collaboration*, 7(2), 1–17.

Kock, N., Davison, R., Ocker, R., & Wazlawick, R. (2001). E-collaboration: A look at past research and future challenges. *Journal of System Information Technology*, 5(1), 1–9. doi:10.1108/13287260180001059

Kock, N., & Nosek, J. (2005). Expanding the boundaries of e-collaboration. *IEEE Transactions on Professional Communication*, 48(1), 1–9. doi:10.1109/TPC.2004.843272

Kock, N., Verville, J., Danesh-Pajou, A., & DeLuca, D. (2009). Communication flow orientation in business process modeling and its effect on redesign success: Results from a field study. *Decision Support Systems*, 46(2), 562–575. doi:10.1016/j.dss.2008.10.002

Kohonen, T. (1982). Self-organized formation of topologically correct feature maps . *Biological Cybernetics*, 43, 59–69. doi:10.1007/BF00337288

Ko, I., Olfman, L., & Choi, S. (2009). The impacts of electronic collaboration and information exploitation capability on firm performance: Focusing on suppliers using buyer-dominated interorganizational systems. *International Journal of e-Collaboration*, 5(2), 1–17. doi:10.4018/jec.2009040101

Kolbe, M., & Boos, M. (2009). Facilitating group decision-making: Facilitator's subjective theories on group coordination. *Forum Qualitative Sozial Forschung*, 10(1), 1–29.

Konradt, U., & Hoch, J. (2007). A work roles and leadership functions of managers in virtual teams. *International Journal of e-Collaboration*, 3(2), 17–35. doi:10.4018/jec.2007040102

Kozinets, R. V. (2002). The field behind the screen: Using netnography for marketing research in online communities. *JMR, Journal of Marketing Research*, 39, 61–72. doi:10.1509/jmkr.39.1.61.18935

Kozlowski, S. W., & Klein, K. J. (2000). *Multilevel theory, research and methods in organizations: Foundations, extensions, and new directions*. San Francisco, CA: Jossey-Bass.

Krippendorf, K. (1986). *A dictionary of cybernetics*. Retrieved February 11, 2010, from http://pespmc1.vub.ac.be/ASC/indexASC.html

Kristensen, K., & Kijl, B. (2010). Collaborative performance: Addressing the ROI of collaboration. *International Journal of e-Collaboration*, 6(1), 53–69. doi:10.4018/jec.2010091104

Krotsch, M., Vrandecic, D., & Volkel, M. (2005). Wikipedia and the Semantic Web—the missing links. *WikiMania Journal*, 53-65.

Krotzsch, M., Vrandecic, V., Volkel, M., Haller, H., & Studer, R. (2007). Semantic Wikipedia. *Journal of Web Semantics: Science . Services and Agents on World Wide Web*, 5, 251–261. doi:10.1016/j.websem.2007.09.001

Kucukyilmaz, T., Cambazoglu, B. B., Aykanat, C., & Can, F. (2008). Chat Mining: Predicting User and Message Attributes in Computer-Mediated Communication. *Information Processing and Management: an International Journal*, 44(4), 1448–1466. doi:10.1016/j.ipm.2007.12.009

Kullback, S., & Leibler, R. A. (1951). On information and sufficiency. *Annals of Mathematical Statistics*, 22(1), 79–86. doi:10.1214/aoms/1177729694

Kumar, N., & Benbasat, I. (2004). The effect of relationship encoding, task type, and complexity on information representation: An empirical evaluation of 2D and 3D line graphs. *Management Information Systems Quarterly*, 28(2), 255–281.

Larman, C., & Vodde, B. (2009). *Scaling lean & agile development: Thinking and organizational tools for large-scale Scrum*. Reading, MA: Addison-Wesley.

Larsern, K. R. T., & Mclnernrey, C. R. (2002). Preparing to work in the virtual organization. *Information & Management*, 39, 445–456. doi:10.1016/S0378-7206(01)00108-2

Latane, B. (1981). The psychology of social impact. *The American Psychologist*, 36(4), 343–356. doi:10.1037/0003-066X.36.4.343

Lawler, E. E. (1986). *High involvement management*. San Francisco, CA: Jossey-Bass.

Lee, J. Y., Seo, D. W., Kim, K., & Kim, H. (2005). A Ubiquitous and Context-Aware Framework for Supporting Virtual Engineering Services. *Computer-Aided Design & Applications*, *2*(6), 769–776.

Leiden, B., Loeh, H., & Katzy, B. (2010). Emerging collaboration routines in knowledge-intensive work process: Insights from three case studies. *International Journal of e-Collaboration*, *6*(1), 33–52. doi:10.4018/jec.2010091103

Leidner, D., Alavi, M., & Kayworth, T. (2006). The Role of Culture in Knowledge Management: A Case Study of Two Global Firms. *International Journal of E-Collaboration*, *2*(1), 17–40.

Lepsinger, R. (2010). *Closing the execution gap: How great leaders and their companies get results*. New York, NY: John Wiley & Sons.

Lesser, E. L., & Storck, J. (2001). Communities of practice and organizational performance. *IBM Systems Journal*, *40*(4), 831–841. doi:10.1147/sj.404.0831

Leuf, B., & Cunningham, W. (2001). *The Wiki way: Quick collaboration on the Web* (pp. 45–59). Reading, MA: Addison-Wesley.

Leventhal, L., & Barnes, J. (2007). *Usability engineering: Process, products, and examples*. Upper Saddle River, NJ: Prentice Hall.

Levin, R. (2009). Tools for multilingual communication. *Multilingual Magazine, 16*(2). Retrieved November 9, 2009, from https://www.multilingual.com/articleDetail.php?id=715

Levy, P. (1997). *Collective intelligence: Mankind's emerging world in cyberspace*. New York: Plenum Publishing.

Lewis, K. (2004). Knowledge and performance in knowledge-worker teams: A longitudinal study of transactive memory systems. *Management Science*, *50*(11), 1519–1533. doi:10.1287/mnsc.1040.0257

Limayem, M., & DeSanctis, G. (2000). Providing decisional guidance for multicriteria decision making in groups. *Information Systems Research*, *11*(4), 386–401. doi:10.1287/isre.11.4.386.11874

Limayem, M., Hirt, S. G., & Cheung, C. M. K. (2007). How habit limits the predictive power of intention: The case of information systems continuance. *Management Information Systems Quarterly*, *31*(4), 705–737.

Lim, J., & Yang, Y. (2008). Exploring computer-based multilingual negotiation support for English-Chinese dyads: Can we negotiate in our native languages? *Behaviour & Information Technology*, *27*(2), 139–151. doi:10.1080/01449290601111135

Lim, J., & Zhong, Y. (2006). The interaction and effects of perceived cultural diversity, group size, leadership, and collaborative learning systems: An experimental study. *Information Resources Management Journal*, *19*(4), 56–71. doi:10.4018/irmj.2006100104

Lin, C., Standing, C., & Liu, Y. C. (2008). A model to develop effective virtual teams. *Journal of Decision Support Systems*, *45*, 1031–1045. doi:10.1016/j.dss.2008.04.002

Lipnack, J., & Stamps, J. (1997). Virtual teams: Reaching across space, time, and organizations with technology. *Strategy and Leadership*, *27*(1), 14–19. doi:10.1108/eb054625

Locke, E. A. (1976). The nature and causes of job satisfaction . In Dunnette, M. D. (Ed.), *Handbook of industrial and organizational psychology* (pp. 1297–1349). Chicago, IL: Rand McNally.

Lodahl, T. M., & Kejner, M. (1965). The definition and a measurement of job involvement. *The Journal of Applied Psychology*, *49*, 24–33. doi:10.1037/h0021692

Lopez, A. (2008). Statistical machine translation. *ACM Computing Surveys*, *40*(3), 1–49. doi:10.1145/1380584.1380586

Luke, D. A. (2004). *Multilevel modeling*. Thousand Oaks, CA: Sage.

MacEachren, A. M. (2001). Cartography and GIS: extending collaborative tools to support virtual teams. *Progress in Human Geography*, *25*(3), 431–444. doi:10.1191/030913201680191763

MacKenzie, S. B., Podsakoff, P. M., & Jarvis, C. B. (2005). The problem of measurement model misspecification in behavioral and organizational research and some recommended solutions. *The Journal of Applied Psychology*, *90*(4), 710–730. doi:10.1037/0021-9010.90.4.710

MacKinnon, D. P. (2008). Multilevel mediation models. In McKinnon, D. P. (Ed.), *Introduction to statistical mediation analysis* (pp. 237–274). New York, NY: Routledge.

MacMillan, J., Entin, E. E., & Serfaty, D. (2004). Communication overhead: The hidden cost of team cognition. In Salas, E., & Fiore, S. M. (Eds.), *Team cognition: Understanding the factors that drive process and performance* (pp. 61–82). Washington, DC: American Psychological Association. doi:10.1037/10690-004

Majchrzac, A., Wagner, C., & Yates, D. (2006). Corporate wiki users: Results of a survey. In *Proceedings of the ACM International Symposium on Wikis*, Odense, Denmark (pp. 452-476).

Majchrzak, A., Beath, C., Lim, R., & Chin, W. (2005). Managing client dialogues during information systems design to facilitate client learning. *Management Information Systems Quarterly*, *29*(4), 653–672.

Malone, T. W., Crowston, K., & Herman, G. A. (2003). *Organizing business knowledge: The MIT process handbook* (pp. 23–36). Cambridge, MA: MIT Press.

Marcoccia, M., Atifi, H., & Gauducheau, N. (2008). Text-Centered versus Multimodal Analysis of Instant Messaging Conversation. *Language@Internet, 5,* article 7. Retrieved from http://www.languageatinternet.de/articles/2008/1621/marcoccia.pdf

Marcoulides, G. A., Chin, W. W., & Saunders, C. (2009). A critical look at partial least squares modeling. *Management Information Systems Quarterly*, *33*(1), 171–175.

Markus, M. L. (1994). Electronic mail as the medium of managerial choice. *Organization Science*, *5*(4), 502–527. doi:10.1287/orsc.5.4.502

Markus, M. L. (2005). Technology-shaping effects of e-collaboration technologies: Bugs and features. *International Journal of e-Collaboration*, *1*(1), 1–23. doi:10.4018/jec.2005010101

Martins, L. L. (2004). Virtual teams: What do we know and where do we go from here? *Journal of Management*, *30*(6), 805–835. doi:10.1016/j.jm.2004.05.002

Martins, L. L., Gilson, L. L., & Maynard, M. T. (2004). Virtual teams: What do we know and where do we go from here? *Journal of Management*, *30*, 805–835. doi:10.1016/j.jm.2004.05.002

Maruyama, G. M. (1998). *Basics of structural equation modeling*. Thousand Oaks, CA: Sage.

Masetti, B., & Zmud, R. W. (1996). Measuring the extend of EDI usage in complex organizations: Strategies and illustrative examples. *Management Information Systems Quarterly*, *4*(1), 95–105.

Mathieu, J. E. (2007). The effects of leader empowering behavior, members' experience, and virtuality on sales team processes and performance. In *Proceedings of the Academy of Management*, Philadelphia, PA.

Mathieu, J. E., Maybard, M. T., Taylor, S. R., Gibson, L. L., & Ruddy, T. M. (2007). An examination of the effects of organizational district and team contexts on team processes and performance: A meso-mediational model. *Journal of Organizational Behavior*, *28*(7), 891–910. doi:10.1002/job.480

Mathieu, J. E., & Taylor, S. R. (2007). A framework for testing meso-mediational relationships in organizational behavior. *Journal of Organizational Behavior*, *28*, 141–172. doi:10.1002/job.436

Mathwave Data Analysis and Simulation. (2009). *EasyFit: Distribution fitting made easy.* Retrieved from http://mathwave.com/

Matsushima, S. (2003). *The grand Louvre, Paris France*. Retrieved from http://isites.harvard.edu/fs/docs/icb.topic30775.files/3-5_Louvre.pdf

Matz, D. C., & Wood, W. (2005). Cognitive dissonance in groups: The consequences of disagreement. *Journal of Personality and Social Psychology*, *88*(1), 22–37. doi:10.1037/0022-3514.88.1.22

McConnell, D. (2002). Action research and distributed problem-based learning in continuing professional education. *Distance Education*, *23*(1), 59–83. doi:10.1080/01587910220123982

McInnerney, J., & Robert, T. S. (2004). Collaborative or cooperative learning? In Roberts, T. S. (Ed.), *Online collaborative learning: Theory and practice* (pp. 203–214). Hershey, PA: IGI Global.

McQueen, J. B. (1967). Some methods for classification and analysis of multivariate observations. In *Proceedings of the Fifth Berkeley Symposium on Mathematical Statistics and Probability* (pp. 281-297).

Mead, J. (1964). *On social psychology: Selected papers.* Chicago, IL: University of Chicago Press.

Meers, D. T., & Nelson, M. (1998). *Using the Internet as a medium to support teachers in the management of students with challenging behaviors.* Lexington, KY: University of Kentucky. Retrieved May 13, 2006, from http://sweb.uky.edu/~dtmeer0/meers98.html

Meroño-Cerdán, A., Soto-Acosta, P., & López-Nicolás, C. (2008). How do collaborative technologies affect innovation in SME's. *International Journal of e-Collaboration, 4*(4), 34–50. doi:10.4018/jec.2008100103

Metcalfe, R. (1995, October 2). Metcalfe's law: A network becomes more valuable as it reaches more users. *Infoworld.*

Meyer, A., & Allen, N. (1991). A three-component conceptualization of organizational commitment. *Human Resource Management Review, 1*, 61–89. doi:10.1016/1053-4822(91)90011-Z

Meyer, J. P., Becker, T. E., & Dick, R. V. (2006). Social identities and commitments at work: Toward an integrative model. *Journal of Organizational Behavior, 27*(5), 665–683. doi:10.1002/job.383

Meyer, J. P., & Herscovitch, L. (2001). Commitment in the workplace: Toward a general model. *Human Resource Management Review, 11*, 299–326. doi:10.1016/S1053-4822(00)00053-X

Miller, R. B., & Wichern, D. W. (1977). *Intermediate business statistics: Analysis of variance, regression and time series.* New York, NY: Holt, Rihehart and Winston.

Miranda, S. M., & Saunders, C. S. (2003). The social construction of meaning: An alternative perspective on information sharing. *Information Systems Research, 14*(1), 87–107. doi:10.1287/isre.14.1.87.14765

Mitchell, T. R., & James, L. R. (2001). Building better theory: Time and the specification of when things happen. *Academy of Management Review, 26*(4), 530–547.

Monticolo, D., Hilaire, V., Koukam, A., & Gomes, S. (2007). OntoDesign: A domain ontology for building and exploiting project memories in product design projects. In *Proceeding of the 2nd International Conference in Knowledge Management in Organizations*, Lecce, Italy (pp. 34-47).

Monticolo, D., Hilaire, V., Gomes, S., & Koukam, A. (2008). A multi agents systems for building project memories to facilitate design process. *International Journal in Integrated Computer Aided Engineering, 15*(1), 3–20.

Morgeson, F. P., & Hofmann, D. A. (1999). The structure and function of collective constructs: Implications for multilevel research and theory development. *Academy of Management Review, 24*(2), 249–265.

Morikawa, H., Suo, Y., Miyata, N., Ishida, T., & Shi, Y. (2008). Supporting remote meeting using multilingual collaboration tool. *Institute of Electronics, Information, and Communication Engineers Technical Report, 107*(428), 19–24.

Morley, D., & Robbins, K. (1996). *Spaces of identity.* London, UK: Rutledge.

Mueller, R. O. (1996). *Basic principles of structural equation modeling.* New York, NY: Springer.

Muthén, B., Asparouhov, T., Hunter, A., & Leuchter, A. (in press). Growth modeling with non-ignorable dropout: Alternative analyses of the STAR*D antidepressant trial. *Psychological Methods.*

Navisworks (2010) *Autodesk navisworks products.* Retrieved from http://usa.autodesk.com/adsk/servlet/pc/index?siteID=123112&id=10571060

Nelson, R. (2008). *Learning and working in the collaborative age: A new model for the workplace.* Video of presentation at the Apple Education Leadership Summit, San Francisco, CA.

Nevitt, J., & Hancock, G. R. (2001). Performance of bootstrapping approaches to model test statistics and parameter standard error estimation in structural equation modeling. *Structural Equation Modeling, 8*(3), 353–377. doi:10.1207/S15328007SEM0803_2

Nikas, A., & Poulymenakou, A. (2008). Technology adaptation: Capturing the appropriation dynamics of web-based collaboration support in a project team. *International Journal of e-Collaboration, 4*(2), 1–27. doi:10.4018/jec.2008040101

Nikas, A., & Poulymenakou, A. (2008). Technology adaptation: Capturing the appropriation dynamics of web-based collaboration support in a project team. *International Journal of e-Collaboration, 4*(2), 1–28.

NIST. (2006). *Machine translation evaluation official results*. Retrieved November 9, 2009 from http://www.itl.nist.gov/iad/mig//tests/mt/2006/doc/mt06eval_official_results.html

Nomura, S., Ishida, T., Yamashita, N., Yasuoka, M., & Funakoshi, K. (2003, June 22-27). Open source software development with your mother language: Intercultural collaboration experiment. In *Proceedings of the International Conference on Human-Computer Interaction (HCI-03)*, Heraklion, Crete, Greece (Vol. 4, pp. 1163-1167).

Norman, D. A., & Draper, S. W. (1986). *User centered system design*. Mahwah, NJ: Lawrence Erlbaum.

Nosek, J. T. (2005). Collaborative sensemaking support: Progressing from portals and tools to Collaboration Envelopes™. *International Journal of e-Collaboration*, *1*(2), 25–39.

Nunamaker, J., Briggs, R., Mittleman, D., Vogel, D., & Balthazard, P. (1996). Lessons from a dozen years of group support systems research: A discussion of lab and field findings. *Journal of Management Information Systems*, *13*(3), 163–207.

Nunnally, J. C. (1978). *Psychometric theory*. New York, NY: McGrawHill.

Nunnally, J. C., & Bernstein, I. H. (1994). *Psychometric theory*. New York, NY: McGrawHill.

Ocker, R. J., & Yaverbaum, G. J. (1999). Asynchronous computer-mediated communication versus face-to-face collaboration: Results on student learning, quality, and satisfaction. *Group Decision and Negotiation*, *8*, 427–440. doi:10.1023/A:1008621827601

Odlyzko, A., & Tilly, B. (2005). *A refutation of Metcalfe's law and a better estimate for the value of networks and network interconnections*. Retrieved February 11, 2010, from http://www.dtc.umn.edu/~odlyzko/doc/metcalfe.pdf

Odom, S. L., & Bailey, D. (2001). Inclusive preschool programs: Classroom ecology and child outcomes . In Guralnick, M. J. (Ed.), *Early childhood inclusion: Focus on change* (pp. 253–276). Baltimore, MD: Brookes.

Ogura, K., Hayashi, Y., Nomura, S., & Ishida, I. (2004). User adaptation in MT-mediated communication. In *Proceedings of the First International Joint Conference on Natural Language Processing* (pp. 596-601).

Okhuysen, G. A., & Eisenhardt, K. M. (2002). Integrating knowledge in groups: How formal interventions enable flexibility. *Organization Science*, *13*(4), 370–386. doi:10.1287/orsc.13.4.370.2947

Orlikowski, W. J. (2000). Using technology and constituting structures: A practice lens for studying technology in organizations. *Organization Science*, *11*(4), 404–428. doi:10.1287/orsc.11.4.404.14600

Ortiz de Guinea, A., Webster, J., & Staples, D. S. (2005). *A meta-analysis of the virtual team literature*. Paper presented at the High Performance Professional Teams Symposium, Industrial Relations Centre, School of Policy Studies, Queen's University, Kingston, ON, Canada.

Ortiz de Guinea, A., & Webster, J. (2011). Are we talking about the task or the computer? An examination of the associated domains of task-specific and computer self-efficacies. *Computers in Human Behavior*, *27*(2), 978–987. doi:10.1016/j.chb.2010.12.002

Osgood, C. E. (1969). The nature and measurement of meaning. In Snider, J. G., & Osgood, C. E. (Eds.), *Semantic differential technique*. Chicago, IL: Aldine Publishing.

Otondo, R. F., Barnett, T., Kellermans, F. W., Pearson, A. W., & Pearson, R. A. (2009). Assessing information technology use over time with growth modeling and hierarchical linear modeling: A tutorial. *Communications of the Association for Information Systems*, *25*(1), 45.

Palmisano, J. (2008). A motivational model of knowledge sharing. In Burstein, F., & Holsapple, C. W. (Eds.), *Handbook on decision support systems* (Vol. 1, pp. 355–370). Berlin, Germany: Springer-Verlag. doi:10.1007/978-3-540-48713-5_18

Pangaea. (2009). *NPO Pangaea*. Retrieved November 9, 2009, from http://www.pangaean.org/

Paullay, I. M., Alliger, G. M., & Stone-Romero, E. F. (1994). Construct validation of two instruments designed to measure job involvement and work centrality. *The Journal of Applied Psychology*, *79*, 224–228. doi:10.1037/0021-9010.79.2.224

Peddibhotla, N. B., & Subramani, M. R. (2007). Contributing to public document repositories: A critical mass theory perspective. *Organization Studies*, *28*(3), 327–346. doi:10.1177/0170840607076002

Pennock, D. M., Flake, G. W., Lawrence, S., Glover, E. J., & Giles, C. L. (2002). Winners don't take all: Characterizing the competition for links on the web. *Proceedings of the National Academy of Sciences of the United States of America, 99*(8), 5207–5211. doi:10.1073/pnas.032085699

Pervan, G. (1998). A review of research in group support systems: Leaders, approaches and directions. *Decision Support Systems, 23*(2), 149–159. doi:10.1016/S0167-9236(98)00041-4

Petter, S., Straub, D., & Rai, A. (2007). Specifying formative constructs in information systems research. *Management Information Systems Quarterly, 31*(4), 623–656.

Peugh, J. L., & Enders, C. K. (2005). Using the spss mixed procedure to fit cross-sectional and longitudinal multilevel models. *Educational and Psychological Measurement, 65*(5), 717–741. doi:10.1177/0013164405278558

Pfafflin, S. (1965). Evaluation of machine translation by reading comprehension tests and subjective judgments. *Machine Translation, 8*(2), 2–8.

Pfeffer, J. (1994). *Competitive advantage through people: Unleashing the power of the work force.* Boston, MA: Harvard Business School Press.

Pick, J. B., Romano, N. C. Jr, & Roztocki, N. (2009). Synthesizing the research advances in electronic collaboration: Theoretical frameworks. *International Journal of e-Collaboration, 5*(1), 1–12.

Pierce, J. L., Kostova, T., & Dirks, K. T. (2001). Toward a theory of psychological ownership. *Academy of Management Review, 26*(2), 298–310. doi:10.2307/259124

Pierce, J. L., Kostova, T., & Dirks, K. T. (2003). The state of psychological ownership: Integrating and extending a century of research. *Review of General Psychology, 7*(1), 84–107. doi:10.1037/1089-2680.7.1.84

Pinchuk, R., Aked, R., de Orus, J.-J., Dessin, E., de Weerdt, D., Focant, G., et al. (2007, October 11-12). Toma – TMQL, TMCL, TMML. In L. Maicher, A. Sigel, & L. M. Garshol (Eds.), *Leveraging the Semantics of Topic Maps: Second International Conference on Topic Maps Research and Applications, TMRA 2006,* Leipzig, Germany (pp. 107-129). Berlin: Springer.

Pinsonneault, A., & Caya, O. (2005). Virtual teams: What we know, what we don't. *International Journal of e-Collaboration, 1*(3), 1–16.

Pizlo, Z. (2007). Human perception of 3D shapes. In W. G. Kropatsch, M. Kampel, & A. Hanbury (Eds.), *Proceedings of the 12th International Conference on Computer Analysis of Images and Patterns* (LNCS 4673, pp. 1-12).

Pizlo, Z. (2001). Perception viewed as an inverse problem. *Vision Research, 41*(24), 3145–3161.

Podsakoff, P. M., MacKenzie, S. B., Paine, J. B., & Bachrach, D. G. (2000). Organizational citizenship behaviors: A critical review of the theoretical and empirical literature and suggestions for future research. *Journal of Management, 26*(3), 513–563. doi:10.1177/014920630002600307

Poling, C. (2005). Blog on: Building communication and collaboration among staff and students. *Learning and Leading with Technology, 32*(6), 12–15.

Postmes, T., & Spears, R. (1998). Deindividuation and antinormative behavior: A meta-analysis. *Psychological Bulletin, 123,* 238–259. doi:10.1037/0033-2909.123.3.238

Powell, A., Piccoli, G., & Ives, B. (2004). Virtual teams: A review of current literature and directions for future research. *The Data Base for Advances in Information Systems, 35*(1), 6–36.

Prahalad, C. K., & Ramaswamy, V. (2004). Co-creation experiences: The next practice in value creation. *Journal of Interactive Marketing, 18*(3), 5–14. doi:10.1002/dir.20015

Preece, J. (1994). *Human-computer interaction.* Reading, MA: Addison-Wesley.

Quigley, N. R., Tekleab, A. G., & Tesluk, P. E. (2007). Comparing consensus- and aggregation-based methods of measuring team-level variables: The role of relationship conflict and conflict management processes. *Organizational Research Methods, 10*(4), 589–606. doi:10.1177/1094428106286853

R Development Core Team. (2007). R: A language and environment for statistical computing. Retrieved from http://www.R-project.org

Raban, D. R., & Rafaeli, S. (2007). Investigating ownership and the willingness to share information online. *Computers in Human Behavior*, 23(5), 2367–2382. doi:10.1016/j.chb.2006.03.013

Rafaeli, S., & Ariel, Y. (2008). Online motivational factors: Incentives for participation and contribution in Wikipedia . In Barak, A. (Ed.), *Psychological aspects of cyberspace: Theory, research, applications* (pp. 243–267). Cambridge, UK: Cambridge University Press.

Rafaeli, S., Hayat, T., & Ariel, Y. (2009). Knowledge building and motivations in Wikipedia: Participation as "Ba" . In Ricardo, F. J. (Ed.), *Cyberculture and new media* (pp. 52–69). New York, NY: Rodopi.

Rafi, A., & Karboulonis, P. (2002). The role of advanced VR interfaces in knowledge management and their relevance to CAD. In *Proceedings of the 7th International Conference on Computer Aided Architectural Design Research in Asia*, Cyberjaya, Malaysia (pp. 277-284).

Ravid, G. (2007, August). *Open large shared knowledge construction systems' dominance: The Wikipedia social structure.* Paper presented at the Academy of Management Annual Meeting, Philadelphia, PA.

Ravid, G., Kalman, Y. M., & Rafaeli, S. (2008). Wikibooks in higher education: Empowerment through online distributed collaboration. *Computers in Human Behavior*, 24(5), 1913–1928. doi:10.1016/j.chb.2008.02.010

Reicher, S. (2004). The context of social identity: Domination, resistance, and change. *Political Psychology*, 25, 921–945. doi:10.1111/j.1467-9221.2004.00403.x

Reinig, B. A. (2003). Toward an understanding of satisfaction with the process and outcomes of teamwork. *Journal of Management Information Systems*, 19(4), 65–83.

Reinig, B., Briggs, R., & Nunamaker, J. (1997). Flaming in the electronic classroom. *Journal of Management Information Systems*, 14(3), 45–59.

Remidez, H. Jr, Stam, A., & Laffey, J. M. (2010). Scaffolding solutions to business problems: Trust development as a learning process. *International Journal of e-Collaboration*, 6(4), 12–31.

Remidez, H., Stam, A., & Laffey, J. (2007). Web-based template-driven communication support systems: Using shadow net workspace to support trust development in virtual teams. *International Journal of e-Collaboration*, 3(1), 65–83. doi:10.4018/jec.2007010104

Rencher, A. C. (1998). *Multivariate statistical inference and applications*. New York, NY: John Wiley & Sons.

Rentsch, J. R., & Woehr, D. R. (2004). Quantifying congruence in cognition: Social relations modeling and team member schema similarity . In Salas, E., & Fiore, S. M. (Eds.), *Team cognition: Understanding the factors that drive process and performance* (pp. 11–31). Washington, DC: American Psychological Association. doi:10.1037/10690-002

Reynolds, C. W. (1987). Flocks, herds, and schools: A distributed behavioral model. *SIGGRAPH '87 Conference Proceedings . Computer Graphics*, 21(4), 25–34. doi:10.1145/37402.37406

Richards, D. (2009). A social software/Web2.0 approach to collaborative knowledge engineering. *International Journal of Information Sciences*, 5, 34–42.

Rico, R., Sánchez-Manzanares, M., Gil, F., & Gibson, C. (2008). Team implicit coordination processes: A team knowledge-based approach. *Academy of Management Review*, 33(1), 163–184. doi:10.5465/AMR.2008.27751276

Riemer, K. (2009). E-Collaboration Systems: Identification of System Classes using Cluster Analysis. *International Journal of E-Collaboration*, 5(3), 1–24.

Rodell, J. B., & Judge, T. A. (2009). Can "good" stressors spark "bad" behaviors? The mediating role of emotions in links of challenge and hindrance stressors with citizenship and counterproductive behaviors. *The Journal of Applied Psychology*, 94(6), 1438–1451. doi:10.1037/a0016752

Rogers, E. M. (1962). *Diffusion of innovations*. Glencoe, IL: Free Press.

Romiszowski, A. J., & Mason, R. (2003). Computer-mediated communication . In Jonassen, D. H. (Ed.), *Handbook of research for educational communications and technology: A project of the Association for Educational Communications and Technology* (2nd ed., pp. 397–431). New York: Lawrence Erlbaum Associates.

Rosa, J. A., Spanjol, J., & Saxon, M. S. (1999). Socio-cognitive Dynamics in a Product Market. *Journal of Marketing*, *63*, 64–77. doi:10.2307/1252102

Roschelle, J., & Teasley, S. (1995). The construction of shared knowledge in collaborative problem solving . In O'Malley, C. E. (Ed.), *Computer supported collaborative learning* (pp. 69–97). Heidelberg, Germany: Springer-Verlag.

Rosen, D. (2002). Flock theory: Cooperative evolution and self-organization of social systems. In *Proceedings of the 2002 CASOS (Computational Analysis of Social and Organizational Systems) Conference*. Pittsburgh, PA: Carnegie Mellon University Press.

Rosenthal, R., & Rosnow, R. L. (1991). *Essentials of behavioral research: Methods and data analysis*. New York, NY: McGrawHill.

Rosson, M. B., & Carroll, J. M. (2002). *Usability engineering: Scenario-based development of human computer interaction*. San Francisco, CA: Morgan Kaufmann.

Rousseau, D. M. (1985). Issues of level in organizational research: Multi-level and cross-level perspectives . In Staw, B. M., & Cummings, L. L. (Eds.), *Research in organizational behavior* (*Vol. 7*, pp. 1–37). Greenwich, CT: JAI Press.

Rubin, A. M. (1994). Media uses and effects: A uses-and-gratifications perspective. J. Bryant & D. Zillmann (Eds.), *Media effects: Advances in theory and research* (pp. 417-436). Mahwah, NJ: Lawrence Erlbaum.

Rulke, D. L., & Galaskiewicz, J. (2000). Distribution of knowledge, group network structure, and group performance. *Management Science*, *46*(5), 612–625. doi:10.1287/mnsc.46.5.612.12052

Rutkowski, A., Saunders, C., & Vogel, D. (2007). Is it already 4 a.m. in your time zone? Focus immersion and temporal dissociation in virtual teams. *Small Group Research*, *38*(1), 98–129. doi:10.1177/1046496406297042

Sagor, R. (2000). *Action Research*. Alexandria, VA: Association for Supervision and Curriculum Development.

Sandor, O., Bogdan, C., & Bowers, J. (1997). Aether: An Awareness Engine for CSCW. In J. A. Hughes, W. Prinz, T. Rodden, & K. Schmidt (Eds.), *Proceedings of the fifth European Conference on Computer-Supported Cooperative Work* (pp. 221-236). Norwell, MA: Kluwer Academic Publishers.

Sarker, S., Valacich, J. S., & Sarker, S. (2005). Technology adoption by groups: A valence perspective. *Journal of the Association for Information Systems*, *6*(2), 37–71.

Sauter, V. (2008). Information technology adoption by groups across time. *International Journal of e-Collaboration*, *4*(3), 51–76.

Schaffert, S. (2006). IkeWiki: A semantic wiki for collaborative knowledge management. In *Proceedings of the 1st International Workshop on Semantic Technologies in Collaborative Applications*, Stanford, CA (pp. 34-45).

Schaupp, L. C., Belanger, F., & Weiguo, F. (2009). Examining the success of websites beyond e-commerce: An extension of the IS success model. *Journal of Computer Information Systems*, *49*(4), 42–52.

Schoberth, T., Heinzl, A., & Rafaeli, S. (2011). *Quantifying the skewed distribution of activity in virtual communities within a longitudinal study*. Retrieved from http://wifo1.bwl.uni-mannheim.de/fileadmin/files/publications/Working%20Paper%203_2009.pdf

Schon, D. A. (1983). *The reflective practitioner: How professionals think in action*. New York: Basic Books.

Schreiber, C. (2006). *Human and organizational risk modeling: critical personnel and leadership in network organizations*. Unpublished doctoral dissertation, Carnegie Mellon University, Pittsburgh.

Scoble, R., & Israel, S. (2006). *Naked conversations*. Hoboken, NJ: John Wiley & Sons.

Scott, J. (2007). *Social network analysis – a handbook*. London, UK: Sage.

Seaborne, A., & Prud'hommeaux, E. (2006). *SPARQL query language for RDF*. Retrieved from http://www.w3.org/TR/2006/CR-rdf-sparql-query-20060406/

Seibert, S. E., Silvert, S. R., & Randolph, W. A. (2004). Taking empowerment to the next level: A multiple-leveled model of empowerment, performance, and satisfaction. *Academy of Management Journal, 47*(3), 332–349. doi:10.2307/20159585

Selwyn, N. (2000). Creating a 'connected' community? Teachers' use of an electronic discussion group. *Teachers College Record, 102*(4), 750–778. doi:10.1111/0161-4681.00076

Serenko, A., Bontis, N., & Detlor, B. (2007). End-user adoption of animated interface agents in everyday work applications. *Behaviour & Information Technology, 26*(2), 119–132. doi:10.1080/01449290500260538

Sert, O., & Açıkgöz, F. (2006). Interlingual machine translation: Prospects and setbacks. *Translation Journal, 10*(3).

Shachaf, P. (2008). Cultural diversity and information and communication technology impacts on global virtual teams: An exploratory study. *Information & Management, 45*(2), 131–142. doi:10.1016/j.im.2007.12.003

Shamir, B., & Kark, R. (2004). A single-item graphic scale for the measurement of organizational identification. *Journal of Occupational and Organizational Psychology, 77*, 115–124. doi:10.1348/096317904322915946

Shang, S., & Seddon, P. B. (2002). Assessing and managing the benefits of enterprise systems: the business manager's perspective. *Information Systems Journal, 12*(4), 271–299. doi:10.1046/j.1365-2575.2002.00132.x

Shannon, C. E. (1948). A mathematical theory of communication. *Bell System Technical Journal, 27*, 379-423 & 623-656.

Shannon, C. E., & Weaver, W. (1969). *The mathematical theory of communication.* Urbana, IL: University of Illinois Press.

Shigenobu, T., Fujii, K., & Yoshino, T. (2007, July 22-27). The role of annotation in intercultural communication. In N. Aykin (Ed.), *Usability and internationalization: HCI and Culture: Proceedings of the Second International Conference on Usability of Internationalization,* Beijing, China (pp. 186-195). Berlin: Springer.

Shin, Y. (2004). A person-environment fit model for virtual organization. *Journal of Management, 30*(5), 725–743. doi:10.1016/j.jm.2004.03.002

Shin, Y. (2005). Conflict resolution in virtual teams. *Organizational Dynamics, 34*(4), 331–345. doi:10.1016/j.orgdyn.2005.08.002

Shirky, C. (2009). *Here comes everybody: The power of organizing without organizations.* New York, NY: Penguin Press.

Short, J. S., Piccolo, G., Powell, A., & Ives, B. (2005). Investigating multilevel relationships in information systems research: An application to virtual teams research using hierarchical linear modeling. *Journal of Information Technology Theory and Application, 7*(3), 1–17.

Shrout, P. E., & Fleiss, J. L. (1979). Intraclass correlations: Uses in assessing rater reliability. *Psychological Bulletin, 86*(2), 420–428. doi:10.1037/0033-2909.86.2.420

Simmel, G., & Levine, D. (1972). *Georg Simmel on individuality and social forms.* Chicago: University of Chicago Press.

Simone, C., & Bandini, S. (2002). Integrating awareness in cooperative applications through the reaction-diffusion metaphor. *Computer Supported Cooperative Work, 11*(3), 495–530. doi:10.1023/A:1021213119071

Singh, A. V., Wombacher, A., & Aberer, K. (2007). Personalized information access in a wiki using structured tagging. In *Proceedings of the Workshop On the Move to Meaningful Internet Systems,* Toronto, ON, Canada (pp. 427-436).

Smidts, A., van Riel, C. B. M., & Pruyn, A. T. H. (2001). The impact of employee communication and perceived external prestige on organizational identification. *Academy of Management Journal, 44*(5), 1051–1062. doi:10.2307/3069448

Smith, S. (1990). Individualized education programs (IEPs) in special education—from intent to acquiescence. *Exceptional Children, 57*(1), 6–14.

Somers, H. (2007). The use of machine translation by law librarians—a reply to Yates. *Law Library Journal, 99*, 611–619.

Souzy, A. (2005). Building a semantic wiki. *IEEE Intelligent Systems, 20*, 87–91. doi:10.1109/MIS.2005.83

Splettstoesser, D. (1998). Electronic decision-making for developing countries. *Group Decision and Negotiation, 7*(5), 417–433. doi:10.1023/A:1008699902917

Stafford, T., Stafford, M., & Schkade, L. (2004). Determining uses and gratifications for the Internet. *Decision Sciences Atlanta, 35*(2), 259–288. doi:10.1111/j.00117315.2004.02524.x

Stassen, H. G., Johannsen, G., & Moray, N. (1990). Internal representation, internal model, human performance model and mental workload. *Automatica, 26*(4), 811–820.

Stowitschek, J. J., & Guest, M. A. (2006). Islands with bridges: Using the web to enhance ongoing problem solving among educators of young children with special needs. *Infants and Young Children, 19*(1), 72–82. doi:10.1097/00001163-200601000-00008

Sugai, G. M., & Tindal, G. A. (1993). *Effective school consultation: An interactive approach*. Belmont, CA: Brooks/Cole.

Surowiecki, J. (2004). *The wisdom of crowds: Why the many are smarter than the few and how collective wisdom shapes business, economies, societies, and nations*. New York, NY: Doubleday.

Tabachnick, B. G., & Fidell, L. S. (2007). *Using multivariate statistics* (5th ed.). Boston, MA: Pearson Education.

Tajfel, H. (1982). *Social identity and intergroup relations*. Cambridge, UK: Cambridge University Press.

Tajfel, H., & Turner, J. C. (1986). *The social identity theory of intergroup behavior: Psychology of intergroup relations* (2nd ed.). Chicago, IL: Nelson-Hall.

Tapscott, D., & Williams, A. D. (2007). *Wikinomics: How mass collaboration changes everything*. New York, NY: Portfolio.

Tenenhaus, M., Vinzi, V. E., Chatelin, Y. M., & Lauro, C. (2005). PLS path modeling. *Computational Statistics & Data Analysis, 48*(1), 159–205. doi:10.1016/j.csda.2004.03.005

Thatcher, S. M. B., & Zhu, X. (2006). Changing identities in a changing workplace: Identification, identity enactment, self-verification, and telecommuting. *Academy of Management Review, 31*(4), 1076–1088.

Thomas, D., & Bostrom, R. (2008). Trust and cooperation through technology adaptation in virtual teams: Empirical field evidence. *Information Systems Management, 25*(1), 45–56. doi:10.1080/10580530701777149

Thomas, K. W., & Kilmann, R. H. (1974). *The conflict mode instrument*. Tuxedo, NY: Xicom.

Tidwell, V. M. (2005). A social identity model of prosocial behaviors within nonprofit organizations. *Nonprofit Management & Leadership, 159*(4), 449–467. doi:10.1002/nml.82

Tiffin, J., & Terashima, N. (2001). *HyperReality: Paradigm for the third millennium*. London: Routledge.

Tjosvold, D., Yu, Z., & Chun, H. (2004). Team learning from mistakes: The contribution of cooperative goals and problem-solving. *Journal of Management Studies, 41*(7), 1223–1245. doi:10.1111/j.1467-6486.2004.00473.x

TOEFL. (2009). *TOEFL Test Review*. Retrieved November 9, 2009, from http://www.toeflprepinfo.com/toefl-reading-comprehension1.htm

Toner, J., & Tu, Y. (1998). Flocks, herds, and schools: A quantitative theory of flocking. *Physical Review E: Statistical Physics, Plasmas, Fluids, and Related Interdisciplinary Topics, 58*(4), 4828–4858. doi:10.1103/PhysRevE.58.4828

Treviño, L. K. W., J., & Stein, E. W. (2000). Making connections: Complementary influences on communication media choices, attitudes, and use. *Organization Science, 11*(2), 163–182. doi:10.1287/orsc.11.2.163.12510

Tullar, W., & Kaiser, P. (2000). The effect of process training on process and outcomes in virtual groups. *Journal of Business Communication, 37*(4), 408–427. doi:10.1177/002194360003700404

Turner, C. J. (1999). *Some current issue in research on social identity and self – social identity context commitment content*. London, UK: Blackwell.

Tyler, T. R., & Blader, S. (2000). *Cooperation in groups: Procedural justice, social identity and behavioral engagement*. New York, NY: Psychology Press.

U.S. Department of Education. (2004). *Individuals with Disabilities Education Improvement Act of 2004.* Retrieved July 1, 2006, from http://frwebgate.access. gpo.gov/cgibin/getdoc.cgi?dbname=108_cong_public_laws&docid=f:publ446.108

UCLA. (2009). *UCLA graduate division English requirements.* Retrieved November 9, 2009, from http://www. gdnet.ucla.edu/gasaa/admissions/ENGREQ.HTM

Ulieru, M., & Verdon, J. (2008). IT revolutions in the industry: From the command economy to the e-networked industrial ecosystem. In *Proceedings of the 6ᵗʰ IEEE International Conference of Industrial Informatics*, Daejoen, Korea (pp. 1315-1320).

Ulieru, M., & Verdon, J. (2009). Organizational transformation in the digital economy. In *Proceedings of the 7ᵗʰ IEEE International Conference of Industrial Informatics*, Cardiff, Wales (pp. 17-24).

Unhelkar, B., Ghanbary, A., & Younessi, H. (2010). *Collaborative business process engineering and global organizations: frameworks for service integration.* Hershey, PA: IGI Global.

Vakola, M., & Wilson, I. E. (2004). The challenge of virtual organization: Critical success factors in dealing with constant change. *Team Performance Management, 10,* 112–120. doi:10.1108/13527590410556836

Valacich, J. S., Sarker, S., Pratt, J., & Groomer, M. (2002). Computer-mediated and face-to-face groups: Who makes riskier decisions? In *Proceedings of the 35th Hawaii International Conference on System Sciences*, Hawaii, HI (pp. 133-142).

van den Hooff, B., & de Ridder, J. A. (2004). Knowledge sharing in context: The influence of organizational commitment, communication climate, and CMC use on knowledge sharing. *Journal of Knowledge Management, 8*(6), 117–130. doi:10.1108/13673270410567675

Van Dick, R., Christ, O., Stellmacher, J., Wagner, U., Ahlswede, O., & Grubba, C. (2004). Should I stay or should I go? Explaining turnover intentions with organizational identification and job satisfaction. *British Journal of Management, 15,* 1–10. doi:10.1111/j.1467-8551.2004.00424.x

Van Ginkel, W. P., & Van Knippenberg, D. (2008). Group information elaboration and group decision making: The role of shared task representations. *Organizational Behavior and Human Decision Processes, 105*(1), 82–97.

Van Knippenberg, D. (2000). Work motivation and performance: A social identity perspective. *Applied Psychology: An International Review, 49,* 357–371. doi:10.1111/1464-0597.00020

Van Knippenberg, D., & Sleebos, E. (2006). Organizational identification versus organizational commitment: Self-definition, social exchange, and job attitudes. *Journal of Organizational Behavior, 27*(5), 571–584. doi:10.1002/job.359

Veerman, A., & Veldhuis-Diermanse, E. (2001). Collaborative learning through computer-mediated communication in academic education. In *Proceedings of Euro CSCL 2001*. Retrieved July 2, 2006, from http://www. ll.unimaas.nl/euro-cscl/Papers/166.doc

Vitvar, T., Peristeras, V., & Tarabanis, K. (Eds.). (2010). *Semantic technologies for e-government.* Berlin, Germany: Springer-Verlag. doi:10.1007/978-3-642-03507-4

Vivacqua, A. S., & Moreira de Souza, J. (2008). The vineyard approach: A computational model for determination of awareness foci in e-mail-based collaboration. *International Journal of e-Collaboration, 4*(1), 41–59.

Vivacqua, A., & Moreira, J. (2008). The vineyard approach: A computational model for determination of awareness foci in e-mail-based collaboration. *International Journal of e-Collaboration, 4*(1), 41–59. doi:10.4018/jec.2008010103

Volkel, M., Krtozsch, M., Vrandecic, D., Haller, H., & Studer, R. (2006). Semantic wikipedia. In *Proceedings of the 15th International Conference on World Wide Web*, New York, NY (pp. 54-67).

Volker, L. (2008). Early design management in architecture . In Smyth, H., & Pryke, S. (Eds.), *Collaborative relationships in construction: Developing frameworks and networks.* London, UK: Blackwell.

Vrandecic, D., & Krötzsch, M. (2006). Reusing ontological background knowledge in semantic wikis. In *Proceedings of the First Workshop on Semantic Wiki: From Wikis to Semantics*, Nice, France (pp. 162-174).

Wakefield, R. L., Leidner, D. E., & Garrison, G. (2008). A model of conflict, leadership, and performance in virtual teams. *Information Systems Research*, *19*(4), 434–455. doi:10.1287/isre.1070.0149

Walczuch, R. M., & Watson, R. T. (2001). Analyzing group data in mis research: Including the effect of the group. *Group Decision and Negotiation*, *10*, 83–94. doi:10.1023/A:1008765029795

Wasserman, S., & Faust, K. (1994). *Social network analysis: Methods and applications*. Cambridge, UK: Cambridge University Press.

Watson, R., Teck, H., & Raman, K. (1994). Culture: A fourth dimension of group support systems. *Communications of the ACM*, *37*(10), 45–55. doi:10.1145/194313.194320

Webster, J., & Staples, D. S. (2006). Comparing virtual teams to traditional teams: An identification of new research opportunities. In Martocchio, J. J. (Ed.), *Research in personnel and human resources management* (*Vol. 25*, pp. 181–215). Oxford, UK: Elsevier.

Webster, J., & Treviño, L. K. (1995). Rational and social theories as complementary explanations of communication media choices: Two policy capturing studies. *Academy of Management Journal*, *38*, 1544–1572. doi:10.2307/256843

Webster, J., & Watson, R. T. (2002). Analyzing the past to prepare for the future: Writing a literature review. *Management Information Systems Quarterly*, *26*(2), xiii–xxiii.

Weick, K. E. (1979). *The social psychology of organizing*. Reading, MA: Addison-Wesley.

Weick, K. E., Sutcliffe, K. M., & Obstfeld, D. (2005). Organizing and the process of sensemaking. *Organization Science*, *16*(4), 409–421. doi:10.1287/orsc.1050.0133

Weinberger, D. (2007). *Everything is miscellaneous: The power of the new digital disorder*. New York, NY: Times Books.

Weiss, H. M. (2002). Deconstructing job satisfaction: Separating evaluations, beliefs and affective experiences. *Human Resource Management Review*, *12*, 173–194. doi:10.1016/S1053-4822(02)00045-1

Welch, M. (1998). Collaboration: Staying on the bandwagon. *Journal of Teacher Education*, *49*(1), 26–37. doi:10.1177/0022487198049001004

Wescott, C. (2001). E-Government in the Asia-Pacific region. *Asian Journal of Political Science*, *9*(2), 1–24. doi:10.1080/02185370108434189

Wetzels, M., Odekerken-Schröder, G., & Van Oppen, C. (2009). Using PLS path modeling for assessing hierarchical construct models: Guidelines and empirical illustration. *Management Information Systems Quarterly*, *33*(1), 177–195.

Whetten, D. A. (1989). What constitutes a theoretical contribution. *Academy of Management Review*, *14*(4), 490–495.

Wickham, K. R., & Joseph, B. W. (2007). Perceived behaviors of emergent and assigned leaders in virtual groups. *International Journal of e-Collaboration*, *3*, 1–18. doi:10.4018/jec.2007010101

Wickham, K., & Walther, J. (2007). Perceived behaviors of emergent and assigned leaders in virtual groups. *International Journal of e-Collaboration*, *3*(1), 1–17. doi:10.4018/jec.2007010101

Wilensky, U. (1999). *NetLogo*. Evanston, IL: Center for Connected Learning and Computer-Based Modeling, Northwestern University. Retrieved February 11, 2010, from http://ccl.northwestern.edu/netlogo/

Williams, S. P., & Schubert, P. (2010). Benefits of Enterprise Systems Use. In R. H. Sprague (Ed.), *Proceedings of the 43rd Hawaii International Conference on System Sciences* (pp. 1-9). Los Alamitos, CA: IEEE Computer Society Press.

Williams, T. C., & Rains, J. (2007). Linking strategy to structure: The power of systematic organization design. *Organization Development Journal*, *25*(2), 163–170.

Wilson, B. (1998). *Wittgenstein's philosophical investigations: A guide*. Edinburgh, UK: Edinburgh University Press.

Winter, E. C., & McGhie-Richmond, D. (2005). Using computer conferencing and case studies to enable collaboration between expert and novice teachers. *Journal of Computer Assisted Learning*, *21*(2), 118–129. doi:10.1111/j.1365-2729.2005.00119.x

Wold, S., Trygg, J., Berglund, A., & Antti, H. (2001). Some recent developments in PLS modeling. *Chemometrics and Intelligent Laboratory Systems, 58*(2), 131–150. doi:10.1016/S0169-7439(01)00156-3

Wolfle, L. M. (1999). Sewall Wright on the method of path coefficients: An annotated bibliography. *Structural Equation Modeling, 6*(3), 280–291. doi:10.1080/10705519909540134

Wright, S. (1934). The method of path coefficients. *Annals of Mathematical Statistics, 5*(3), 161–215. doi:10.1214/aoms/1177732676

Wright, S. (1960). Path coefficients and path regressions: Alternative or complementary concepts? *Biometrics, 16*(2), 189–202. doi:10.2307/2527551

Yamashita, N., & Ishida, T. (2006, November 4-8). Effects of machine translation on collaborative work. In *Proceedings of the 2006 20th Anniversary Conference on Computer Supported Cooperative Work,* Banff, Alberta, Canada (pp. 515-524).

Yamashita, N., Inaba, R., Kuzuoka, H., & Ishida, T. (2009, April 4-9). Difficulties in establishing common ground in multiparty groups using machine translation. In *Proceedings of the 27th International Conference on Human factors in Computing Systems,* Boston (pp. 679-688).

Yammarino, F. J., & Markham, S. E. (1992). On the application of within and between analysis: Are absence and affect really group-based phenomena? *The Journal of Applied Psychology, 77,* 168–176. doi:10.1037/0021-9010.77.2.168

Yang, J., & Lange, E. (1998, October 28-31). SYSTRAN on AltaVista: A user study on real-time machine translation on the Internet. In *Proceedings of the 3rd Conference of the Association for Machine Translation in the Americas,* Langhorne, PA (pp. 275-285).

Yang, S. C., & Liu, S. F. (2004). Case study of online workshop for the professional development of teachers. *Computers in Human Behavior, 20*(6), 733–761. doi:10.1016/j.chb.2004.02.005

Yoo, Y., & Alavi, M. (2001). Media and group cohesion: Relative influences on social presence, task participation, and group consensus. *Management Information Systems Quarterly, 25*(3), 371–391. doi:10.2307/3250922

Yufik, Y. M., & Georgopoulos, A. P. (2002). Understanding understanding: Modeling cognitive mechanisms of comprehension in complex dynamic tasks. In *Proceedings of the Technology for Command and Control Workshop: Cognitive Elements of Effective Collaboration* (pp. 91-96).

Yukl, G., Seifert, C. F., & Chaver, C. (2008). Validation of the extended influence behavior questionnaire. *The Leadership Quarterly, 19,* 609–621. doi:10.1016/j.leaqua.2008.07.006

Zhang, S., Tremaine, M., Egan, R., Milewski, A., O'Sullivan, P., & Fjermestad, J. (2009). Occurrence and effects of leader delegation in virtual software teams. *International Journal of e-Collaboration, 5*(1), 47–68. doi:10.4018/jec.2009010104

Zhao, Y., Alvarez-Torres, M. J., Smith, B., & Tan, H. S. (2004). The non-neutrality of technology: A theoretical analysis and empirical study of computer mediated communication technologies. *Journal of Educational Computing Research, 30*(1-2), 23–55. doi:10.2190/5N93-BJQR-3H4Q-7704

Zuckerman, O., Blau, I., & Monroy-Hernández, A. (2009). Children's participation patterns in online communities: An analysis of Israeli learners in the Scratch online community. *Interdisciplinary Journal of E-Learning and Learning Objects, 5*(1), 263–274.

About the Contributors

Ned Kock is Professor of Information Systems and Director of the Collaborative for International Technology Studies at Texas A&M International University. He holds degrees in Electronics Engineering (B.E.E.), Computer Science (M.S.), and Management Information Systems (Ph.D.). Ned has authored and edited several books, including the bestselling Sage Publications book titled *Systems Analysis and Design Fundamentals: A Business Process Redesign Approach*. He has published his research in a number of high-impact journals including *Communications of the ACM*, *Decision Support Systems*, *European Journal of Information Systems*, *European Journal of Operational Research*, *IEEE Transactions (various)*, *Information & Management*, *Information Systems Journal*, *Journal of the Association for Information Systems*, *MIS Quarterly*, and *Organization Science*. He is the Founding Editor-in-Chief of the *International Journal of e-Collaboration*, Associate Editor for Information Systems of the journal *IEEE Transactions on Professional Communication*, and Associate Editor of the *Journal of Systems and Information Technology*. His main research interests are biological and cultural influences on human-technology interaction, nonlinear structural equation modeling, electronic communication and collaboration, action research, ethical and legal issues in technology research and management, and business process improvement.

* * *

Milam Aiken is Professor of Management Information Systems in the School of Business Administration at the University of Mississippi. He holds degrees in business, engineering, and computer science (B.S.), business (M.B.A.), and management information systems (Ph.D.). Milam has been ranked as a leading researcher in the field of electronic meeting systems, and his current research is focused on how machine translation can support groups.

Hayward Andres is an Associate Professor of Management Information Systems in the Department of Management at North Carolina A&T State University. He earned his Ph.D. in Management Information Systems at Florida State University. His current research focuses on virtual teams, technology-mediated collaboration, human-computer interaction, organizational computing, and project management. His research has been published in Journal of Management Information Systems, the Information Resources Management Journal, Journal of End User Computing, Journal of Information Systems Education, Journal of Educational Technology Systems, and Team Performance Management.

Ina Blau holds a PhD in CyberPsychology and E-Learning from the University of Haifa, Israel. She teaches courses in the Graduate Programs for Technologies in Education and for Information and Knowledge Management at the University of Haifa. She is also a member of Research Center for Innovation in Learning Technologies at the Open University of Israel. Her research interests include social aspects of Internet use, e-collaboration and e-communication, as well as online participation patterns, and integration of innovative technologies in organizations.

Robyn Catagnus is adjunct Professor of Education at Arcadia University with additional adjunct experience at Temple University. She holds degrees in psychology (B.S), curriculum, instruction, & technology in education (M.S.Ed.), and special education (Ed.D.). She is a Board Certified Behavior Analyst with extensive expertise in autism, behavior disorders, and positive behavior supports. As founder and former owner of a special education service agency, she clinically supervised cases, developed staff training programs, and conducted regular workshops and training events. Her current work includes special education consultation, online course development and instruction in Arcadia University's Autism Certification and Behavior Analysis Certification programs. Her research interests include class-wide interventions, action research, online professional development of teachers, e-collaboration for education and behavioral health teams, and staff performance.

Shibnath Chakrabarty is Professor of civil engineering at Jadavpur University, India. He is associated with this institution since 1991 as a teaching faculty. He received a bachelor degree (1983) and a master degree (1986) in civil engineering. His primary areas of research and work are pollution control, environmental impact assessment and design collaborations. He has more than forty papers published in reputed journals.

Sean Cox is currently working for a Hedge Fund Management where he is responsible for company research and alpha generation of trading algorithms for their quantitative fund of hedge funds. After receiving a B.S. in Mathematics as well as a B.A. In Philosophy from Indiana University in 2007, Cox pursued such topics as dynamical systems, computational complexity, probability theory and vector calculus further at the Universiteit van Amsterdam's Institute for Logic, Language and Computation. Upon completing work at Amsterdam, Cox moved to New York to apply his academic research into the financial field. His interests outside of the industry include developmental economics, econometrics, operations research, exploratory data analysis and web-metrics. Sean spends free time as a manager and producer for a musical collaboration in Boston, Massachusetts.

Darleen DeRosa, Ph.D. is a managing partner at OnPoint Consulting. Darleen brings ten years of consulting experience, with expertise in talent management, executive assessment, virtual teams, and organizational assessment. Darleen previously was an Executive Director in the Assessment practice at Russell Reynolds Associates. Darleen conducted assessments of senior executives and worked closely with CEOs and Boards. Darleen previously served as Assessment Practice Leader for Right Management, where she grew the assessment practice. Darleen provided assessment solutions to help organizations facilitate selection, succession, and leadership development initiatives. Darleen received her B.A. from the College of the Holy Cross and her M.A. and Ph.D. in social/organizational psychology from Temple University. Darleen is a member of The Society for Industrial and Organizational Psychology (SIOP) and other professional organizations. She has published book chapters and articles in journals, and recently co-authored *Virtual Team Success: A Practical Guide to Working and Leading From a Distance.*

Paul Dwyer is an Assistant Professor of Marketing at the Atkinson Graduate School of Management at Willamette University. He holds degrees in computer engineering (BSCE) and marketing (MBA, PhD). His research generally focuses on consumer behavior as revealed in social networks, word-of-mouth, participation in virtual communities, and the managerial implications of that behavior. His work in this research stream has been published in the Marketing Science Institute's Working Paper Series and the Journal of Interactive Marketing. Additionally, he is interested in cognitive modeling, the emergence of complex behavior in groups of individuals, computational modeling, data visualization and agent-based simulation.

Jennifer Forgie is a managing partner at OnPoint Consulting. She has over 13 years of experience designing and delivering solutions to enhance leadership and organizational effectiveness in a range of industries, including pharmaceuticals, manufacturing, consumer, financial services, and non-profit. The focus of her work has been on helping companies close the gap between strategy and execution. Specifically, Jennifer has deep expertise in organizational assessment, designing and implementing performance management systems, designing large-scale leadership development programs, and developing competency models to enhance human resource management systems. Some of her clients include: Terex, Acadia Realty Trust, Eisai, Forest Laboratories, Eduventures, Boston Medical Center Healthnet Plan, NJM Insurance Group, New Horizons, Pfizer, Siemens Medical Solutions, and New York Life. Earlier in her career, Jennifer held organizational consulting positions with Right Management Consultants and Manus. She began her career in clinical research at the Yale School of Medicine. She holds a bachelor's degree in neuroscience/psychology from Yale University.

Samuel Gomes received his PhD in Mechanical Engineering from Belfort-Montbéliard University of Technology (France) in 1999. He is currently Assistant Professor at the Department of Mechanical Engineering in the same University. His current research interest includes Product Lifecycle Management, Collaborative Engineering and Knowledge Engineering.

Linwu Gu is an Associate Professor of Management Information Systems in the Eberly College of Business and Information Technology. She holds an M.S. degree in computer science and a Ph.D. degree in management information systems, both from the University of Mississippi. Her research interests include electronic meeting systems and online business.

Shaheli Guha works in Product Development in BigMachines, an enterprise software company based in Chicago. Previously, she has held positions in Product Management. She is working in the field of software development for about three years. Shaheli graduated from Wellesley College, Massachusetts with a dual major in Computer Science and Economics. Her interests lie in the area of entrepreneurship and the use of software tools in diverse industries.

Ana Ortiz de Guinea is an assistant professor in the Department of Information Technologies of HEC Montréal. She holds a Ph.D. in Information Systems from Queen's University, a M.Sc. in Management from the University of Lethbridge, and a graduate degree in Computer Science and Engineering from the Universidad de Deusto. Her research has been published in *MIS Quarterly, Computers in Human Behavior*, and the *Journal of Global Information Management*.

Donald A. Hantula, is an organizational psychologist, associate professor of Psychology and director of the Decision Making Laboratory at Temple University. He holds degrees. in Religion and Psychology (B.A.) from Emory University and Psychology (M.A & Ph.D.) from the University of Notre Dame. He is the past Executive Editor of the Journal of Social Psychology, current Associate Editor of the Journal of Organizational Behavior Management, and has edited special issues of other journals on topics such as: experiments in e-commerce, evolutionary perspectives on consumption, Darwinian Perspectives on Electronic Communication, and Consumer Behavior Analysis. His work appears in many high impact journals including the Journal of the American Medical Association, IEEE Transactions on Professional Communication, Journal of Applied Psychology, Journal of Economic Psychology, Organizational Behavior and Human Decision Processes and Behavior Research Methods. Current research interests include evolutionary behavioral economics, consumer and financial decision making, organizational behavior analysis and human/technology interactions.

Tuhin Subhra Konar is an Assistant Professor in the department of civil engineering of Camellia School of Engineering and Technology in Kolkata. He received a bachelor degree (2008) and a master degree (2010) in civil engineering. His research fields are pollution control, engineering systems and application of information technology in civil engineering. He has six articles published in journals and symposiums.

Davy Monticolo is an associate professor in Informatics and Computer Science in the National Polytechnic Institute of Lorraine, France. He has a Ph.D. in Informatics and Computer Science. His professional interests include: Knowledge Engineering and Modelling, Semantic Web, Ontologies, Web Services and Multi-Agents Systems. His main domain of application is knowledge engineering dedicated to mechanical design projects and knowledge management in general. His personal objectives are to re-search and teach in the field of applied computer science and informatics, in an international environment.

John Nosek is Professor of Computer & Information Sciences at Temple University. His seminal work in collaborative programming has influenced major software engineering areas, including eXtreme Programming and Agile Development. He continues to focus on development of collaboration theories and theory-based technology that will improve anytime, anyplace collaborative work by better managing the social, cognitive, and procedural complexities inherent in joint effort. He is Senior Editor of the Journal of Information Systems Management; Associate Editor of the International Journal of e-Collaboration; and Associate Editor of the Advances in e-Collaboration (AECOB) Book Series. He has guest co-edited two recent special issues on collaboration technology. He completed successive appointments as Scholar-in-Residence in Collaborative Work at Hong Kong Polytechnic University; and was a Research Fellow at Curtin University of Technology. Dr. Nosek is a retired Navy Captain and holds degrees from The United States Naval Academy, Villanova University, and Temple University.

Joseph G. P. Paolillo is Professor of Management in the School of Business Administration at the University of Mississippi. He holds degrees in chemistry (B.S.), business (MBA), and organization and management (PhD). Joseph has published articles in peer reviewed journals in the fields of management, marketing, accounting, and management information systems.

Eldar Sultanow is currently active at the University of Potsdam as an external Ph.D candidate. He graduated with a Bachelor of Software Systems Engineering at the Hasso-Plattner-Institut (an institution at the University of Potsdam) which he attended from October 2001 to April 2005. Simultaneously, Eldar earned a diploma in Computer Science at the University of Potsdam in December 2005. Since 2006 he acts as a software engineer and JEE-architect in the industry. Eldar has authored one book and published at a number of conferences including those from the *World Academy of Science, Engineering and Technology (WASET)*, *Institute of Electrical and Electronics Engineers (IEEE)*, *International Institute of Informatics and Systemics (IIIS)*, and *Association for Information Systems (AIS)*. Sultanow's primary research interests preside in the areas of web development, e-Collaboration, and geographic information systems (GIS).

Biswajit Thakur is working as the Assistant Professor in the department of civil engineering of Meghnad Saha Institute of Technology in Kolkata, India for about five years. Before joining MSIT he worked as a senior research fellow in the civil engineering department of Jadavpur University, Kolkata. He received a bachelor degree (1999) and a master degree (2001) in civil engineering and is currently engaged in his doctoral research. His research areas are pollution control, sustainable development and collaboration in engineering design. He has more than twenty papers published in research journals.

Jianfeng Wang is an Associate Professor of Management Information Systems in the Eberly College of Business and Information Technology. He holds a Ph.D. degree in management information systems from the University of Mississippi. His research interests includes electronic meeting systems, e-business, financial information technology, and economics of information technology.

Edzard Weber studied business informatics in Münster and computer science at Carl von Ossietzky University in Oldenburg. He is a research assistant at the University of Potsdam. His main fields of interests are knowledge management, communication theories and collaboration systems. Edzard published at a number of conferences including those from the *Institute of Electrical and Electronics Engineers (IEEE), International Institute of Informatics and Systemics (IIIS)*, and *Association for Information Systems (AIS)*.

Index

A

Action Regulation Theory (ART) 127
    evaluation 1, 4, 8, 10-12, 14, 26-27, 31, 34-35, 42, 97-98, 100, 125, 127, 140, 143-144, 148, 152, 182, 187, 218, 220-221, 225
    implementation 3-4, 8, 12-14, 35, 42, 97-99, 110, 127, 223
    orientation 44, 127
agent-based model (ABM) 54
AmiChat 20
ANCOVA 63, 66
AnnoChat 18
ANOVA 63, 65-66, 119, 218-219
APC (the average path coefficient, a model fit index) 115
architectural design 97
Architectural Learning Expert (ALEX) 98
ARS (the average R-squared, another model fit index) 115
attunement 212
available affordances 206
Average Measure Intraclass Correlation 131
average path coefficient (APC) 68
average R-squared (ARS) 68, 118
Average variances extracted (AVE) 73

B

bag-of-words 50-51
barriers to change 30, 35-36, 41
behavior intervention plan 30-31, 33, 35, 37, 40-42
beneficial augmentation 30, 35
betweenness 102
blog 47, 51-54, 57-58, 191
blogsphere 51
bootstrapping 68, 118

C

Chi-Squared goodness test 104
closeness 102
Collaboration Action (CoAct) 205
collaboration envelope 53, 58
collaboration triangle 99
collective cognition 46
collective intelligence 47
collinearity 123
Comma Separated Values 10
communication medium 197
Communities of Practice (CoP) 193
comparative fit index (CFI) 89-90
composite reliabilities (CR) 133
compositional models 172
computer mediated communication (CMC) 189
connectedness 102
consultation 32-33, 35, 39, 45, 232-234, 236
contextual fallacies 171
cooperation 190
cross-level fallacies 171
CryptoHeaven 33
cultural dispersion 81
Cultural Tribalism 48-49

D

Development Decision Centers (DDC) 18

E

echo chamber 46
e-collaboration 2
ECU 64-65, 70, 113-116, 122-123
ECUVar 64, 113, 115-116
Effe 64-65, 113
Effi 64, 72, 113-116, 122

Eigenvector 104
electronic meetings 20
Enterprise Resource Planning 2

F

fandom 47
Flocking Theory 49-51
focus group 34, 36
folk models 205
free riders 196
frog-pond models 174

G

Global Fit Measure (GoF) 135
Google Translate 18-19, 21, 24
group decision-making 140, 204, 226
group support systems 17, 27-28, 43

H

Health Insurance Portability and Accountability Act
    (HIPAA) 33

I

identity acquisition 82-85, 87, 89, 91
ID'EST 98
IEP Team Surveys 33
IEP Team Time Tracking 34, 39
Individual Action (IAct) 205, 209-210
Individualized Education Plan (IEP) 31
Individuals with Disabilities Act of 1997 (IDEA) 31
information and communication technologies (ICT)
    190
Information Systems (IS) 173
information technology (IT) 97
information warfare 168
internal representations 205
International Journal of e-Collaboration (IJeC) 166
internet forum 96
inter-observer agreement (IOA) 34
interpersonal relationships 160

J

jacknifing 67
job satisfaction 86

K

KATRAS 146
knowledge creation 144
Knowledge Management System 145
Knowledge Modeling and Description Language
    (KMDL) 6
Knowledge Persistent Layer 146
knowledge sharing 189
Kullback-Leibler divergence 50-51, 57

L

latent variables (LVs) 63
least effective tactics 234
        coalition 4, 234
        legitimating 234
        pressure 47, 49, 126, 234, 236
level paradox 167
local education agency specialists (LEA) 31
lurkers 196

M

machine translation (MT) 18
macro view 4-6, 13
MANCOVA 63
MANOVA 63
matrix organization 228
mediating effect significance test 114
meso-mediational models 175
meso view 4-5, 9
Metcalfe's Law 49
micro view 4-5
Model of Modulated Awareness (MoMA) 3
moderately effective tactics 234
        apprising 234
        exchange 8, 20, 22, 47, 95, 126, 143-144, 188-
        191, 193-194, 198-199, 234-235
        ingratiation 234
        personal appeals 234
moderator models 174
Monte Carlos simulation (MCS) 103

N

Near Term Analysis (NTA) 105
Need-for-Cognition and Co-Creation 47
NetLogo 54, 61
netnography 51

nonlinear analysis 62, 112-113, 119
non-normed fit index (NNFI) 89

O

online discussion board 34
online platform 32
OnPoint 155-156, 228, 234
OntoDesign 145-150, 152, 154
OrgaDesign 145-146
organizational dispersion 81
Organizational Risk Analyzer (ORA) 96, 101

P

partial least squares 62-63, 77, 112, 125, 132, 138, 141
participation culture 47
participatory culture 189
perceived affordances 206
Platypus Wiki 151
PLS Regression algorithm 66-67, 76, 117
power-low distribution 192
proactive influence tactic 232
Proc 64, 70, 72, 113-116, 120-122
psychological ownership 190

R

Radio Frequency Identification (RFID) 2
Random Network Theory 196
rational persuasion 232-233
Real-time collaboration (RTC) 2
Real World Awareness (RWA) 2
redefinition 127, 129
reflective practice 30, 35, 37, 41-42
Robust Path Analysis algorithm 67, 117-118
root mean square error of approximation (RMSEA) 89-90

S

screen scraping 51
self-reflection 32, 208-212
semantic knowledge 144, 222-223
SemanticTalk 7
semantic wiki 144
Sensemaking 46-48, 54, 61, 205, 226-227
shared mental model 127
silhouette coefficicent 51
simple request 232

single-level research 167, 181
social capital 193-194, 200
social identity 80, 82
Social Impact Theory (SIT) 127
 immediacy 127, 136
 number 2, 7, 11, 20, 22, 34, 36-38, 46-53, 58, 64, 66-68, 70, 72, 99, 101-102, 106, 113, 118, 120, 125-127, 129, 132, 148, 151, 155-156, 159, 178-179, 187, 192, 194-196, 221, 233
 strength 70, 110, 127, 129, 136, 173, 211
social life 85
source actor 210-216
spatial dispersion 81
StarDesign 145
steering behaviors 49
 alignment 49, 204, 209, 225, 231-232
 cohesion 37, 49
 separation 49
structural equation modeling (SEM) 63, 89-90, 112
 covariance-based 63
 variance-based 63
Supply Chain Management (SCM) 2
syntactic knowledge 222-223

T

tag dictionary 50
target actor 210-216
team cognition 126
team mental model 127
technology use 168
 group behavior 136, 168, 170-171, 173, 179
 individual behavior 168
 intra-organizational behavior 168
temporal dispersion 81
Test of English as a Foreign Language (TOEFL) 19
Topic Map Query (TMQL) 3
Topic Maps (TM) 3
Topics, Associations and Occurrences (TAO) 3
TransBBS 20

U

U-curve 66, 117
usability engineering 204, 221-222, 225-227
user-generated content networks 192
user-generated tags 192

V

variance inflation factor (VIF) 68
virtual IEP team 31
virtuality 81
virtual organizations 80
virtual team collaboration 158
virtual team inventory 156
virtual team performance 140, 155-156, 163, 184
virtual teams 83
virtual teamwork 156

W

WarpPLS 62, 64, 112
Web 2.0 189-190
Web3D 3
wiki 143
WikiDesign 149
wiki markup language (WikiML) 144
WikiSar 151
wikitext 144